WHISTLE!™

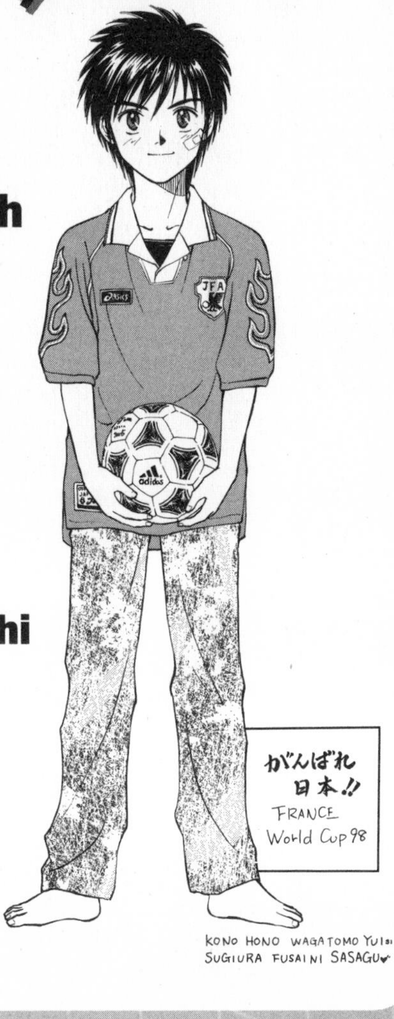
がんばれ
日本!!
FRANCE
World Cup 98
KONO HONO WAGATOMO YUISI
SUGIURA FUSAINI SASAGU

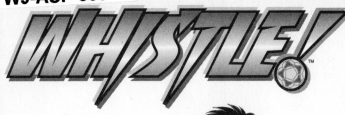

Vol. 1

Break Through

Story and Art by

Daisuke Higuchi

WHISTLE!

**Vol. 1
Break Through**

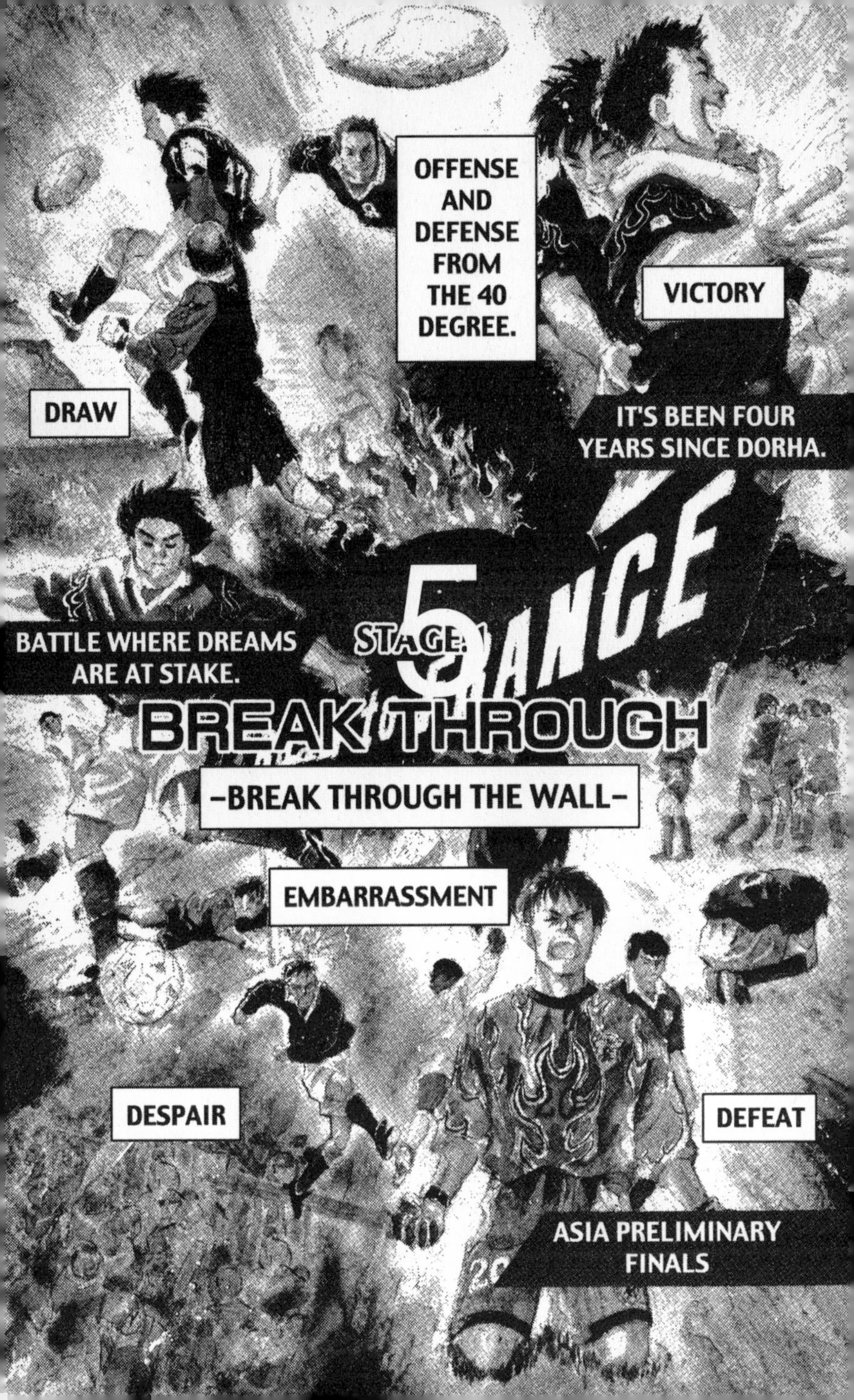
OFFENSE AND DEFENSE FROM THE 40 DEGREE.
VICTORY
IT'S BEEN FOUR YEARS SINCE DORHA.
DRAW
STAGE. 5
BREAK THROUGH
BATTLE WHERE DREAMS ARE AT STAKE.
-BREAK THROUGH THE WALL-
EMBARRASSMENT
DEFEAT
DESPAIR
ASIA PRELIMINARY FINALS

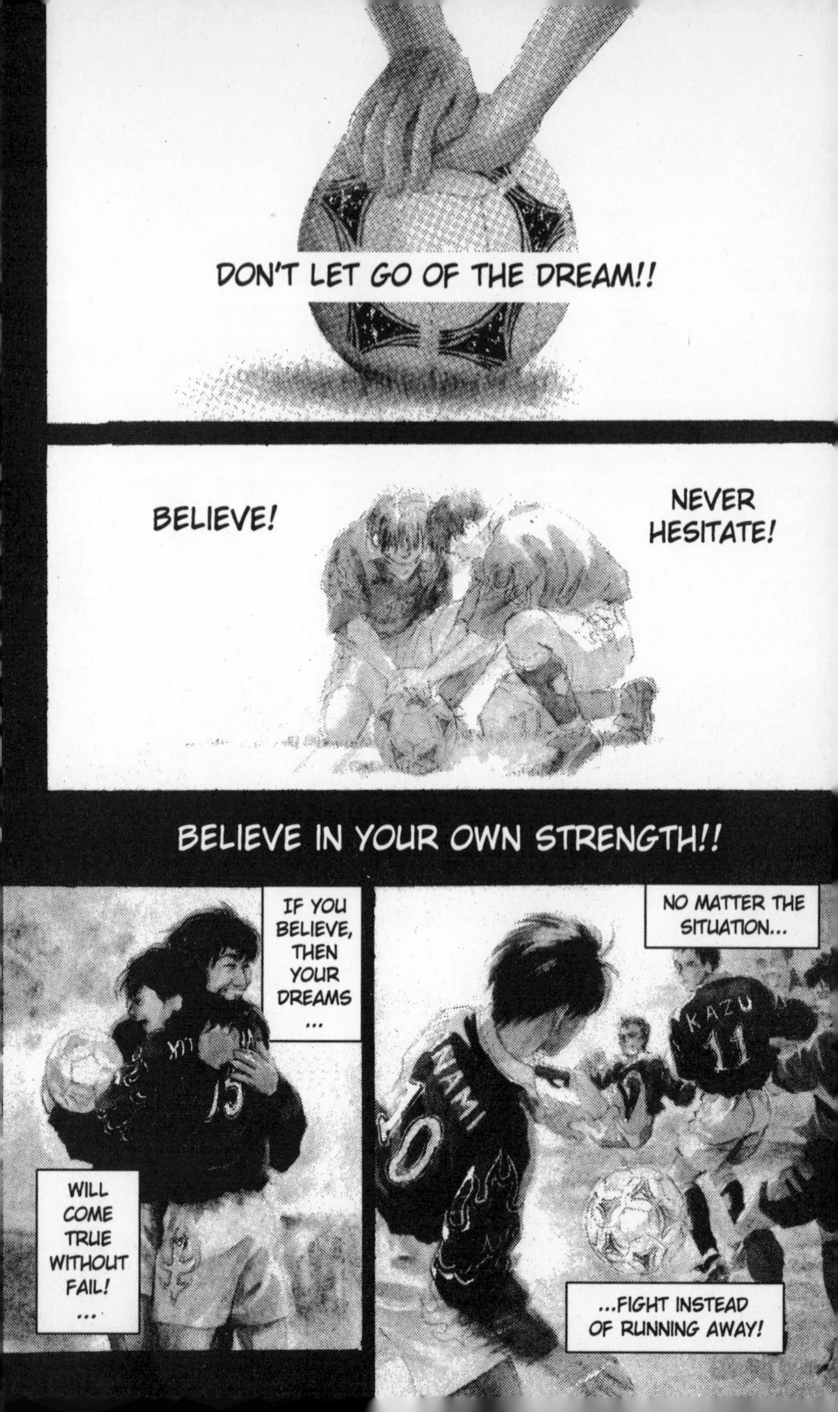

DON'T LET GO OF THE DREAM!!
NEVER HESITATE!
BELIEVE!
BELIEVE IN YOUR OWN STRENGTH!!
NO MATTER THE SITUATION...
...FIGHT INSTEAD OF RUNNING AWAY!
IF YOU BELIEVE, THEN YOUR DREAMS ...
WILL COME TRUE WITHOUT FAIL! ...

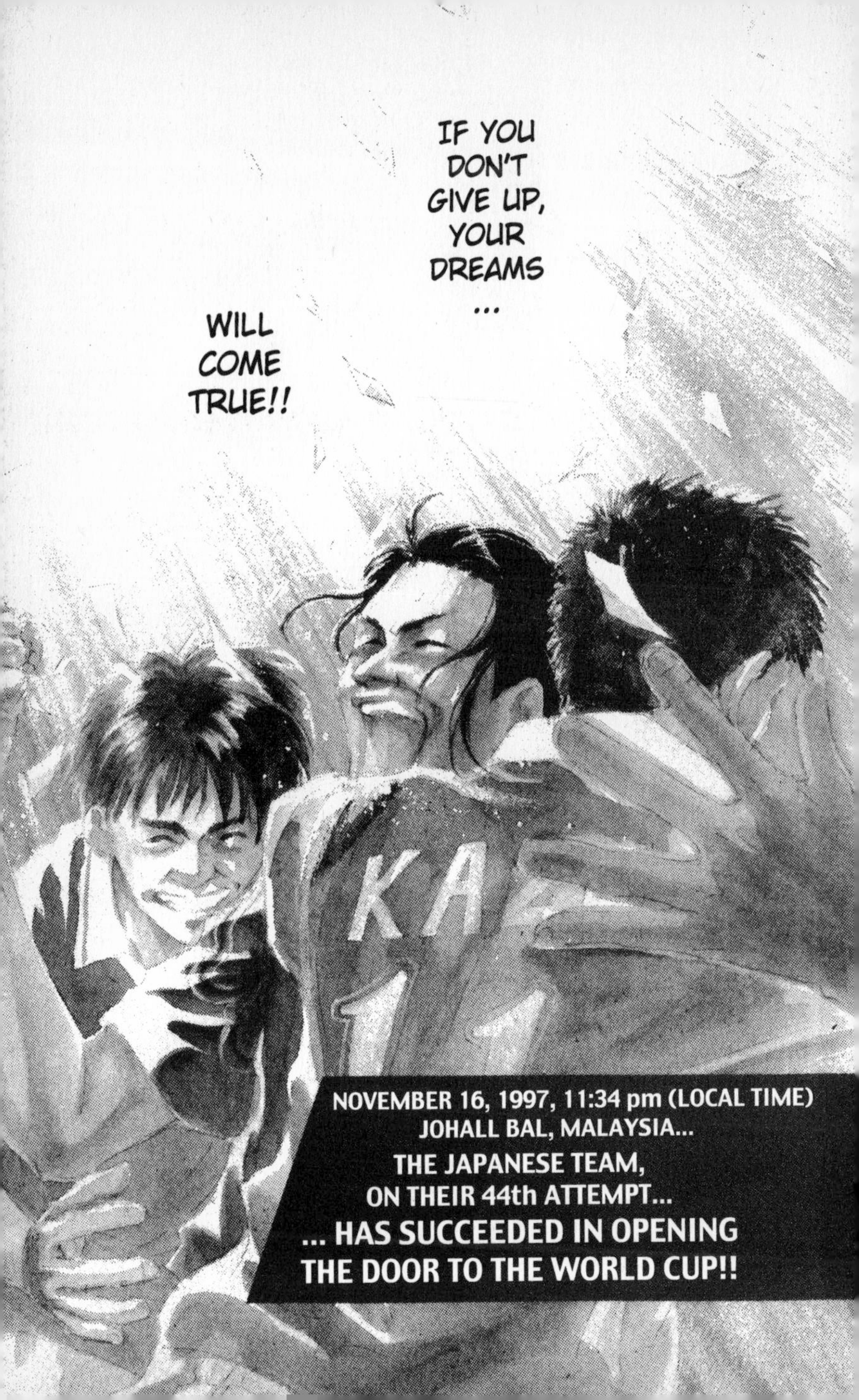
IF YOU DON'T GIVE UP, YOUR DREAMS ...
WILL COME TRUE!!
KA
NOVEMBER 16, 1997, 11:34 pm (LOCAL TIME)
JOHALL BAL, MALAYSIA...
THE JAPANESE TEAM,
ON THEIR 44th ATTEMPT...
... HAS SUCCEEDED IN OPENING
THE DOOR TO THE WORLD CUP!!

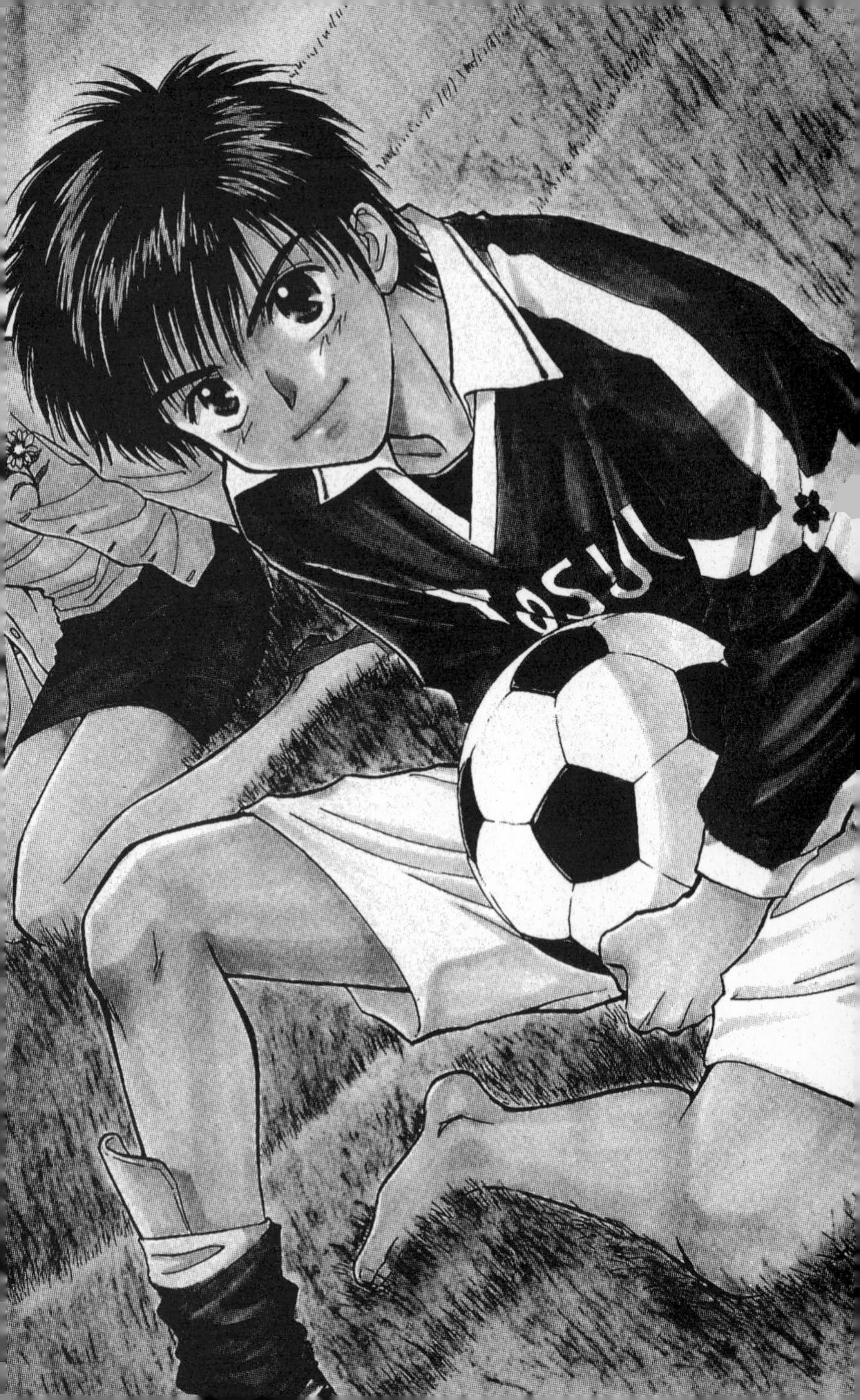

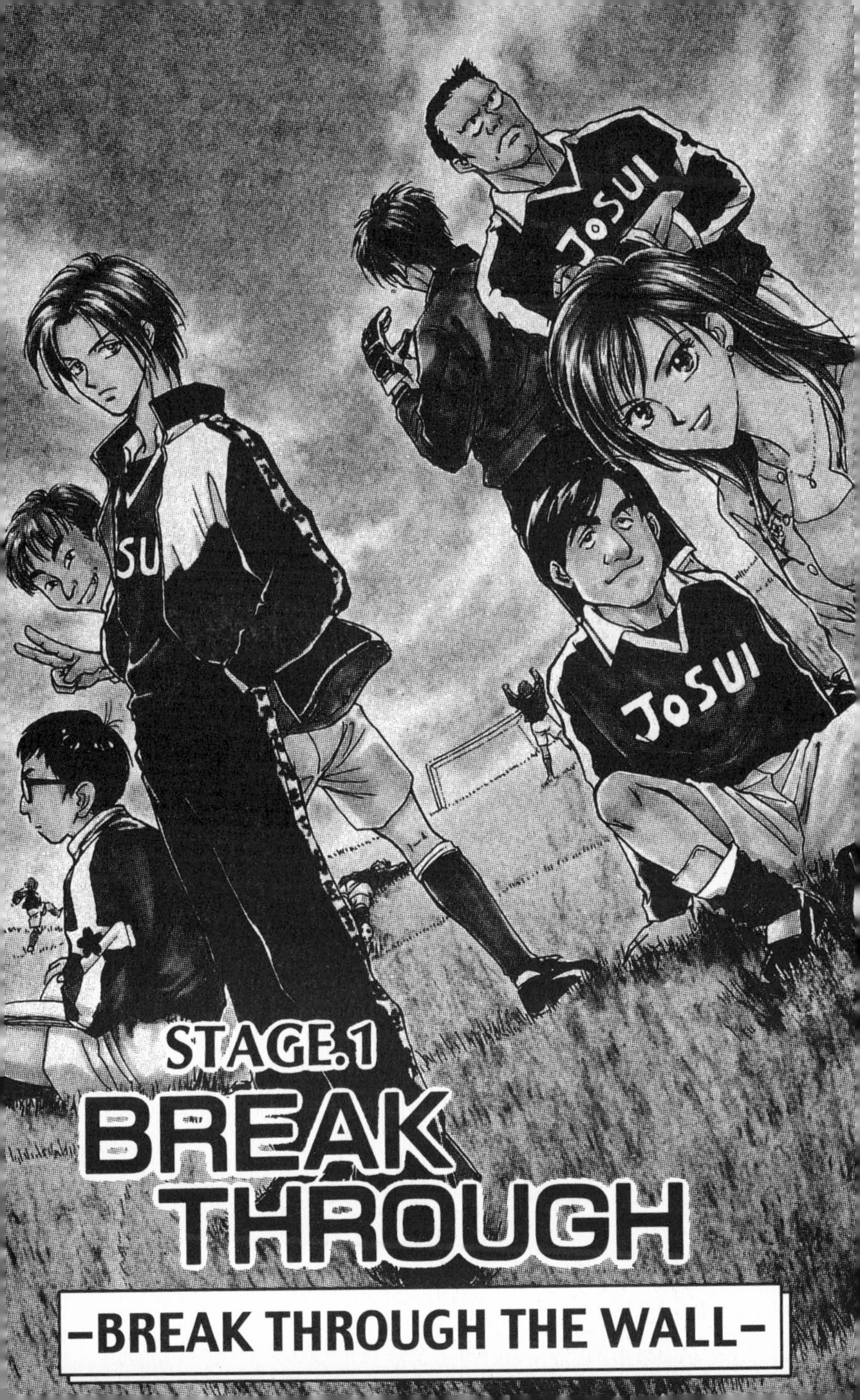
JOSUI
STAGE.1
BREAK THROUGH
-BREAK THROUGH THE WALL-

● INTRODUCTION ●

SOCCER IS A SPORT IN WHICH THE PLAYER'S TEAM STEALS THE BALL FROM THE OPPONENT'S TEAM THEN PASSES IT FROM PLAYER TO PLAYER UNTIL IT IS SHOT INTO THE OTHER TEAM'S GOAL. IT MAY SOUND EASY, BUT YOUR OPPONENTS WILL INTERFERE, MAKING IT DIFFICULT TO SCORE.

TO MAKE A GOAL, TEAMS ESTABLISH POSITIONS, INITIATE PASSES, SET UP COMPLICATED FORMATIONS AND TRY TO OUT-MANEUVER OPPONENTS.

THESE DAYS, THE PLAYERS, EXCLUDING GOALKEEPERS, CHANGE POSITIONS SO RAPIDLY AND CONSTANTLY THAT IT'S OFTEN HARD TO KEEP TRACK OF WHO IS POSITIONED WHERE. SINCE, UNLIKE BASEBALL, PLAYERS' POSITIONS ARE NOT FIXED, IT IS NOT NECESSARY TO KNOW WHERE THEY ARE AS YOU WATCH THEM PLAY. ALL YOU NEED TO DO IS KEEP IN MIND WHICH PLAYER TAKES WHAT POSITION WITHIN A FORMATION SUCH AS 4-4-2 OR 3-5-2.

BEYOND THAT, FOCUS ON FIGURING OUT HOW TO GAIN POINTS AND WHEN TO STEAL THE BALL. YOU MUST NOT ONLY WATCH THE GOAL BUT ALSO THE PROCESS OF GETTING THERE.

YOU WILL ENJOY SOCCER IF YOU CAN UNDERSTAND, AS AN EXAMPLE, THAT JOE'S GOAL WAS THE RESULT OF YAMAGUCHI'S PASS-CUT, OR THAT THE GOAL WAS POSSIBLE BECAUSE OF THE LAST PASS.

SOCCER ALLOWS PLAYERS TO USE ANY PART OF THEIR BODIES EXCEPT FOR THEIR HANDS. USING VARIOUS PARTS OF A PLAYER'S LEG, APPLYING DIVERSE INTENSITIES AS WELL AS DIFFERENT ANGLES, ALLOWS FOR A GREAT MANY WAYS TO PASS A BALL. ADDING BOTH LEGS AND FEET AS WELL AS YOUR HEAD, AND YOU'LL FIND IT IMPOSSIBLE TO COUNT HOW MANY WAYS A PLAYER CAN MAKE A PASS. ISN'T IT ALREADY EXCITING TO THINK ABOUT IT?

--TATSUYA WATANABE (WINNING RUN)

DID IT!

TWINK

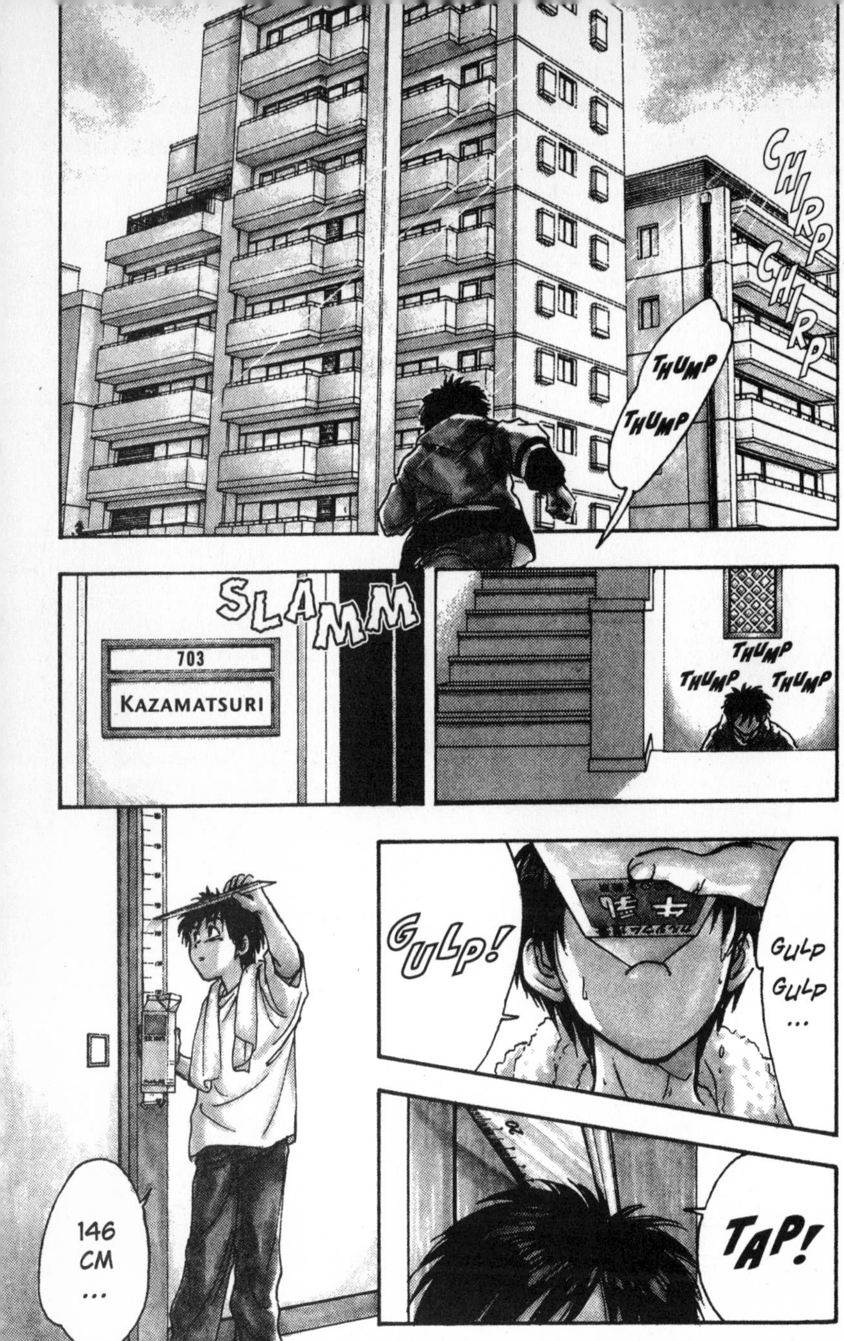
CHIRP CHIRP
THUMP THUMP
THUMP THUMP THUMP
SLAMM
703
KAZAMATSURI
GULP GULP ...
GULP!
TAP!
146 CM ...

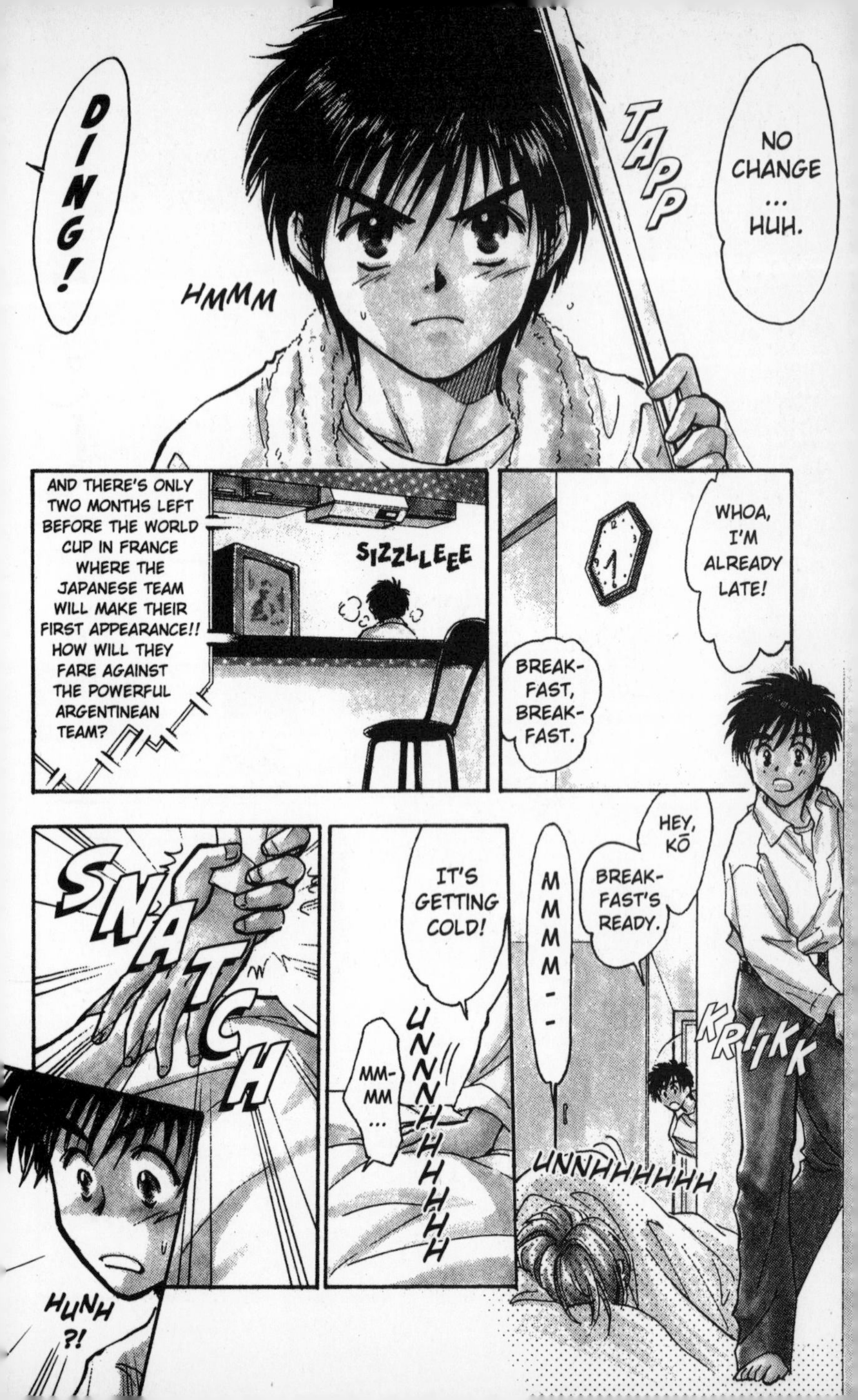
NO CHANGE ... HUH.
TAPP
DING!
HMMM
WHOA, I'M ALREADY LATE!
BREAK-FAST, BREAK-FAST.
SIZZLLEEE
AND THERE'S ONLY TWO MONTHS LEFT BEFORE THE WORLD CUP IN FRANCE WHERE THE JAPANESE TEAM WILL MAKE THEIR FIRST APPEARANCE!! HOW WILL THEY FARE AGAINST THE POWERFUL ARGENTINEAN TEAM?
HEY, KŌ
BREAK-FAST'S READY.
MMMMM--
KRIIKK
UNNHHHHHHH
IT'S GETTING COLD!
UNNNHHHHHHH
MM-MM ...
SNATCH
HUNH ?!

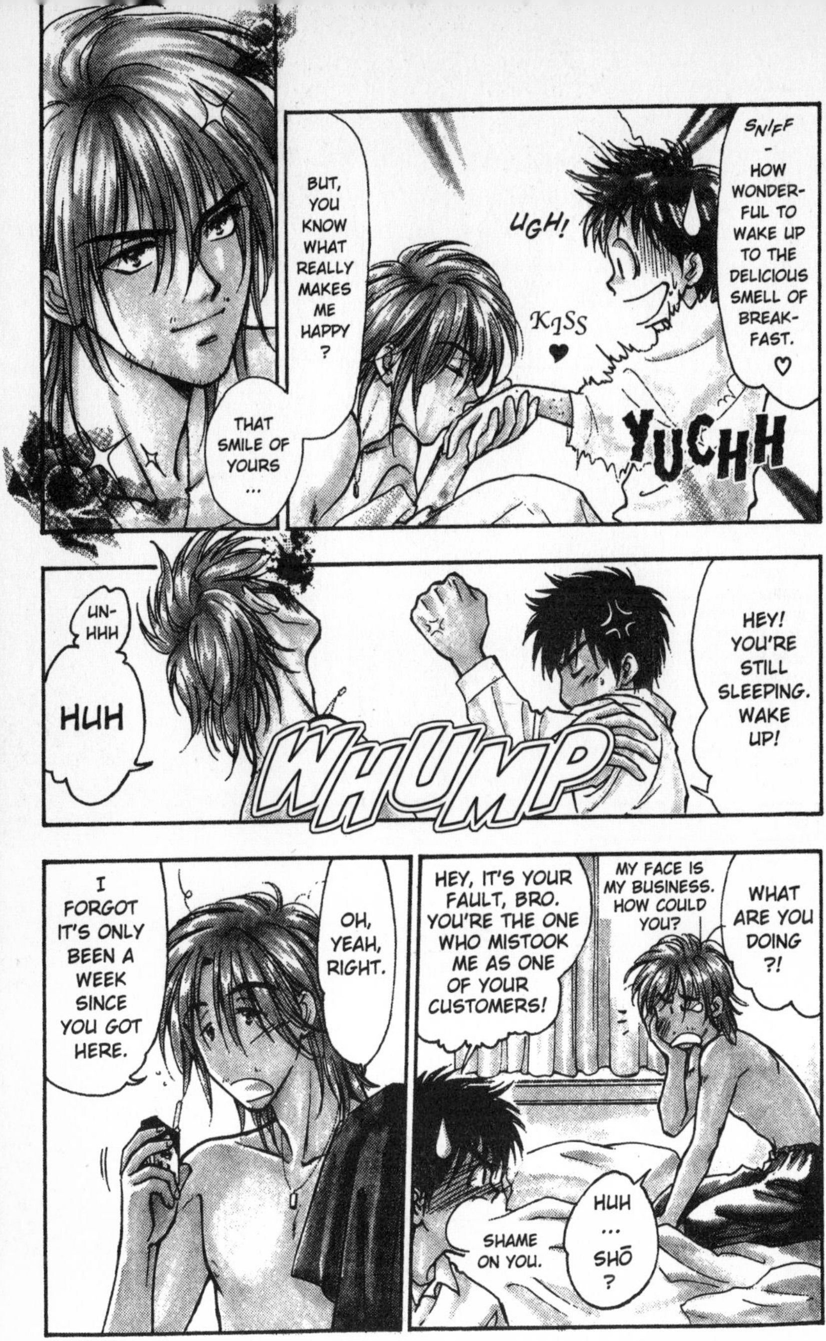
SNIFF - HOW WONDERFUL TO WAKE UP TO THE DELICIOUS SMELL OF BREAKFAST. ♡
UGH!
KISS ♥
YUCHH
BUT, YOU KNOW WHAT REALLY MAKES ME HAPPY?
THAT SMILE OF YOURS ...
HEY! YOU'RE STILL SLEEPING. WAKE UP!
WHUMP
UN-HHH
HUH
WHAT ARE YOU DOING?!
MY FACE IS MY BUSINESS. HOW COULD YOU?
HEY, IT'S YOUR FAULT, BRO. YOU'RE THE ONE WHO MISTOOK ME AS ONE OF YOUR CUSTOMERS!
HUH ... SHŌ?
SHAME ON YOU.
OH, YEAH, RIGHT.
I FORGOT IT'S ONLY BEEN A WEEK SINCE YOU GOT HERE.

READ THIS WAY

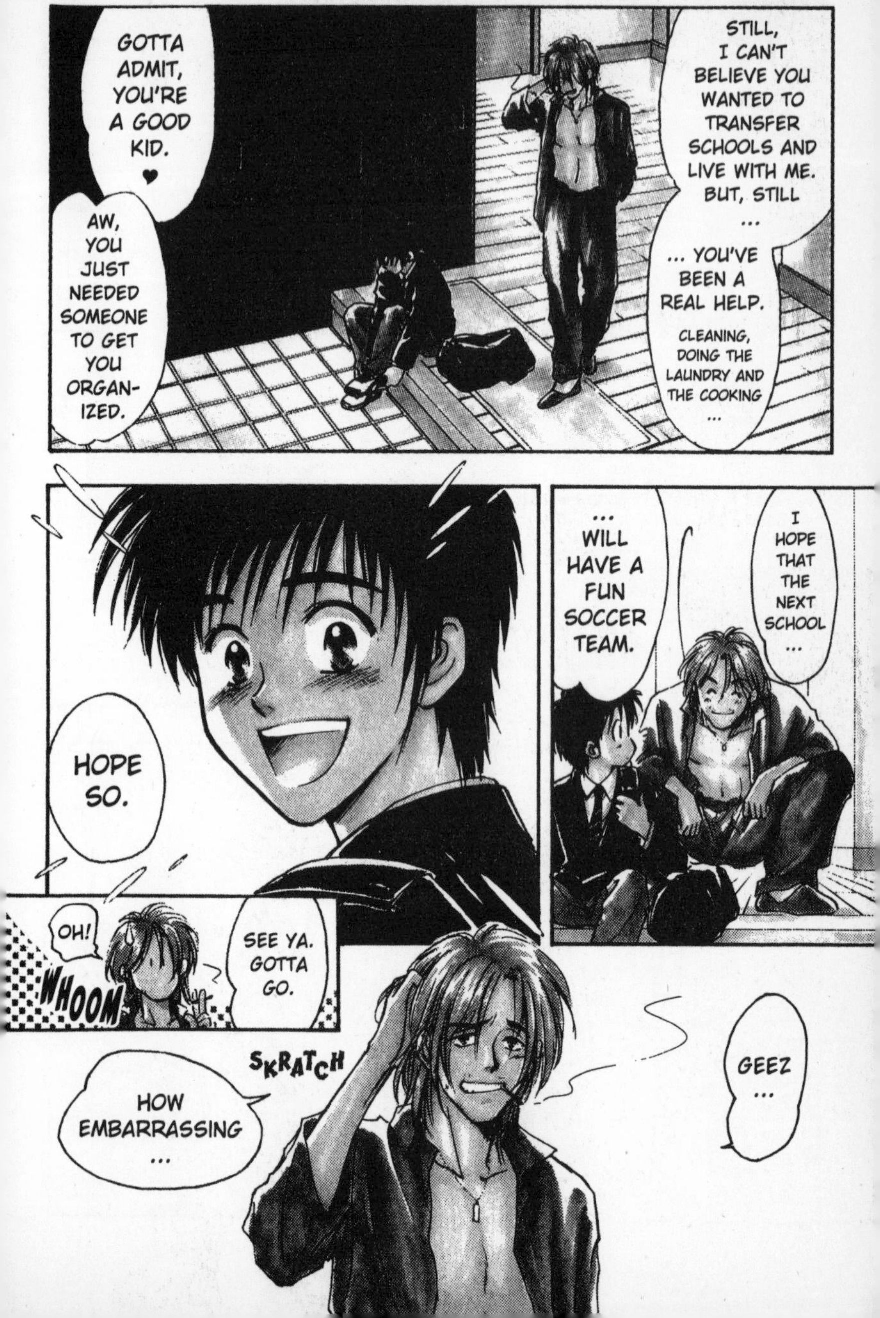

STILL, I CAN'T BELIEVE YOU WANTED TO TRANSFER SCHOOLS AND LIVE WITH ME. BUT, STILL ...
... YOU'VE BEEN A REAL HELP.
CLEANING, DOING THE LAUNDRY AND THE COOKING ...
GOTTA ADMIT, YOU'RE A GOOD KID. ♥
AW, YOU JUST NEEDED SOMEONE TO GET YOU ORGANIZED.
I HOPE THAT THE NEXT SCHOOL ...
... WILL HAVE A FUN SOCCER TEAM.
HOPE SO.
SEE YA. GOTTA GO.
OH!
WHOOM
GEEZ ...
SKRATCH
HOW EMBARRASSING ...

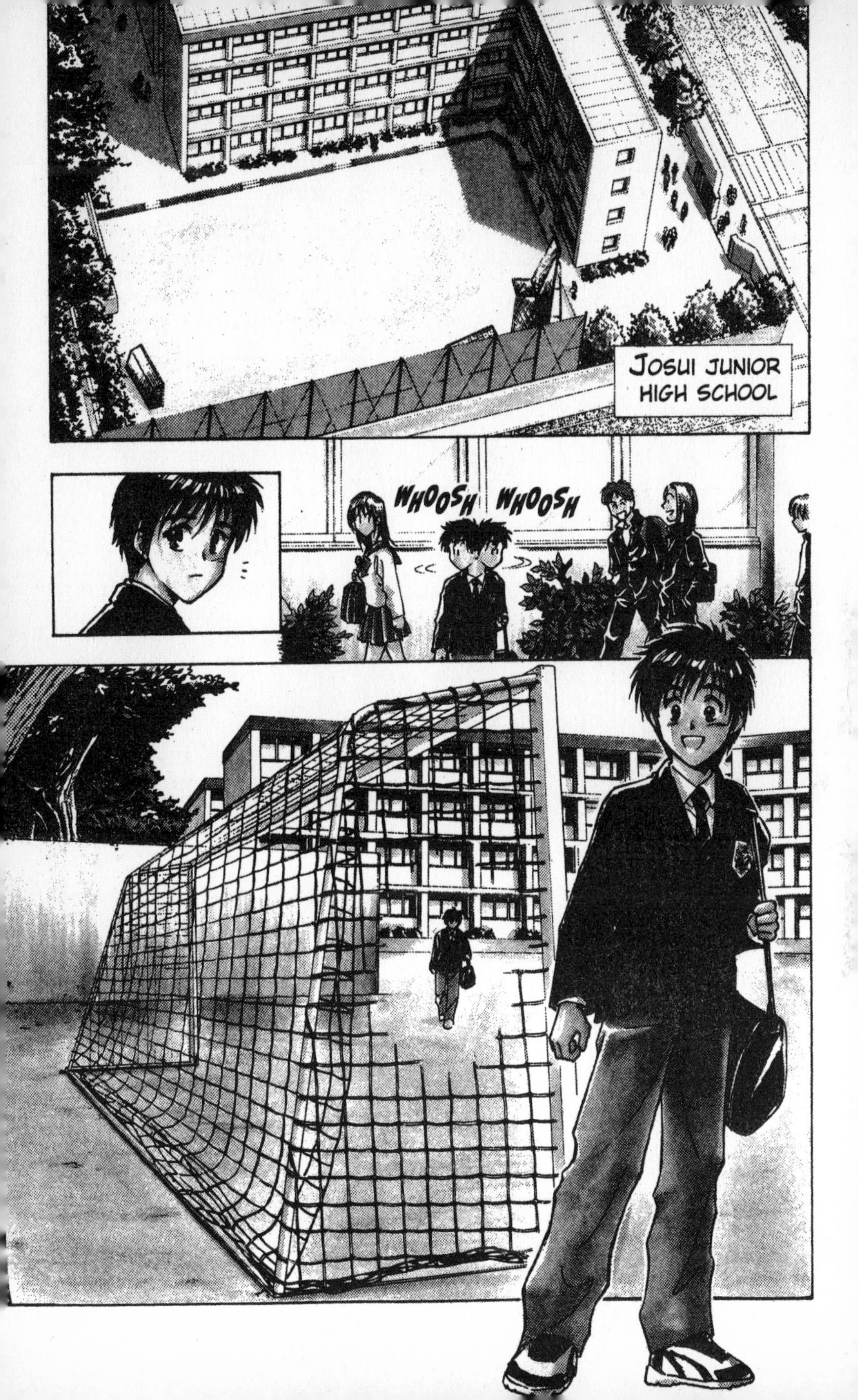
JOSUI JUNIOR HIGH SCHOOL
WHOOSH
WHOOSH

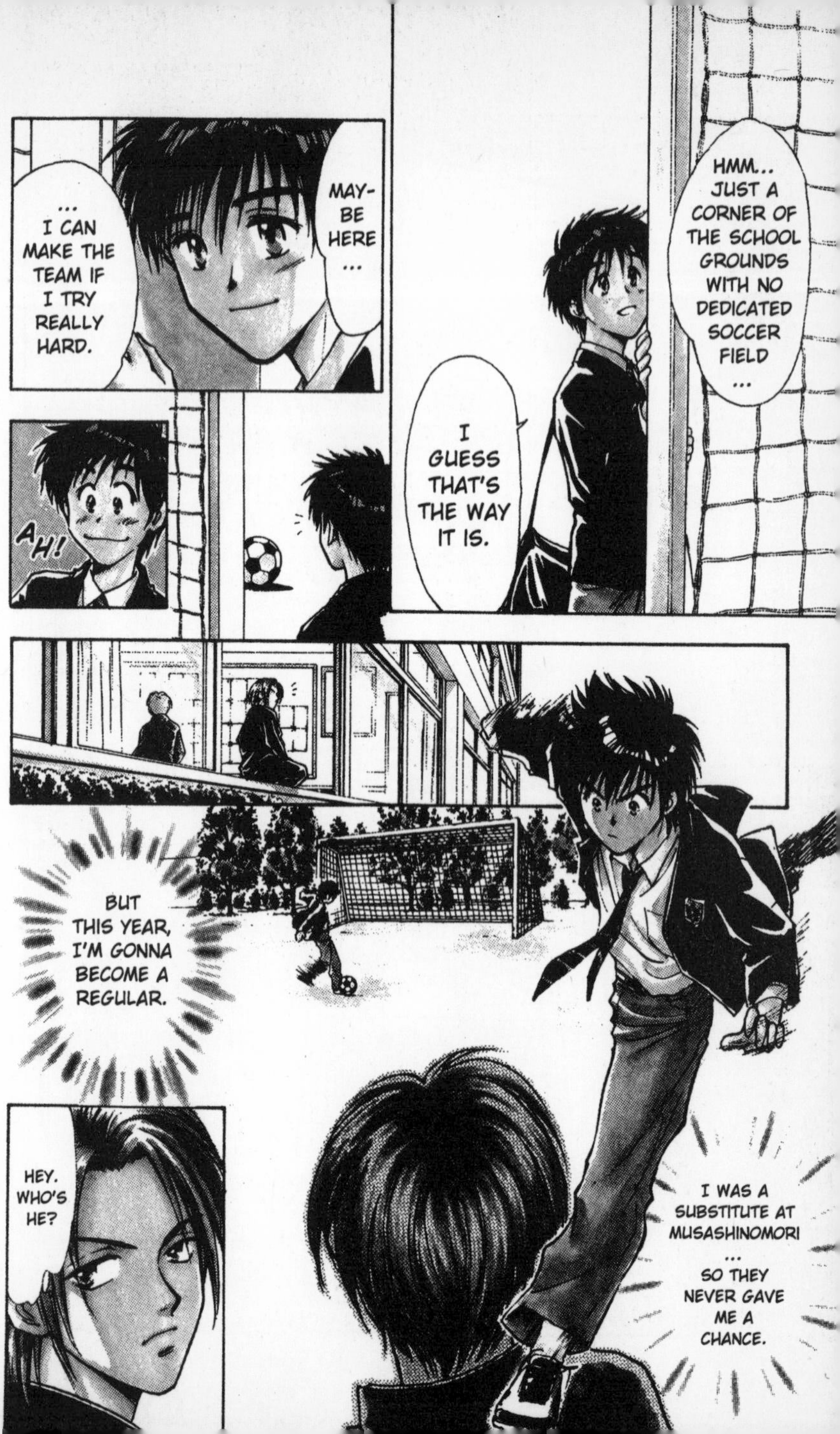
HMM... JUST A CORNER OF THE SCHOOL GROUNDS WITH NO DEDICATED SOCCER FIELD ...
I GUESS THAT'S THE WAY IT IS.
MAY-BE HERE ...
... I CAN MAKE THE TEAM IF I TRY REALLY HARD.
AH!
I WAS A SUBSTITUTE AT MUSASHINOMORI ... SO THEY NEVER GAVE ME A CHANCE.
BUT THIS YEAR, I'M GONNA BECOME A REGULAR.
HEY. WHO'S HE?

READ THIS WAY

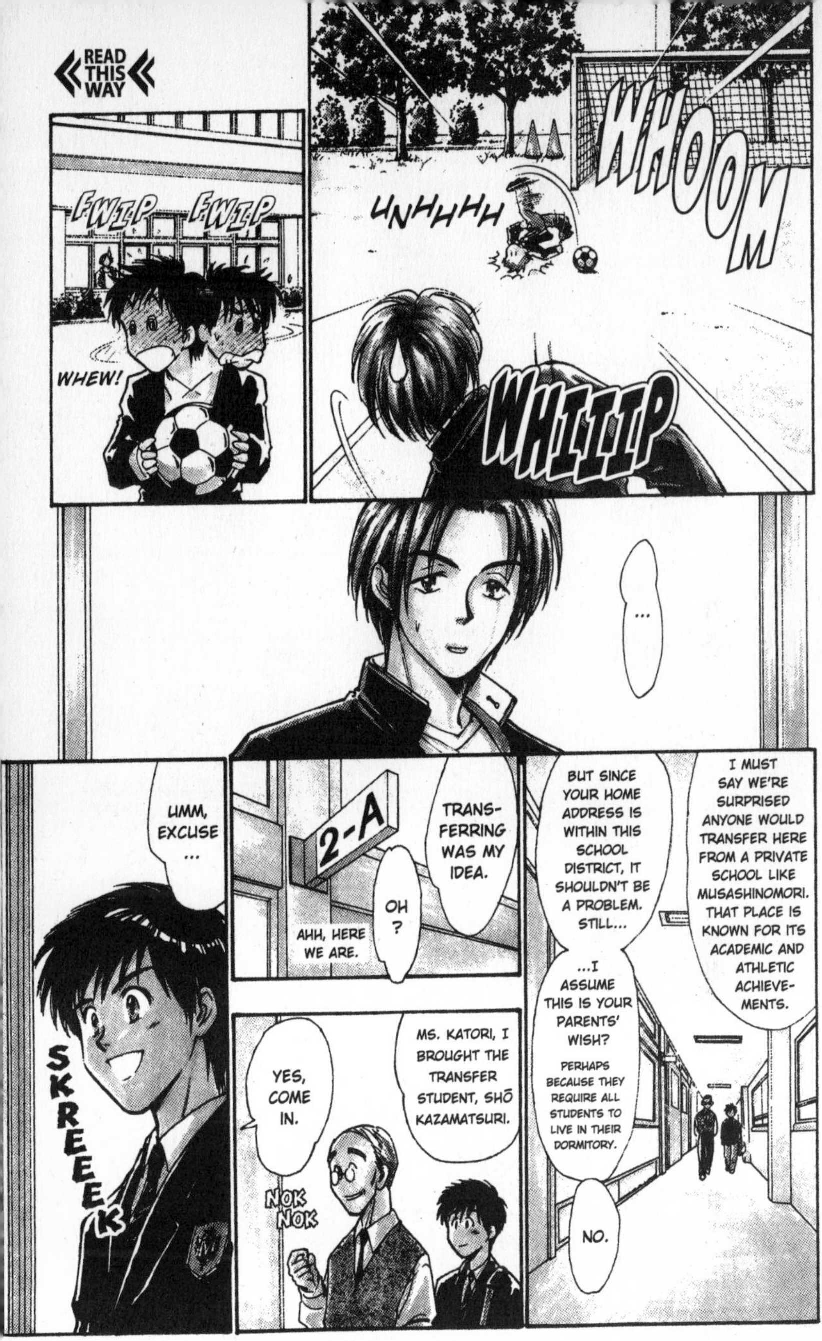
WHOOM
UNHHHH
WHIIIP
FWIP FWIP
WHEW!
...
I MUST SAY WE'RE SURPRISED ANYONE WOULD TRANSFER HERE FROM A PRIVATE SCHOOL LIKE MUSASHINOMORI. THAT PLACE IS KNOWN FOR ITS ACADEMIC AND ATHLETIC ACHIEVEMENTS.
BUT SINCE YOUR HOME ADDRESS IS WITHIN THIS SCHOOL DISTRICT, IT SHOULDN'T BE A PROBLEM. STILL...
...I ASSUME THIS IS YOUR PARENTS' WISH?
PERHAPS BECAUSE THEY REQUIRE ALL STUDENTS TO LIVE IN THEIR DORMITORY.
NO.
2-A
TRANSFERRING WAS MY IDEA.
OH?
AHH, HERE WE ARE.
MS. KATORI, I BROUGHT THE TRANSFER STUDENT, SHŌ KAZAMATSURI.
YES, COME IN.
NOK NOK
UMM, EXCUSE ...
SKREEEK

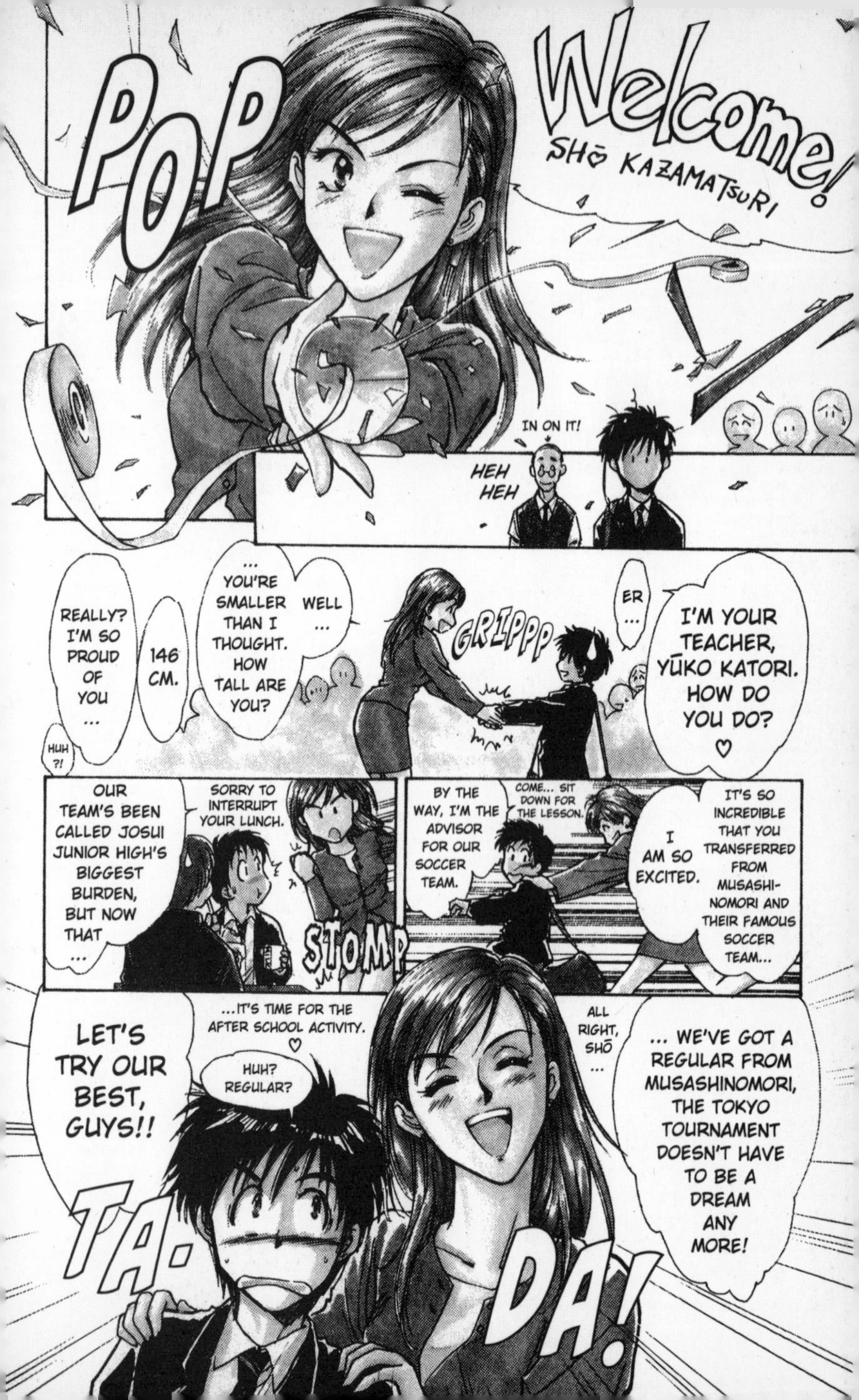
POP
Welcome! SHŌ♡ KAZAMATSURI
IN ON IT!
HEH HEH
I'M YOUR TEACHER, YŪKO KATORI. HOW DO YOU DO? ♡
ER ...
GRIPPP
WELL ...
... YOU'RE SMALLER THAN I THOUGHT. HOW TALL ARE YOU?
146 CM.
REALLY? I'M SO PROUD OF YOU ...
HUH ?!
IT'S SO INCREDIBLE THAT YOU TRANSFERRED FROM MUSASHI-NOMORI AND THEIR FAMOUS SOCCER TEAM...
I AM SO EXCITED.
COME... SIT DOWN FOR THE LESSON.
BY THE WAY, I'M THE ADVISOR FOR OUR SOCCER TEAM.
SORRY TO INTERRUPT YOUR LUNCH.
OUR TEAM'S BEEN CALLED JOSUI JUNIOR HIGH'S BIGGEST BURDEN, BUT NOW THAT ...
STOMP
... WE'VE GOT A REGULAR FROM MUSASHINOMORI, THE TOKYO TOURNAMENT DOESN'T HAVE TO BE A DREAM ANY MORE!
ALL RIGHT, SHŌ ...
HUH? REGULAR?
...IT'S TIME FOR THE AFTER SCHOOL ACTIVITY. ♡
LET'S TRY OUR BEST, GUYS!!
TA-DA!

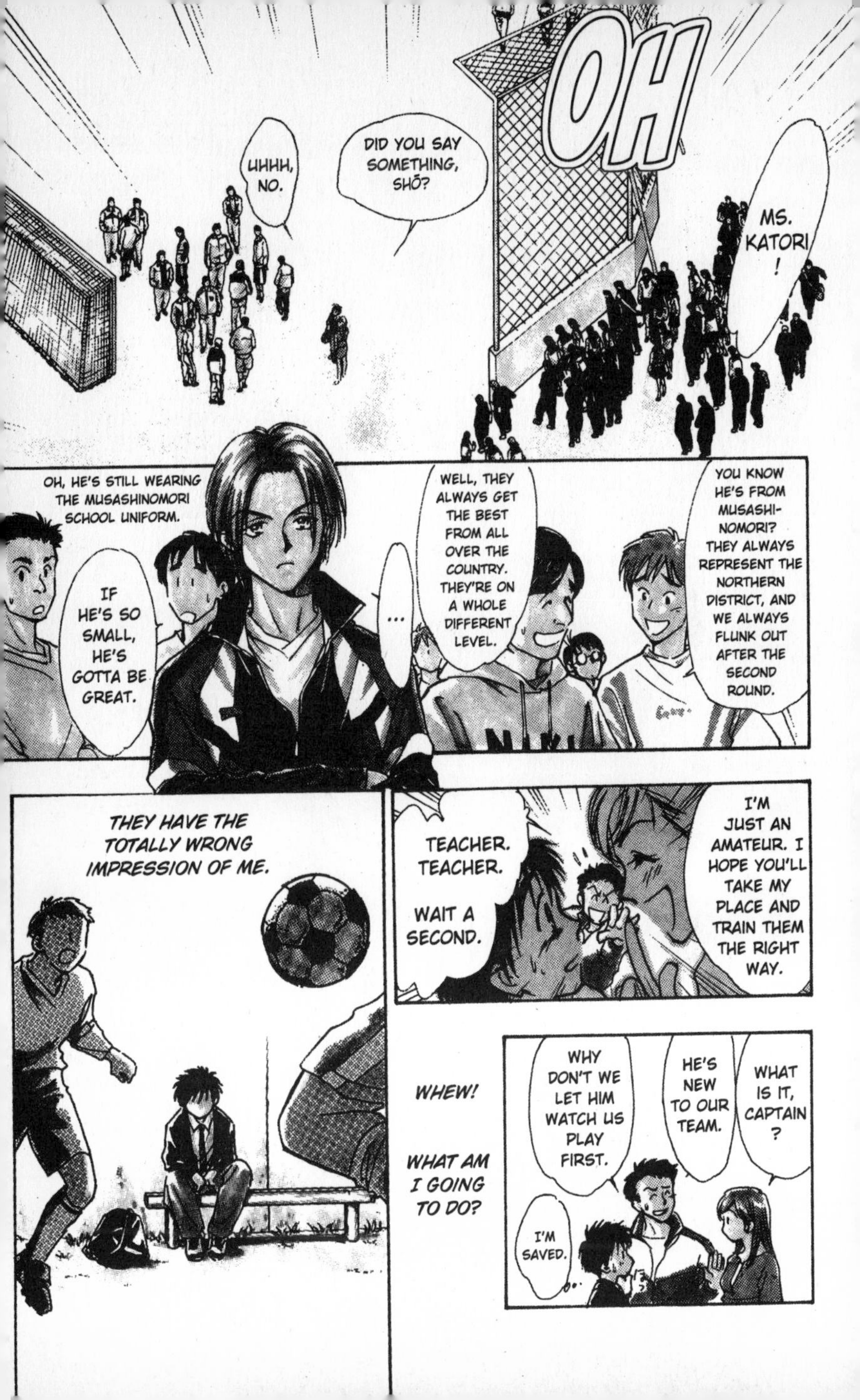
OH
MS. KATORI!
DID YOU SAY SOMETHING, SHŌ?
UHHH, NO.
YOU KNOW HE'S FROM MUSASHI-NOMORI? THEY ALWAYS REPRESENT THE NORTHERN DISTRICT, AND WE ALWAYS FLUNK OUT AFTER THE SECOND ROUND.
WELL, THEY ALWAYS GET THE BEST FROM ALL OVER THE COUNTRY. THEY'RE ON A WHOLE DIFFERENT LEVEL.
...
OH, HE'S STILL WEARING THE MUSASHINOMORI SCHOOL UNIFORM.
IF HE'S SO SMALL, HE'S GOTTA BE GREAT.
I'M JUST AN AMATEUR. I HOPE YOU'LL TAKE MY PLACE AND TRAIN THEM THE RIGHT WAY.
TEACHER. TEACHER.
WAIT A SECOND.
WHAT IS IT, CAPTAIN?
HE'S NEW TO OUR TEAM.
WHY DON'T WE LET HIM WATCH US PLAY FIRST.
I'M SAVED.
WHEW!
WHAT AM I GOING TO DO?
THEY HAVE THE TOTALLY WRONG IMPRESSION OF ME.

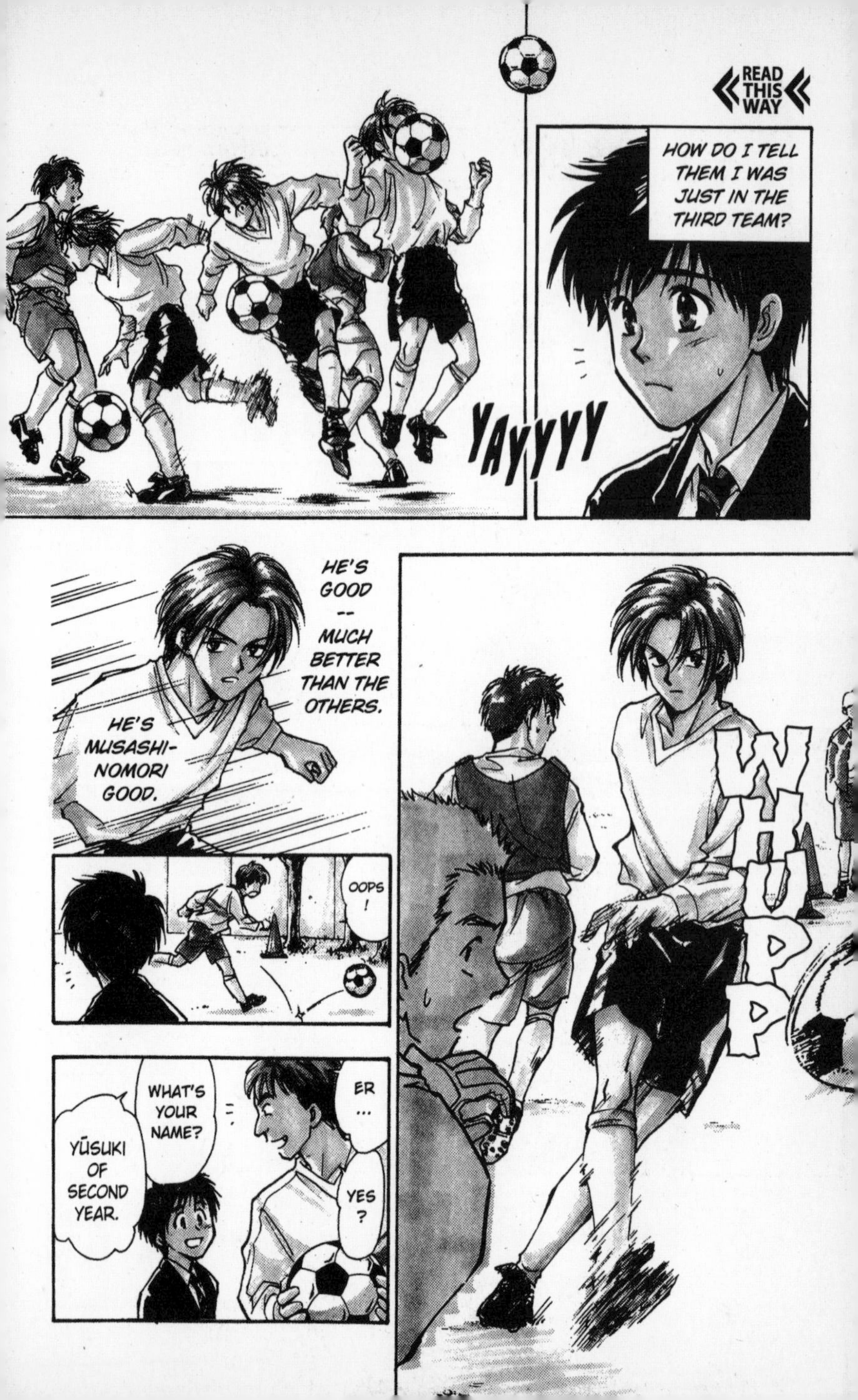
READ THIS WAY
HOW DO I TELL THEM I WAS JUST IN THE THIRD TEAM?
YAYYYY
WHUPP
HE'S GOOD -- MUCH BETTER THAN THE OTHERS.
HE'S MUSASHI-NOMORI GOOD.
OOPS!
ER ...
WHAT'S YOUR NAME?
YES ?
YŪSUKI OF SECOND YEAR.

READ THIS WAY

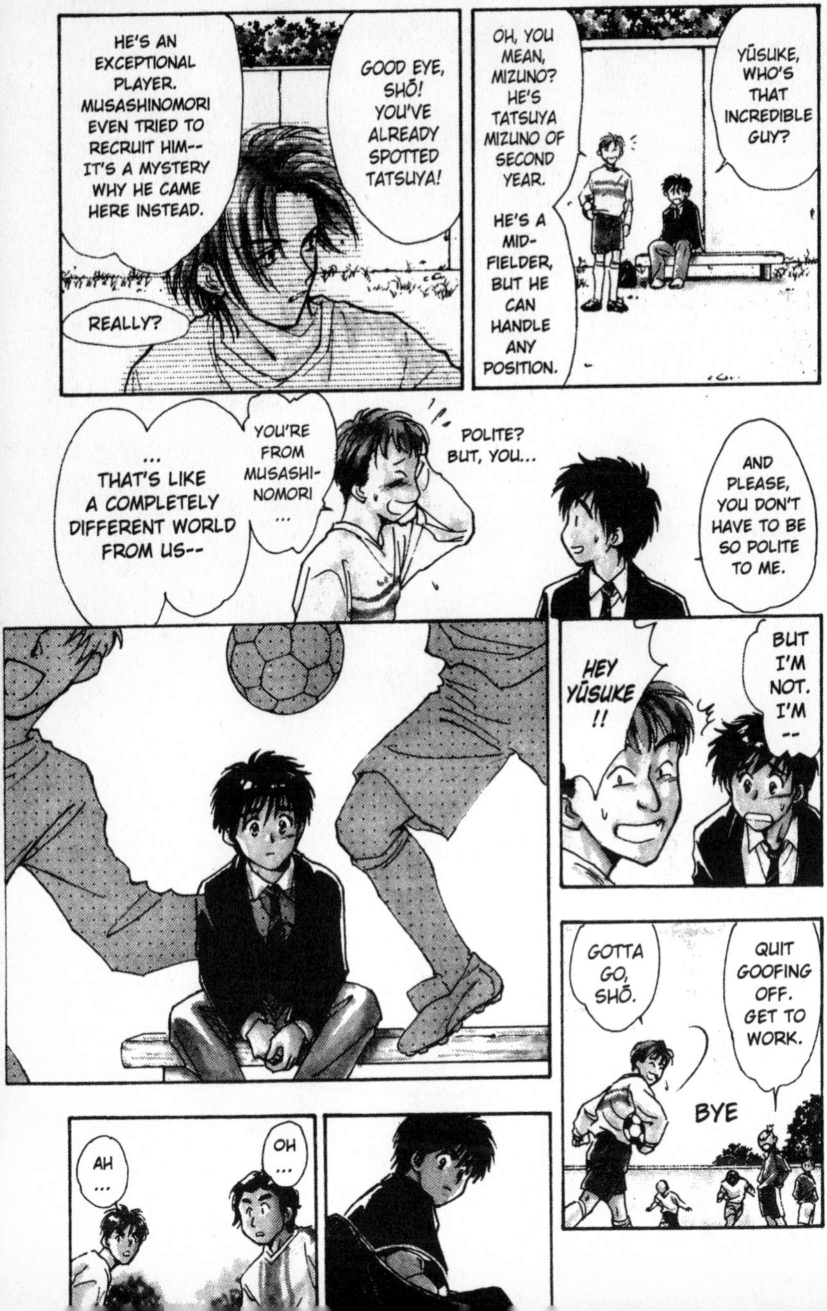
YŪSUKE, WHO'S THAT INCREDIBLE GUY?
OH, YOU MEAN, MIZUNO? HE'S TATSUYA MIZUNO OF SECOND YEAR.
HE'S A MID-FIELDER, BUT HE CAN HANDLE ANY POSITION.
GOOD EYE, SHŌ! YOU'VE ALREADY SPOTTED TATSUYA!
HE'S AN EXCEPTIONAL PLAYER. MUSASHINOMORI EVEN TRIED TO RECRUIT HIM-- IT'S A MYSTERY WHY HE CAME HERE INSTEAD.
REALLY?
AND PLEASE, YOU DON'T HAVE TO BE SO POLITE TO ME.
POLITE? BUT, YOU...
YOU'RE FROM MUSASHI-NOMORI ...
... THAT'S LIKE A COMPLETELY DIFFERENT WORLD FROM US--
BUT I'M NOT. I'M --
HEY YŪSUKE !!
QUIT GOOFING OFF. GET TO WORK.
GOTTA GO, SHŌ.
BYE
OH ...
AH ...

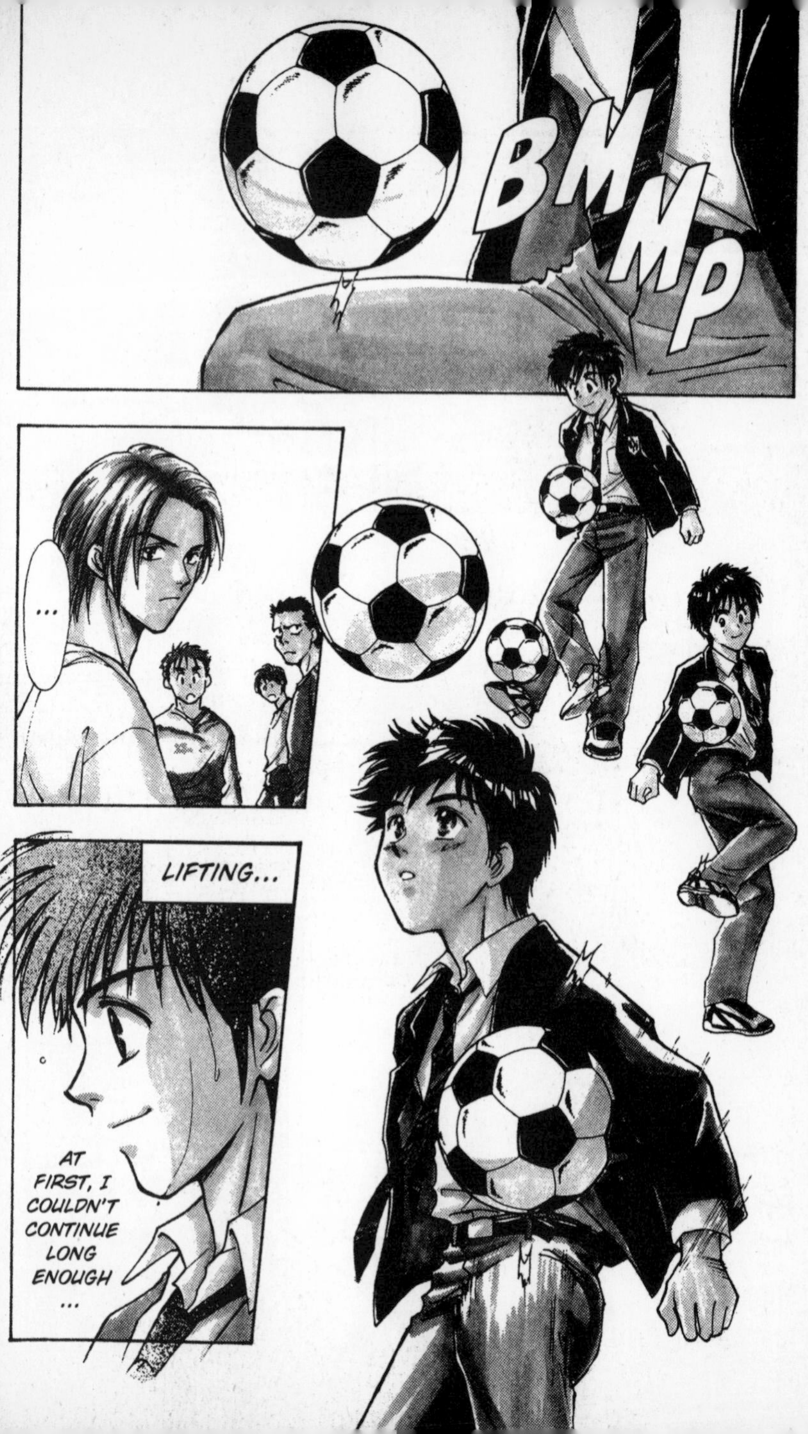
BMMP
...
LIFTING...
AT FIRST, I COULDN'T CONTINUE LONG ENOUGH ...

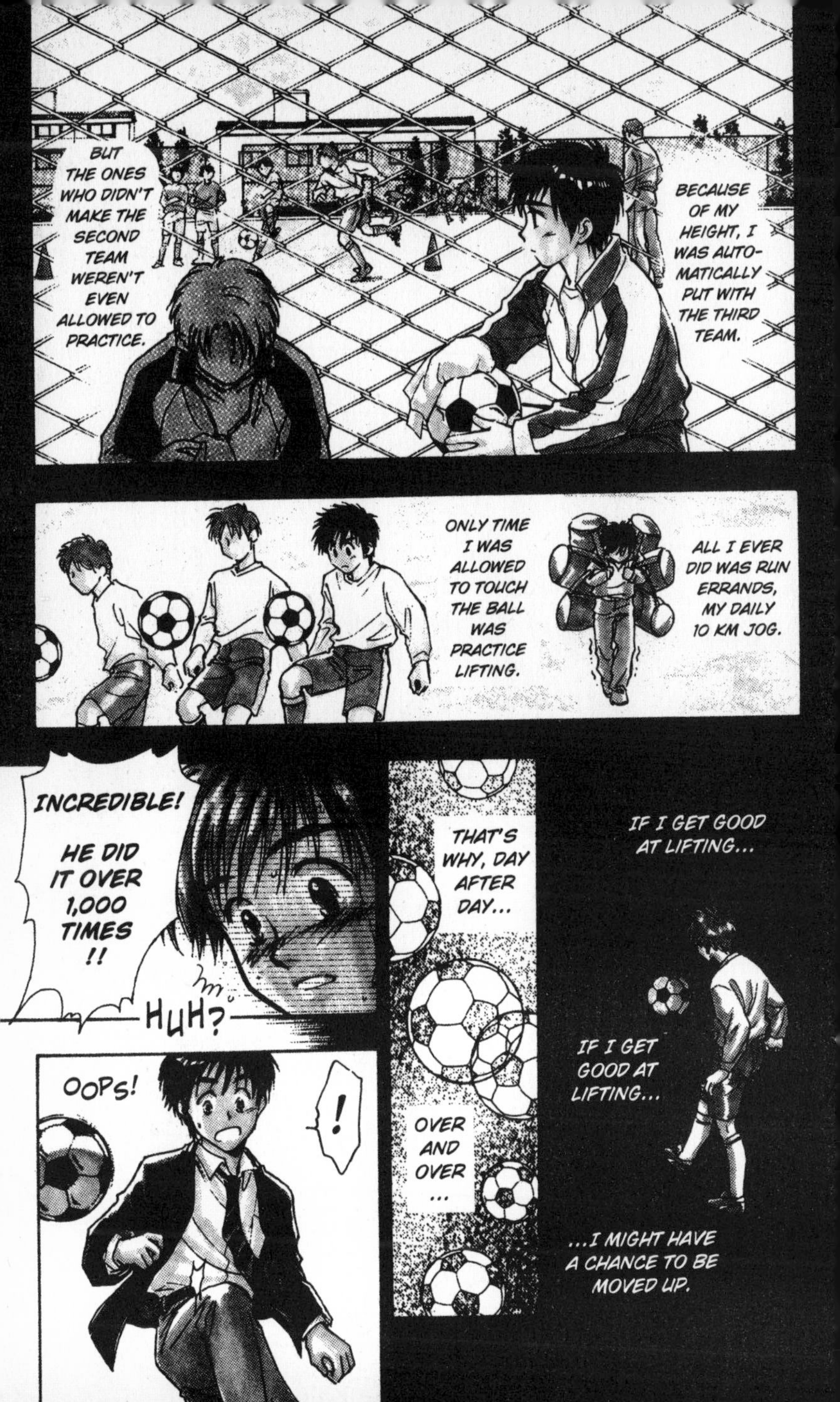
BECAUSE OF MY HEIGHT, I WAS AUTOMATICALLY PUT WITH THE THIRD TEAM.
BUT THE ONES WHO DIDN'T MAKE THE SECOND TEAM WEREN'T EVEN ALLOWED TO PRACTICE.
ALL I EVER DID WAS RUN ERRANDS, MY DAILY 10 KM JOG.
ONLY TIME I WAS ALLOWED TO TOUCH THE BALL WAS PRACTICE LIFTING.
IF I GET GOOD AT LIFTING...
IF I GET GOOD AT LIFTING...
...I MIGHT HAVE A CHANCE TO BE MOVED UP.
THAT'S WHY, DAY AFTER DAY...
OVER AND OVER ...
INCREDIBLE!
HE DID IT OVER 1,000 TIMES !!
HUH?
!
OOPS!

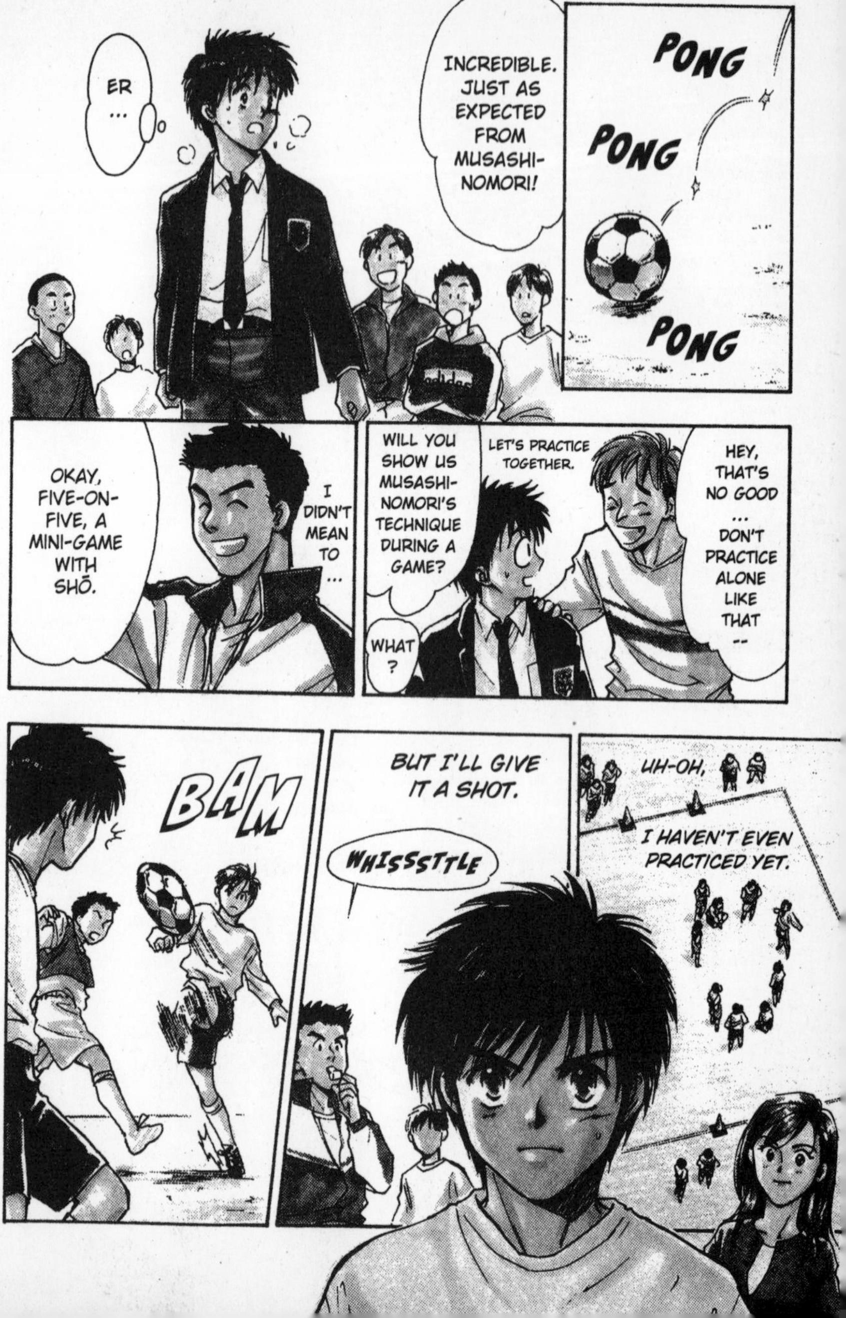

PONG
PONG
PONG
INCREDIBLE. JUST AS EXPECTED FROM MUSASHI-NOMORI!
ER ...
HEY, THAT'S NO GOOD ... DON'T PRACTICE ALONE LIKE THAT --
LET'S PRACTICE TOGETHER.
WILL YOU SHOW US MUSASHI-NOMORI'S TECHNIQUE DURING A GAME?
WHAT ?
I DIDN'T MEAN TO ...
OKAY, FIVE-ON-FIVE, A MINI-GAME WITH SHŌ.
UH-OH,
I HAVEN'T EVEN PRACTICED YET.
BUT I'LL GIVE IT A SHOT.
WHISSSTTLE
BAM

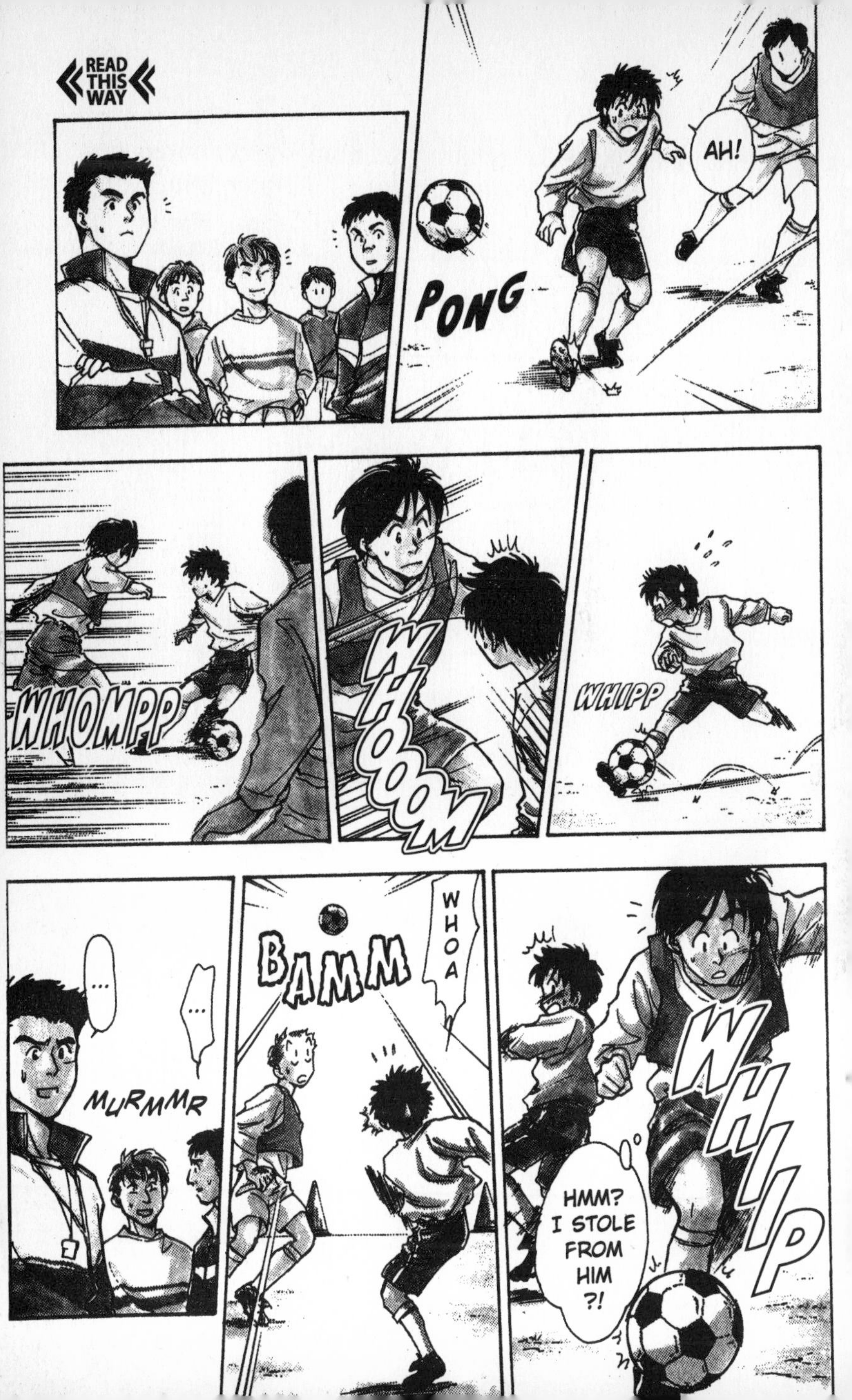
READ THIS WAY
AH!
PONG
WHIPP
WHOOOM
WHOMPP
WHIP
HMM? I STOLE FROM HIM ?!
BAMM
WHOA
...
...
MURMMR

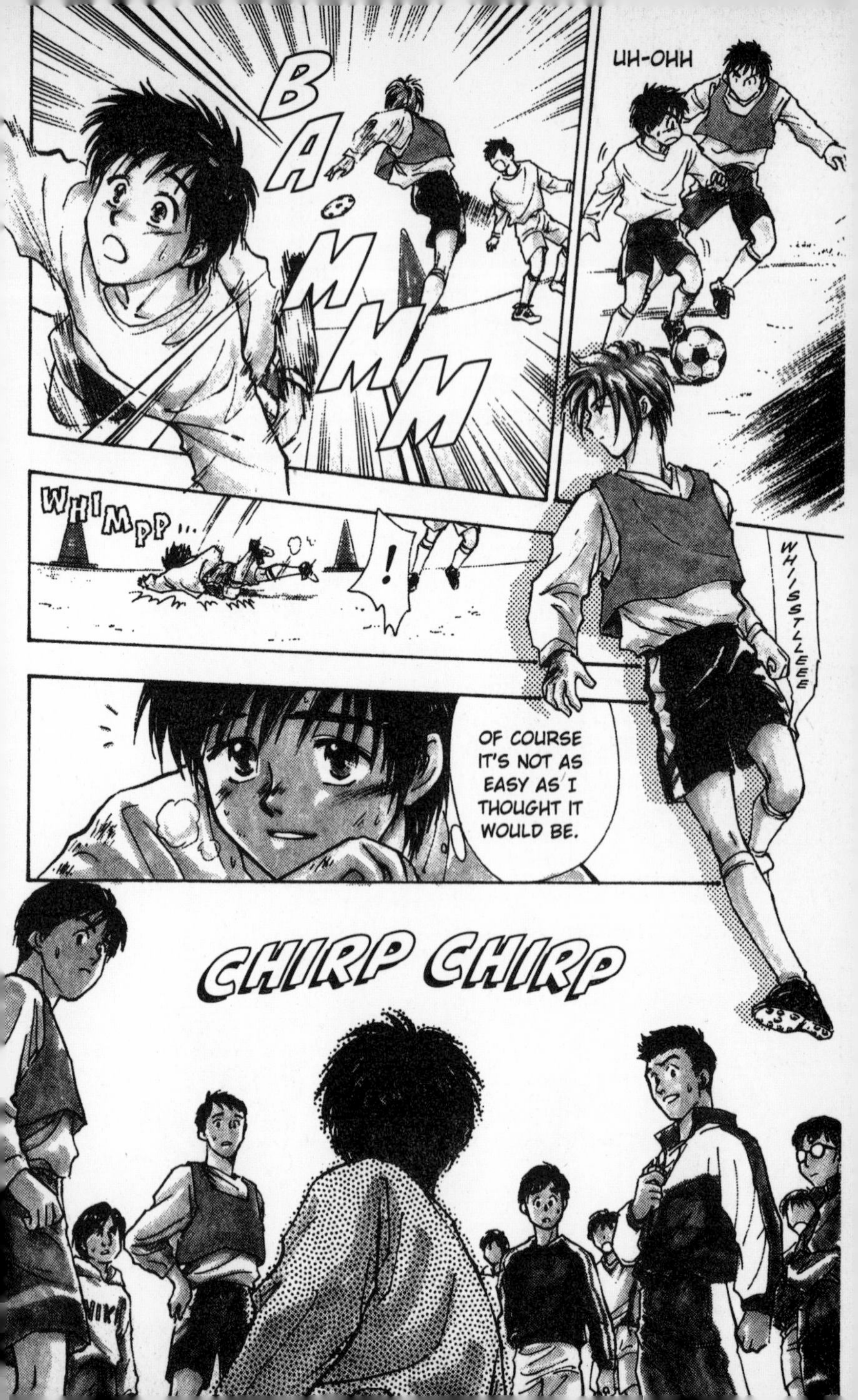
UH-OHH
BAMMM
WHIISSTLLEEE
WHIMPP...
!
OF COURSE IT'S NOT AS EASY AS I THOUGHT IT WOULD BE.
CHIRP CHIRP

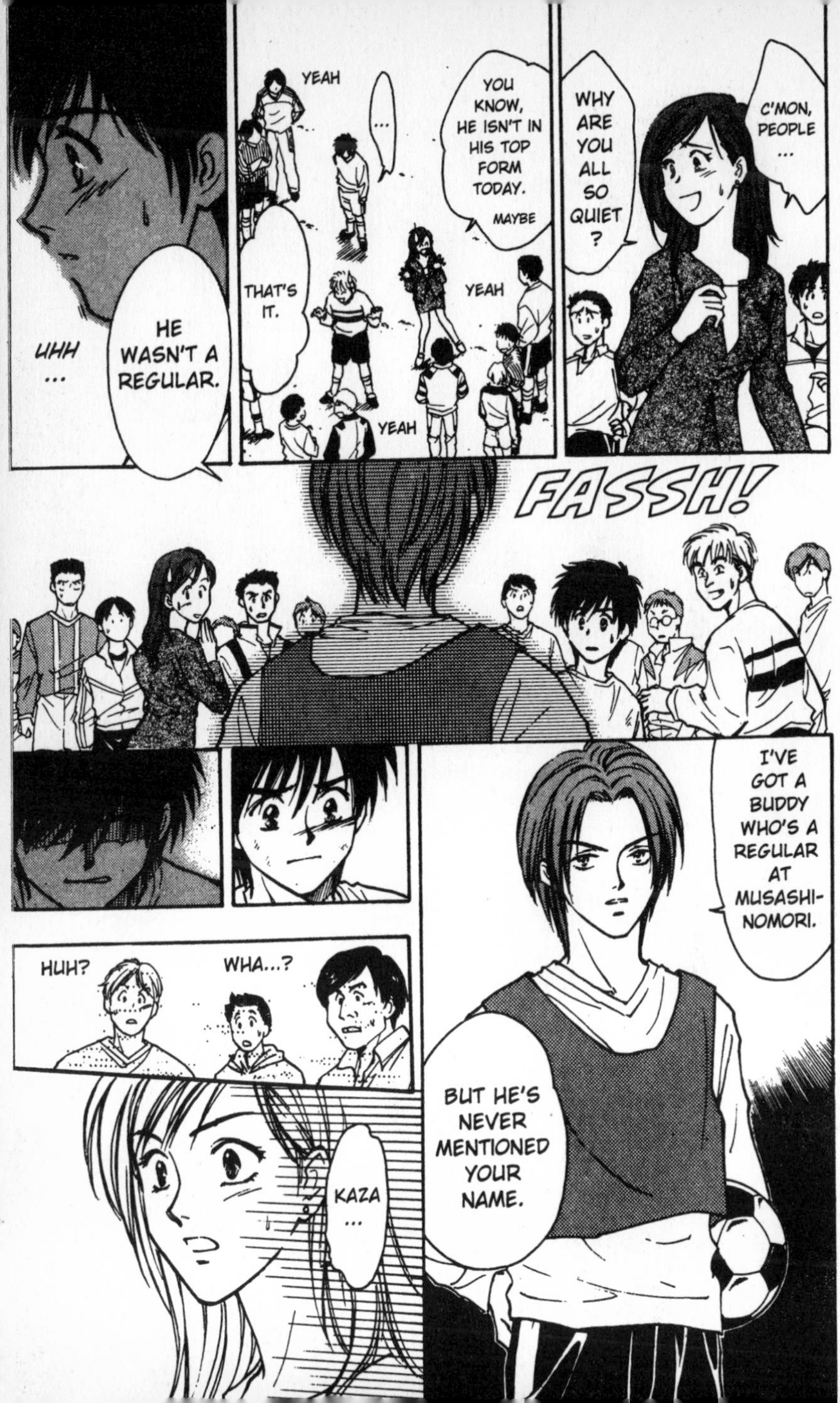
C'MON, PEOPLE ...
WHY ARE YOU ALL SO QUIET ?
YOU KNOW, HE ISN'T IN HIS TOP FORM TODAY.
MAYBE
...
YEAH
YEAH
THAT'S IT.
YEAH
HE WASN'T A REGULAR.
UHH ...
FASSH!
I'VE GOT A BUDDY WHO'S A REGULAR AT MUSASHI-NOMORI.
BUT HE'S NEVER MENTIONED YOUR NAME.
WHA...?
HUH?
KAZA ...

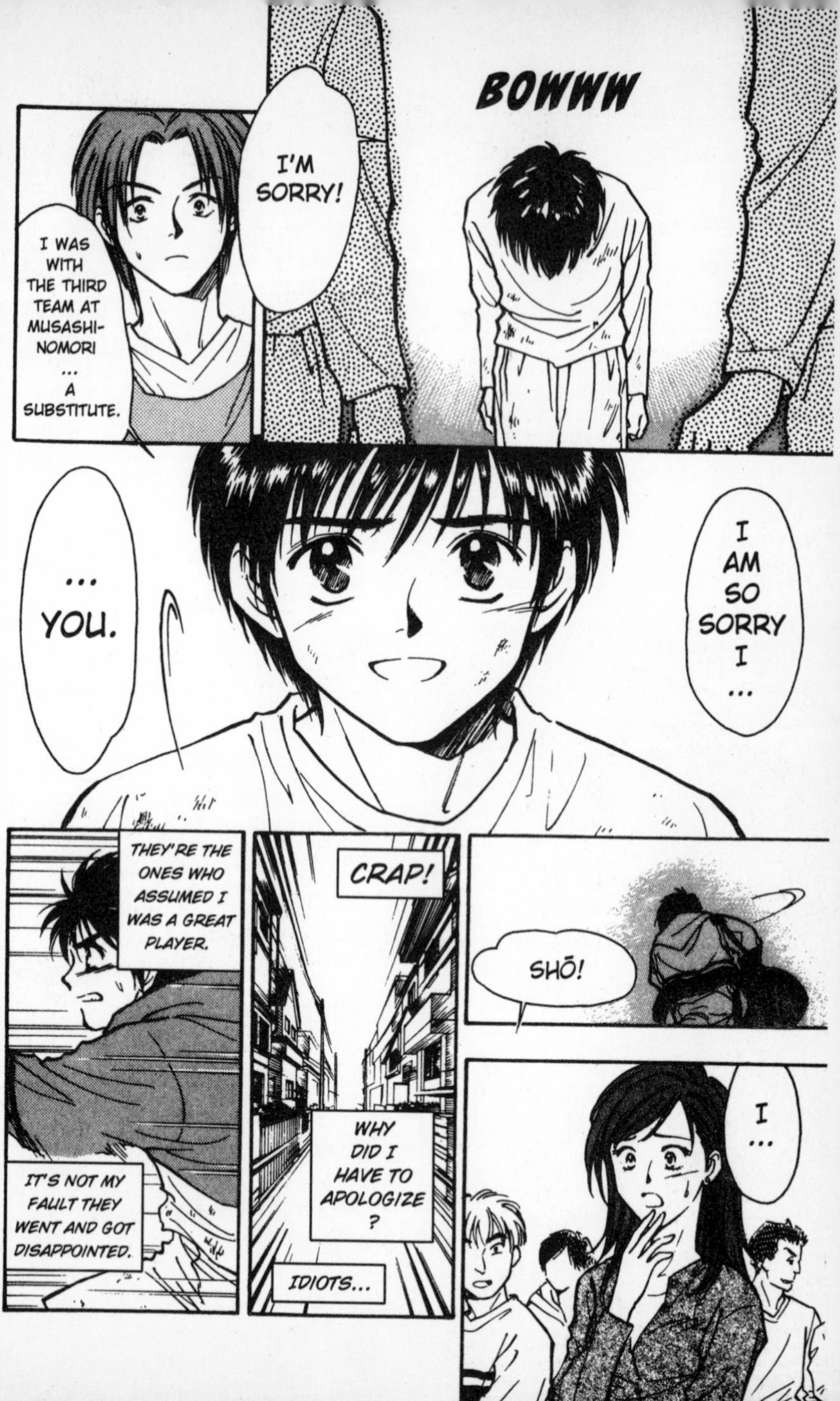
BOWWW
I'M SORRY!
I WAS WITH THE THIRD TEAM AT MUSASHI-NOMORI ... A SUBSTITUTE.
I AM SO SORRY I ...
... YOU.
SHŌ!
I ...
CRAP!
WHY DID I HAVE TO APOLOGIZE?
IDIOTS...
THEY'RE THE ONES WHO ASSUMED I WAS A GREAT PLAYER.
IT'S NOT MY FAULT THEY WENT AND GOT DISAPPOINTED.

READ THIS WAY

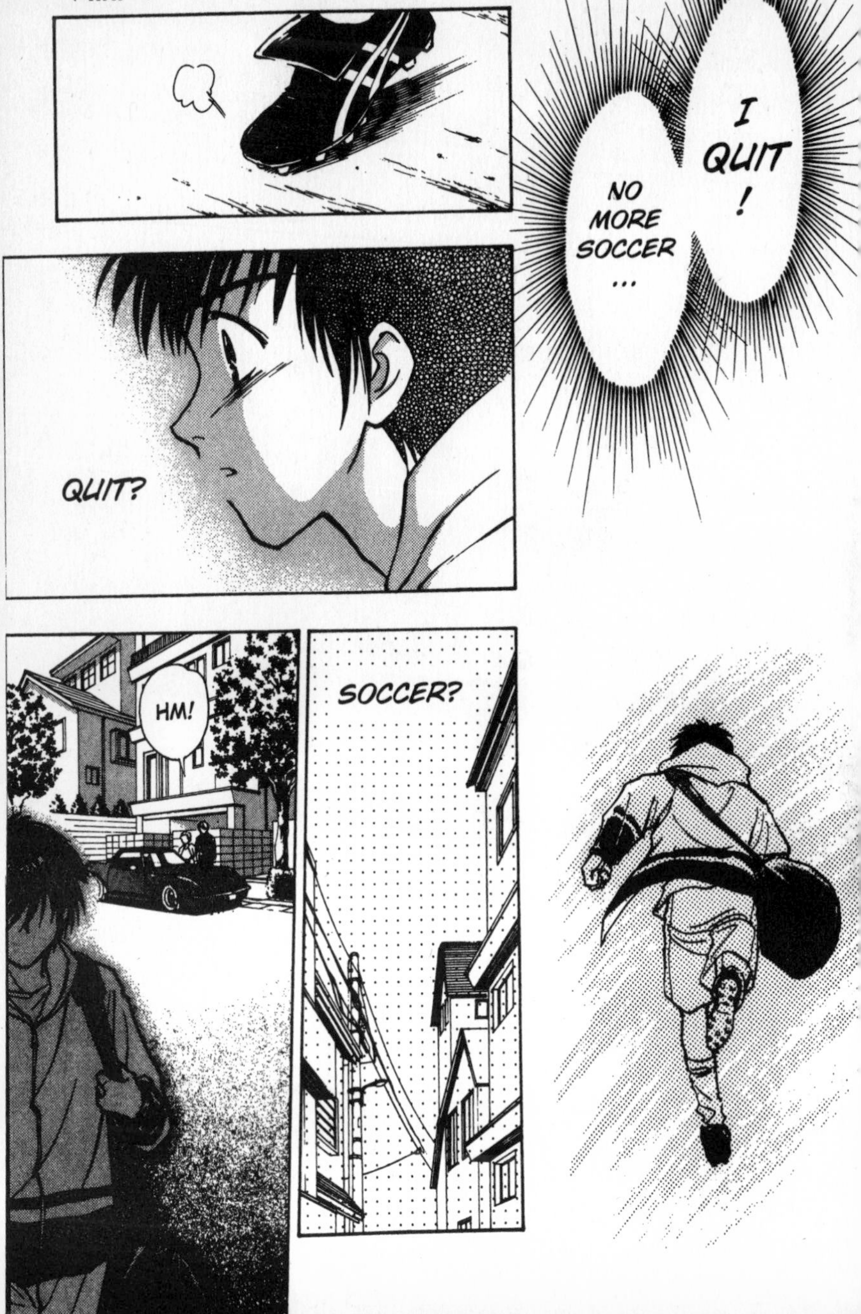
I QUIT!
NO MORE SOCCER...
QUIT?
SOCCER?
HM!

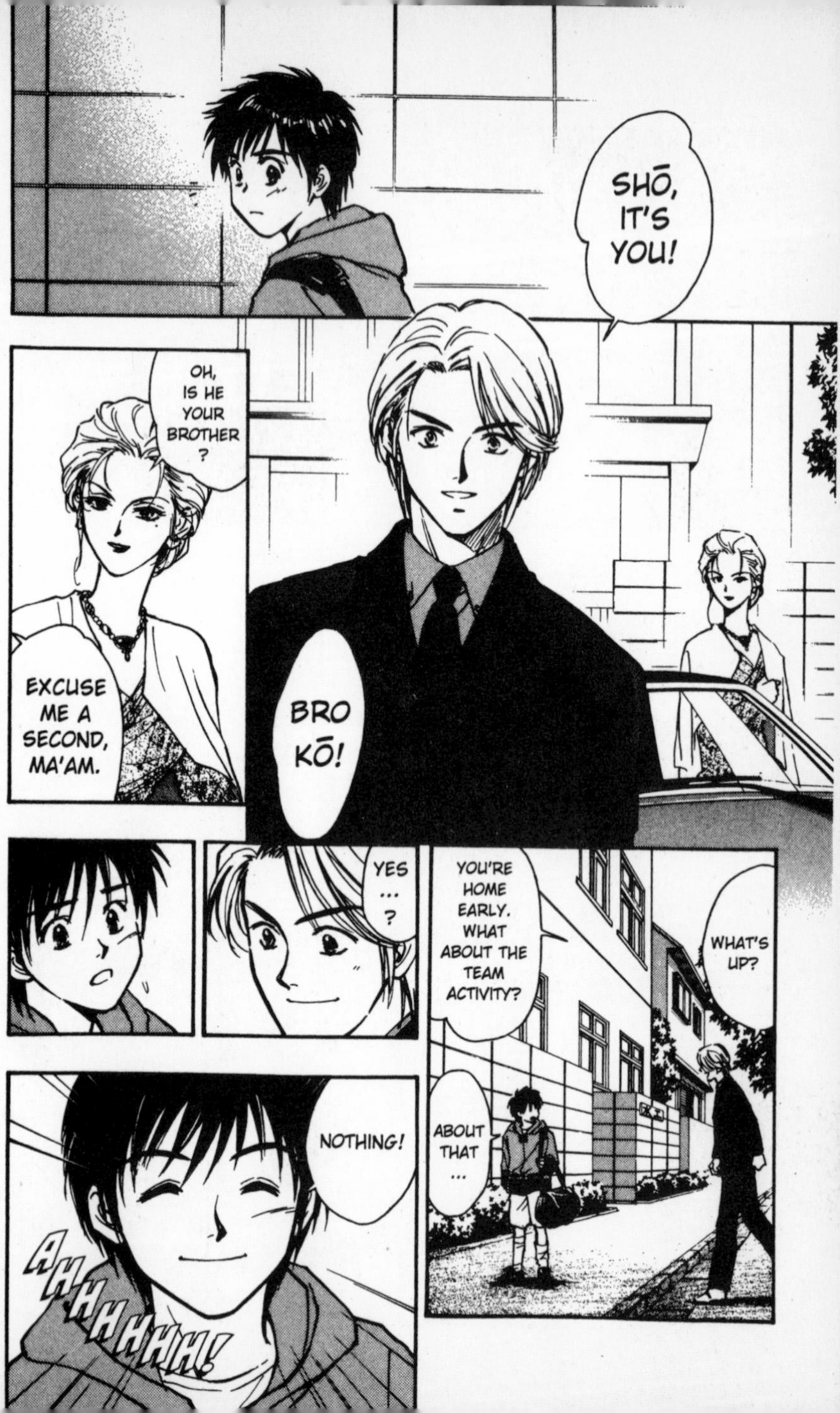
SHŌ, IT'S YOU!
BRO KŌ!
OH, IS HE YOUR BROTHER?
EXCUSE ME A SECOND, MA'AM.
WHAT'S UP?
YOU'RE HOME EARLY. WHAT ABOUT THE TEAM ACTIVITY?
ABOUT THAT ...
YES ... ?
NOTHING!
AHHHHHHH!

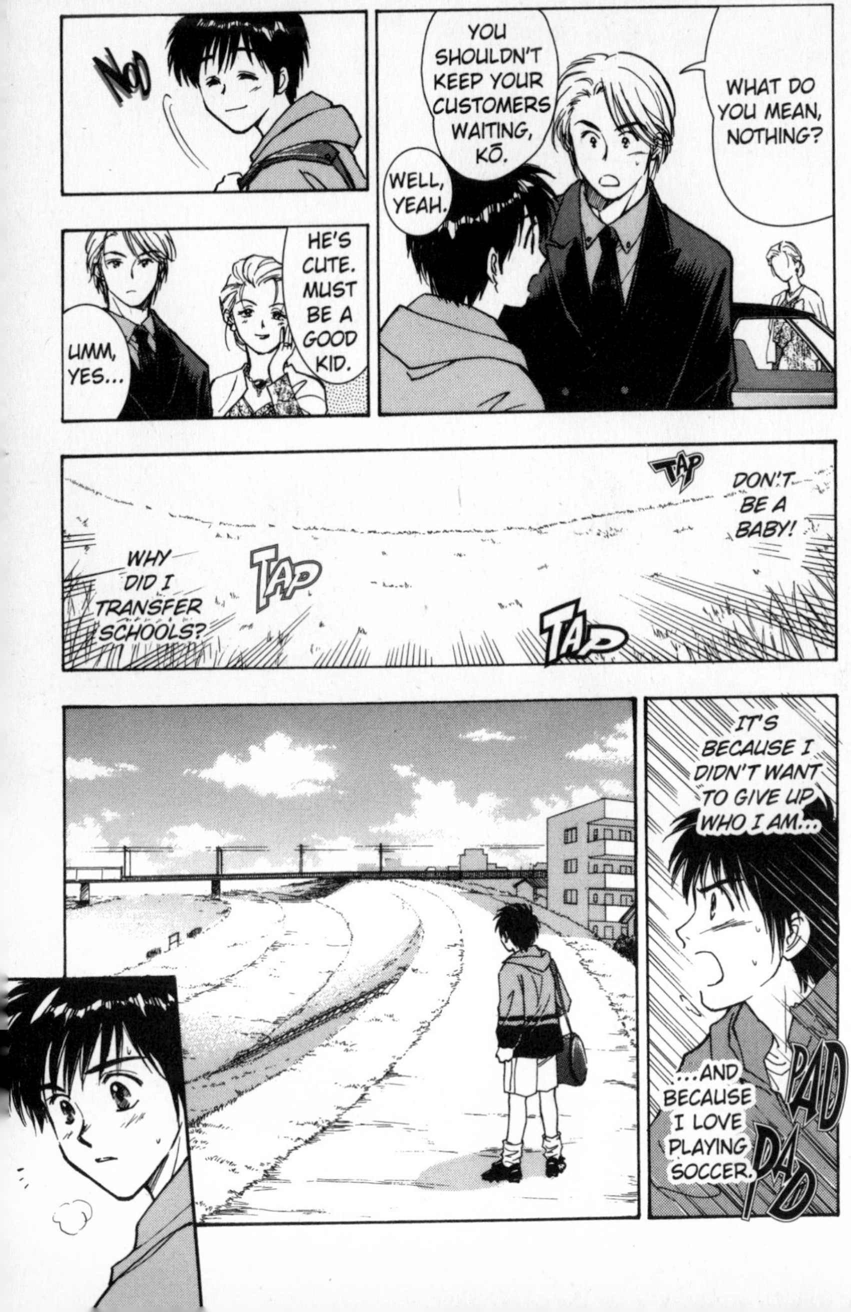
WHAT DO YOU MEAN, NOTHING?
YOU SHOULDN'T KEEP YOUR CUSTOMERS WAITING, KŌ.
WELL, YEAH.
NOD
HE'S CUTE. MUST BE A GOOD KID.
UMM, YES...
TAP
DON'T BE A BABY!
TAP
WHY DID I TRANSFER SCHOOLS?
TAP
IT'S BECAUSE I DIDN'T WANT TO GIVE UP WHO I AM...
...AND BECAUSE I LOVE PLAYING SOCCER.
PAD PAD
PAD PAD

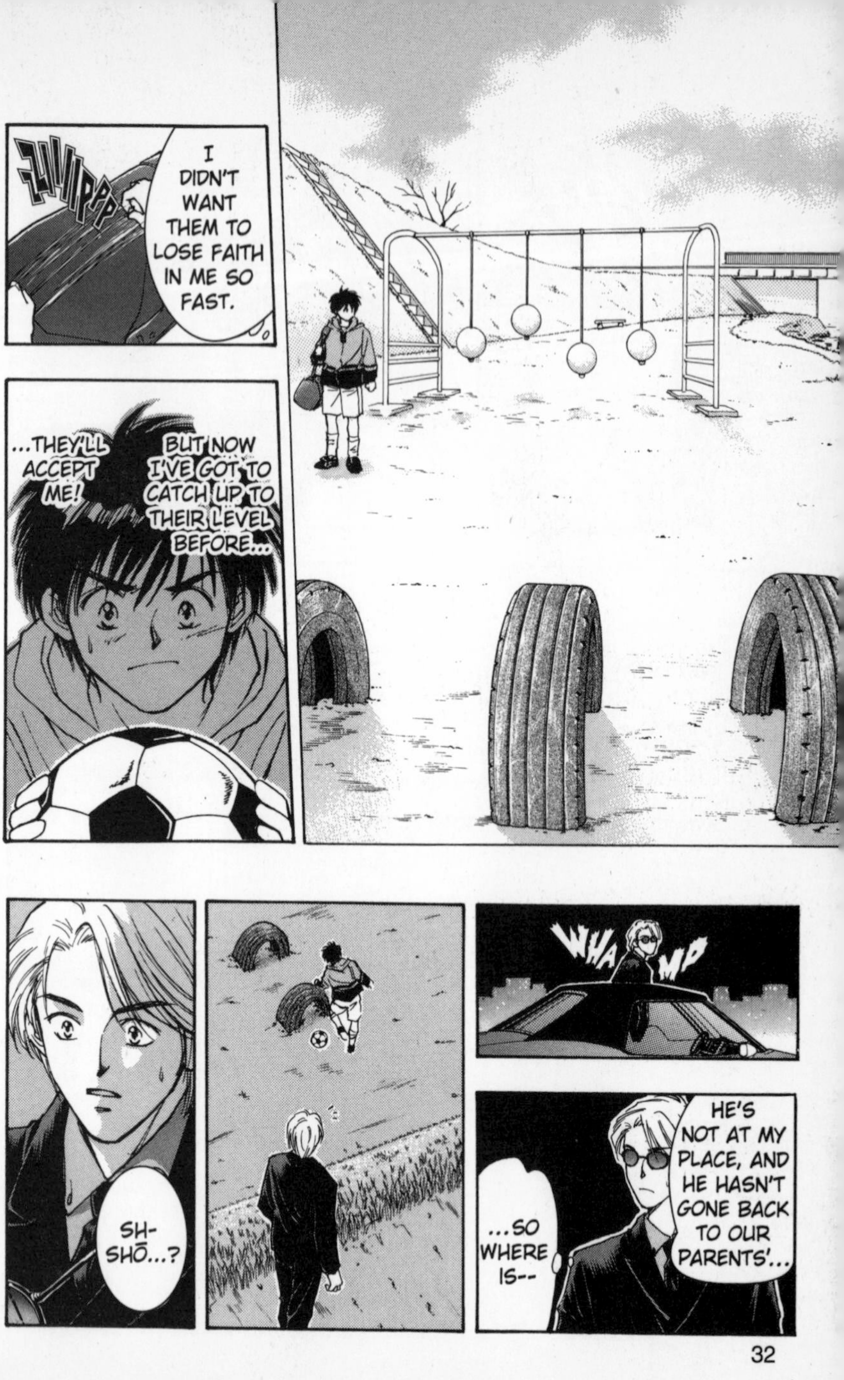
ZIIIIPPP
I DIDN'T WANT THEM TO LOSE FAITH IN ME SO FAST.
BUT NOW I'VE GOT TO CATCH UP TO THEIR LEVEL BEFORE...
...THEY'LL ACCEPT ME!
WHAMP
HE'S NOT AT MY PLACE, AND HE HASN'T GONE BACK TO OUR PARENTS'...
...SO WHERE IS--
SH-SHŌ...?

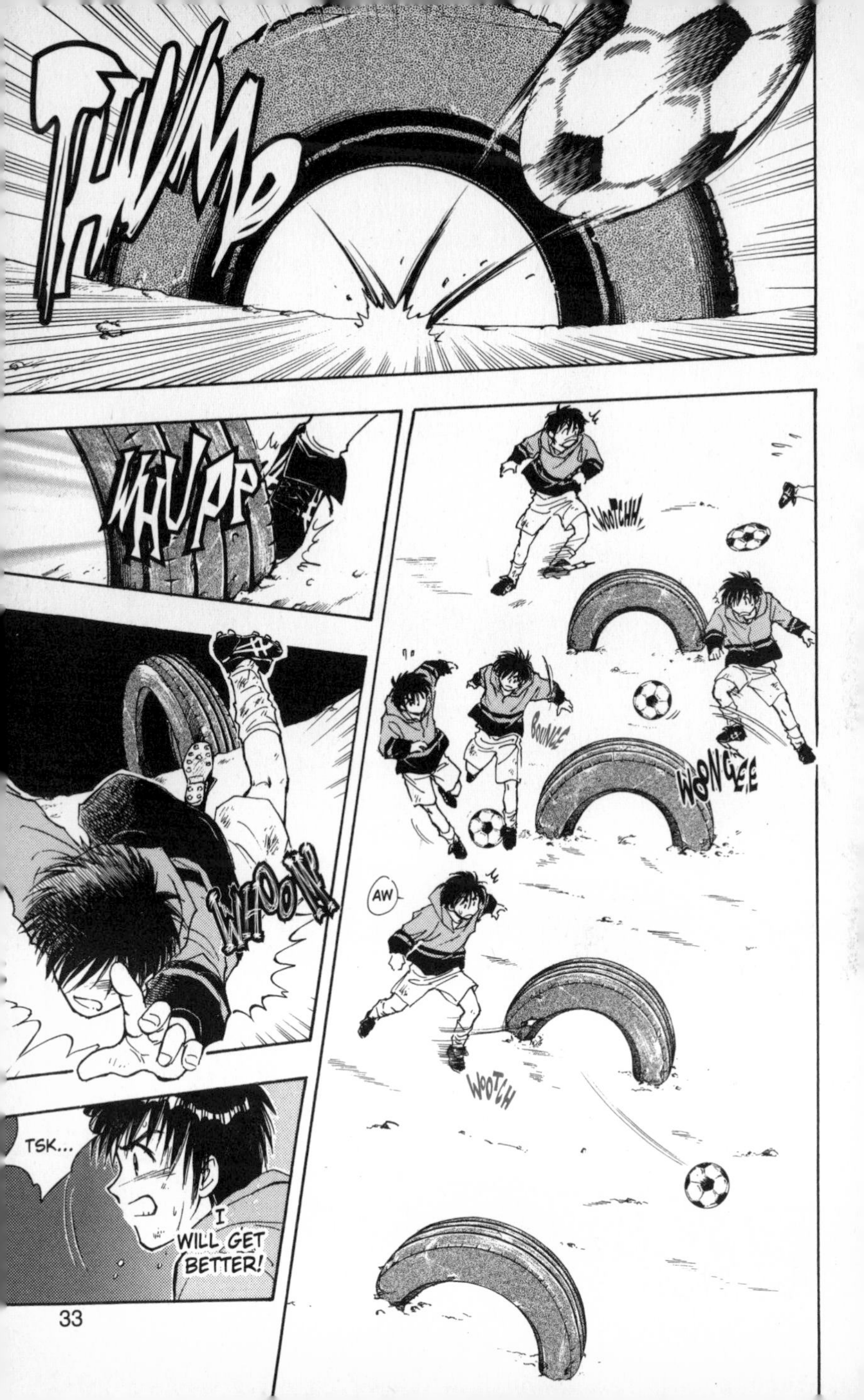
THUMP
WOOTCHH
BOUNCE
WOONGEE
AW
WOOTCH
WHUPP
WHOOM
TSK...
I WILL GET BETTER!

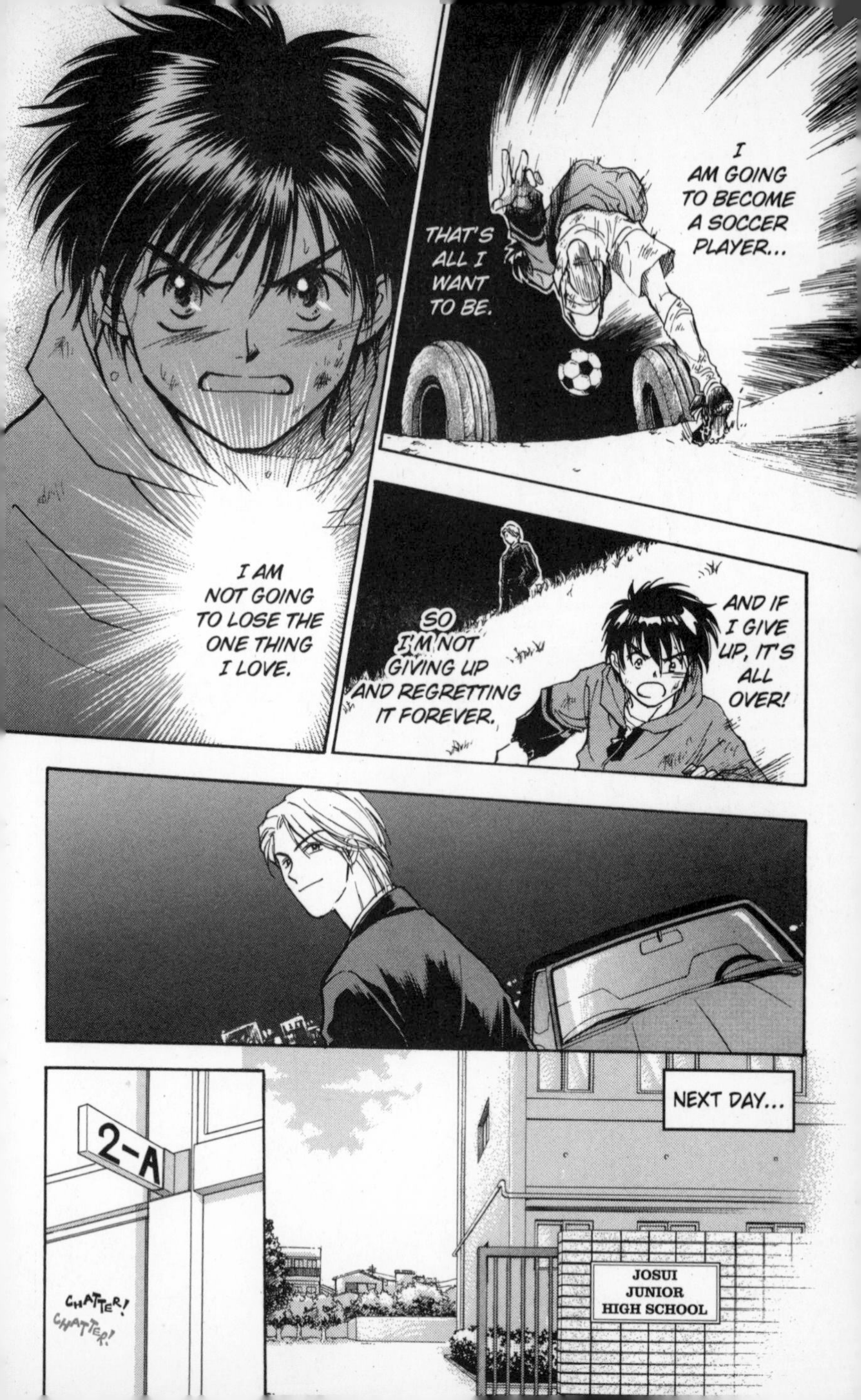
I AM GOING TO BECOME A SOCCER PLAYER...
THAT'S ALL I WANT TO BE.
AND IF I GIVE UP, IT'S ALL OVER!
SO I'M NOT GIVING UP AND REGRETTING IT FOREVER.
I AM NOT GOING TO LOSE THE ONE THING I LOVE.
NEXT DAY...
JOSUI JUNIOR HIGH SCHOOL
2-A
CHATTER!
CHATTER!

READ THIS WAY

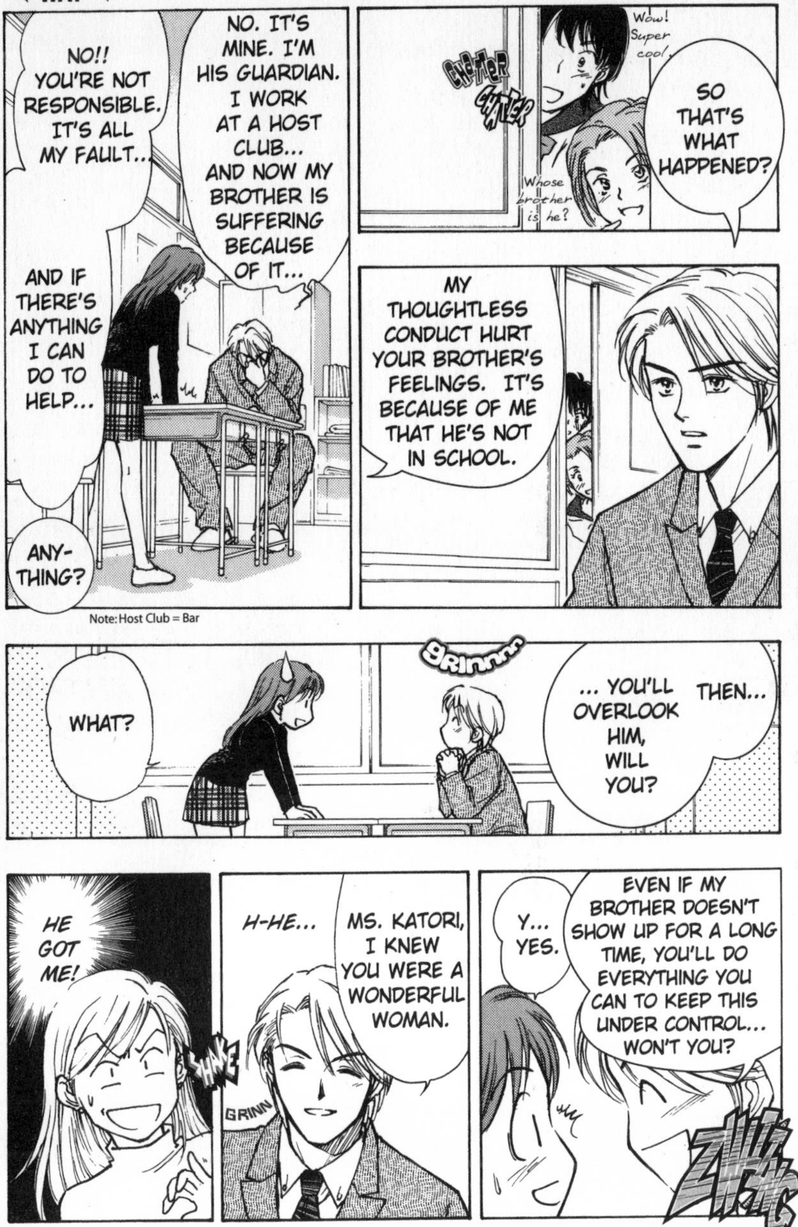

CHATTER CHATTER
Wow! Super cool.
Whose brother is he?
SO THAT'S WHAT HAPPENED?
MY THOUGHTLESS CONDUCT HURT YOUR BROTHER'S FEELINGS. IT'S BECAUSE OF ME THAT HE'S NOT IN SCHOOL.
NO!! YOU'RE NOT RESPONSIBLE. IT'S ALL MY FAULT...
NO. IT'S MINE. I'M HIS GUARDIAN. I WORK AT A HOST CLUB... AND NOW MY BROTHER IS SUFFERING BECAUSE OF IT...
AND IF THERE'S ANYTHING I CAN DO TO HELP...
ANY-THING?
Note: Host Club = Bar
GRINnnn
THEN...
... YOU'LL OVERLOOK HIM, WILL YOU?
WHAT?
EVEN IF MY BROTHER DOESN'T SHOW UP FOR A LONG TIME, YOU'LL DO EVERYTHING YOU CAN TO KEEP THIS UNDER CONTROL... WON'T YOU?
Y... YES.
ZHING
MS. KATORI, I KNEW YOU WERE A WONDERFUL WOMAN.
H-HE...
GRINN
HE GOT ME!

READ THIS WAY

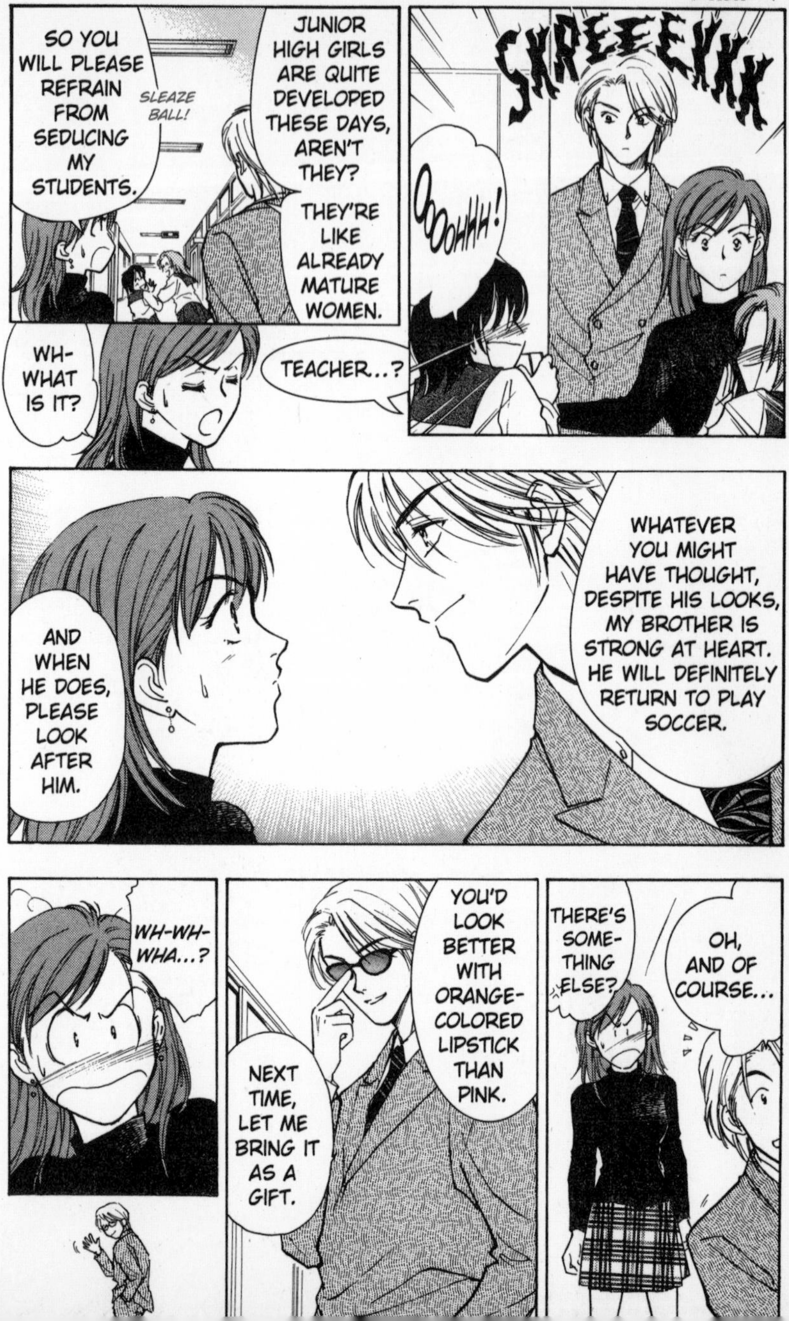
SKREEEEKKK
OOOOHHH!
TEACHER...?
JUNIOR HIGH GIRLS ARE QUITE DEVELOPED THESE DAYS, AREN'T THEY?
THEY'RE LIKE ALREADY MATURE WOMEN.
SLEAZE BALL!
SO YOU WILL PLEASE REFRAIN FROM SEDUCING MY STUDENTS.
WH-WHAT IS IT?
WHATEVER YOU MIGHT HAVE THOUGHT, DESPITE HIS LOOKS, MY BROTHER IS STRONG AT HEART. HE WILL DEFINITELY RETURN TO PLAY SOCCER.
AND WHEN HE DOES, PLEASE LOOK AFTER HIM.
OH, AND OF COURSE...
THERE'S SOME-THING ELSE?
YOU'D LOOK BETTER WITH ORANGE-COLORED LIPSTICK THAN PINK.
NEXT TIME, LET ME BRING IT AS A GIFT.
WH-WH-WHA...?

READ THIS WAY

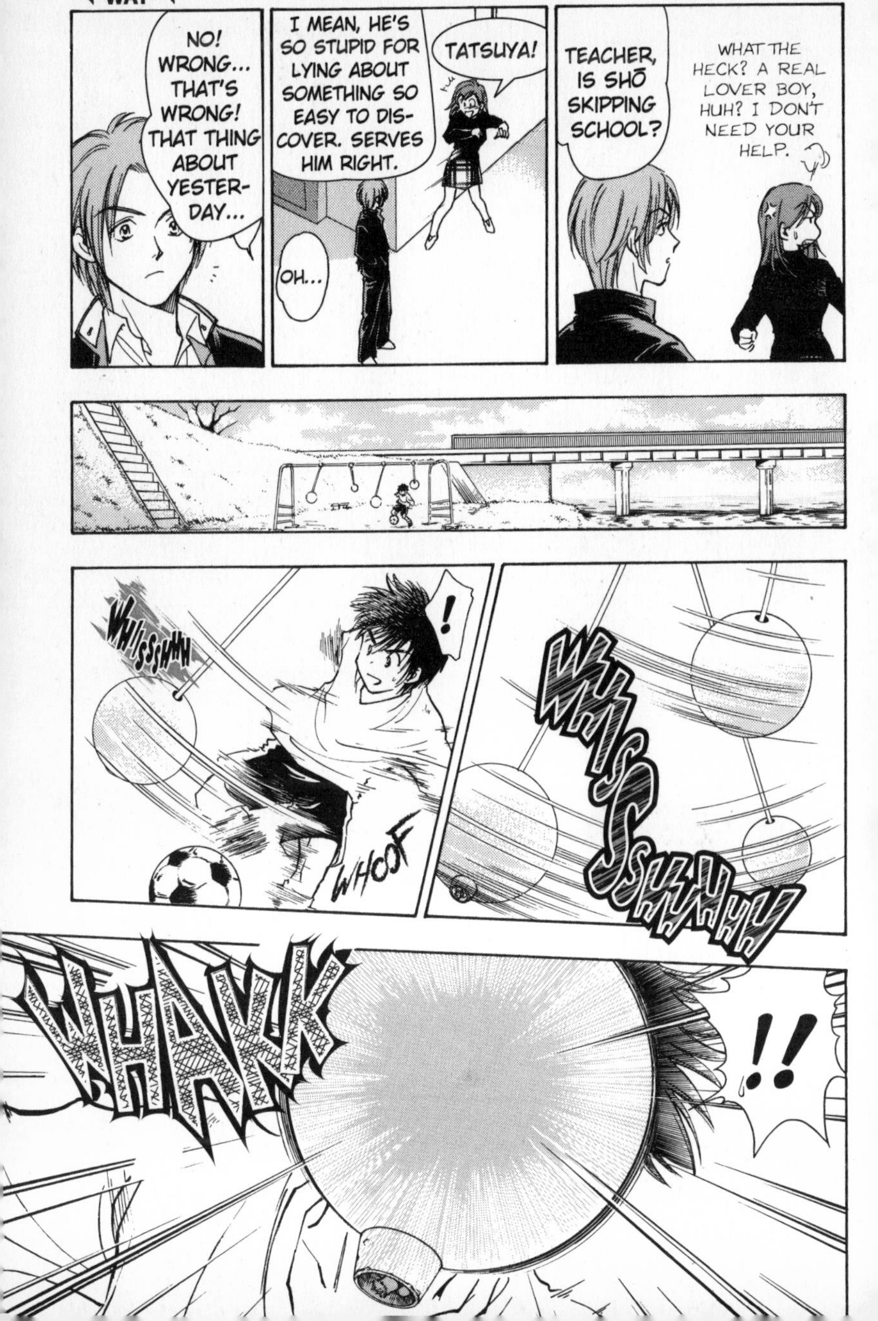
WHAT THE HECK? A REAL LOVER BOY, HUH? I DON'T NEED YOUR HELP.
TEACHER, IS SHŌ SKIPPING SCHOOL?
TATSUYA!
I MEAN, HE'S SO STUPID FOR LYING ABOUT SOMETHING SO EASY TO DISCOVER. SERVES HIM RIGHT.
OH...
NO! WRONG... THAT'S WRONG! THAT THING ABOUT YESTERDAY...
WHISSSHHHH
!
WHISSHHH
WHOOF
!!
WHACK

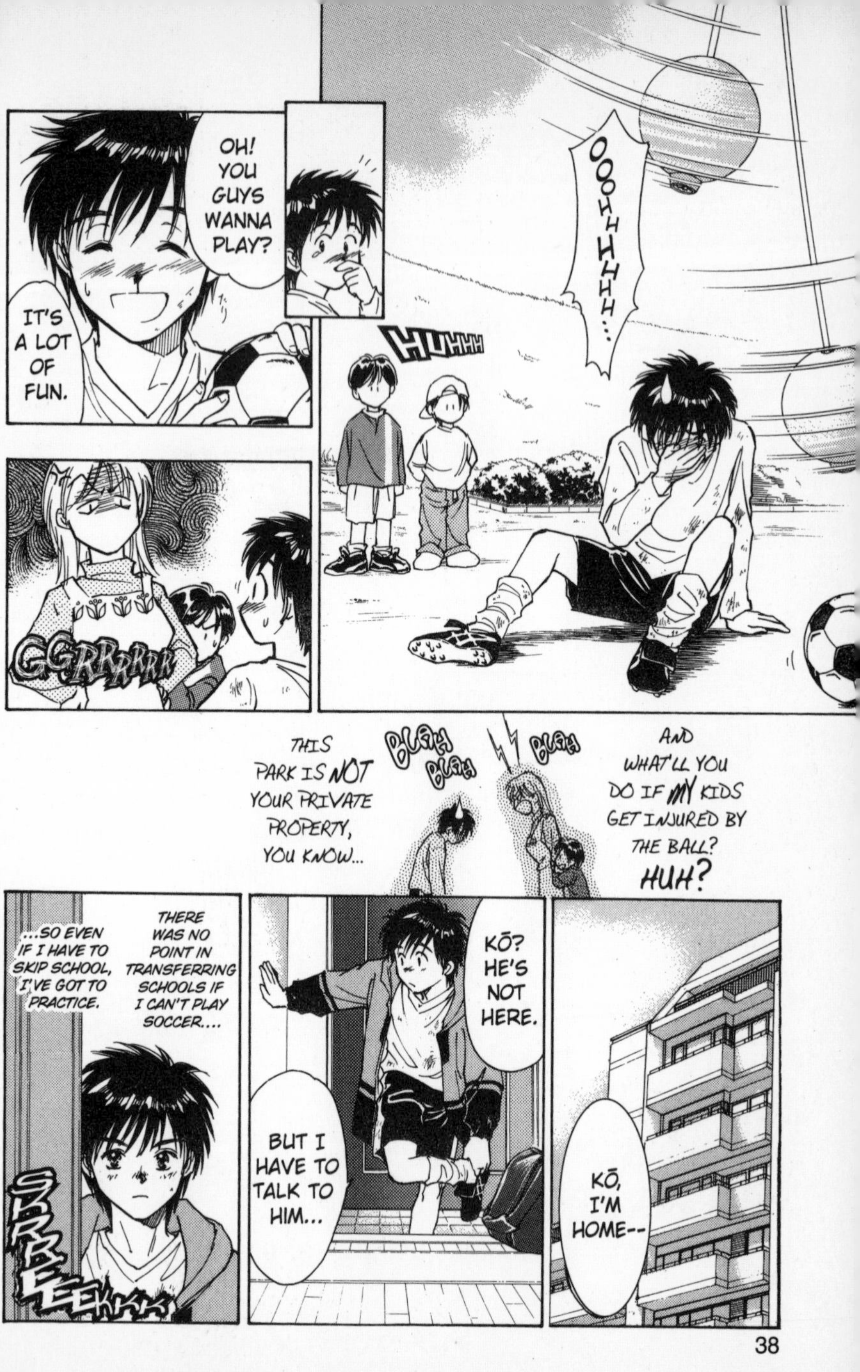
OOOHHHHHH...
HUHHH
OH! YOU GUYS WANNA PLAY?
IT'S A LOT OF FUN.
GGRRRRRR
AND WHAT'LL YOU DO IF MY KIDS GET INJURED BY THE BALL? HUH?
BLAH
BLAH BLAH
THIS PARK IS NOT YOUR PRIVATE PROPERTY, YOU KNOW...
KŌ, I'M HOME--
KŌ? HE'S NOT HERE.
BUT I HAVE TO TALK TO HIM...
THERE WAS NO POINT IN TRANSFERRING SCHOOLS IF I CAN'T PLAY SOCCER....
...SO EVEN IF I HAVE TO SKIP SCHOOL, I'VE GOT TO PRACTICE.
SKRREEEKKK

READ THIS WAY

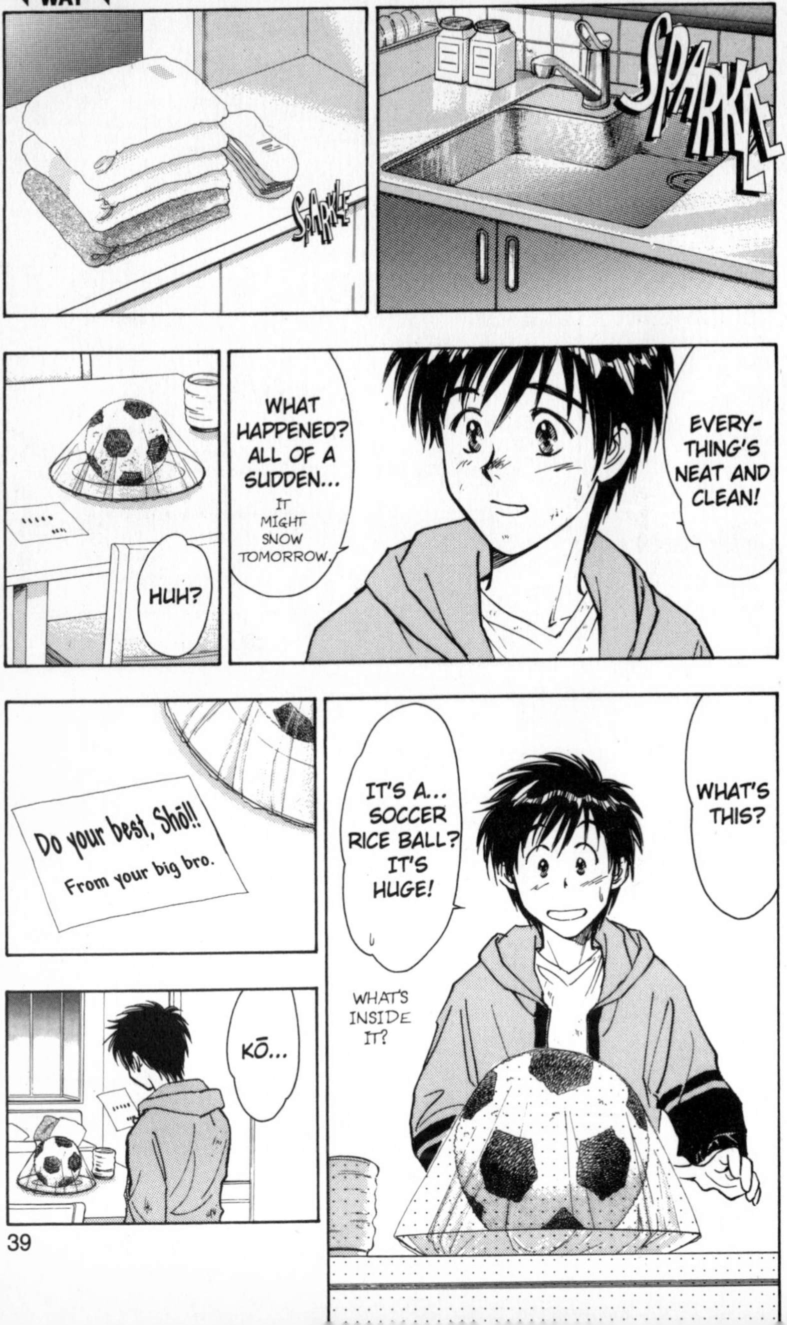
SPARKLE
SPARKLE
EVERYTHING'S NEAT AND CLEAN!
WHAT HAPPENED? ALL OF A SUDDEN...
IT MIGHT SNOW TOMORROW.
HUH?
WHAT'S THIS?
IT'S A... SOCCER RICE BALL? IT'S HUGE!
WHAT'S INSIDE IT?
Do your best, Shō!!
From your big bro.
KŌ...

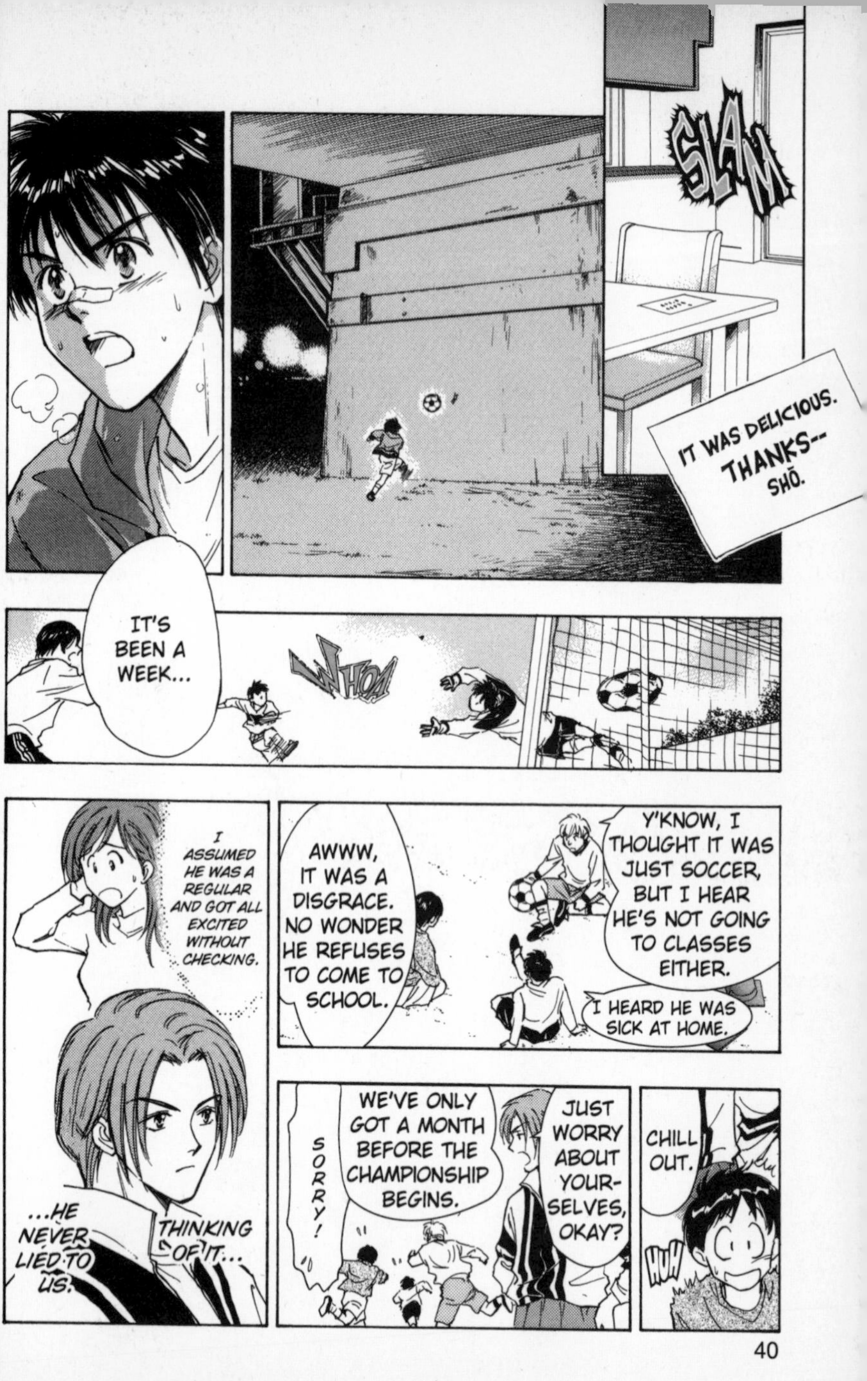
SLAM
IT WAS DELICIOUS. THANKS-- SHŌ.
WHOA
IT'S BEEN A WEEK...
Y'KNOW, I THOUGHT IT WAS JUST SOCCER, BUT I HEAR HE'S NOT GOING TO CLASSES EITHER.
I HEARD HE WAS SICK AT HOME.
AWWW, IT WAS A DISGRACE. NO WONDER HE REFUSES TO COME TO SCHOOL.
CHILL OUT.
HUH
JUST WORRY ABOUT YOURSELVES, OKAY?
WE'VE ONLY GOT A MONTH BEFORE THE CHAMPIONSHIP BEGINS.
SORRY!
I ASSUMED HE WAS A REGULAR AND GOT ALL EXCITED WITHOUT CHECKING.
THINKING OF IT...
...HE NEVER LIED TO US.

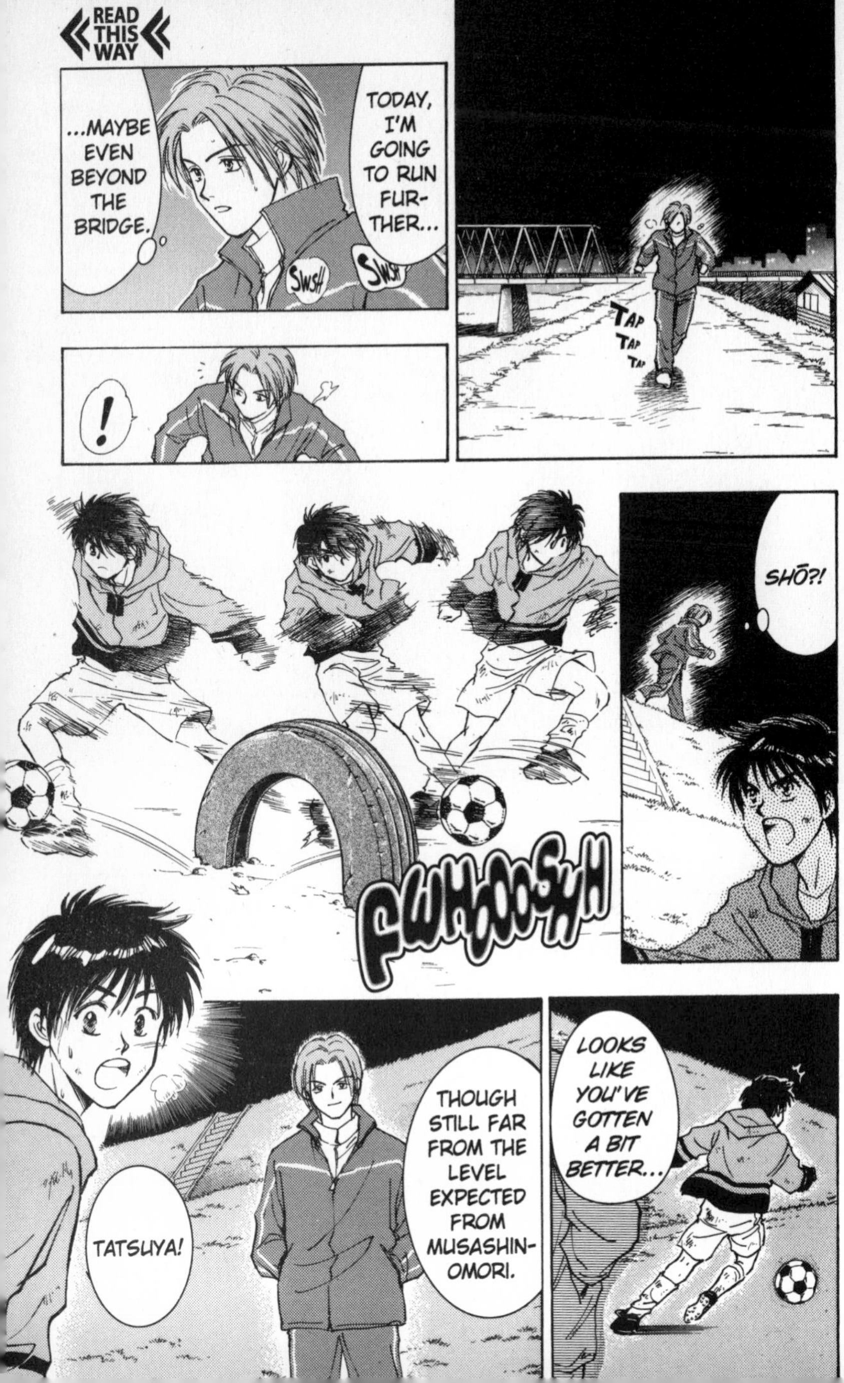
READ THIS WAY
TAP TAP TAP
TODAY, I'M GOING TO RUN FUR-THER...
...MAYBE EVEN BEYOND THE BRIDGE.
SWSH
SWSH
!
SHŌ?!
FWHOOOSHH
LOOKS LIKE YOU'VE GOTTEN A BIT BETTER...
THOUGH STILL FAR FROM THE LEVEL EXPECTED FROM MUSASHIN-OMORI.
TATSUYA!

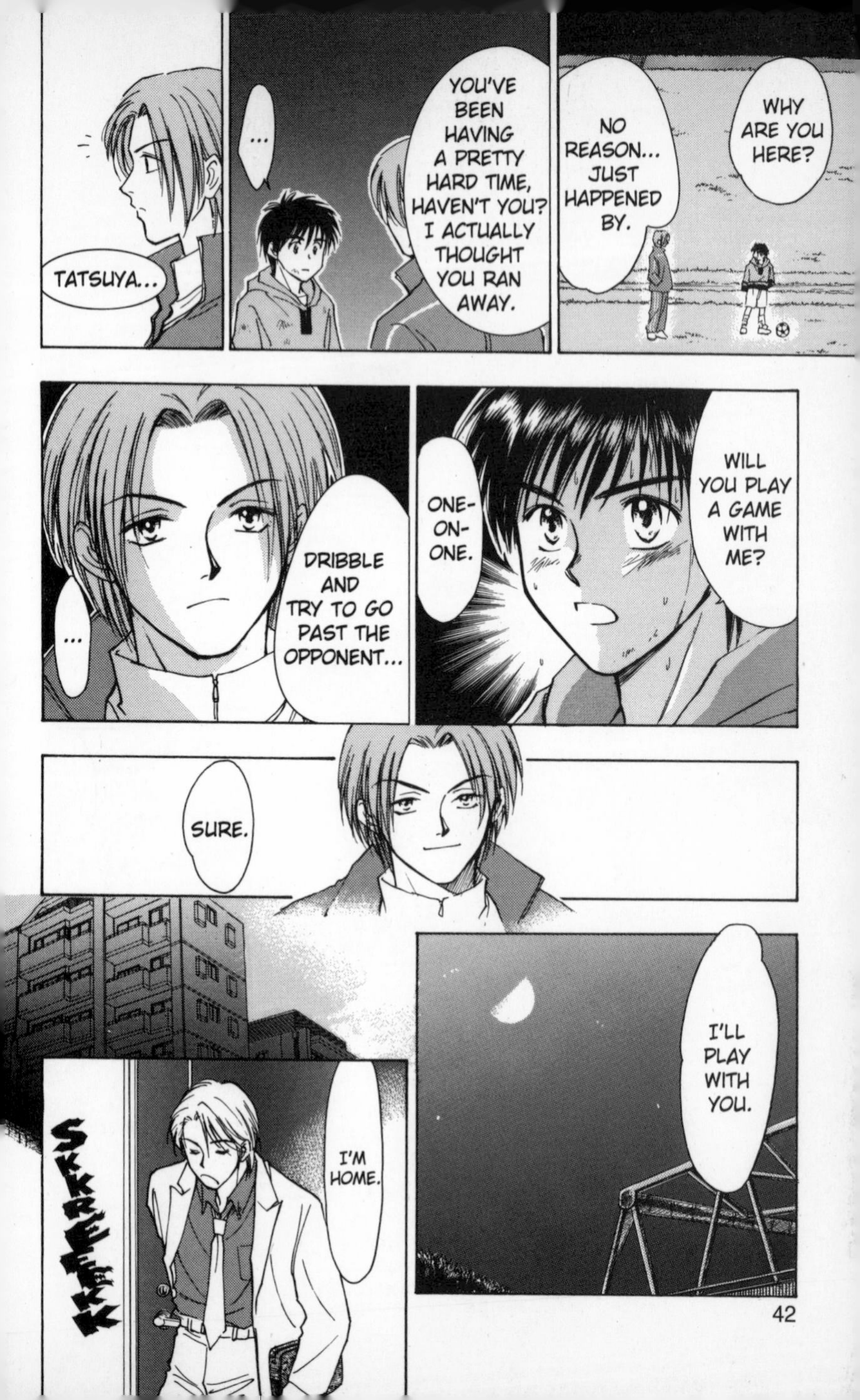
WHY ARE YOU HERE?
NO REASON... JUST HAPPENED BY.
YOU'VE BEEN HAVING A PRETTY HARD TIME, HAVEN'T YOU? I ACTUALLY THOUGHT YOU RAN AWAY.
...
TATSUYA...
WILL YOU PLAY A GAME WITH ME?
ONE-ON-ONE.
DRIBBLE AND TRY TO GO PAST THE OPPONENT...
...
SURE.
I'LL PLAY WITH YOU.
I'M HOME.
SKKREEEKK

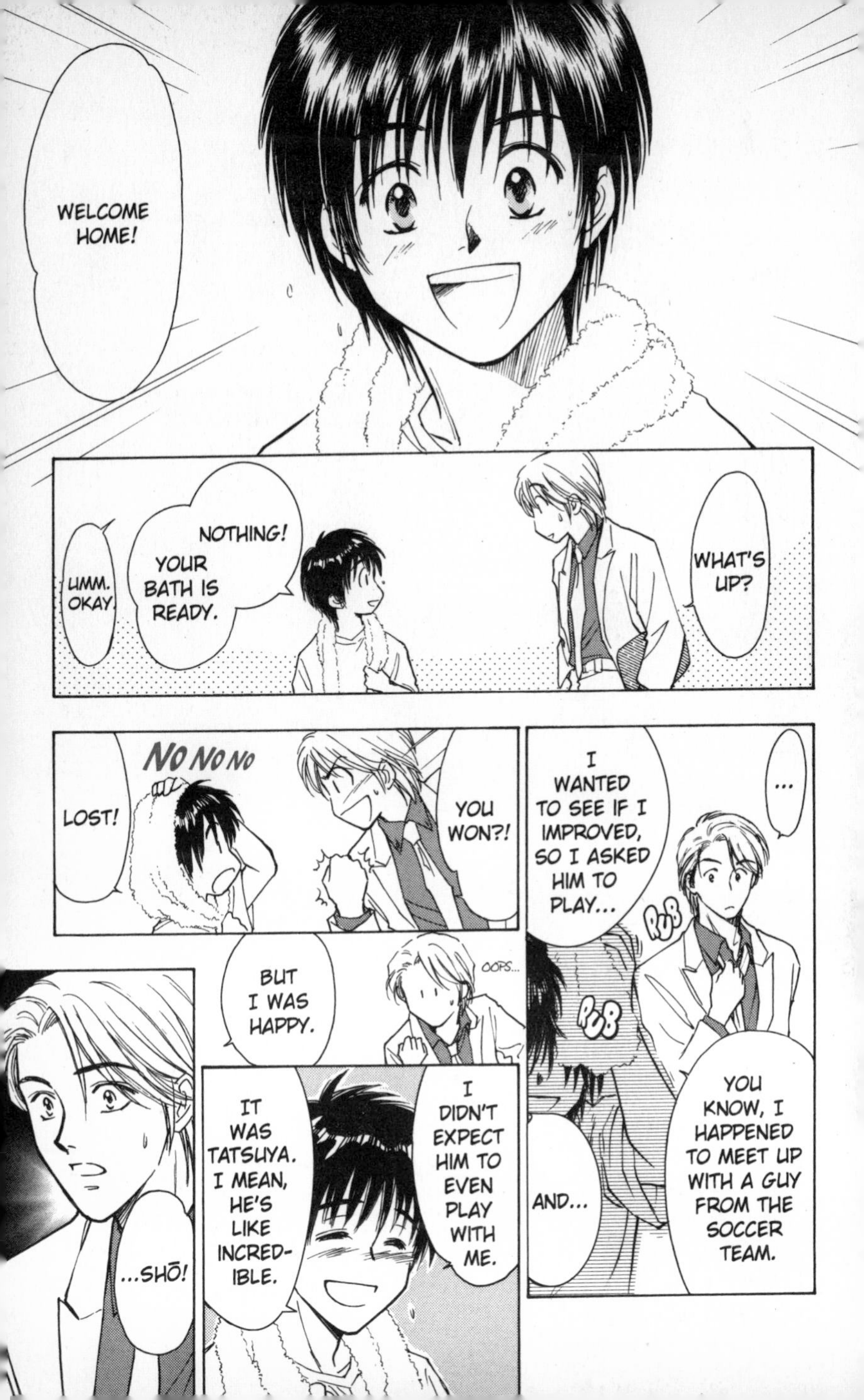
WELCOME HOME!
WHAT'S UP?
NOTHING! YOUR BATH IS READY.
UMM. OKAY.
...
I WANTED TO SEE IF I IMPROVED, SO I ASKED HIM TO PLAY...
RUB
RUB
YOU KNOW, I HAPPENED TO MEET UP WITH A GUY FROM THE SOCCER TEAM.
AND...
YOU WON?!
NO NO NO
LOST!
OOPS...
BUT I WAS HAPPY.
I DIDN'T EXPECT HIM TO EVEN PLAY WITH ME.
IT WAS TATSUYA. I MEAN, HE'S LIKE INCRED-IBLE.
...SHŌ!

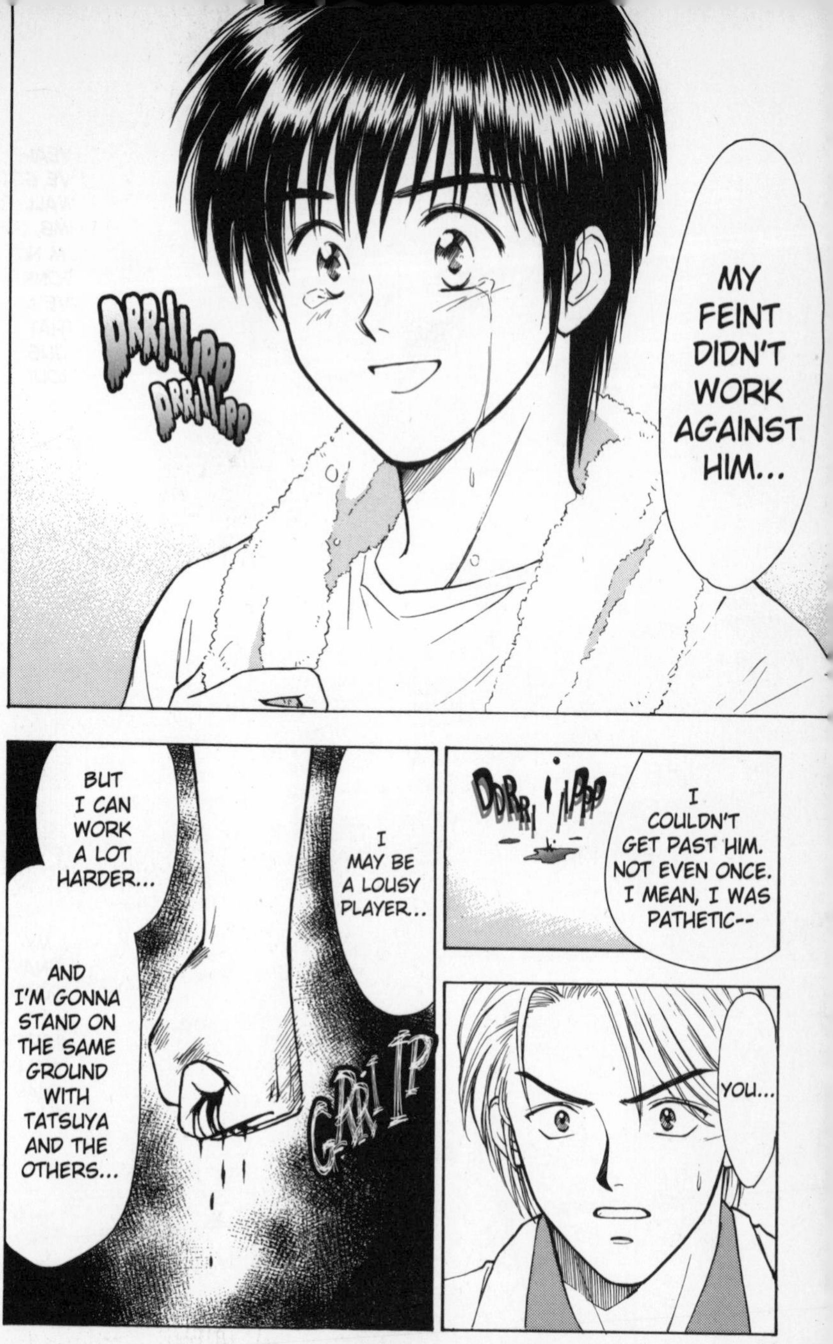
MY FEINT DIDN'T WORK AGAINST HIM...
I COULDN'T GET PAST HIM. NOT EVEN ONCE. I MEAN, I WAS PATHETIC--
YOU...
I MAY BE A LOUSY PLAYER...
BUT I CAN WORK A LOT HARDER...
AND I'M GONNA STAND ON THE SAME GROUND WITH TATSUYA AND THE OTHERS...
GRRIP

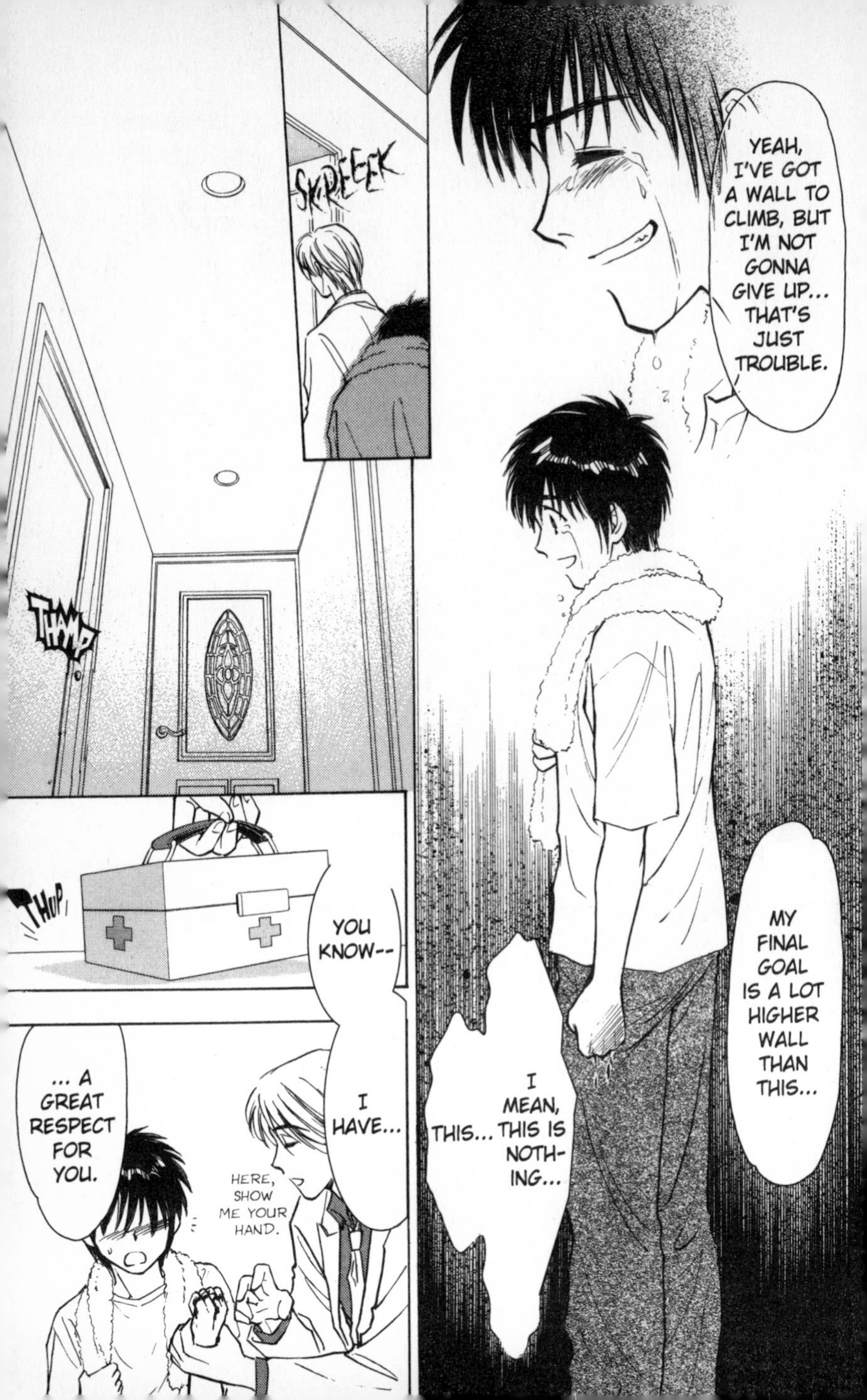
YEAH, I'VE GOT A WALL TO CLIMB, BUT I'M NOT GONNA GIVE UP... THAT'S JUST TROUBLE.
MY FINAL GOAL IS A LOT HIGHER WALL THAN THIS...
I MEAN, THIS IS NOTH-ING...
THIS...
SKREEEK
THAMP
THUP
YOU KNOW--
I HAVE...
... A GREAT RESPECT FOR YOU.
HERE, SHOW ME YOUR HAND.

READ THIS WAY

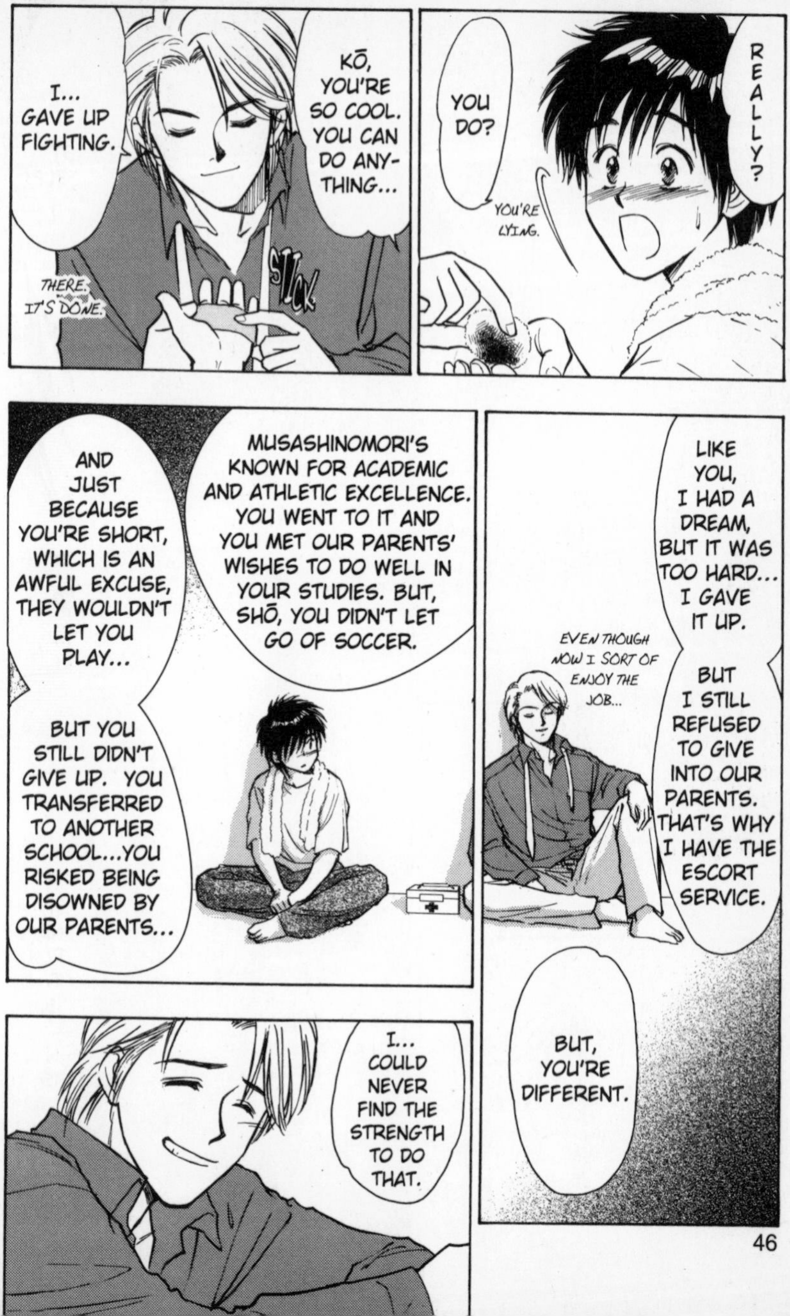
REALLY?
YOU DO?
YOU'RE LYING.
KŌ, YOU'RE SO COOL. YOU CAN DO ANY-THING...
I... GAVE UP FIGHTING.
THERE. IT'S DONE.
STICK
LIKE YOU, I HAD A DREAM, BUT IT WAS TOO HARD... I GAVE IT UP.
EVEN THOUGH NOW I SORT OF ENJOY THE JOB...
BUT I STILL REFUSED TO GIVE INTO OUR PARENTS. THAT'S WHY I HAVE THE ESCORT SERVICE.
BUT, YOU'RE DIFFERENT.
MUSASHINOMORI'S KNOWN FOR ACADEMIC AND ATHLETIC EXCELLENCE. YOU WENT TO IT AND YOU MET OUR PARENTS' WISHES TO DO WELL IN YOUR STUDIES. BUT, SHŌ, YOU DIDN'T LET GO OF SOCCER.
AND JUST BECAUSE YOU'RE SHORT, WHICH IS AN AWFUL EXCUSE, THEY WOULDN'T LET YOU PLAY...
BUT YOU STILL DIDN'T GIVE UP. YOU TRANSFERRED TO ANOTHER SCHOOL...YOU RISKED BEING DISOWNED BY OUR PARENTS...
I... COULD NEVER FIND THE STRENGTH TO DO THAT.

READ THIS WAY

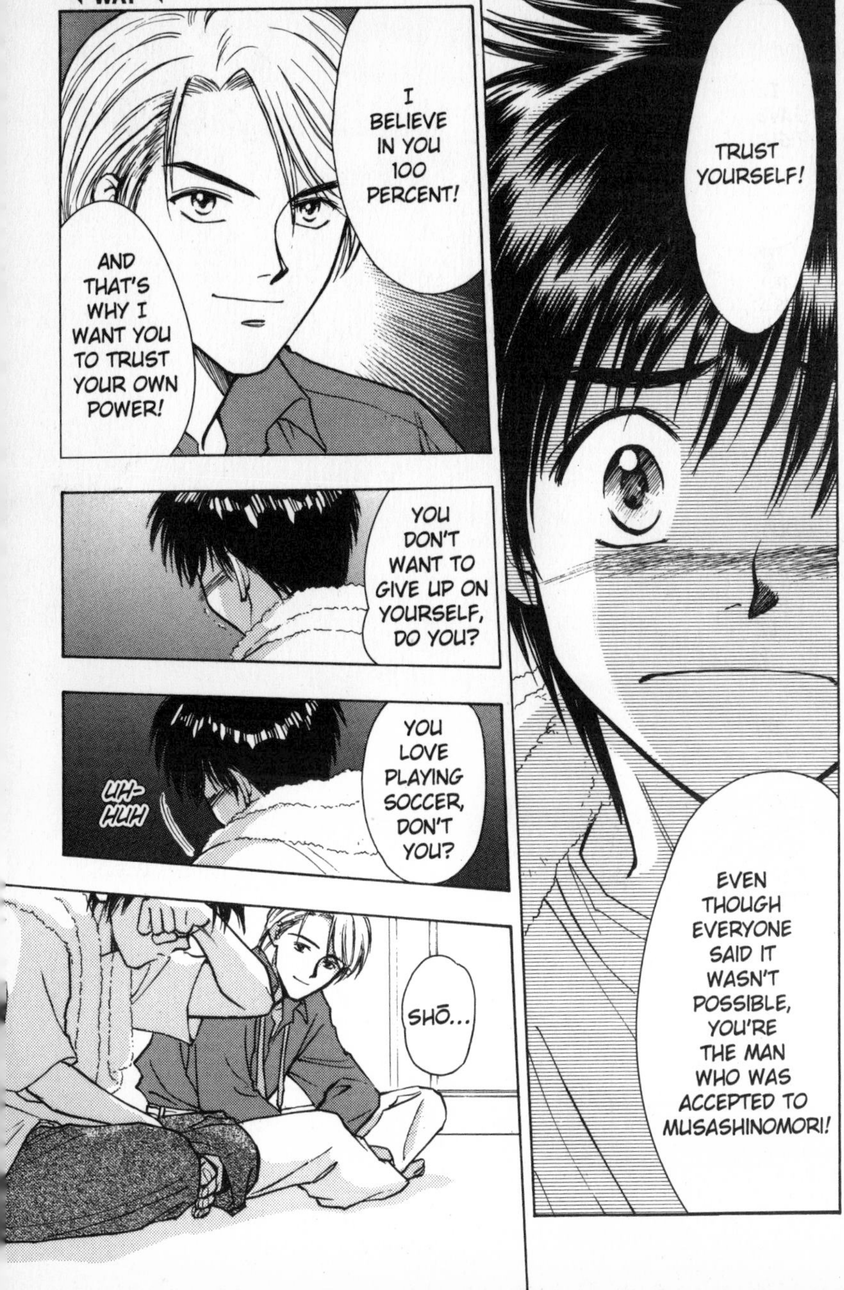

TRUST YOURSELF!
EVEN THOUGH EVERYONE SAID IT WASN'T POSSIBLE, YOU'RE THE MAN WHO WAS ACCEPTED TO MUSASHINOMORI!
I BELIEVE IN YOU 100 PERCENT!
AND THAT'S WHY I WANT YOU TO TRUST YOUR OWN POWER!
YOU DON'T WANT TO GIVE UP ON YOURSELF, DO YOU?
YOU LOVE PLAYING SOCCER, DON'T YOU?
UH-HUH
SHŌ...

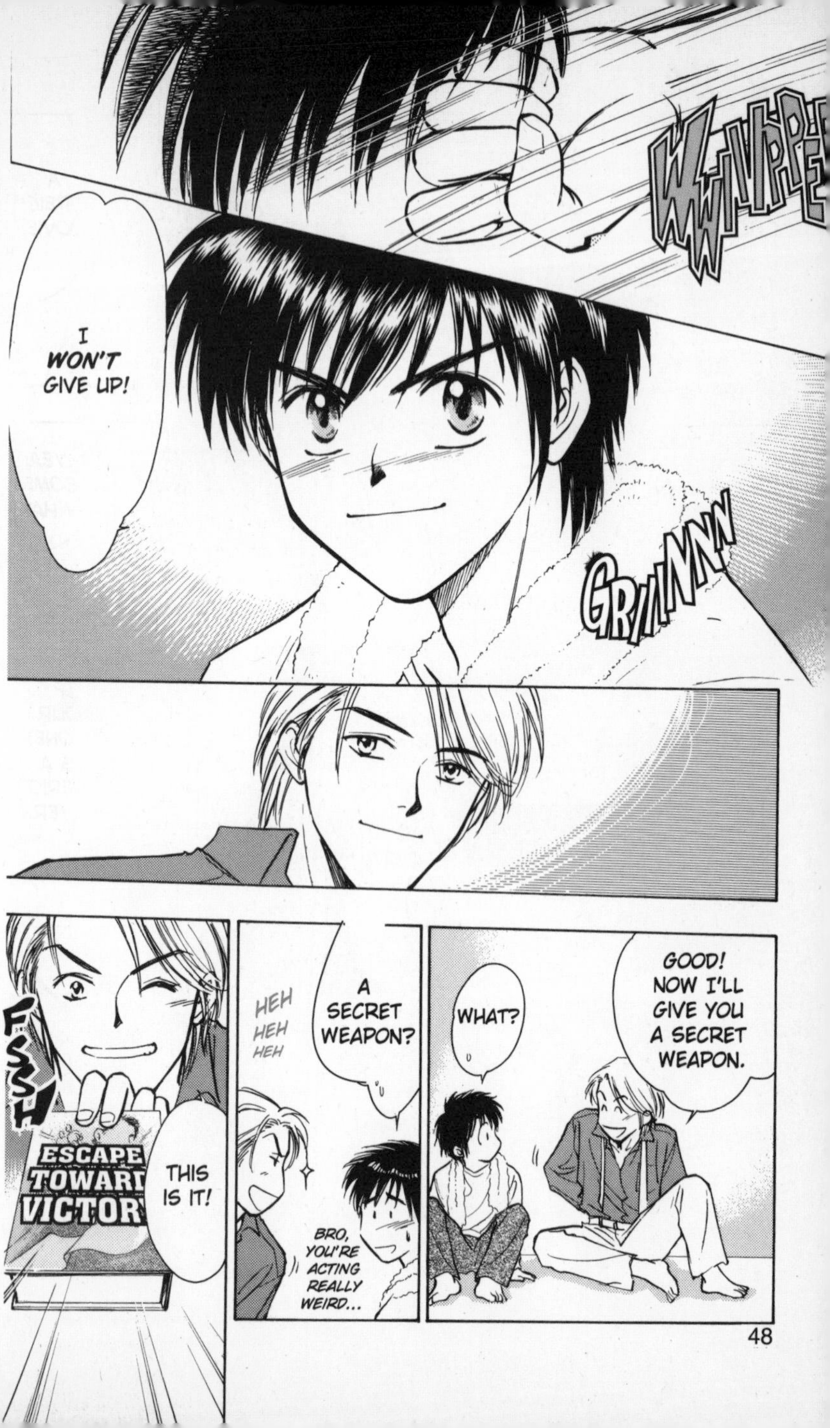
I WON'T GIVE UP!
GRIIINNN
GOOD! NOW I'LL GIVE YOU A SECRET WEAPON.
WHAT?
A SECRET WEAPON?
HEH HEH HEH
BRO, YOU'RE ACTING REALLY WEIRD...
FSSH
THIS IS IT!
ESCAPE

READ THIS WAY

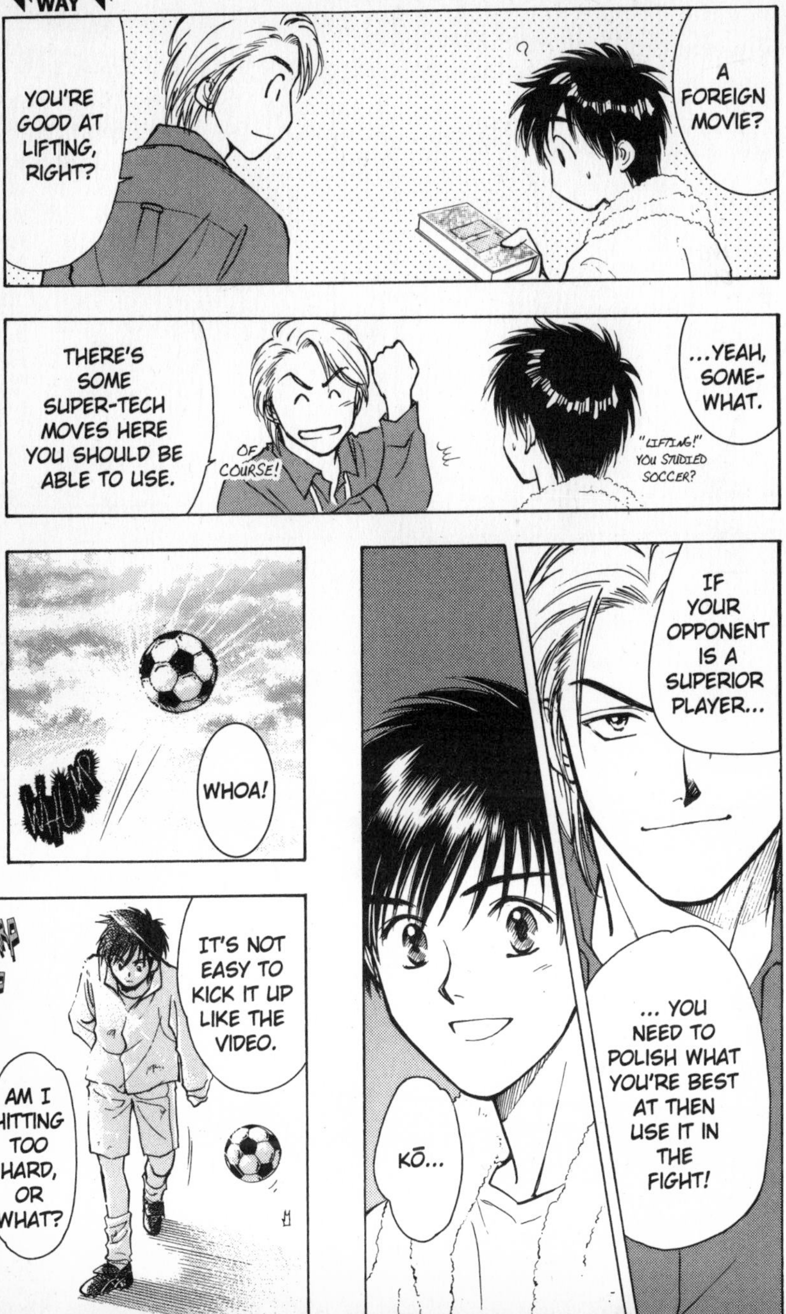
A FOREIGN MOVIE?
YOU'RE GOOD AT LIFTING, RIGHT?
...YEAH, SOME-WHAT.
"LIFTING!" YOU STUDIED SOCCER?
OF COURSE!
THERE'S SOME SUPER-TECH MOVES HERE YOU SHOULD BE ABLE TO USE.
IF YOUR OPPONENT IS A SUPERIOR PLAYER...
... YOU NEED TO POLISH WHAT YOU'RE BEST AT THEN USE IT IN THE FIGHT!
KŌ...
WHOA!
IT'S NOT EASY TO KICK IT UP LIKE THE VIDEO.
AM I HITTING TOO HARD, OR WHAT?
CHIRP CHIRP

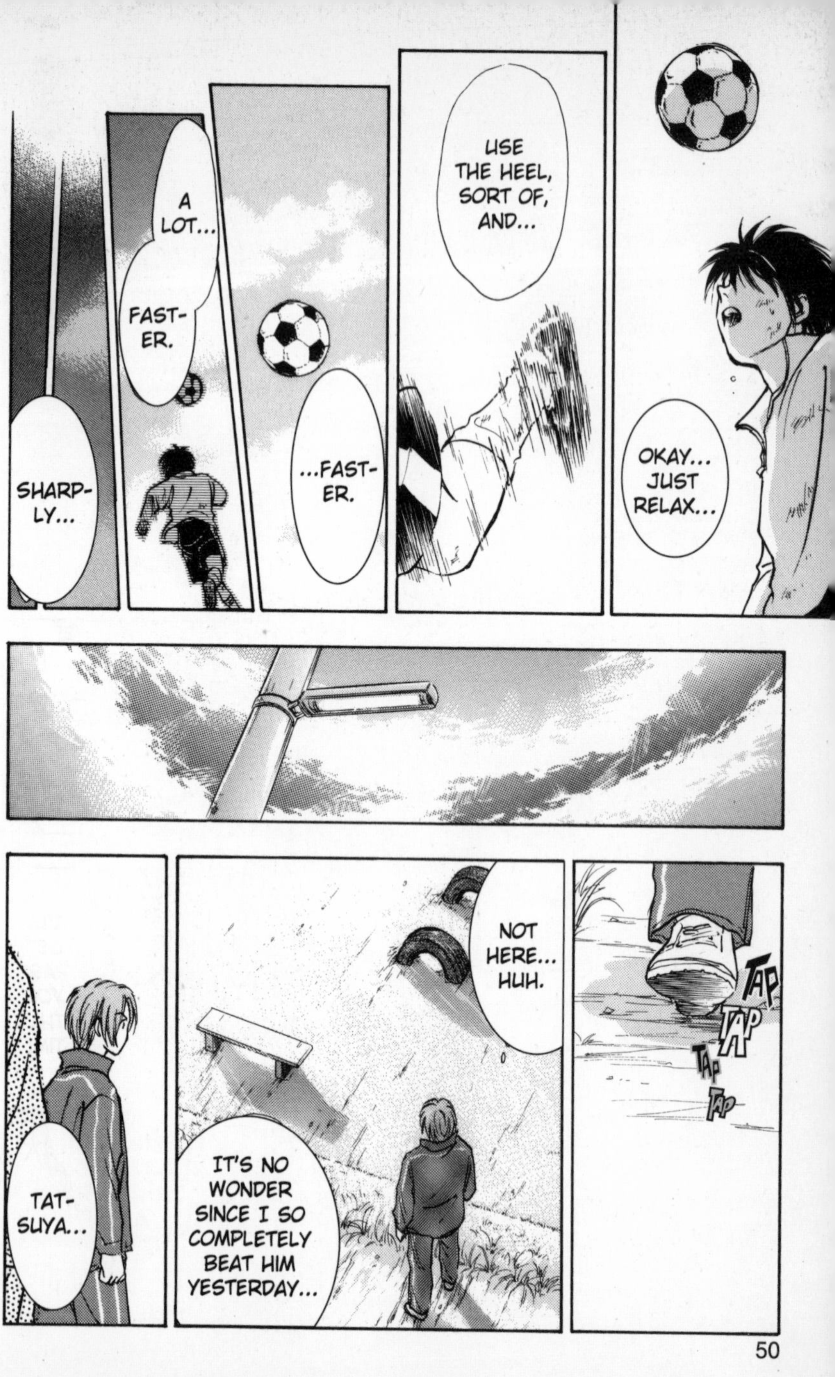
OKAY... JUST RELAX...
USE THE HEEL, SORT OF, AND...
...FAST-ER.
A LOT...
FAST-ER.
SHARP-LY...
TAP
TAP
TAP
TAP
NOT HERE... HUH.
IT'S NO WONDER SINCE I SO COMPLETELY BEAT HIM YESTERDAY...
TAT-SUYA...

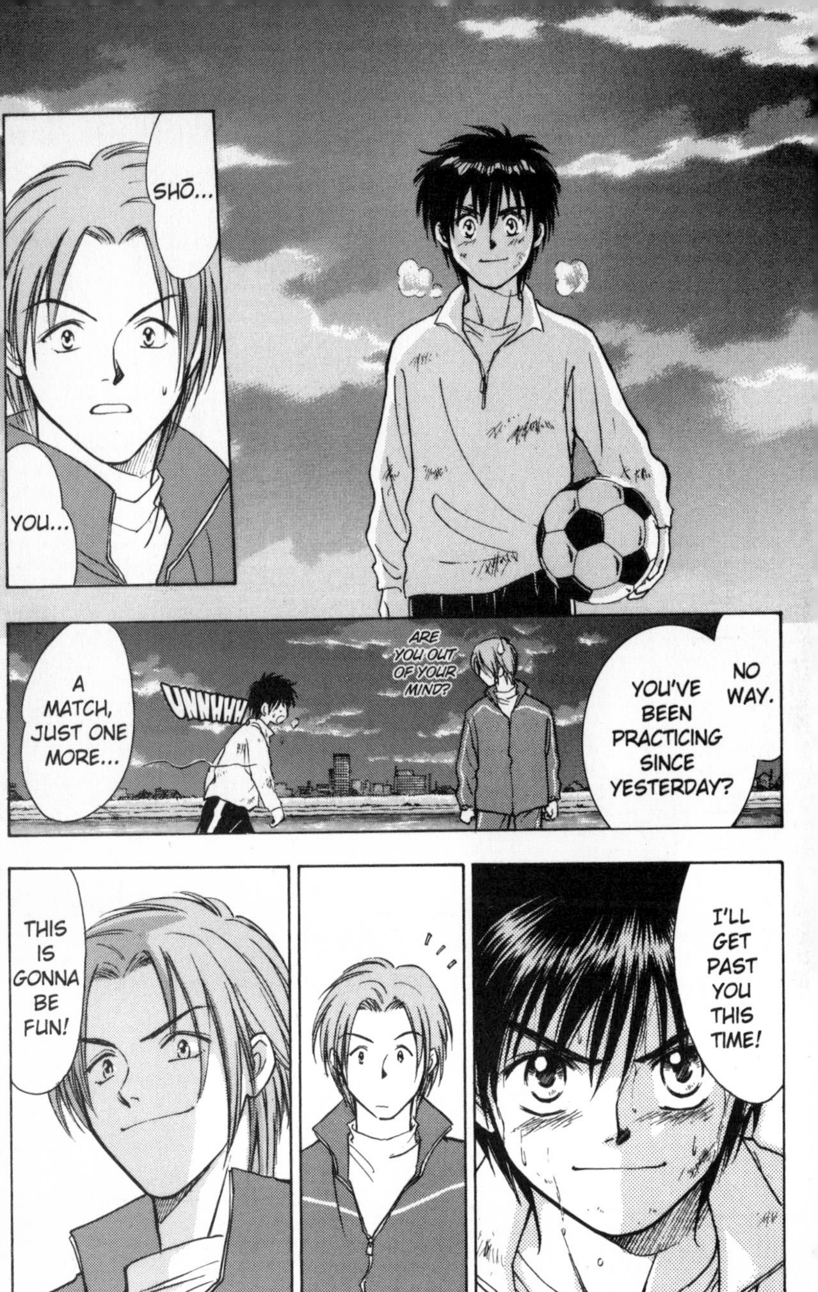
SHŌ...
YOU...
NO WAY.
YOU'VE BEEN PRACTICING SINCE YESTERDAY?
ARE YOU OUT OF YOUR MIND?
UNNHHH
A MATCH, JUST ONE MORE...
I'LL GET PAST YOU THIS TIME!
THIS IS GONNA BE FUN!

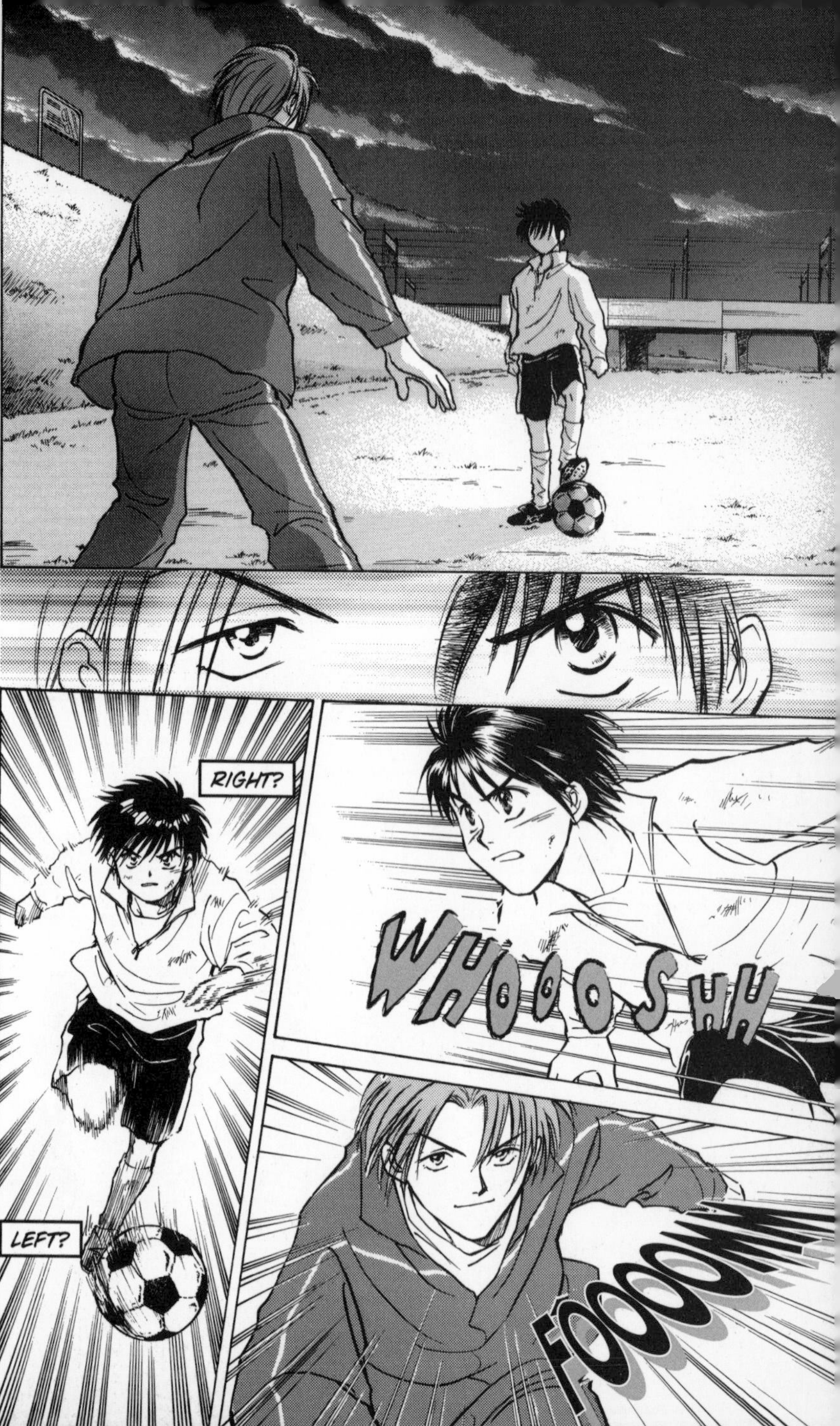
WHOOOSHH
FOOOOM
RIGHT?
LEFT?

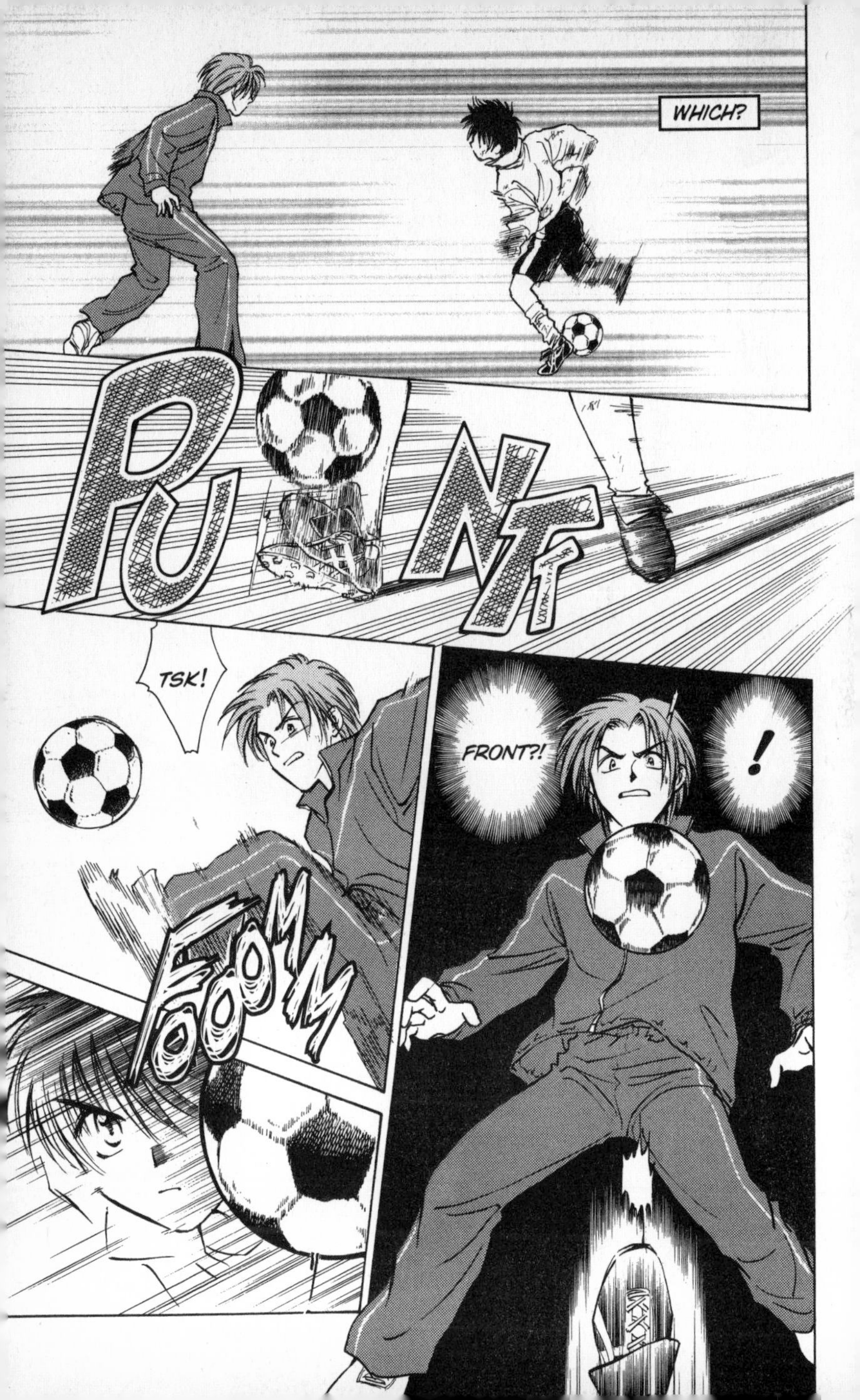
WHICH?
PUNT
FRONT?!
!
TSK!
FOOOMM

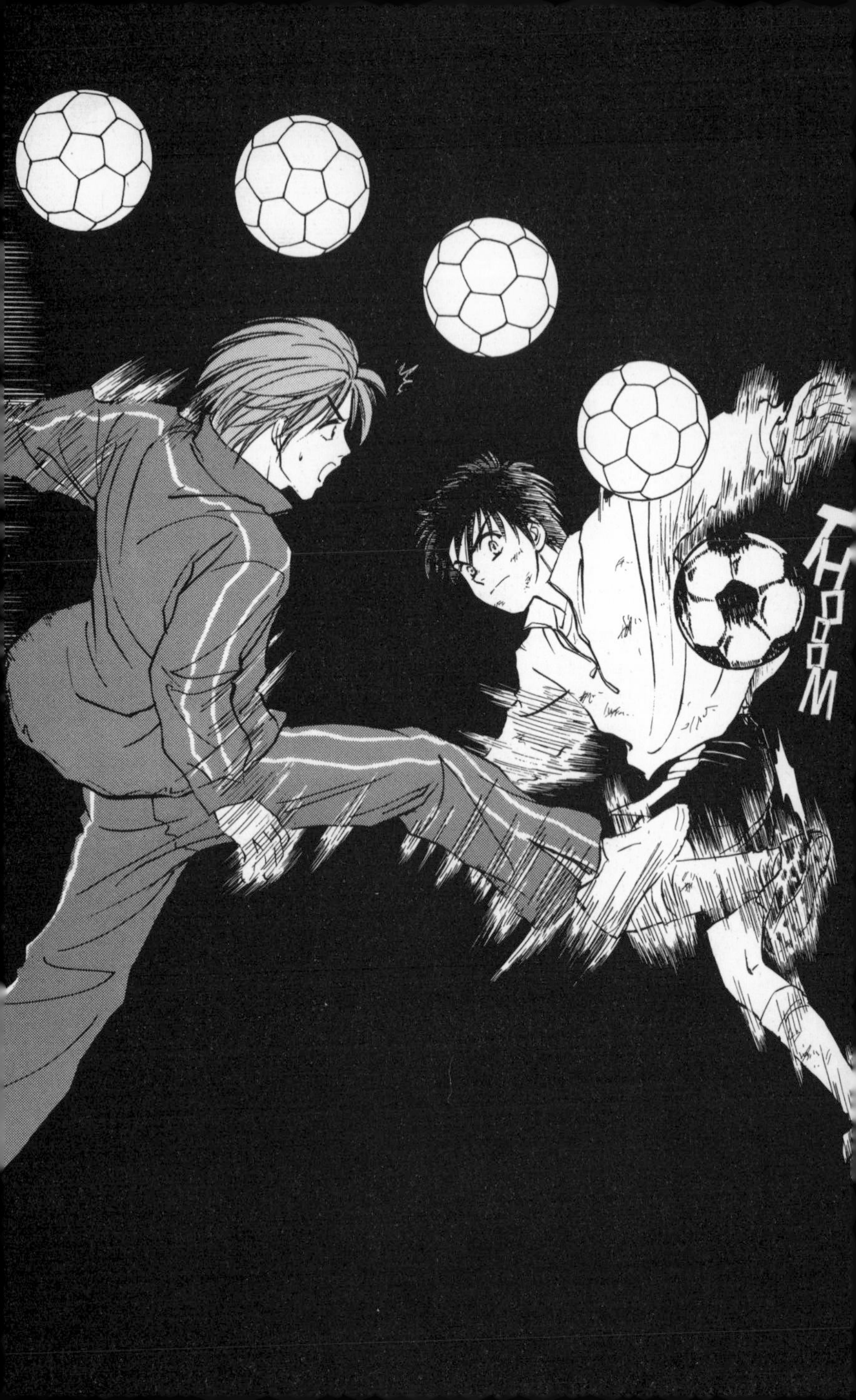
THOOOM

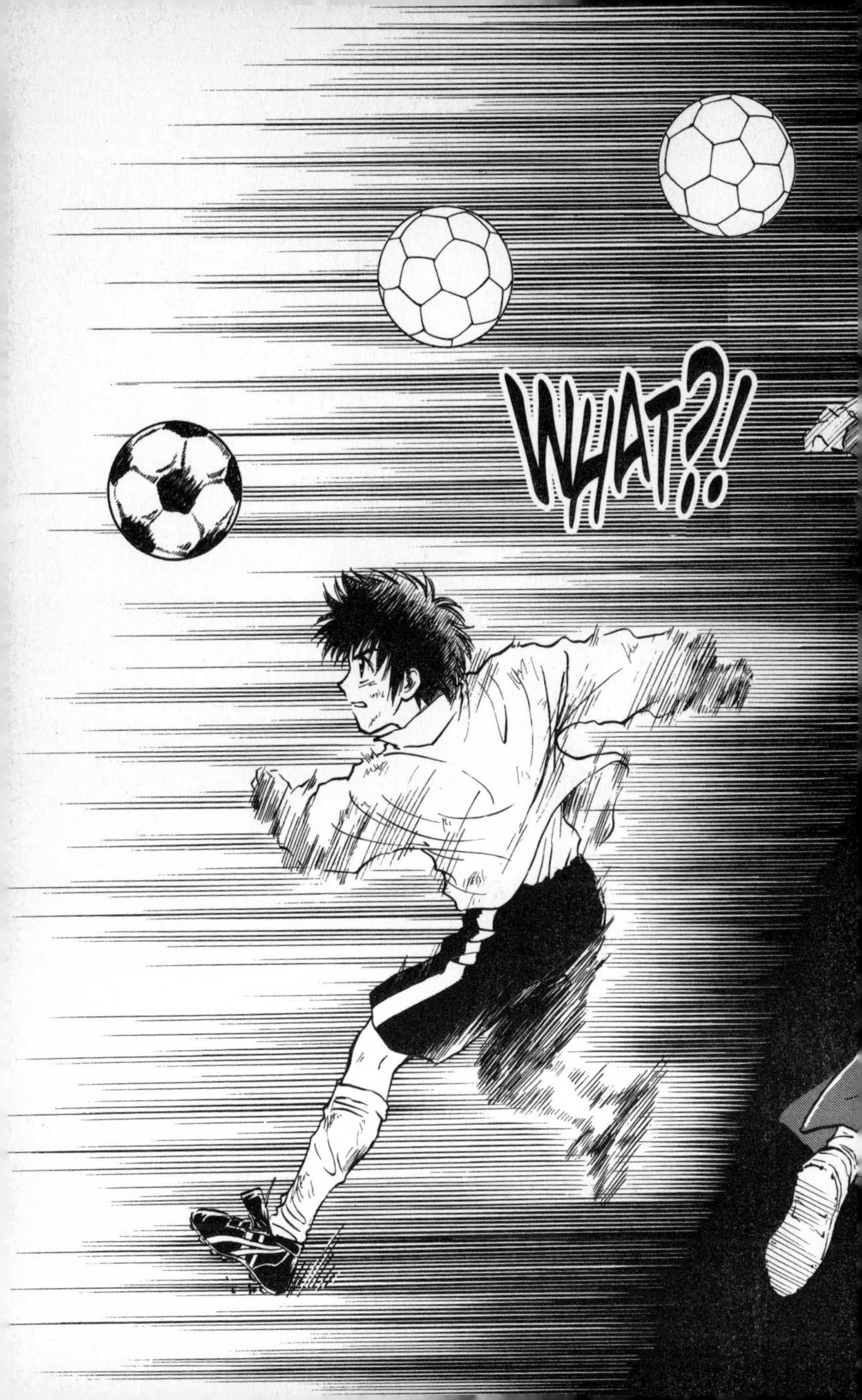
WHAT?!

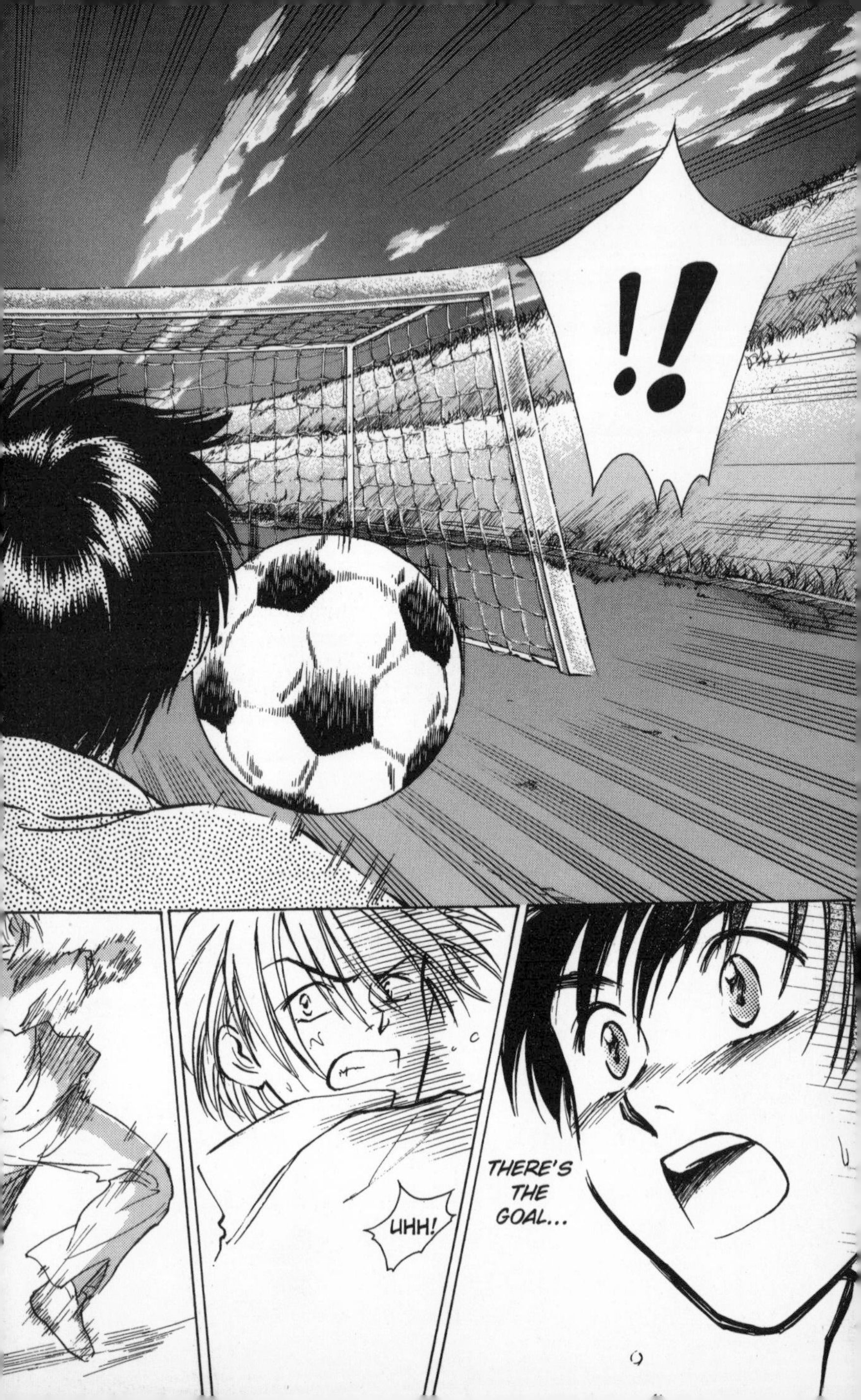
!!
THERE'S THE GOAL...
UHH!

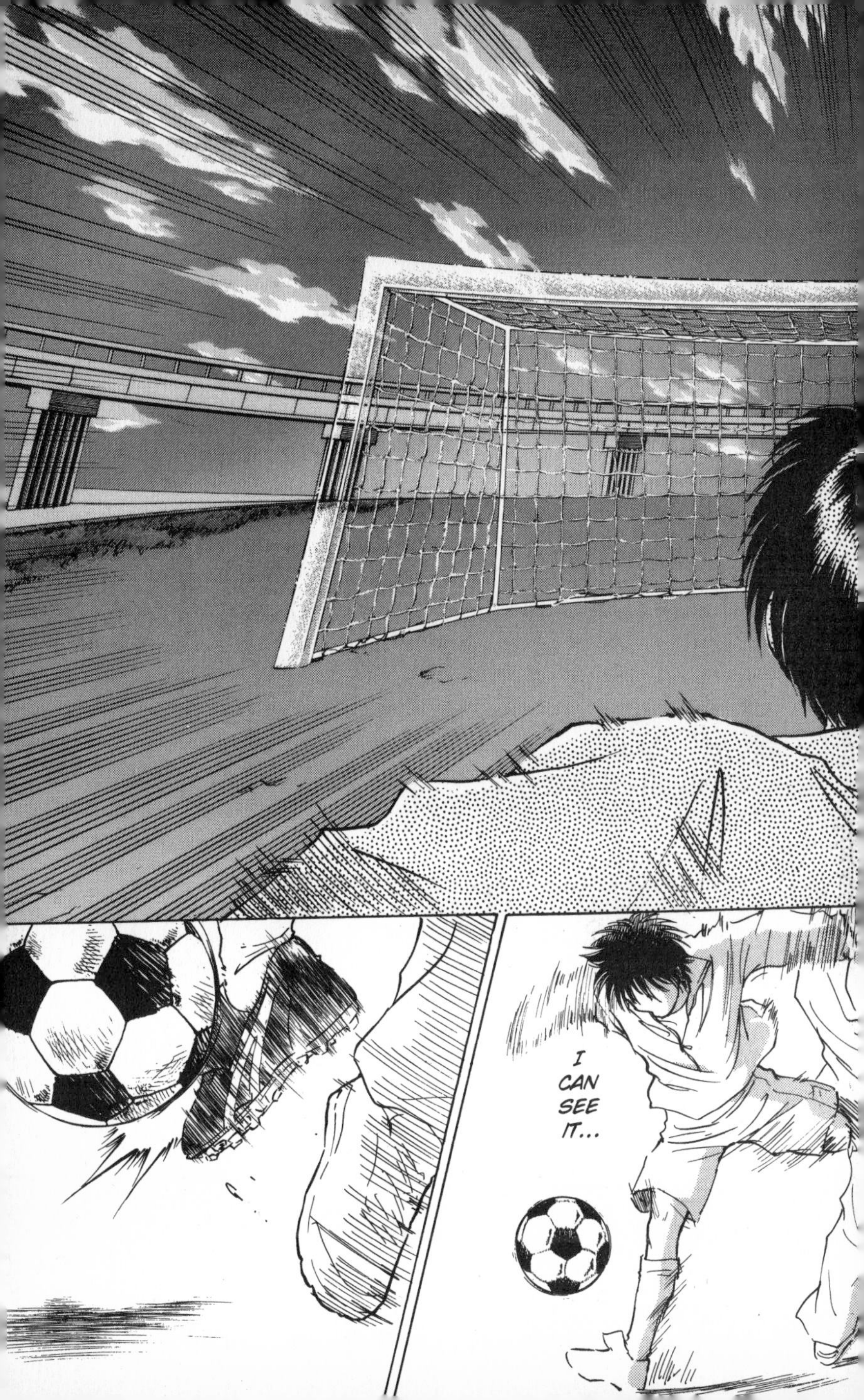
I CAN SEE IT...

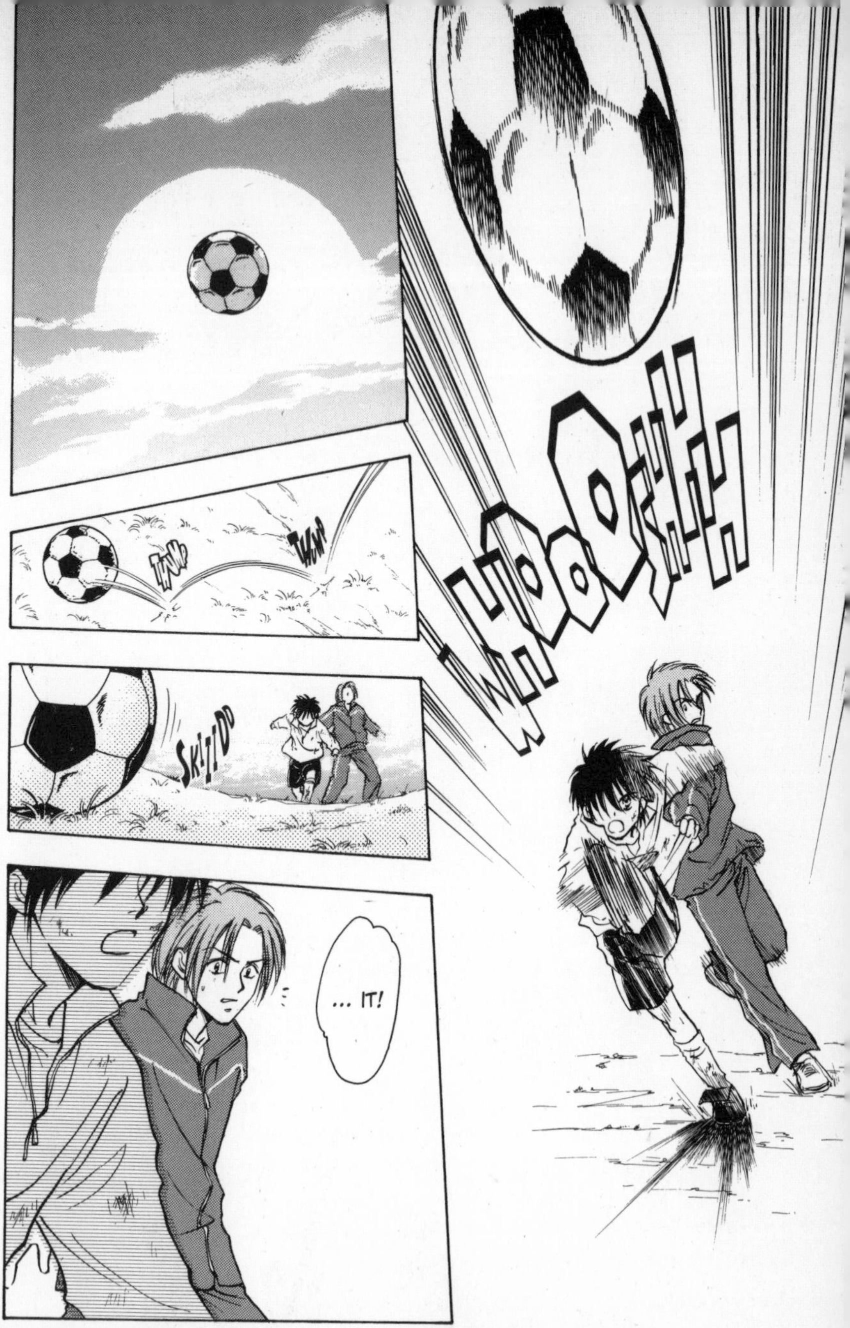
WHOOOSH
... IT!

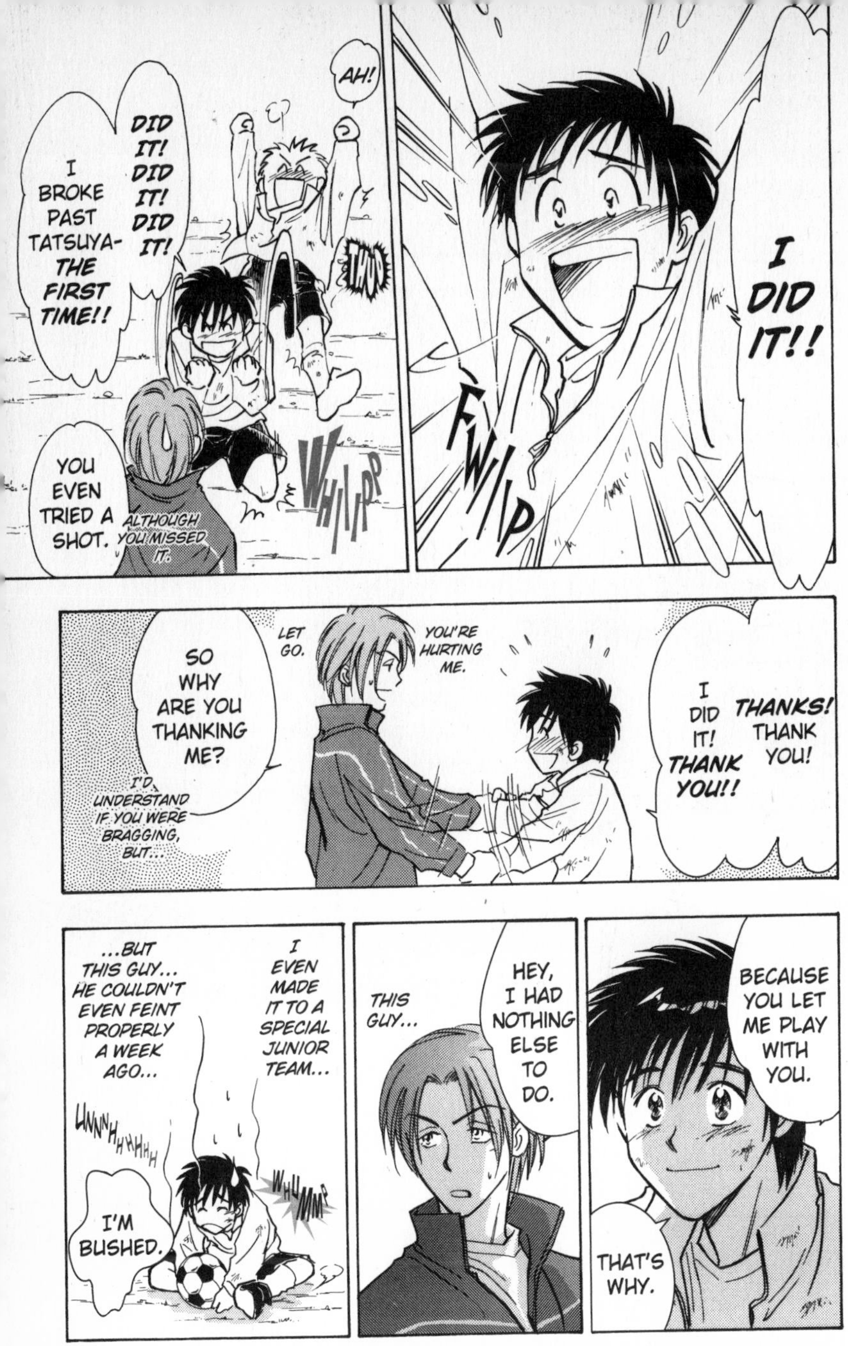
I DID IT!!
FWIP
AH!
DID IT! DID IT! DID IT!
I BROKE PAST TATSUYA- THE FIRST TIME!!
THUD
WHIRRRP
YOU EVEN TRIED A SHOT.
ALTHOUGH YOU MISSED IT.
THANKS! THANK YOU!
I DID IT! THANK YOU!!
YOU'RE HURTING ME.
LET GO.
SO WHY ARE YOU THANKING ME?
I'D UNDERSTAND IF YOU WERE BRAGGING, BUT...
BECAUSE YOU LET ME PLAY WITH YOU.
THAT'S WHY.
HEY, I HAD NOTHING ELSE TO DO.
THIS GUY...
I EVEN MADE IT TO A SPECIAL JUNIOR TEAM...
...BUT THIS GUY... HE COULDN'T EVEN FEINT PROPERLY A WEEK AGO...
WHUMMP
UNNNHHHHHH
I'M BUSHED.

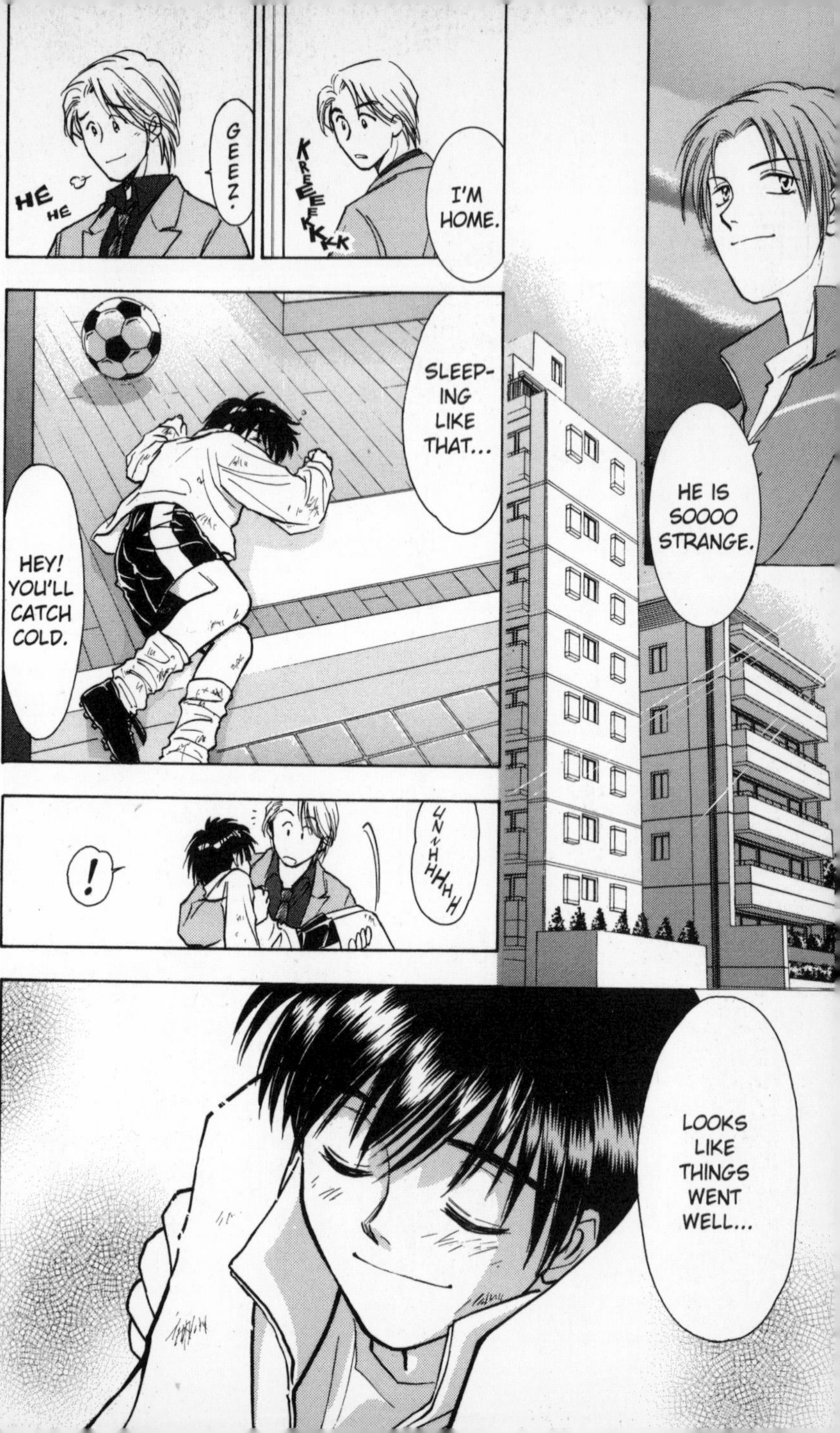
HE IS SOOOO STRANGE.
KREEEEKKKK
I'M HOME.
GEEZ.
HE HE
SLEEPING LIKE THAT...
HEY! YOU'LL CATCH COLD.
UNNHHHHHH
!
LOOKS LIKE THINGS WENT WELL...

STAGE.2 SPECIAL NIGHT TRAINING

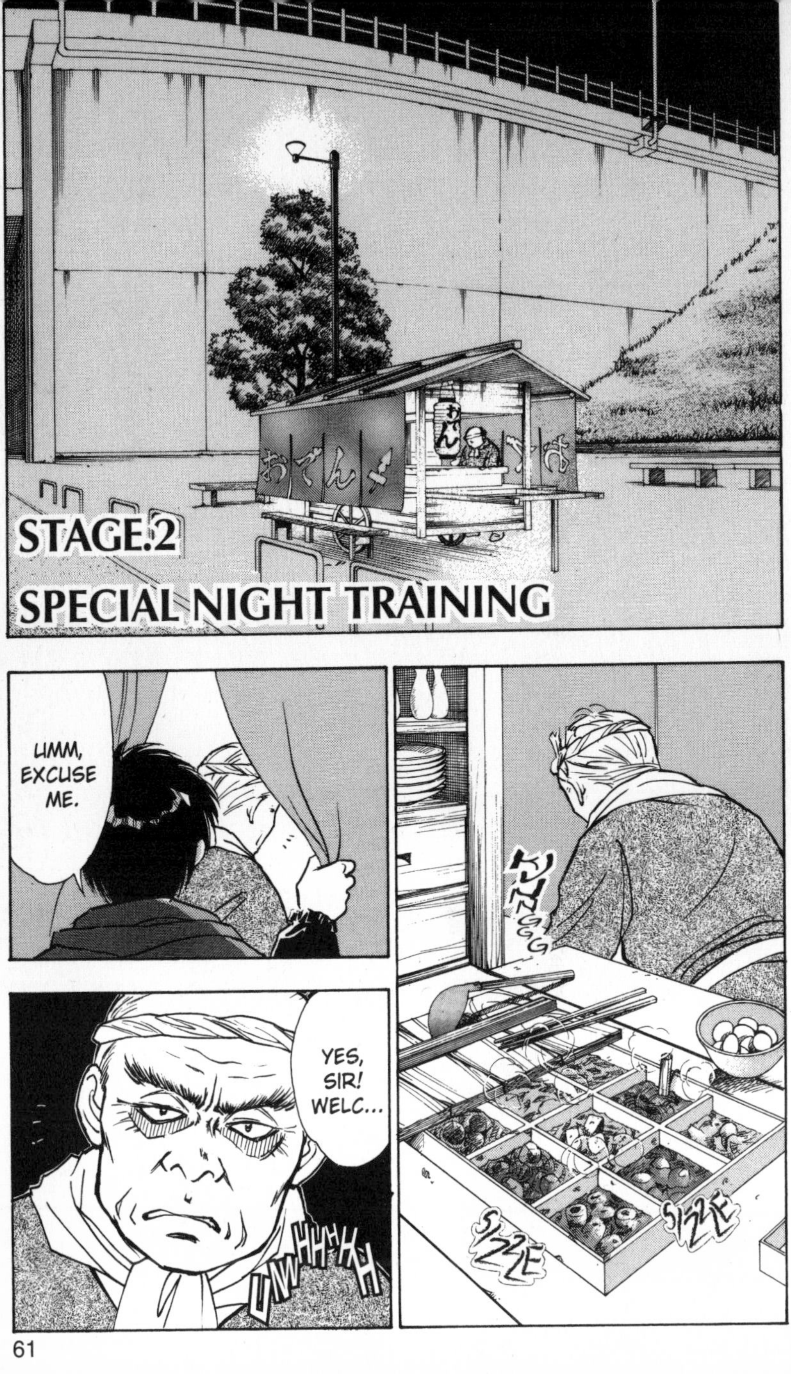
おでん
SIZZLE
SIZZLE
UMM, EXCUSE ME.
YES, SIR! WELC...

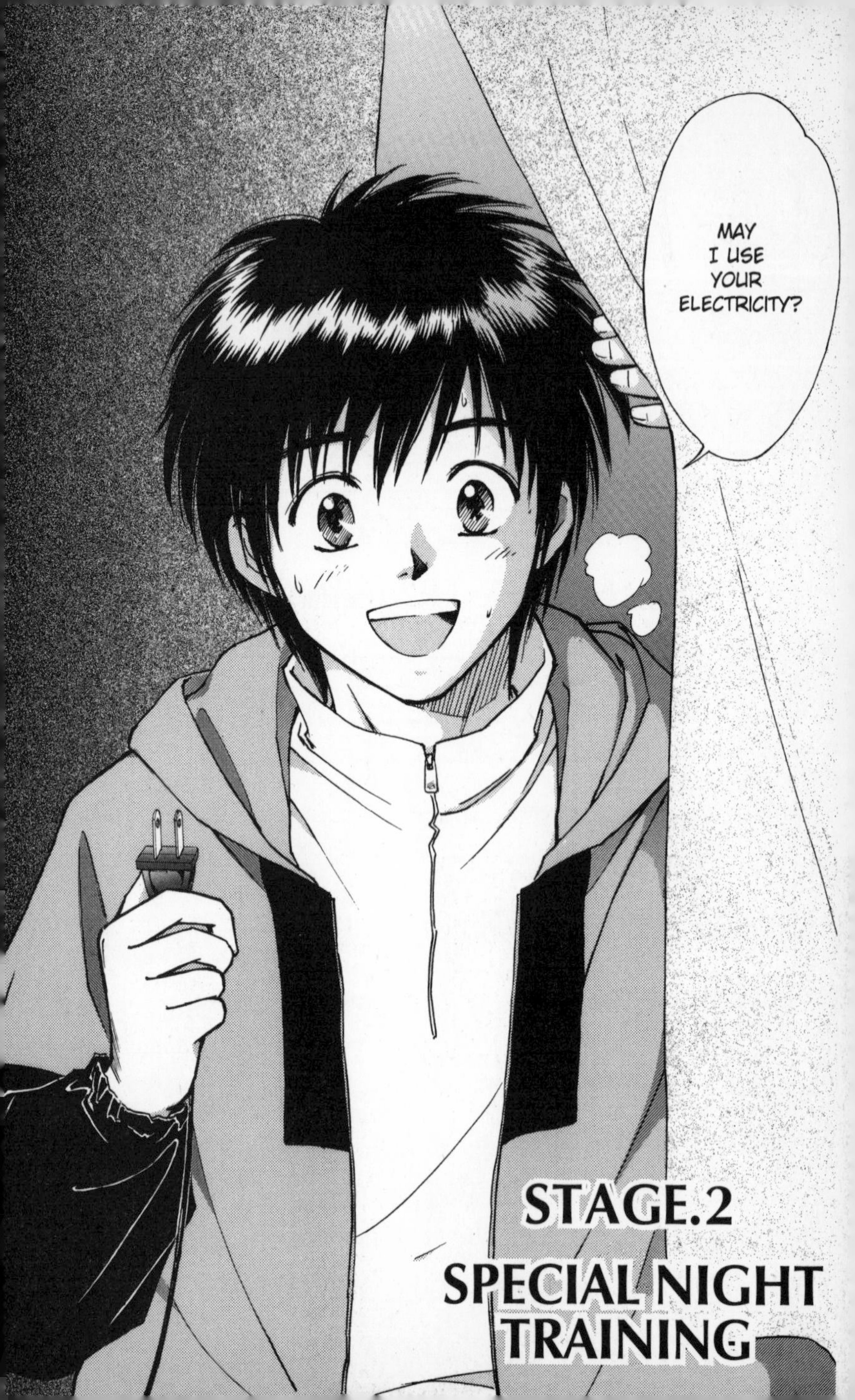
MAY I USE YOUR ELECTRICITY?
STAGE.2
SPECIAL NIGHT TRAINING

READ THIS WAY

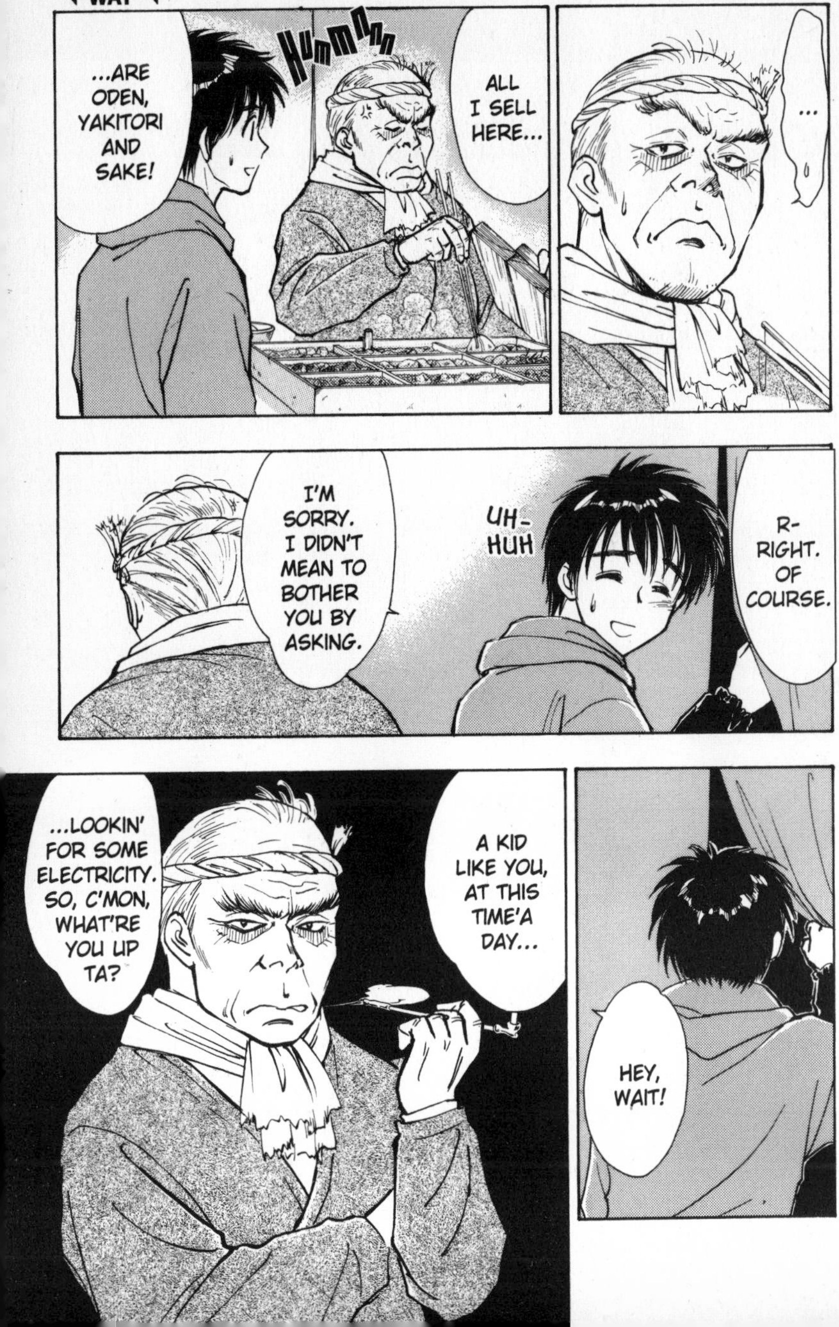
...
ALL I SELL HERE...
HUMMNNN
...ARE ODEN, YAKITORI AND SAKE!
R-RIGHT. OF COURSE.
UH-HUH
I'M SORRY. I DIDN'T MEAN TO BOTHER YOU BY ASKING.
HEY, WAIT!
A KID LIKE YOU, AT THIS TIME'A DAY...
...LOOKIN' FOR SOME ELECTRICITY. SO, C'MON, WHAT'RE YOU UP TA?

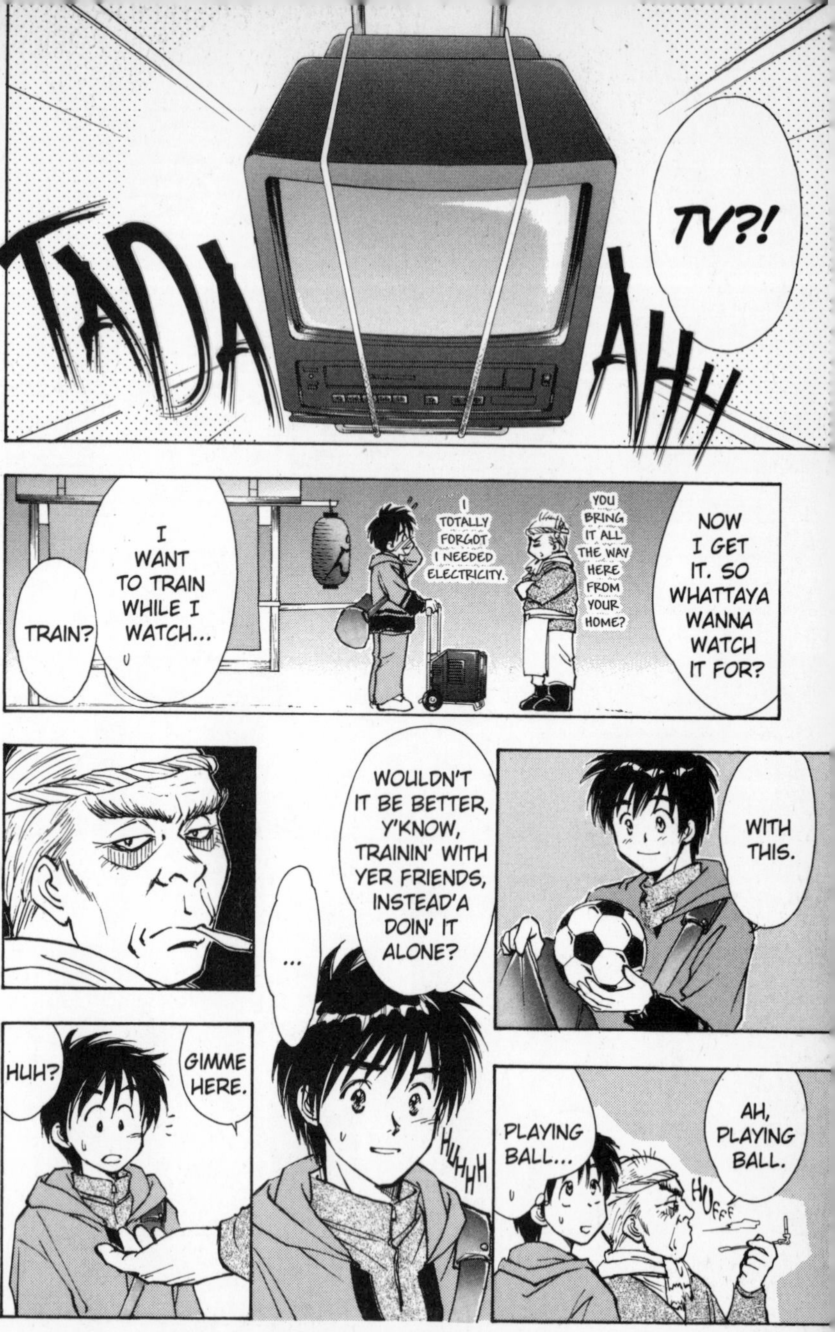
TV?!
TADA AHH
NOW I GET IT. SO WHATTAYA WANNA WATCH IT FOR?
YOU BRING IT ALL THE WAY HERE FROM YOUR HOME?
I TOTALLY FORGOT I NEEDED ELECTRICITY.
I WANT TO TRAIN WHILE I WATCH...
TRAIN?
WITH THIS.
WOULDN'T IT BE BETTER, Y'KNOW, TRAININ' WITH YER FRIENDS, INSTEAD'A DOIN' IT ALONE?
...
HUHHH
AH, PLAYING BALL.
HUFFF
PLAYING BALL...
GIMME HERE.
HUH?

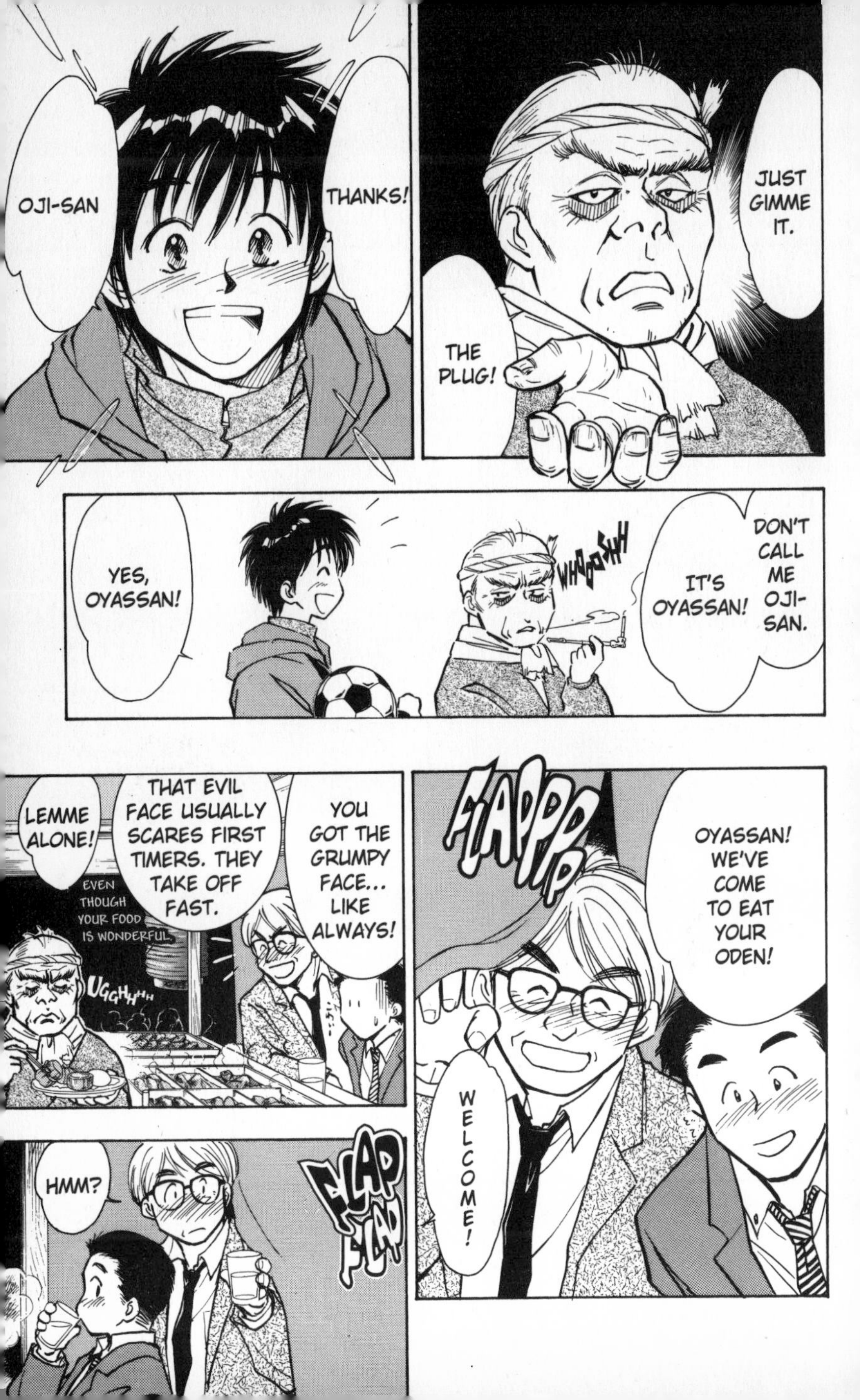
JUST GIMME IT.
THE PLUG!
THANKS!
OJI-SAN
DON'T CALL ME OJI-SAN.
IT'S OYASSAN!
WHOOOSHH
YES, OYASSAN!
FLAPPP
OYASSAN! WE'VE COME TO EAT YOUR ODEN!
WELCOME!
YOU GOT THE GRUMPY FACE... LIKE ALWAYS!
THAT EVIL FACE USUALLY SCARES FIRST TIMERS. THEY TAKE OFF FAST.
LEMME ALONE!
EVEN THOUGH YOUR FOOD IS WONDERFUL.
UGGHHHH
FLAP FLAP
HMM?

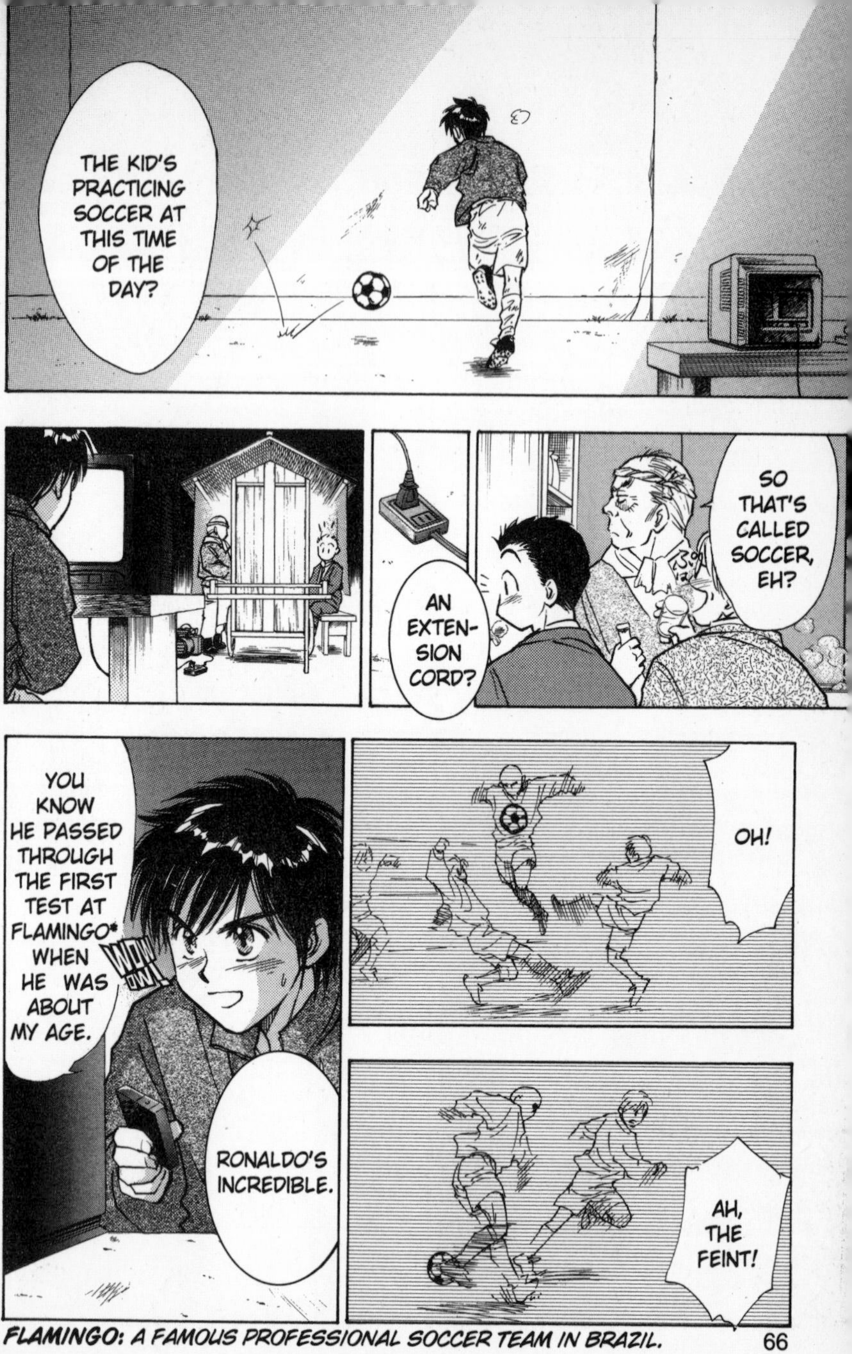
THE KID'S PRACTICING SOCCER AT THIS TIME OF THE DAY?
SO THAT'S CALLED SOCCER, EH?
AN EXTEN-SION CORD?
OH!
AH, THE FEINT!
YOU KNOW HE PASSED THROUGH THE FIRST TEST AT FLAMINGO* WHEN HE WAS ABOUT MY AGE.
RONALDO'S INCREDIBLE.

FLAMINGO: A FAMOUS PROFESSIONAL SOCCER TEAM IN BRAZIL.

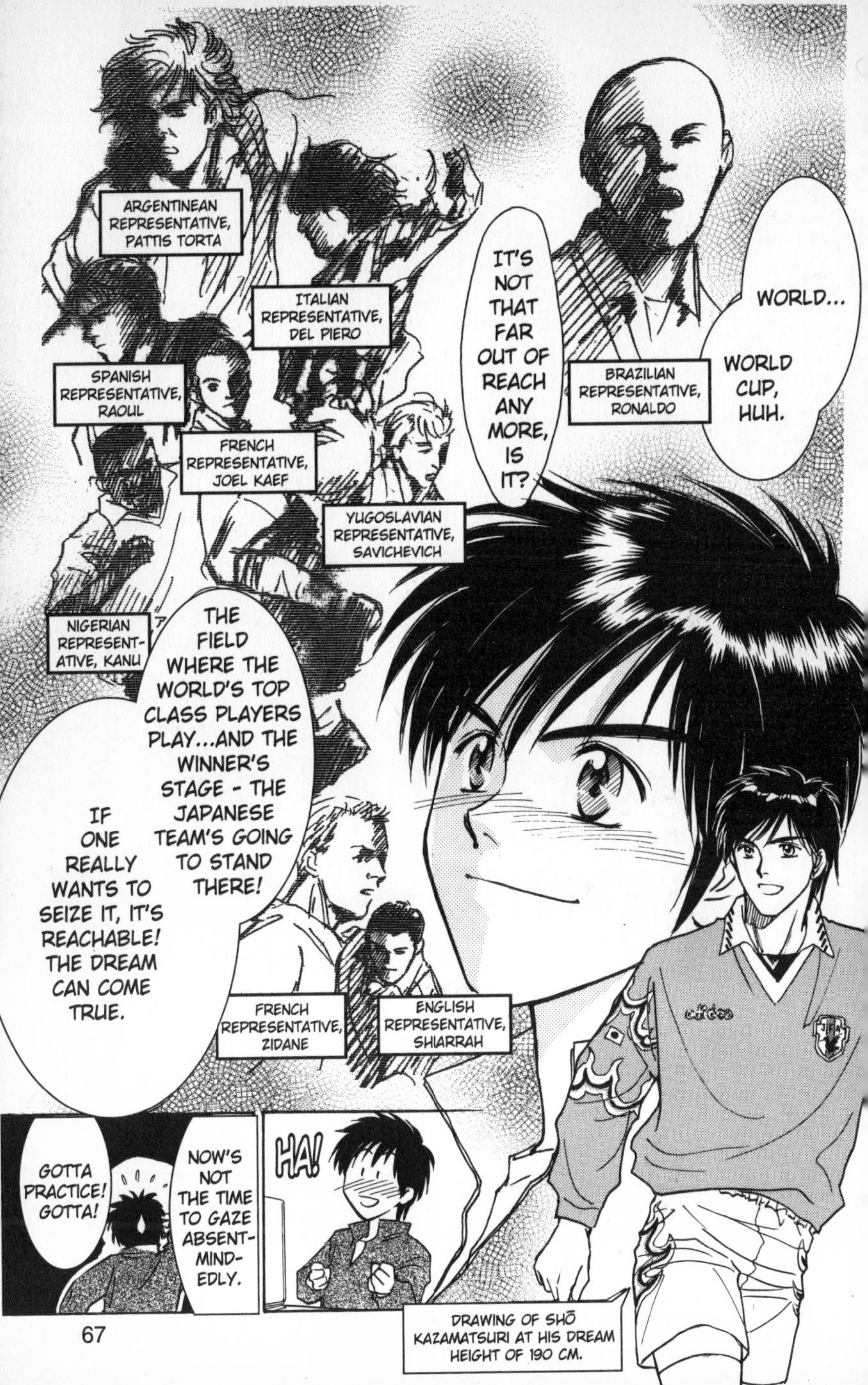
WORLD... WORLD CUP, HUH.
IT'S NOT THAT FAR OUT OF REACH ANY MORE, IS IT?
BRAZILIAN REPRESENTATIVE, RONALDO
ARGENTINEAN REPRESENTATIVE, PATTIS TORTA
ITALIAN REPRESENTATIVE, DEL PIERO
SPANISH REPRESENTATIVE, RAOUL
FRENCH REPRESENTATIVE, JOEL KAEF
YUGOSLAVIAN REPRESENTATIVE, SAVICHEVICH
NIGERIAN REPRESENTATIVE, KANU
THE FIELD WHERE THE WORLD'S TOP CLASS PLAYERS PLAY...AND THE WINNER'S STAGE - THE JAPANESE TEAM'S GOING TO STAND THERE!
IF ONE REALLY WANTS TO SEIZE IT, IT'S REACHABLE! THE DREAM CAN COME TRUE.
ENGLISH REPRESENTATIVE, SHIARRAH
FRENCH REPRESENTATIVE, ZIDANE
DRAWING OF SHŌ KAZAMATSURI AT HIS DREAM HEIGHT OF 190 CM.
HA!
NOW'S NOT THE TIME TO GAZE ABSENT-MINDEDLY.
GOTTA PRACTICE! GOTTA!

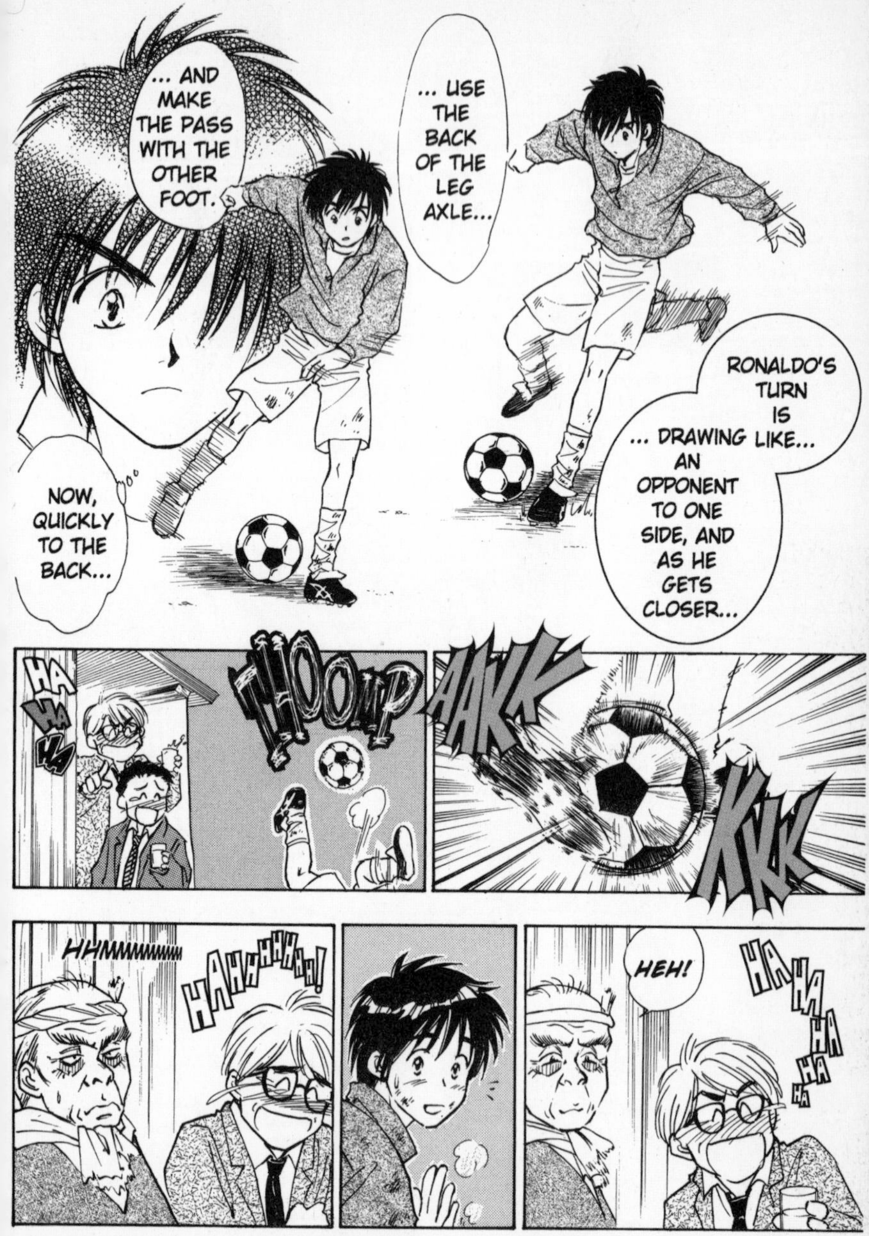
RONALDO'S TURN IS ... DRAWING LIKE... AN OPPONENT TO ONE SIDE, AND AS HE GETS CLOSER...
... USE THE BACK OF THE LEG AXLE...
... AND MAKE THE PASS WITH THE OTHER FOOT.
NOW, QUICKLY TO THE BACK...
AAKK
KKK
THOOMP
HA HA HA
HEH!
HA HA HA HA HA
HAHHHHHHH!
HHMMMMMMM

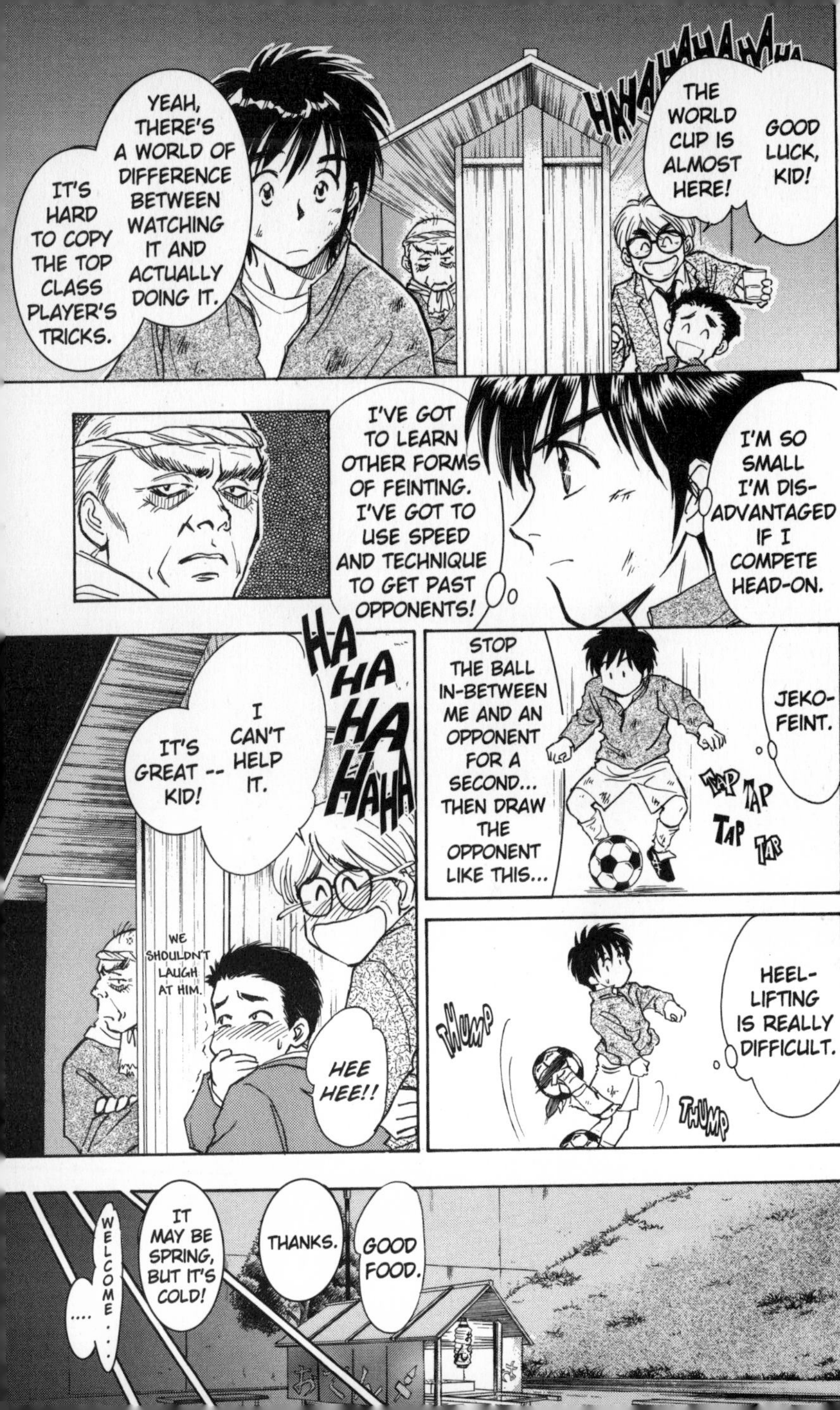
HAHAHAHAHAHAHA
GOOD LUCK, KID!
THE WORLD CUP IS ALMOST HERE!
YEAH, THERE'S A WORLD OF DIFFERENCE BETWEEN WATCHING IT AND ACTUALLY DOING IT.
IT'S HARD TO COPY THE TOP CLASS PLAYER'S TRICKS.
I'M SO SMALL I'M DIS-ADVANTAGED IF I COMPETE HEAD-ON.
I'VE GOT TO LEARN OTHER FORMS OF FEINTING. I'VE GOT TO USE SPEED AND TECHNIQUE TO GET PAST OPPONENTS!
JEKO-FEINT.
TAP TAP TAP TAP
STOP THE BALL IN-BETWEEN ME AND AN OPPONENT FOR A SECOND... THEN DRAW THE OPPONENT LIKE THIS...
HEEL-LIFTING IS REALLY DIFFICULT.
THUMP
THUMP
HA HA HA HA HAHA
I CAN'T HELP IT.
IT'S GREAT -- KID!
WE SHOULDN'T LAUGH AT HIM.
HEE HEE!!
GOOD FOOD.
THANKS.
IT MAY BE SPRING, BUT IT'S COLD!
WELCOME . . .
....

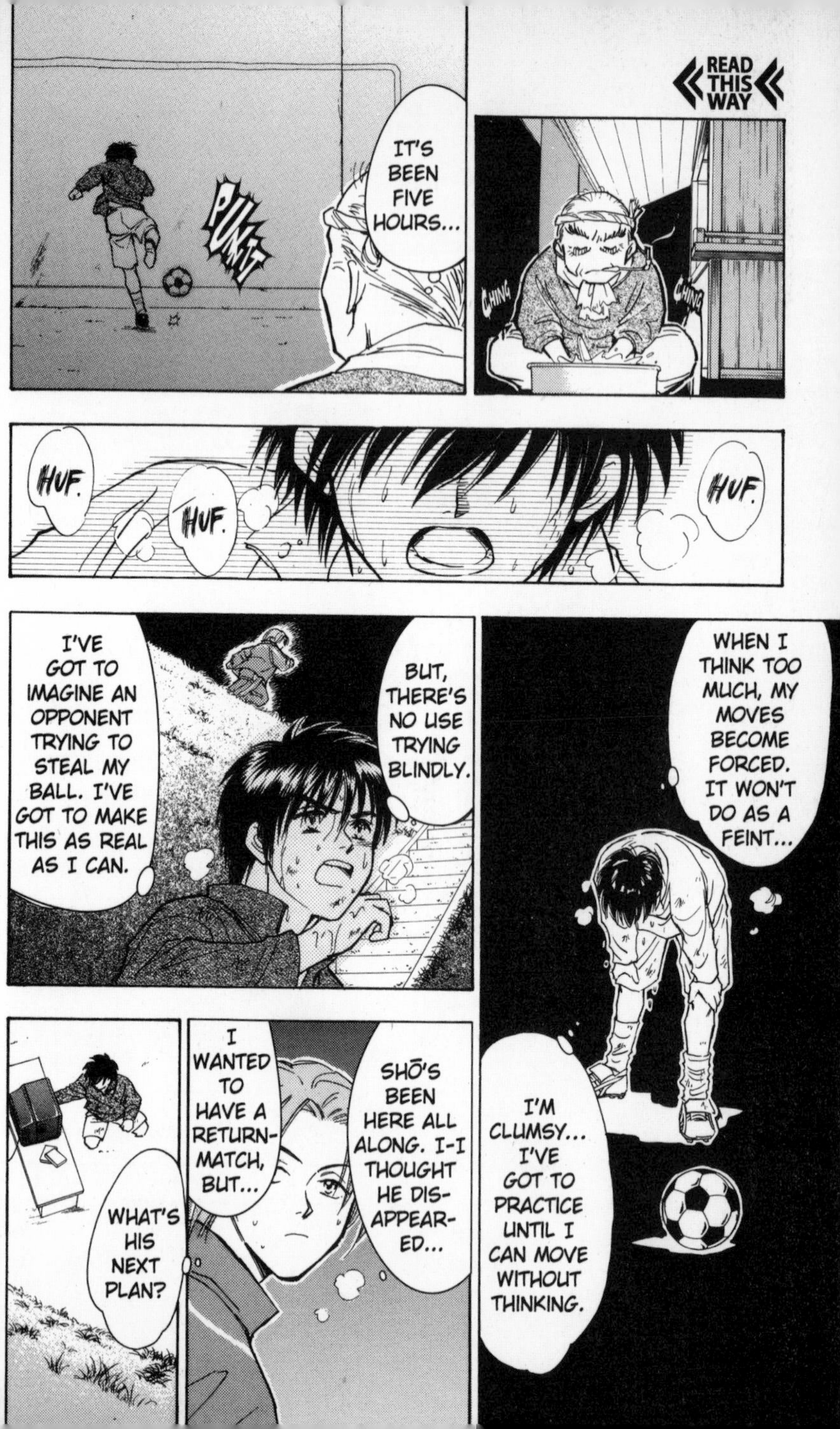
READ THIS WAY
CHING
CHING
IT'S BEEN FIVE HOURS...
PUNT
HUF.
HUF.
HUF.
WHEN I THINK TOO MUCH, MY MOVES BECOME FORCED. IT WON'T DO AS A FEINT...
I'M CLUMSY... I'VE GOT TO PRACTICE UNTIL I CAN MOVE WITHOUT THINKING.
BUT, THERE'S NO USE TRYING BLINDLY.
I'VE GOT TO IMAGINE AN OPPONENT TRYING TO STEAL MY BALL. I'VE GOT TO MAKE THIS AS REAL AS I CAN.
SHŌ'S BEEN HERE ALL ALONG. I-I THOUGHT HE DIS-APPEAR-ED...
I WANTED TO HAVE A RETURN-MATCH, BUT...
WHAT'S HIS NEXT PLAN?

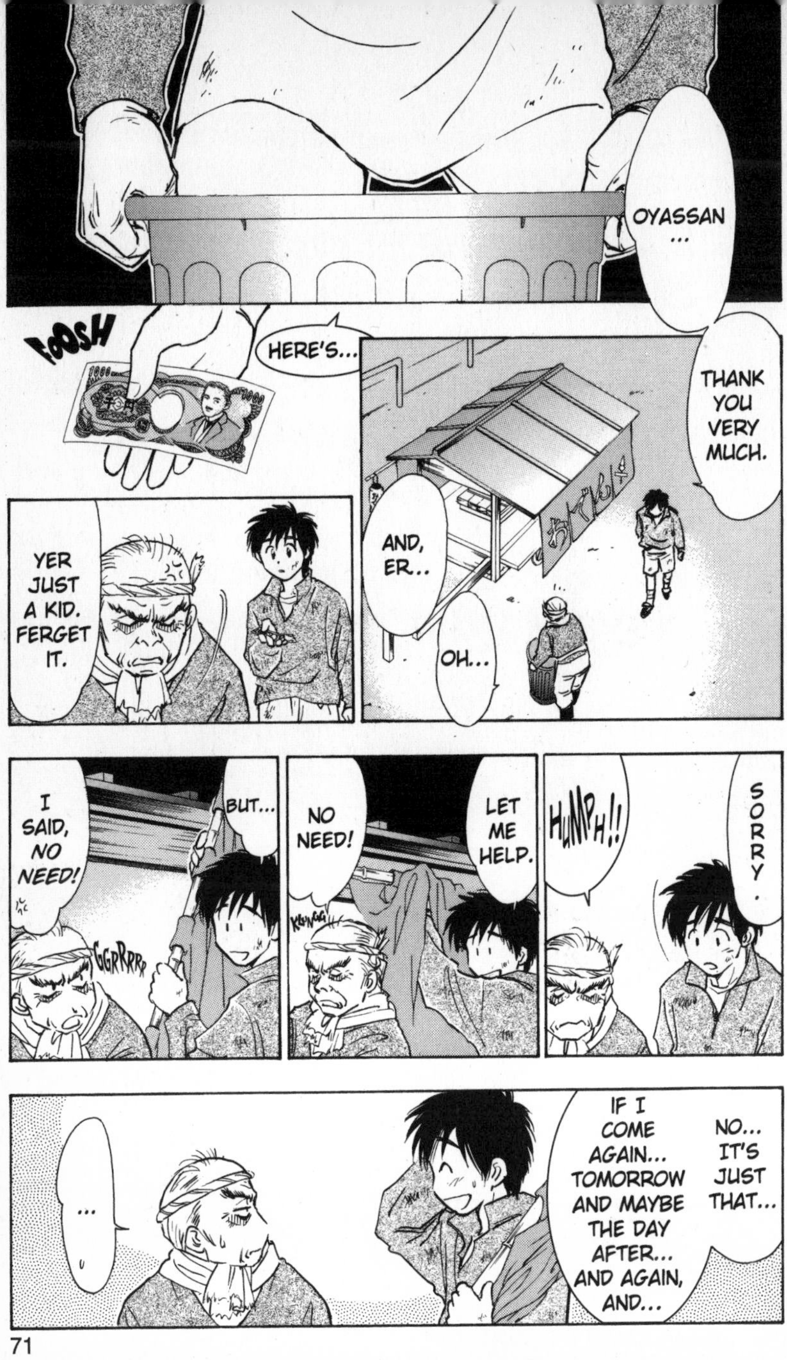
OYASSAN ...
THANK YOU VERY MUCH.
AND, ER...
OH...
HERE'S...
FOOSH
YER JUST A KID. FERGET IT.
SORRY.
HUMPH!!
LET ME HELP.
NO NEED!
BUT...
I SAID, NO NEED!
GGRRRR
NO... IT'S JUST THAT...
IF I COME AGAIN... TOMORROW AND MAYBE THE DAY AFTER... AND AGAIN, AND...
...

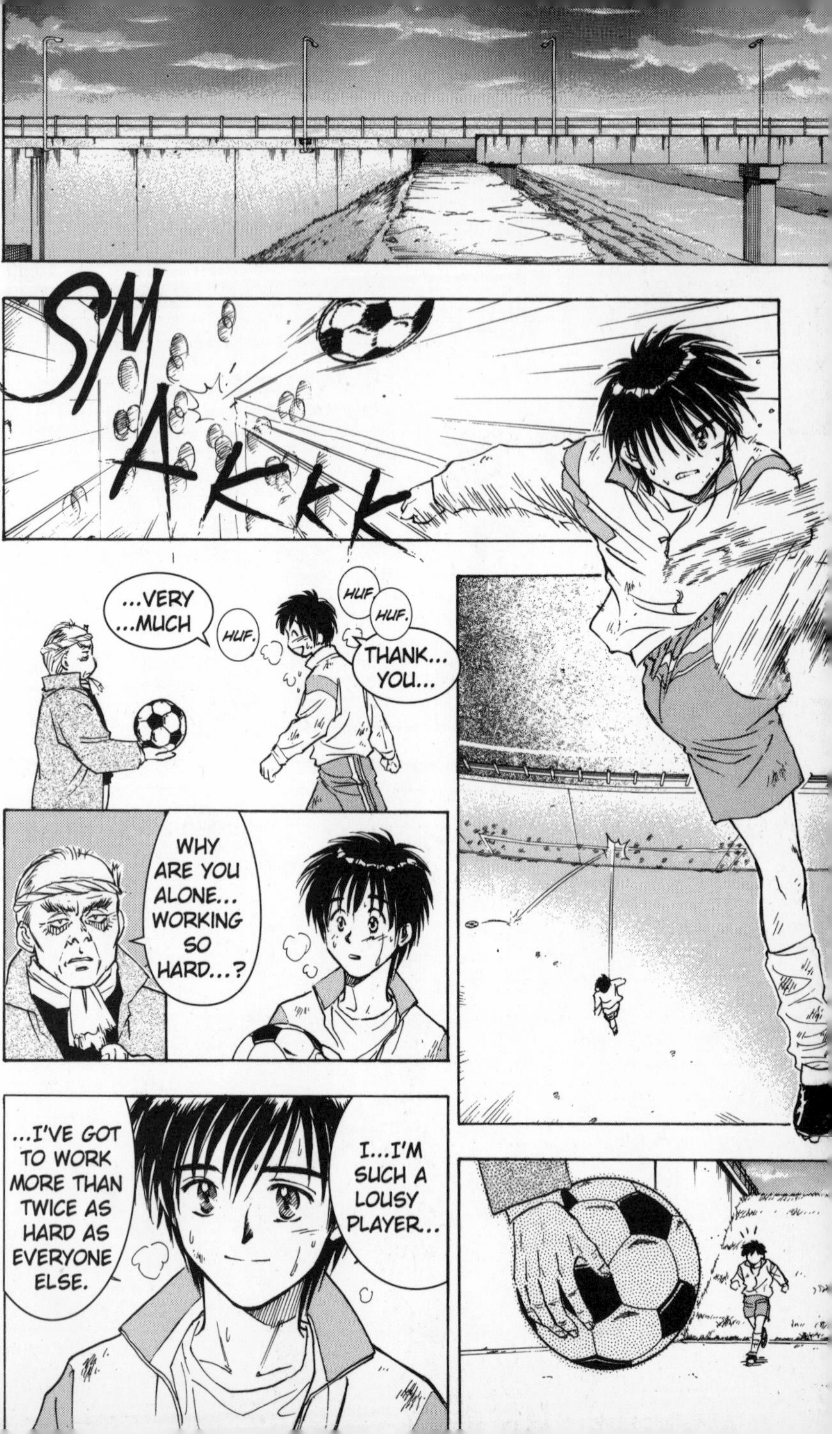
SMAKKK
HUF.
HUF.
THANK... YOU...
HUF.
...VERY ...MUCH
WHY ARE YOU ALONE... WORKING SO HARD...?
I...I'M SUCH A LOUSY PLAYER...
...I'VE GOT TO WORK MORE THAN TWICE AS HARD AS EVERYONE ELSE.

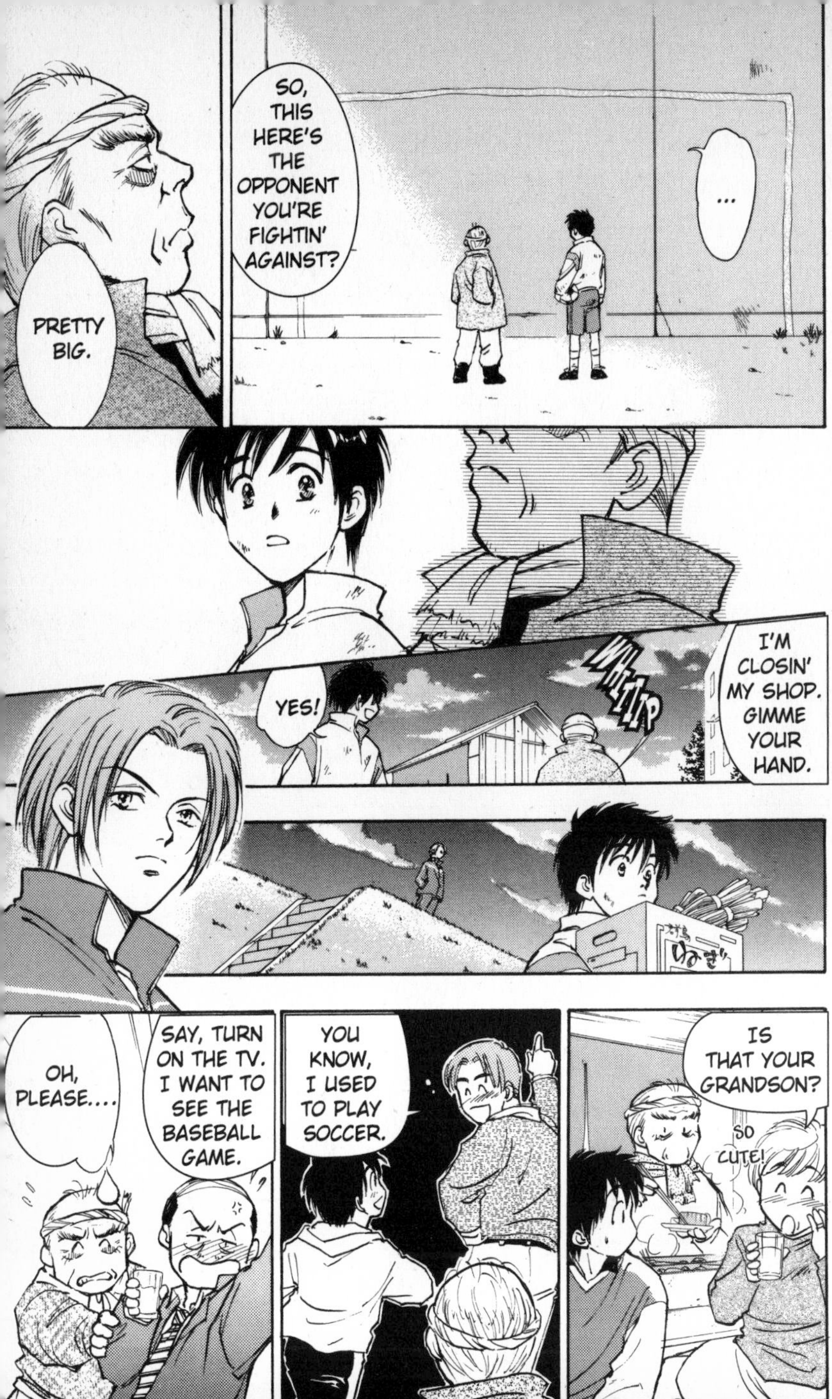
SO, THIS HERE'S THE OPPONENT YOU'RE FIGHTIN' AGAINST?
...
PRETTY BIG.
I'M CLOSIN' MY SHOP. GIMME YOUR HAND.
WHAP
YES!
IS THAT YOUR GRANDSON?
SO CUTE!
YOU KNOW, I USED TO PLAY SOCCER.
SAY, TURN ON THE TV. I WANT TO SEE THE BASEBALL GAME.
OH, PLEASE....

READ THIS WAY

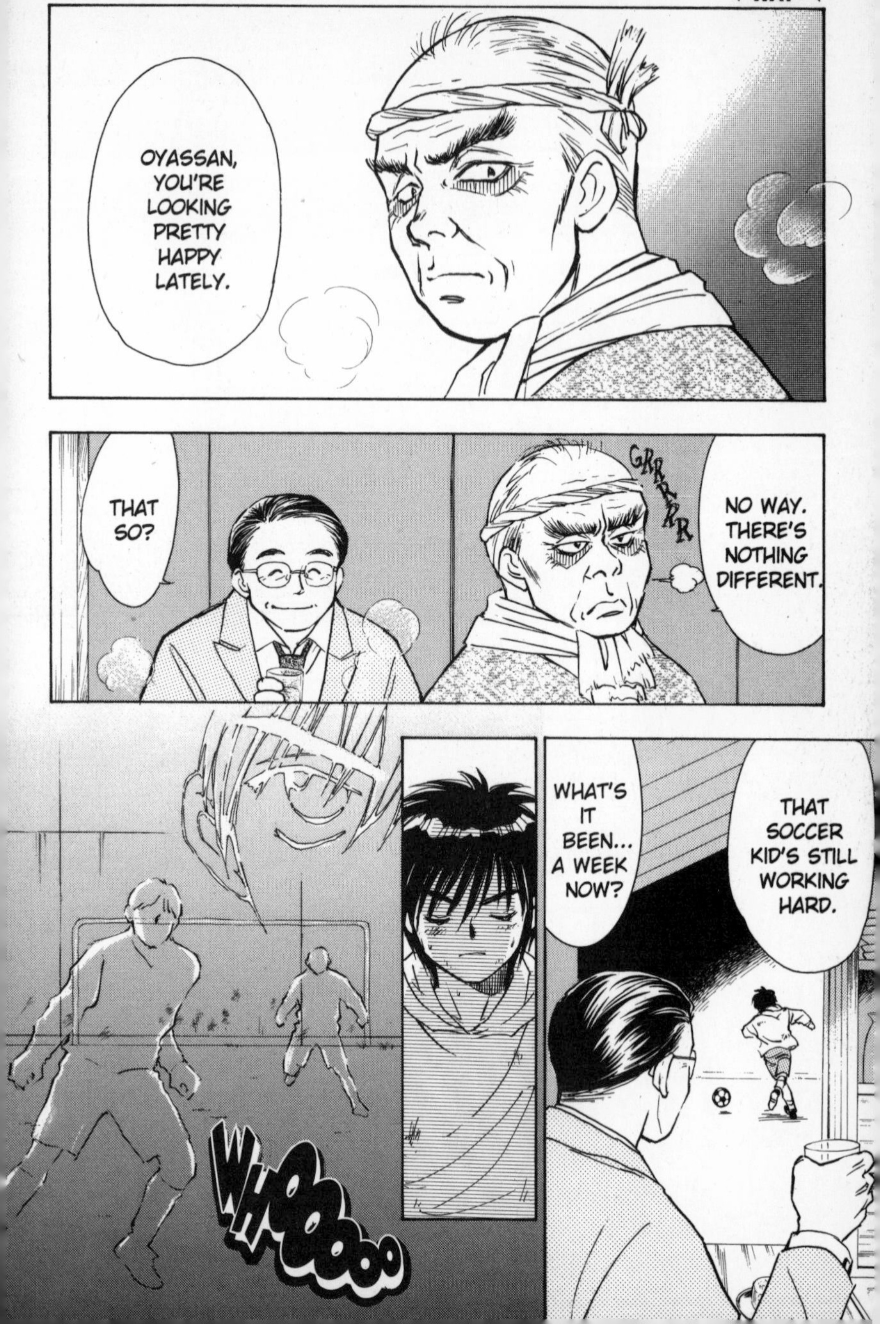

OYASSAN, YOU'RE LOOKING PRETTY HAPPY LATELY.
GRRRRRR
NO WAY. THERE'S NOTHING DIFFERENT.
THAT SO?
THAT SOCCER KID'S STILL WORKING HARD.
WHAT'S IT BEEN... A WEEK NOW?
WHOOOOOO

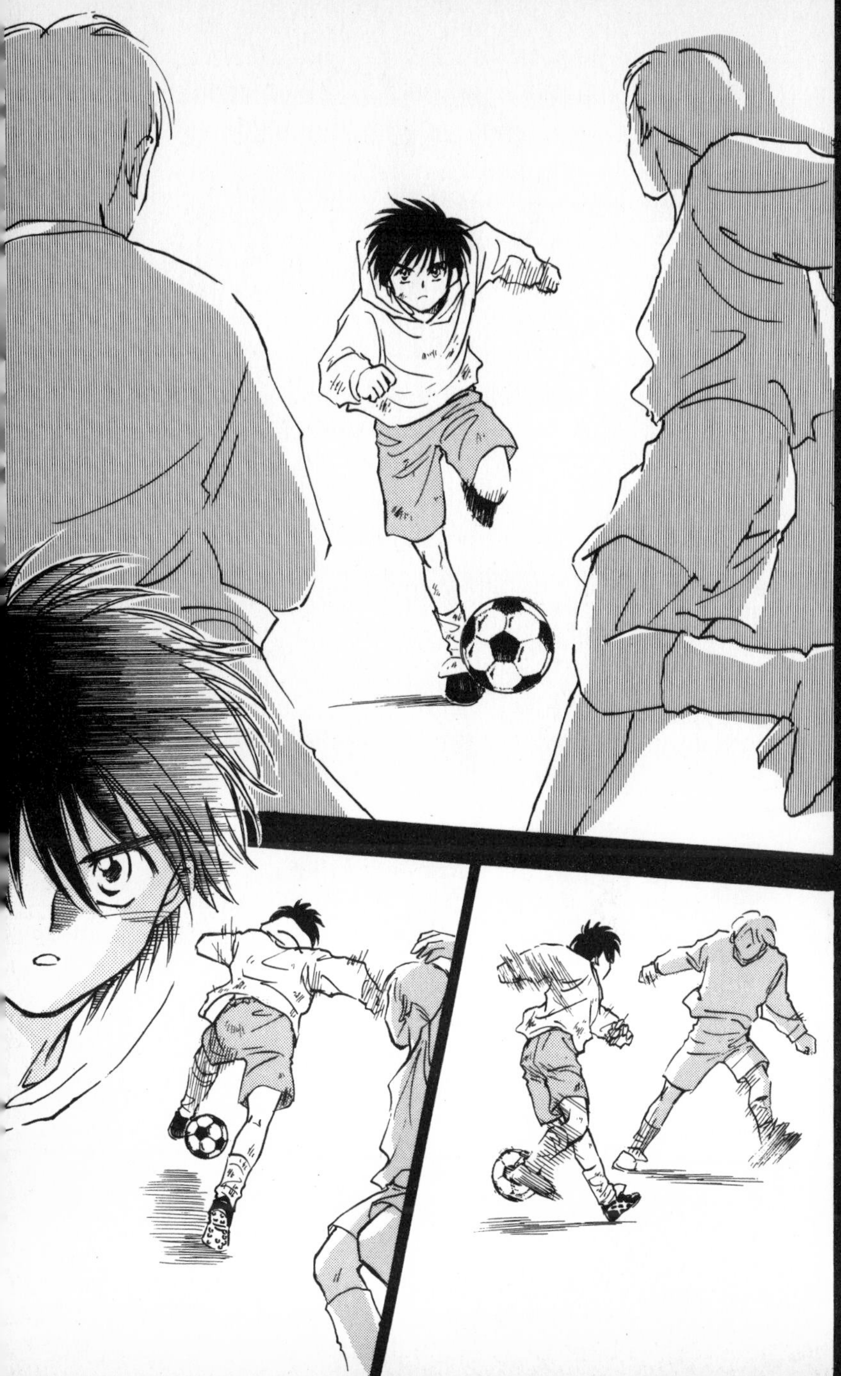

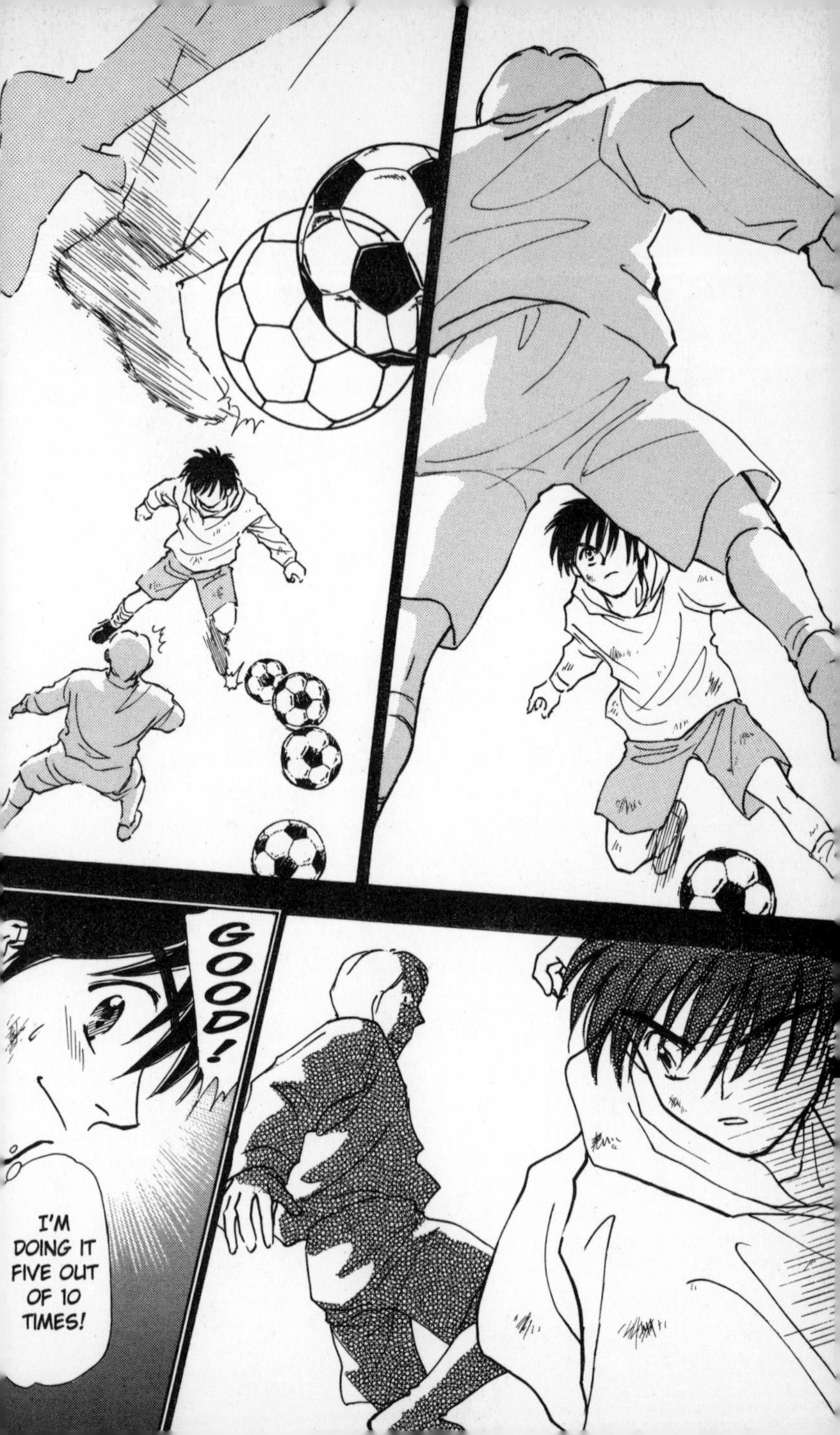
GOOD!
I'M DOING IT FIVE OUT OF 10 TIMES!

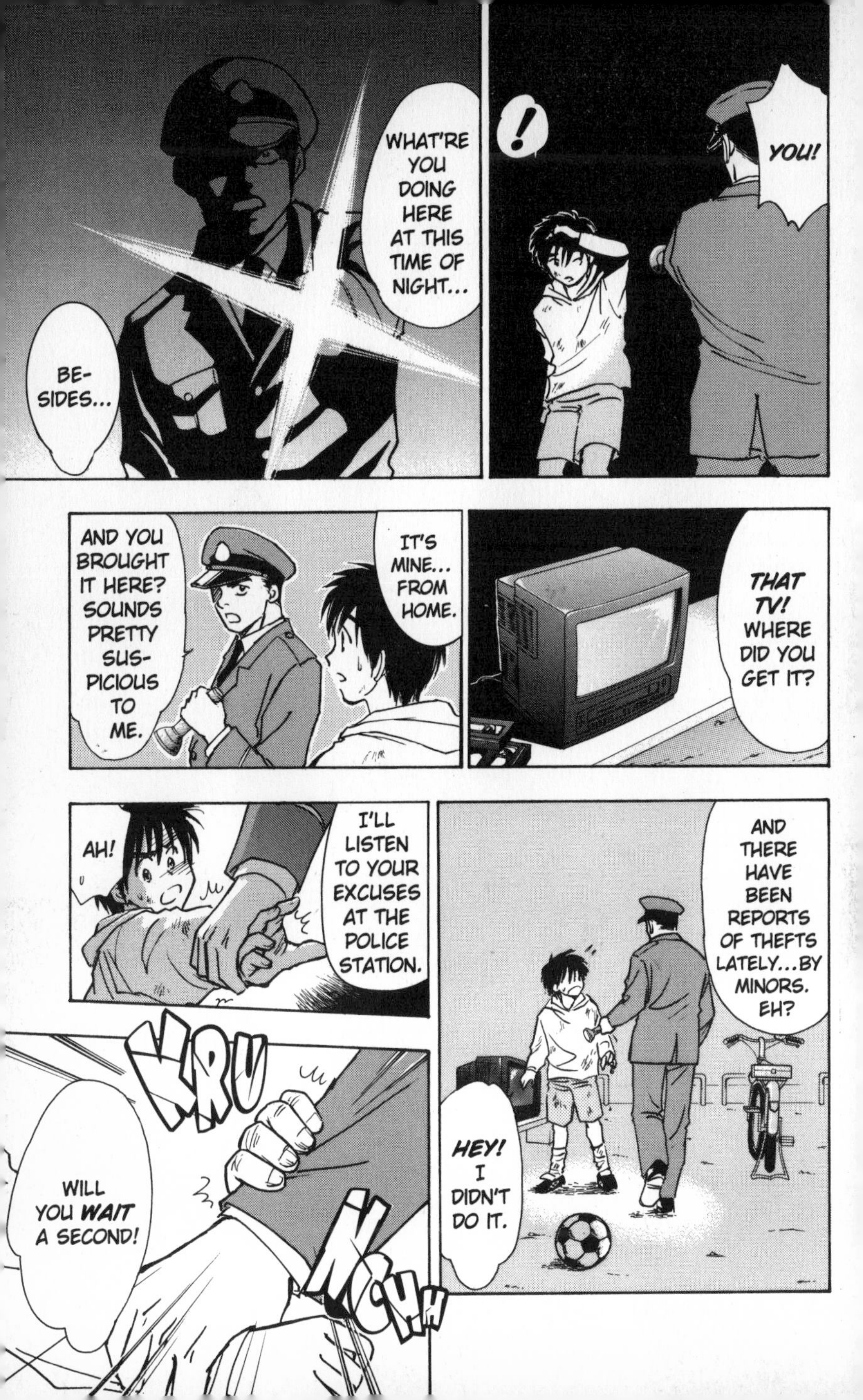
!
YOU!
WHAT'RE YOU DOING HERE AT THIS TIME OF NIGHT...
BE-SIDES...
THAT TV! WHERE DID YOU GET IT?
IT'S MINE... FROM HOME.
AND YOU BROUGHT IT HERE? SOUNDS PRETTY SUS-PICIOUS TO ME.
AND THERE HAVE BEEN REPORTS OF THEFTS LATELY...BY MINORS. EH?
HEY! I DIDN'T DO IT.
I'LL LISTEN TO YOUR EXCUSES AT THE POLICE STATION.
AH!
WILL YOU WAIT A SECOND!

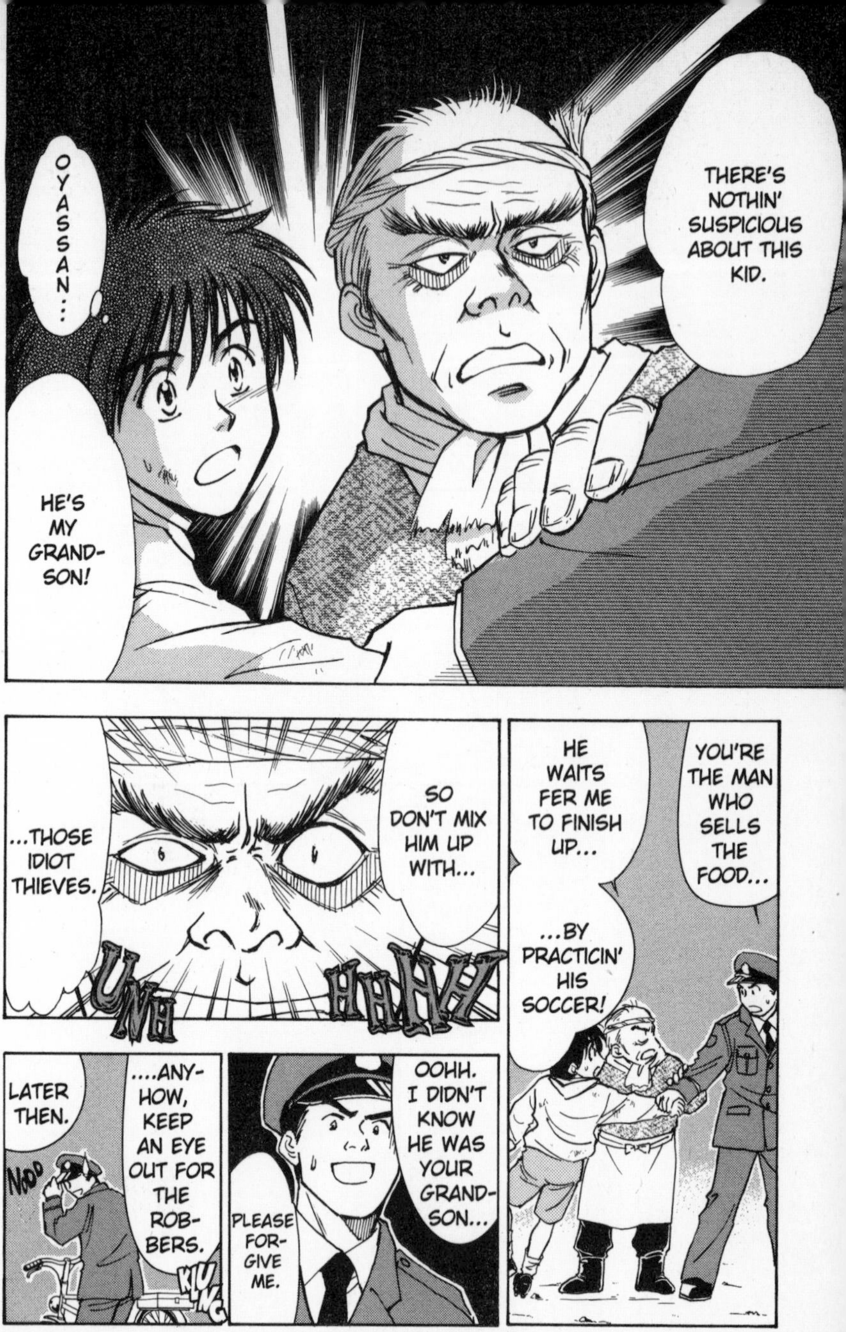
THERE'S NOTHIN' SUSPICIOUS ABOUT THIS KID.
OYASSAN...
HE'S MY GRAND-SON!
YOU'RE THE MAN WHO SELLS THE FOOD...
HE WAITS FER ME TO FINISH UP...
...BY PRACTICIN' HIS SOCCER!
SO DON'T MIX HIM UP WITH...
...THOSE IDIOT THIEVES.
UNH
HHHH
OOHH. I DIDN'T KNOW HE WAS YOUR GRAND-SON...
PLEASE FOR-GIVE ME.
....ANY-HOW, KEEP AN EYE OUT FOR THE ROB-BERS.
LATER THEN.
NOD
KLUNG

READ THIS WAY

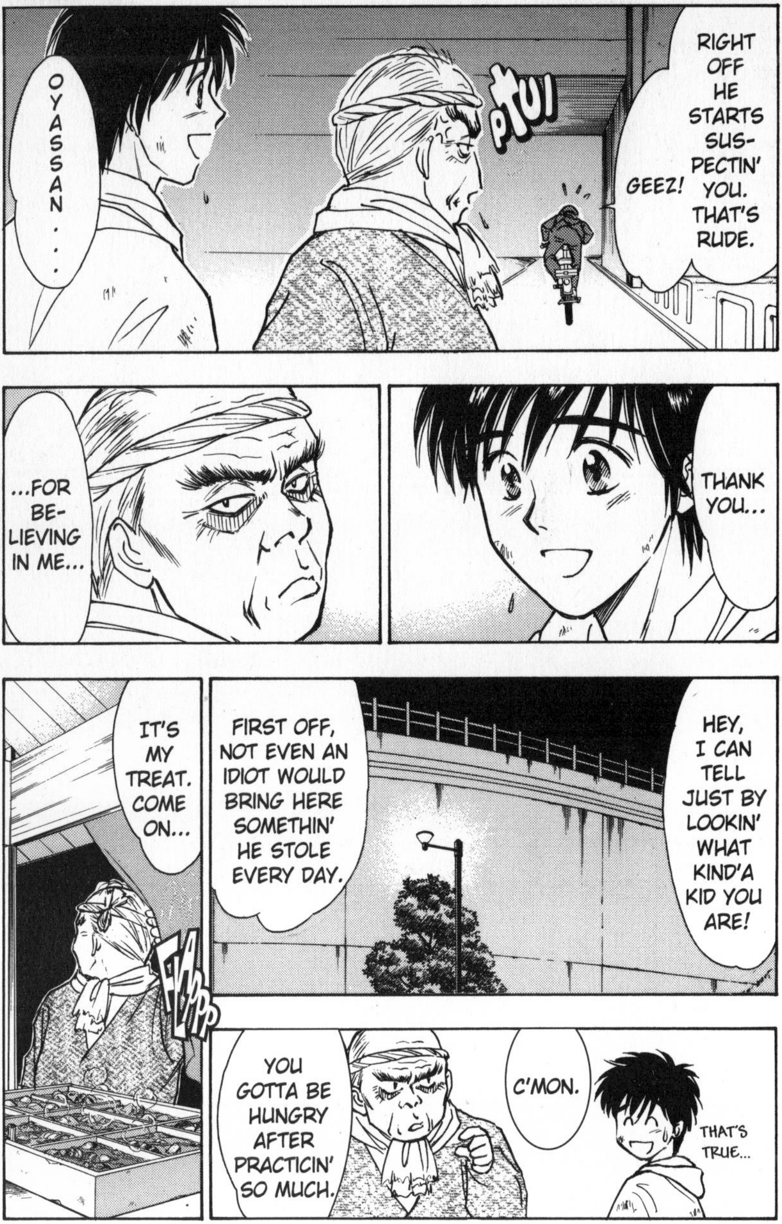
RIGHT OFF HE STARTS SUS-PECTIN' YOU. THAT'S RUDE.
GEEZ!
PTUI
OYASSAN...
THANK YOU...
...FOR BE-LIEVING IN ME...
HEY, I CAN TELL JUST BY LOOKIN' WHAT KIND'A KID YOU ARE!
FIRST OFF, NOT EVEN AN IDIOT WOULD BRING HERE SOMETHIN' HE STOLE EVERY DAY.
THAT'S TRUE...
C'MON.
YOU GOTTA BE HUNGRY AFTER PRACTICIN' SO MUCH.
IT'S MY TREAT. COME ON...

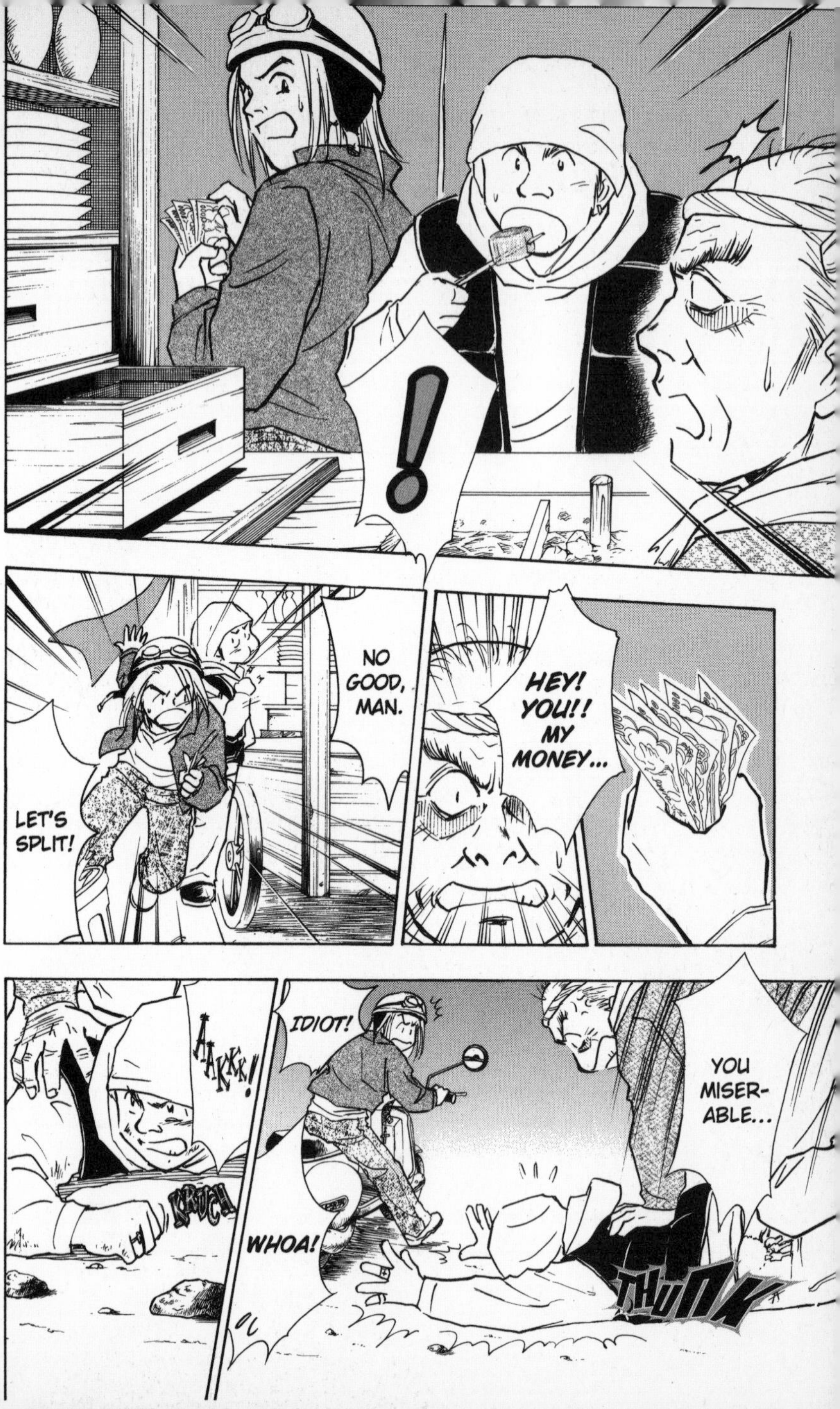
!
HEY! YOU!! MY MONEY...
NO GOOD, MAN.
LET'S SPLIT!
YOU MISER-ABLE...
IDIOT!
THUNK
WHOA!
AAKKK!!
KRUCH

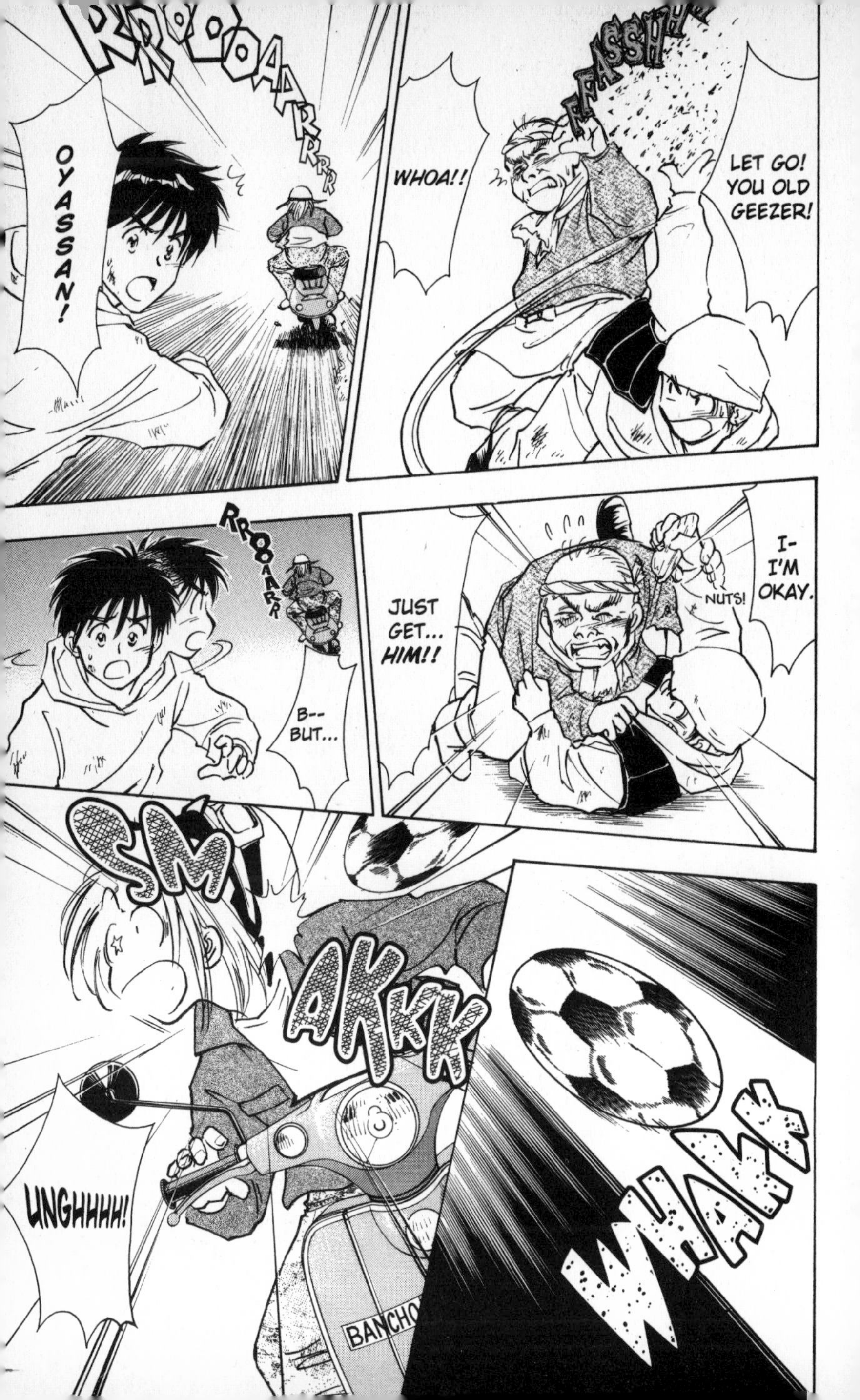
FFASSH!!
LET GO! YOU OLD GEEZER!
WHOA!!
RROOOAARRRR
OYASSAN!
I- I'M OKAY.
NUTS!
JUST GET... HIM!!
RROOAARR
B-- BUT...
WHAKK
SMAKKK
UNGHHHH!
BANCHO

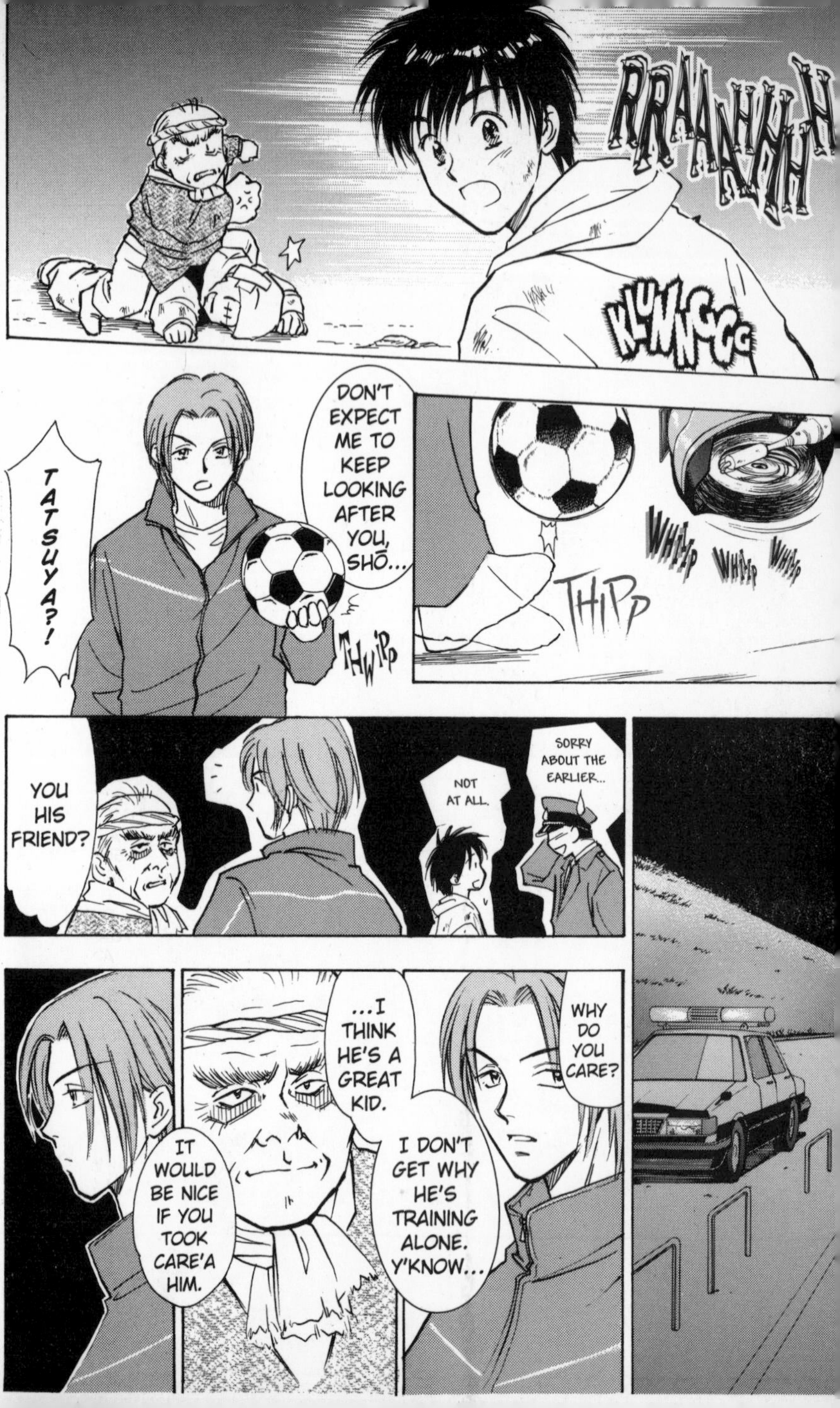
RRAAHHHH
KLUNNGGG
WHIIP WHIIP WHIIP
THIPP
DON'T EXPECT ME TO KEEP LOOKING AFTER YOU, SHŌ...
THWIPP
TATSUYA?!
SORRY ABOUT THE EARLIER...
NOT AT ALL.
YOU HIS FRIEND?
WHY DO YOU CARE?
...I THINK HE'S A GREAT KID.
I DON'T GET WHY HE'S TRAINING ALONE. Y'KNOW...
IT WOULD BE NICE IF YOU TOOK CARE'A HIM.

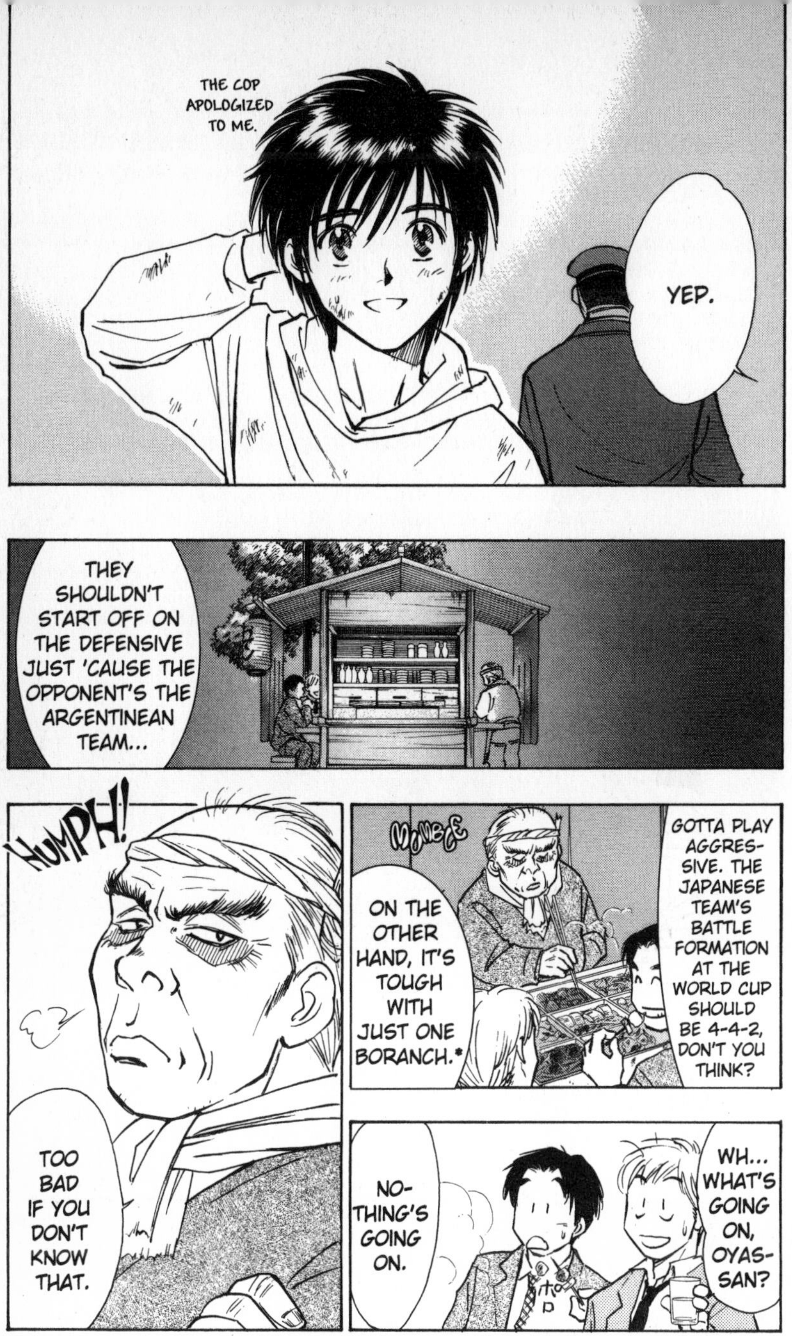
THE COP APOLOGIZED TO ME.
YEP.
THEY SHOULDN'T START OFF ON THE DEFENSIVE JUST 'CAUSE THE OPPONENT'S THE ARGENTINEAN TEAM...
GOTTA PLAY AGGRES-SIVE. THE JAPANESE TEAM'S BATTLE FORMATION AT THE WORLD CUP SHOULD BE 4-4-2, DON'T YOU THINK?
MUMBLE
ON THE OTHER HAND, IT'S TOUGH WITH JUST ONE BORANCH.*
WH... WHAT'S GOING ON, OYAS-SAN?
NO-THING'S GOING ON.
HUMPH!
TOO BAD IF YOU DON'T KNOW THAT.

Boranch: Middle Fielder who is in charge of defending when the game/play/battle reaches it's highest intensity. Player named Motohiro Yamaguchi of Japanese team is known as Boranch.

● WORLD'S SUPER STARS ●

THE WORLD CUP IS A STAGE WHERE THE WORLD'S SUPER STARS WILL SHOW THEIR BEST PLAYS TO EVERYONE ACROSS THE GLOBE. NOW, LET ME INTRODUCE THE PLAYERS SHŌ IDOLIZES.

FIRST OF ALL, RONALDO. AT THE AGE OF 17, HE MADE HIS DEBUT AS A BRAZILIAN REPRESENTATIVE, AND HE WENT ON TO RECEIVE GLORIES AS THE KING SCORER AT THE DUTCH LEAGUE, AS WELL AS THE SPANISH LEAGUE. CURRENTLY, HE PLAYS AT ITALIAN SERIE A INTEL. HE'S A FIRST CLASS PLAYER ON EVERY FRONT, AND IT'S NOT AN EXAGGERATION TO SAY THAT ONCE HE GETS A BALL FREE, NO ONE WILL BE ABLE TO GET IT BACK FROM HIM.

NEXT, THE ITALIAN REPRESENTATIVE, DEL PIERO. ALTHOUGH SMALL IN SIZE, HE HAS KEEN, STRATEGIC EYES. THE LEFT SIDE OF THE PENALTY AREA IS ESPECIALLY CALLED "DEL PIERO ZONE" BECAUSE IF HE SHOOTS FROM THAT SPOT, HE NEVER FAILS TO MAKE A GOAL.

THE ARGENTINEAN REPRESENTATIVE, PATTIS TORTA, IS A GENUINE STRIKER. HIS POWERFUL SHOT USING HIS RIGHT FOOT IS WORTH SEEING AT LEAST ONCE.

IN ADDITION, THERE ARE MANY GREAT PLAYERS, SUCH AS THE FRENCH REPRESENTATIVES, ZIDANE AND JOEL KAEF, THE ENGLISH REPRESENTATIVE, SHIARRAH, THE SPANISH REPRESENTATIVE, RAOUL, AND THE NIGERIAN REPRESENTATIVE, KANU.

--TATSUYA WATANABE *(WINNING RUN)*

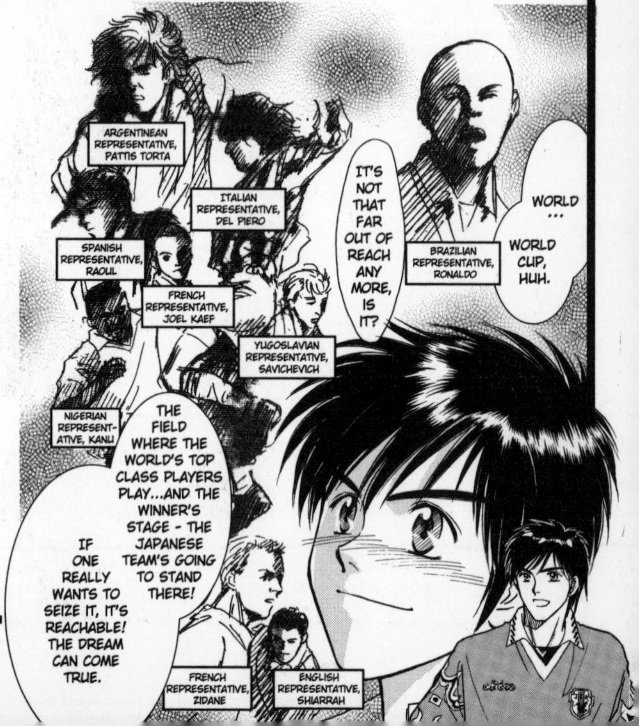
WORLD ... WORLD CUP, HUH.
IT'S NOT THAT FAR OUT OF REACH ANY MORE, IS IT?
BRAZILIAN REPRESENTATIVE, RONALDO
ARGENTINEAN REPRESENTATIVE, PATTIS TORTA
ITALIAN REPRESENTATIVE, DEL PIERO
SPANISH REPRESENTATIVE, RAOUL
FRENCH REPRESENTATIVE, JOEL KAEF
YUGOSLAVIAN REPRESENTATIVE, SAVICHEVICH
NIGERIAN REPRESENT-ATIVE, KANU
THE FIELD WHERE THE WORLD'S TOP CLASS PLAYERS PLAY...AND THE WINNER'S STAGE - THE JAPANESE TEAM'S GOING TO STAND THERE!
IF ONE REALLY WANTS TO SEIZE IT, IT'S REACHABLE! THE DREAM CAN COME TRUE.
ENGLISH REPRESENTATIVE, SHIARRAH
FRENCH REPRESENTATIVE, ZIDANE

STAGE.3 TEAM MATE

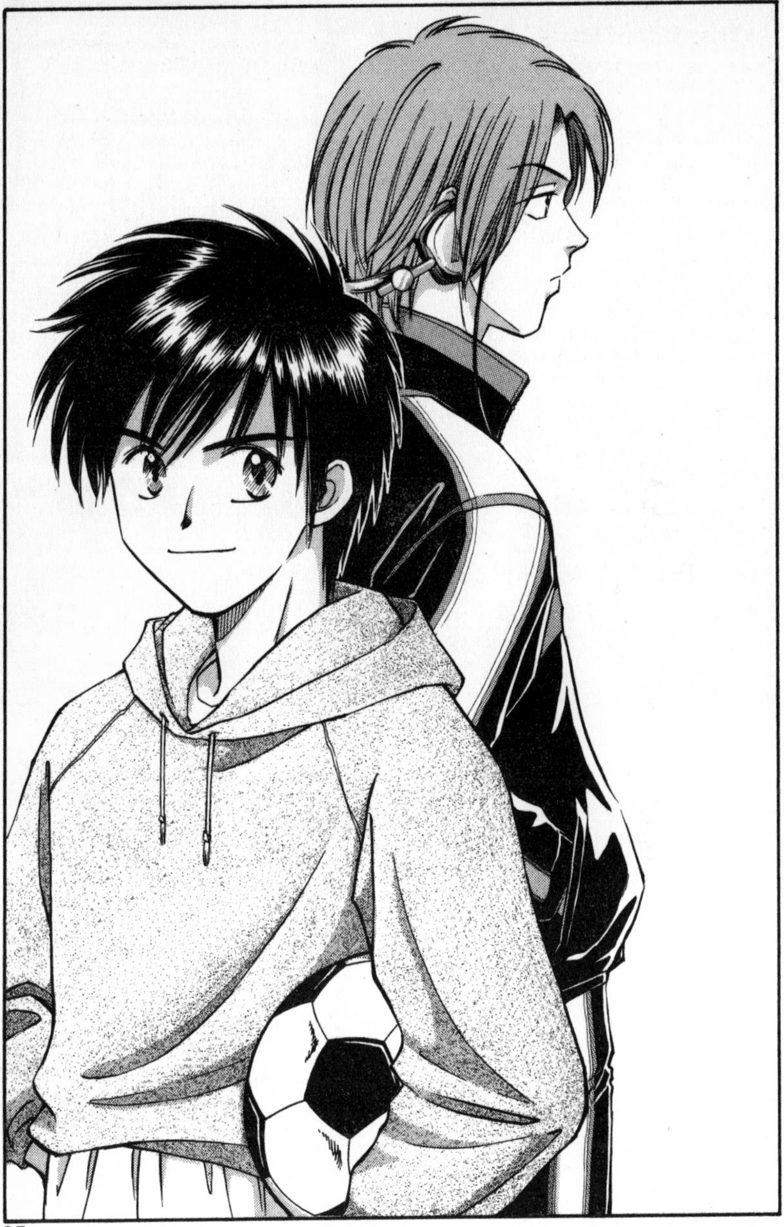

READ THIS WAY

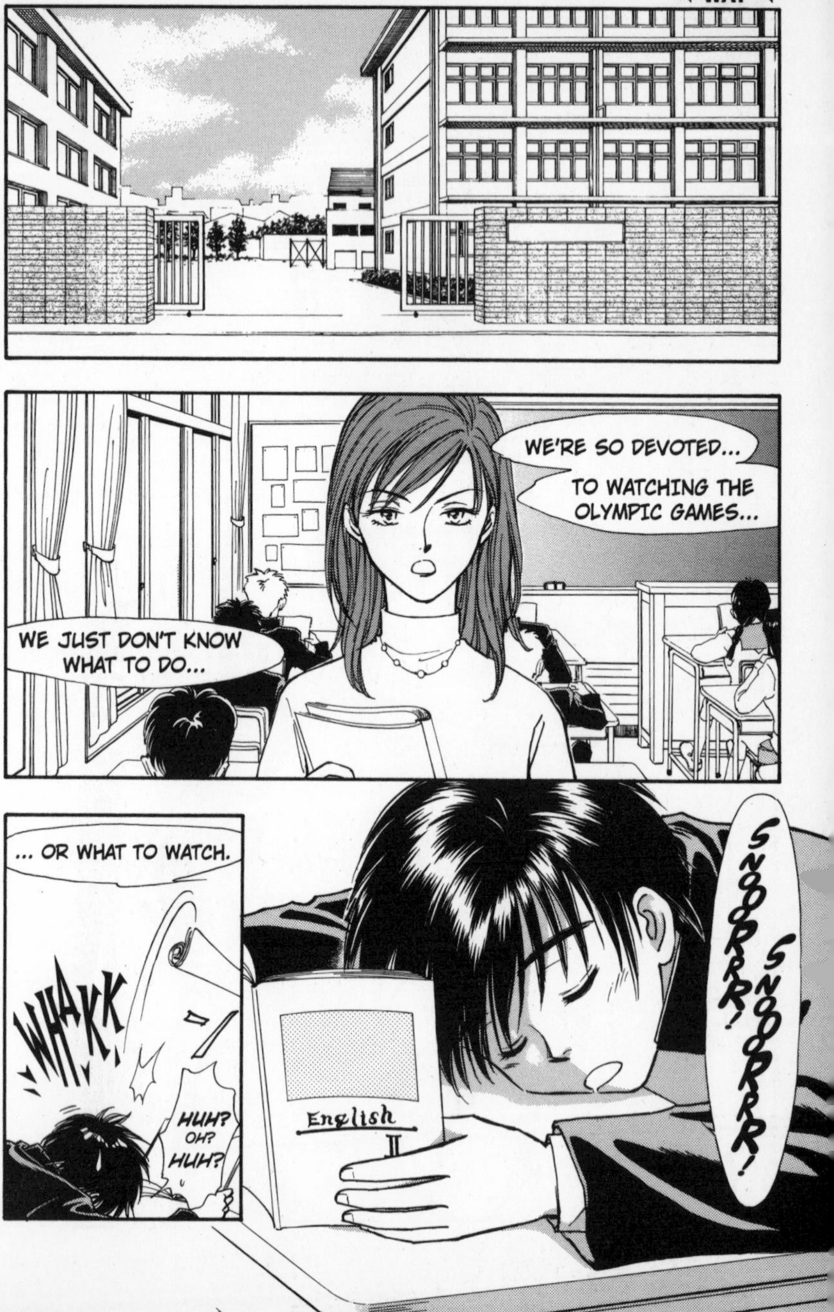

WE'RE SO DEVOTED...
TO WATCHING THE OLYMPIC GAMES...
WE JUST DON'T KNOW WHAT TO DO...
SNOOORRR!
SNOOORRR!
English II
... OR WHAT TO WATCH.
WHAKK!
HUH? OH? HUH?

READ THIS WAY

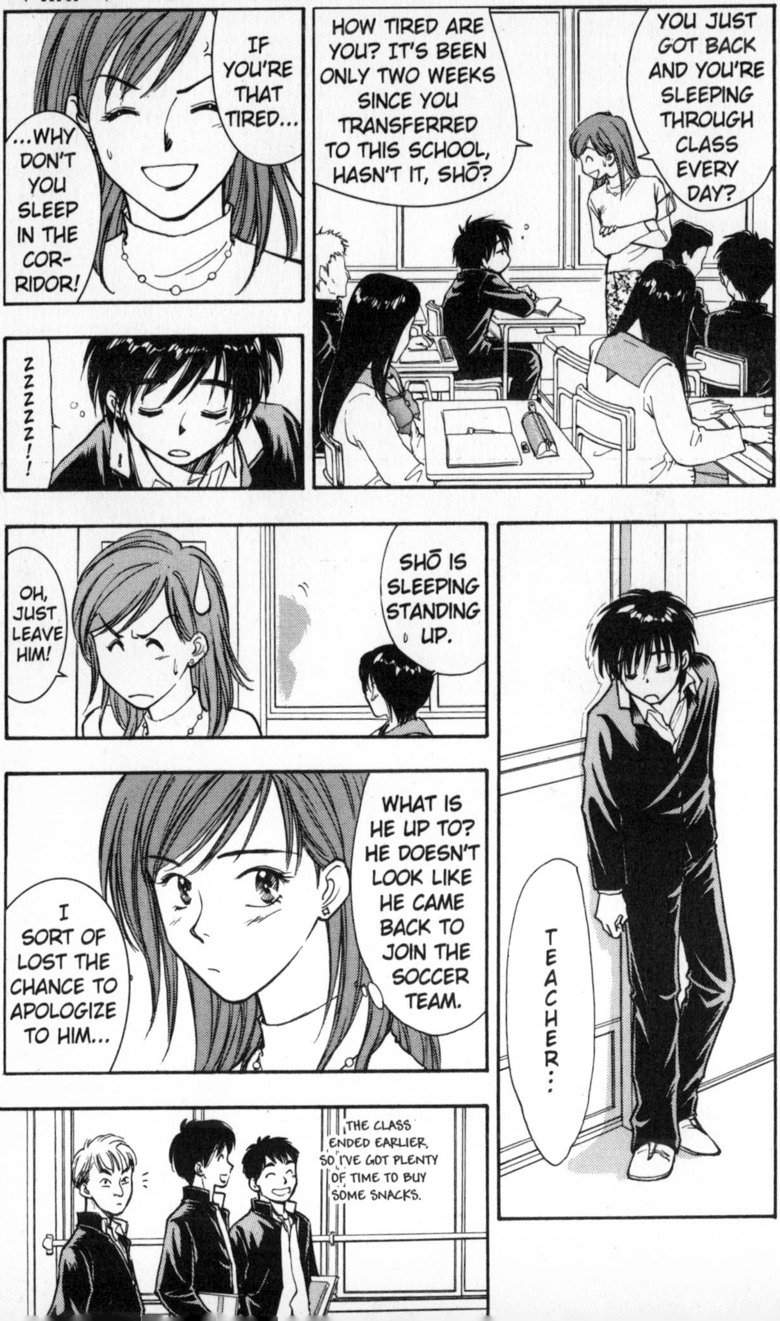
YOU JUST GOT BACK AND YOU'RE SLEEPING THROUGH CLASS EVERY DAY?
HOW TIRED ARE YOU? IT'S BEEN ONLY TWO WEEKS SINCE YOU TRANSFERRED TO THIS SCHOOL, HASN'T IT, SHŌ?
IF YOU'RE THAT TIRED...
...WHY DON'T YOU SLEEP IN THE CORRIDOR!
ZZZZZ!!
TEACHER...
SHŌ IS SLEEPING STANDING UP.
OH, JUST LEAVE HIM!
WHAT IS HE UP TO? HE DOESN'T LOOK LIKE HE CAME BACK TO JOIN THE SOCCER TEAM.
I SORT OF LOST THE CHANCE TO APOLOGIZE TO HIM...
THE CLASS ENDED EARLIER, SO I'VE GOT PLENTY OF TIME TO BUY SOME SNACKS.

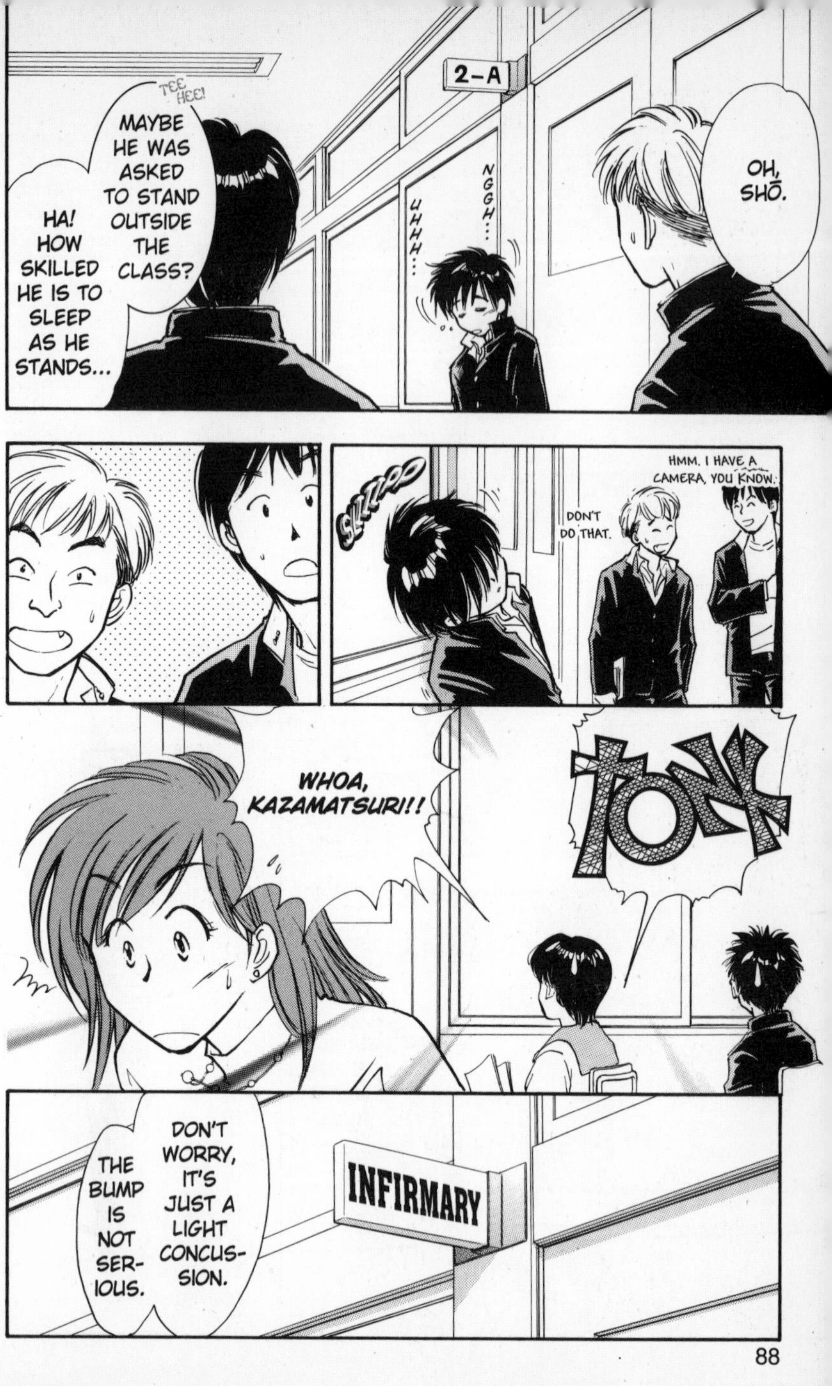
2-A
OH, SHŌ.
NGGH...
UHHH...
TEE HEE!
MAYBE HE WAS ASKED TO STAND OUTSIDE THE CLASS?
HA! HOW SKILLED HE IS TO SLEEP AS HE STANDS...
HMM. I HAVE A CAMERA, YOU KNOW.
DON'T DO THAT.
SLLLIP
TON
WHOA, KAZAMATSURI!!
INFIRMARY
DON'T WORRY, IT'S JUST A LIGHT CONCUSSION.
THE BUMP IS NOT SERIOUS.

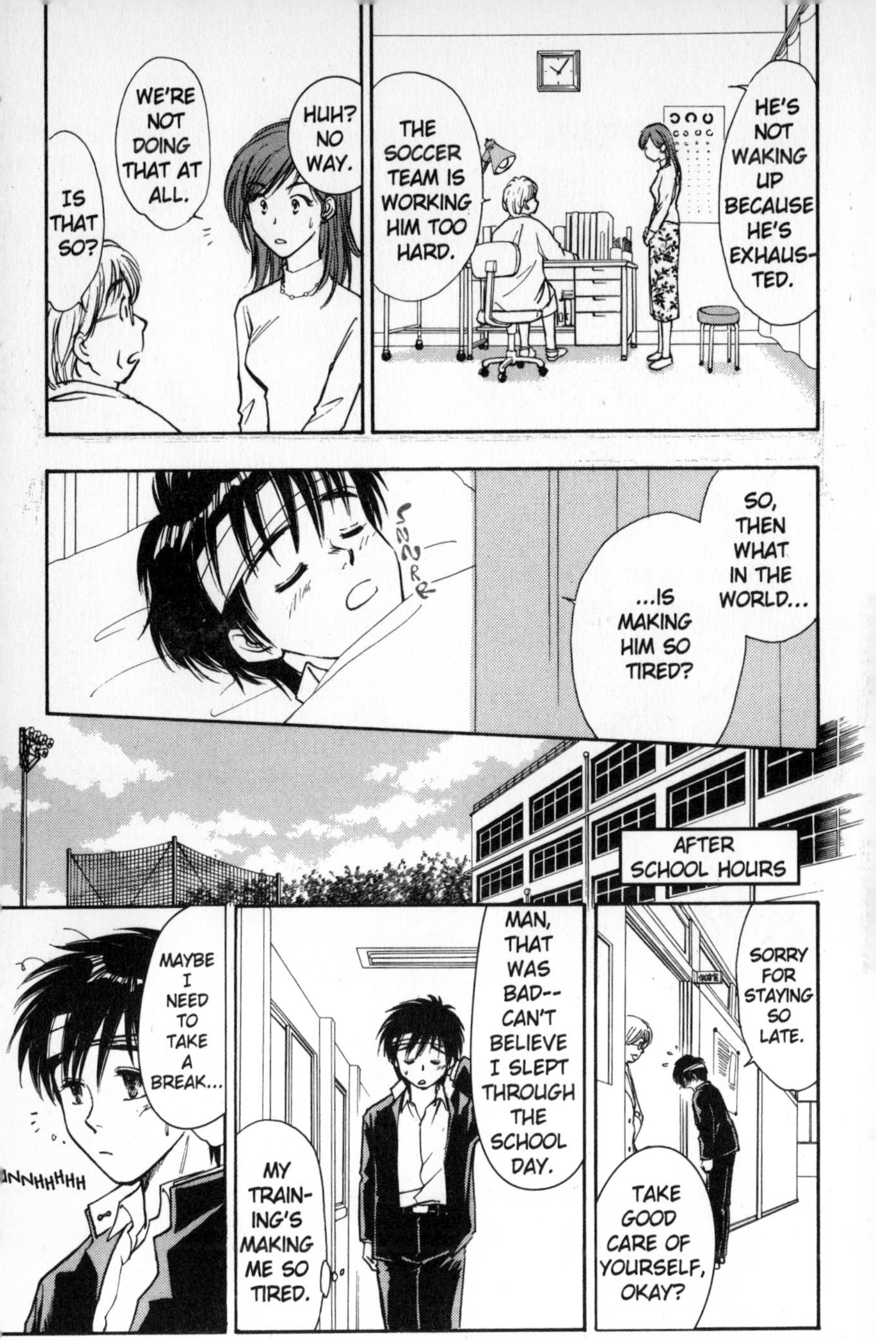
HE'S NOT WAKING UP BECAUSE HE'S EXHAUSTED.
THE SOCCER TEAM IS WORKING HIM TOO HARD.
HUH? NO WAY.
WE'RE NOT DOING THAT AT ALL.
IS THAT SO?
SO, THEN WHAT IN THE WORLD...
...IS MAKING HIM SO TIRED?
AFTER SCHOOL HOURS
SORRY FOR STAYING SO LATE.
TAKE GOOD CARE OF YOURSELF, OKAY?
MAN, THAT WAS BAD-- CAN'T BELIEVE I SLEPT THROUGH THE SCHOOL DAY.
MY TRAIN-ING'S MAKING ME SO TIRED.
MAYBE I NEED TO TAKE A BREAK...
NNNHHHHH

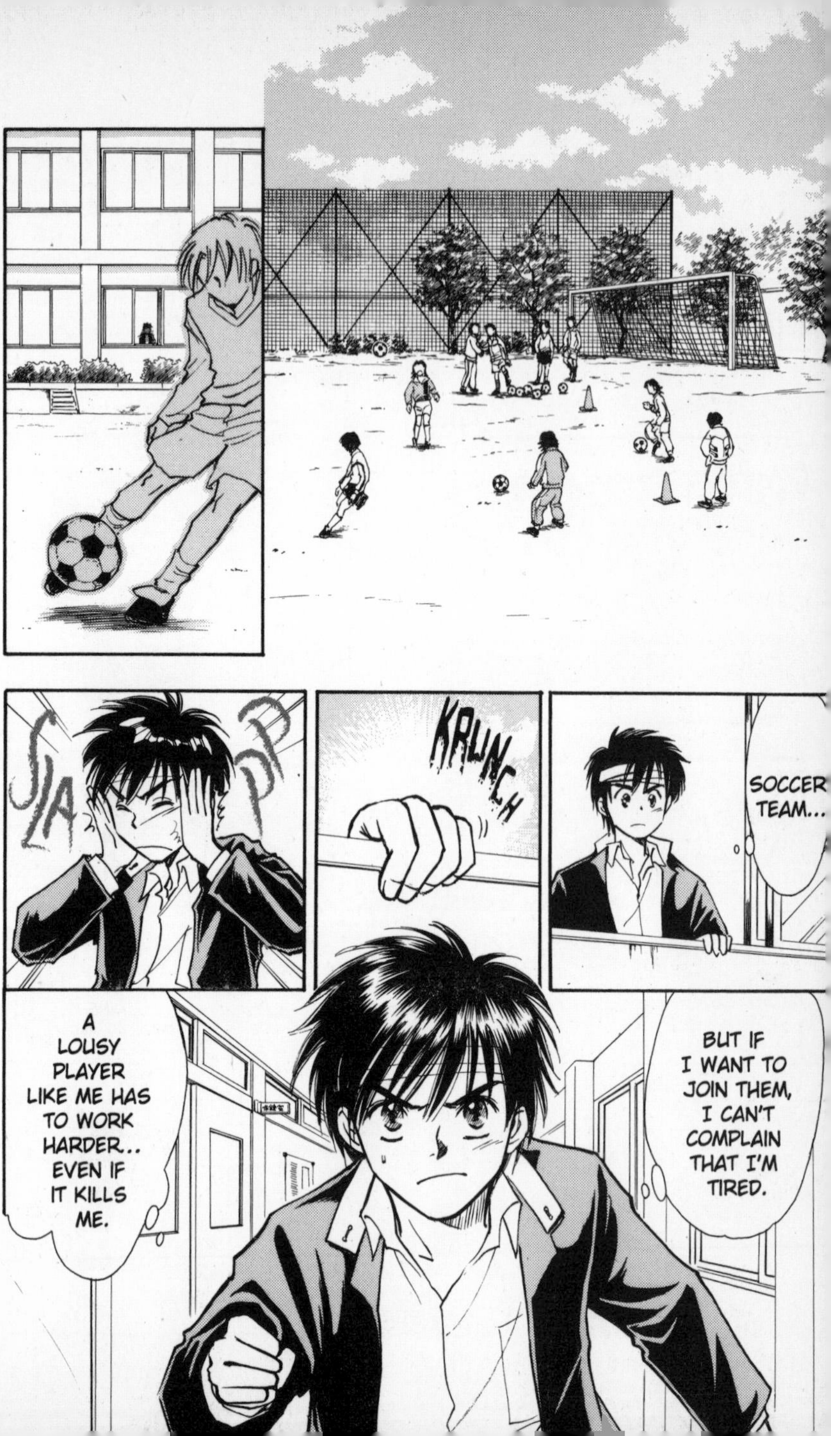
SOCCER TEAM...
KRUNCH
BUT IF I WANT TO JOIN THEM, I CAN'T COMPLAIN THAT I'M TIRED.
A LOUSY PLAYER LIKE ME HAS TO WORK HARDER... EVEN IF IT KILLS ME.

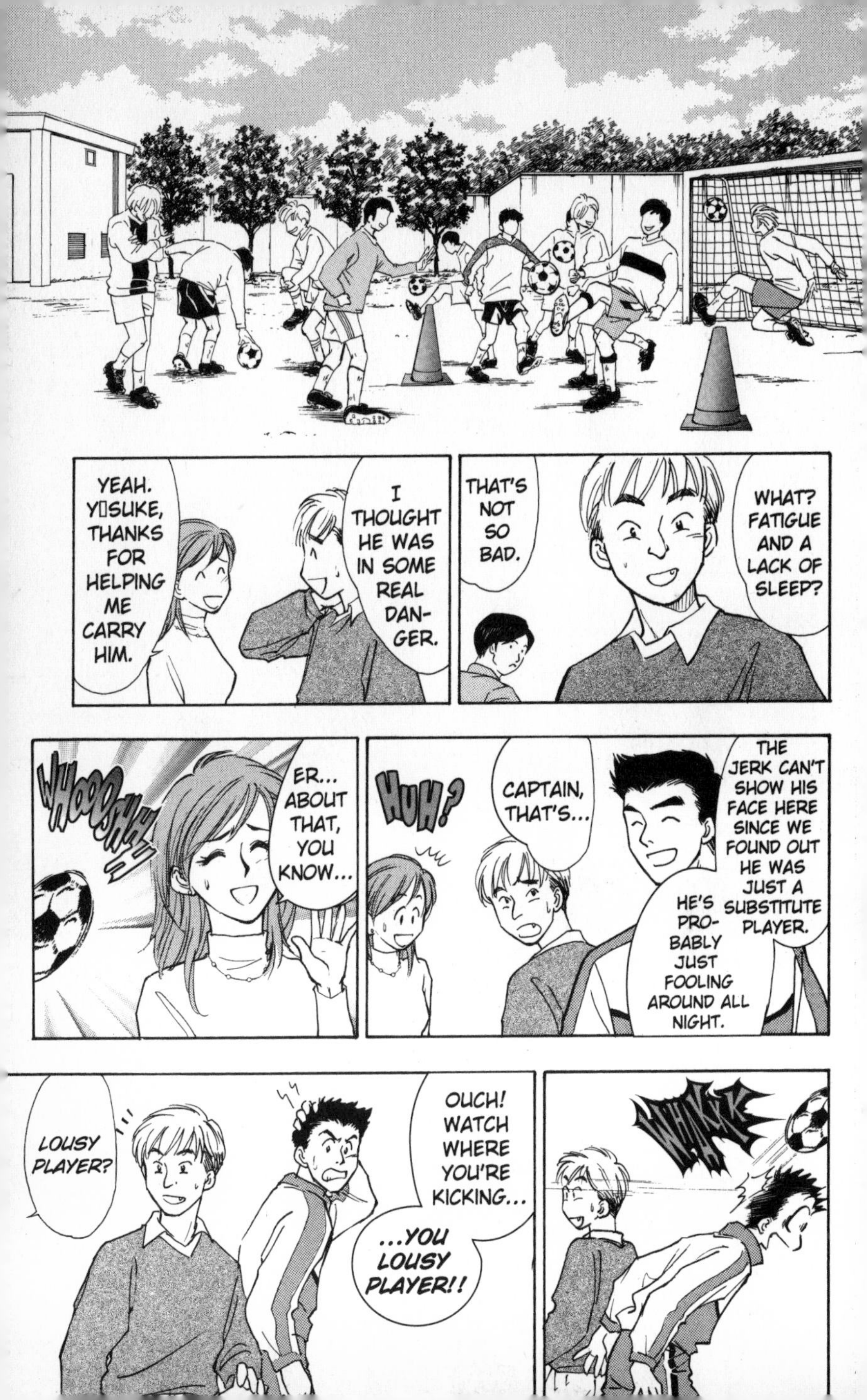
WHAT? FATIGUE AND A LACK OF SLEEP?
THAT'S NOT SO BAD.
I THOUGHT HE WAS IN SOME REAL DAN-GER.
YEAH. Y□SUKE, THANKS FOR HELPING ME CARRY HIM.
THE JERK CAN'T SHOW HIS FACE HERE SINCE WE FOUND OUT HE WAS JUST A SUBSTITUTE PLAYER.
HE'S PRO-BABLY JUST FOOLING AROUND ALL NIGHT.
CAPTAIN, THAT'S...
HUH?
ER... ABOUT THAT, YOU KNOW...
WHOOOSH
WHACK
OUCH! WATCH WHERE YOU'RE KICKING...
...YOU LOUSY PLAYER!!
LOUSY PLAYER?

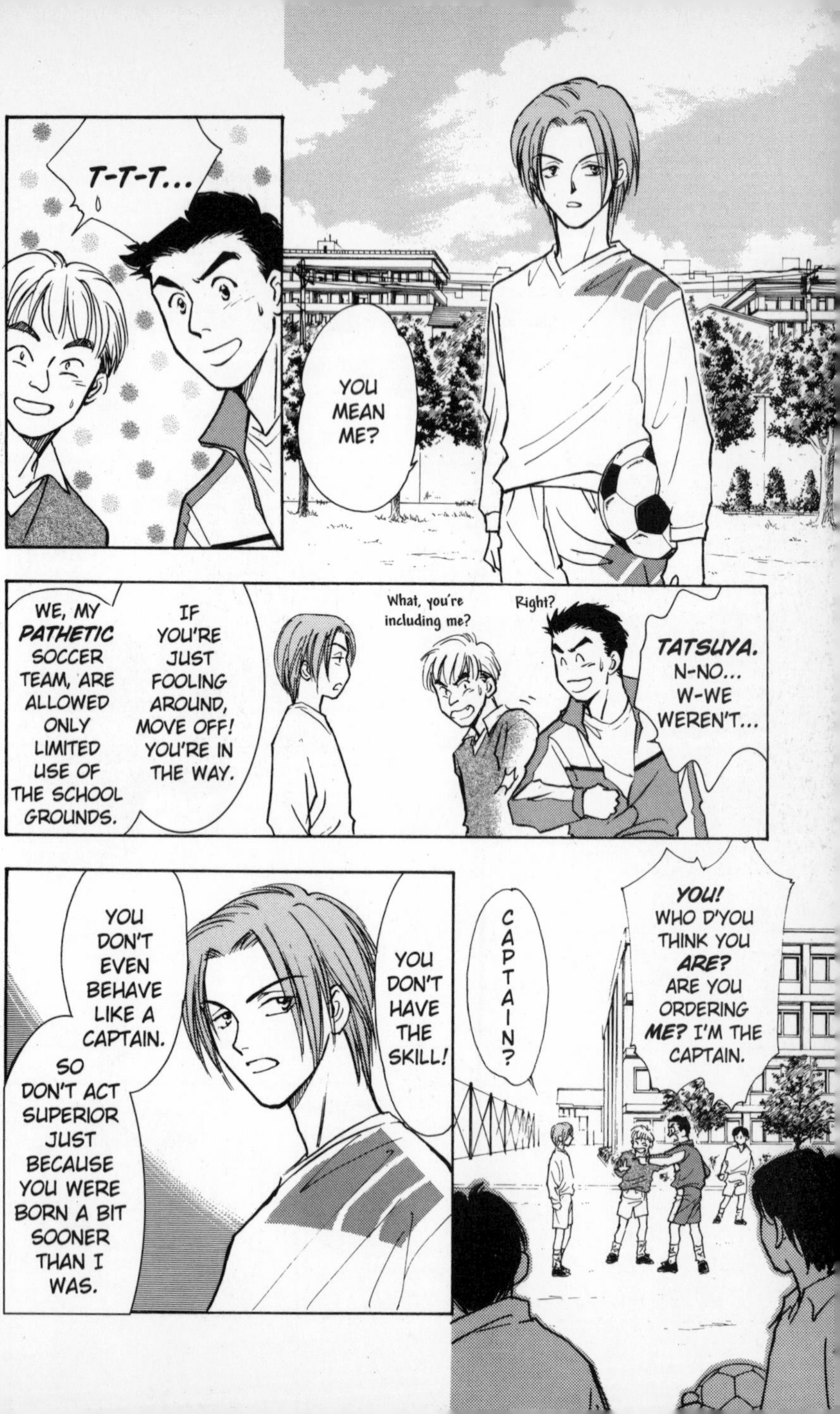
YOU MEAN ME?
T-T-T...
TATSUYA. N-NO... W-WE WEREN'T...
Right?
What, you're including me?
IF YOU'RE JUST FOOLING AROUND, MOVE OFF! YOU'RE IN THE WAY.
WE, MY PATHETIC SOCCER TEAM, ARE ALLOWED ONLY LIMITED USE OF THE SCHOOL GROUNDS.
YOU! WHO D'YOU THINK YOU ARE? ARE YOU ORDERING ME? I'M THE CAPTAIN.
CAPTAIN?
YOU DON'T HAVE THE SKILL!
YOU DON'T EVEN BEHAVE LIKE A CAPTAIN.
SO DON'T ACT SUPERIOR JUST BECAUSE YOU WERE BORN A BIT SOONER THAN I WAS.

READ THIS WAY

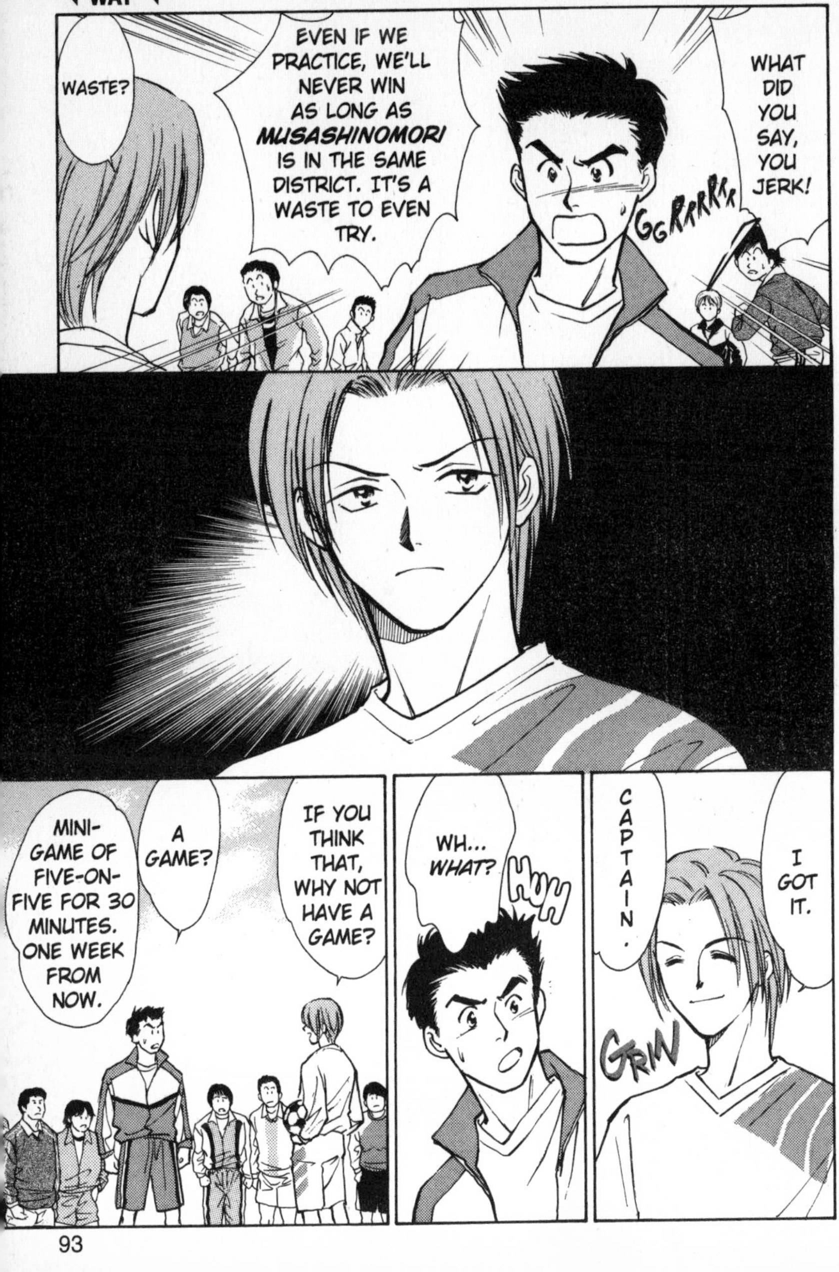
WHAT DID YOU SAY, YOU JERK!
GGRRRRRR
EVEN IF WE PRACTICE, WE'LL NEVER WIN AS LONG AS MUSASHINOMORI IS IN THE SAME DISTRICT. IT'S A WASTE TO EVEN TRY.
WASTE?
I GOT IT.
CAPTAIN.
GRIN
WH... WHAT?
HUH
IF YOU THINK THAT, WHY NOT HAVE A GAME?
A GAME?
MINI-GAME OF FIVE-ON-FIVE FOR 30 MINUTES. ONE WEEK FROM NOW.

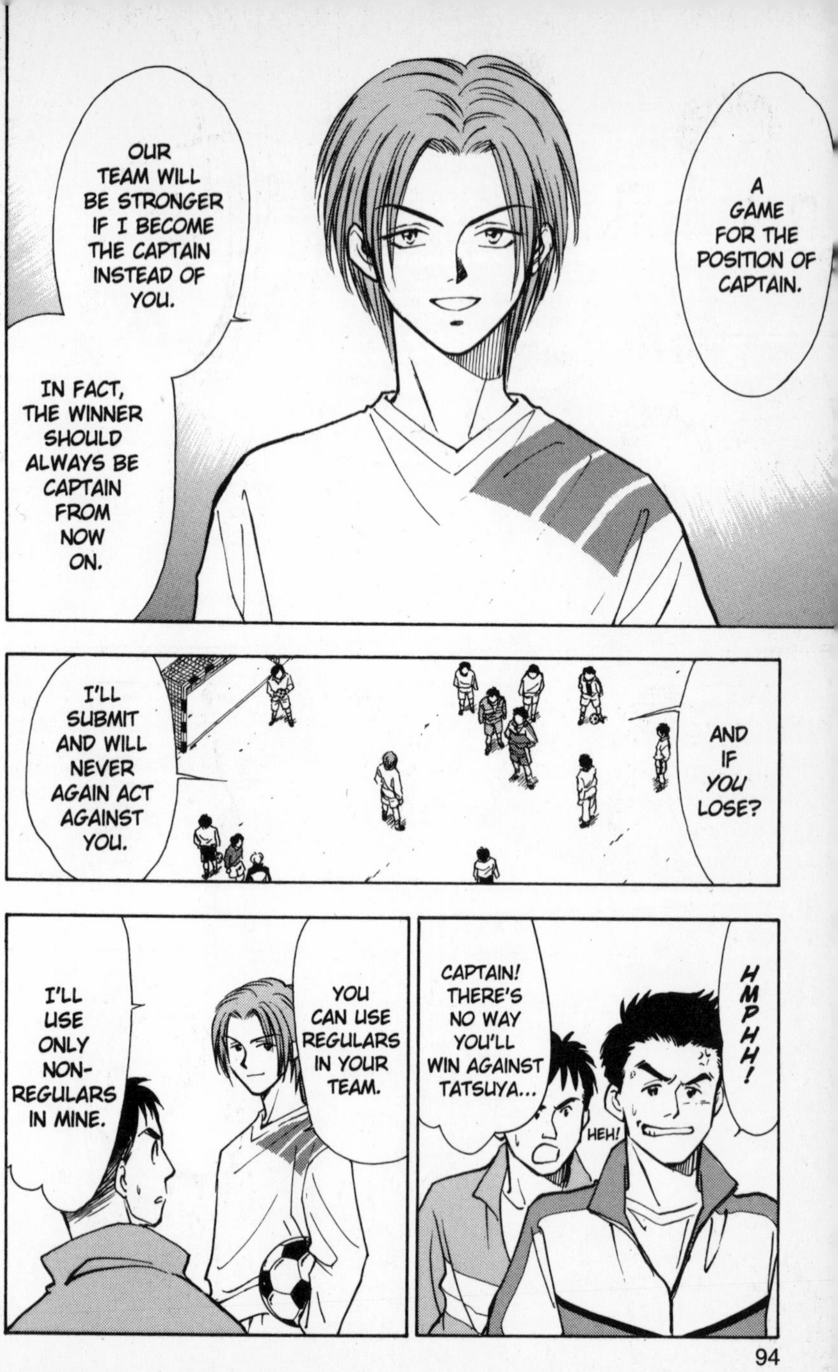
A GAME FOR THE POSITION OF CAPTAIN.
OUR TEAM WILL BE STRONGER IF I BECOME THE CAPTAIN INSTEAD OF YOU.
IN FACT, THE WINNER SHOULD ALWAYS BE CAPTAIN FROM NOW ON.
AND IF YOU LOSE?
I'LL SUBMIT AND WILL NEVER AGAIN ACT AGAINST YOU.
HMPHH!
CAPTAIN! THERE'S NO WAY YOU'LL WIN AGAINST TATSUYA...
HEH!
YOU CAN USE REGULARS IN YOUR TEAM.
I'LL USE ONLY NON-REGULARS IN MINE.

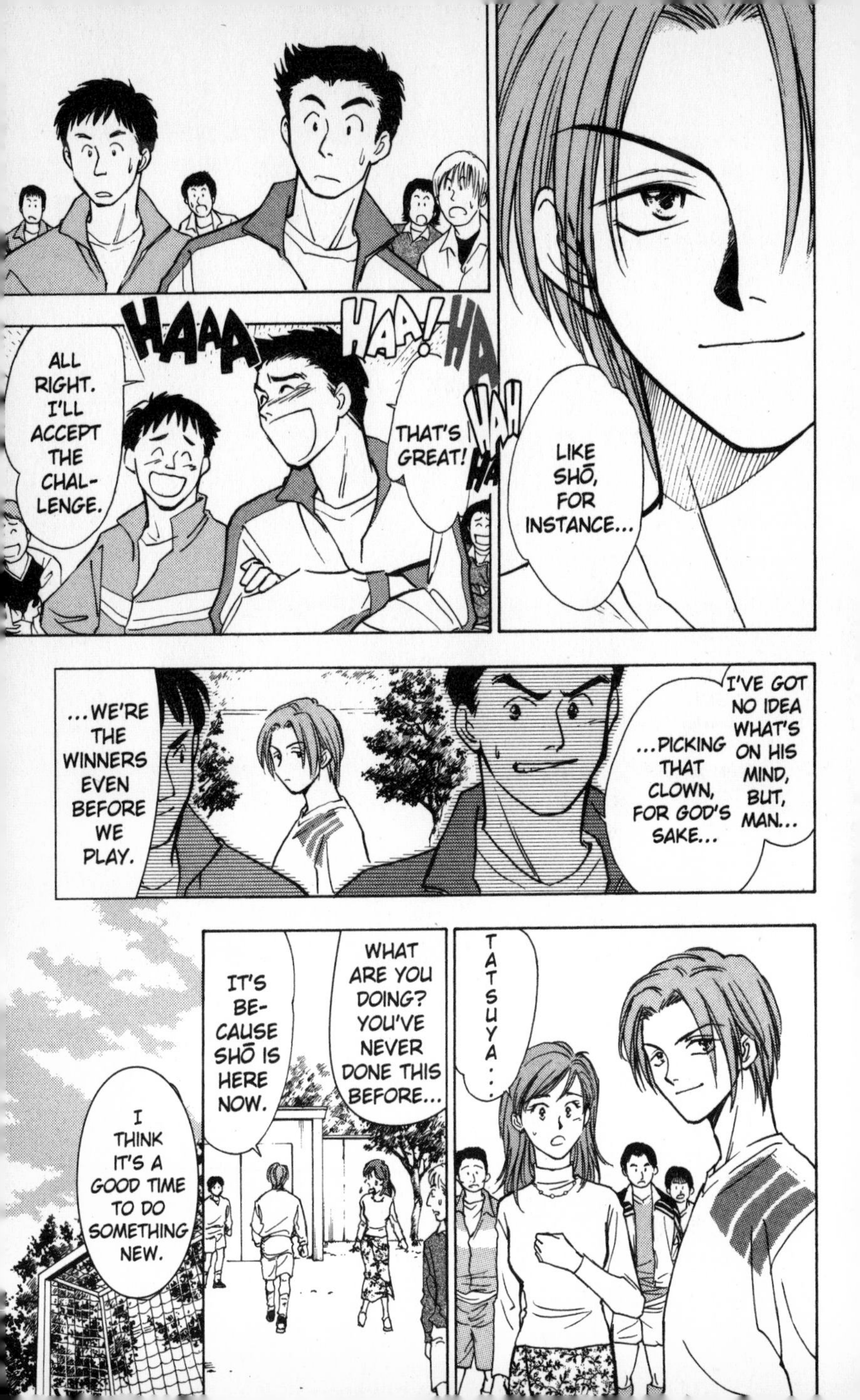
LIKE SHŌ, FOR INSTANCE...
HAA! HA
HAH HA
THAT'S GREAT!
HAAA
ALL RIGHT. I'LL ACCEPT THE CHAL- LENGE.
I'VE GOT NO IDEA WHAT'S ON HIS MIND, BUT, MAN...
...PICKING THAT CLOWN, FOR GOD'S SAKE...
...WE'RE THE WINNERS EVEN BEFORE WE PLAY.
TATSUYA...
WHAT ARE YOU DOING? YOU'VE NEVER DONE THIS BEFORE...
IT'S BE- CAUSE SHŌ IS HERE NOW.
I THINK IT'S A GOOD TIME TO DO SOMETHING NEW.

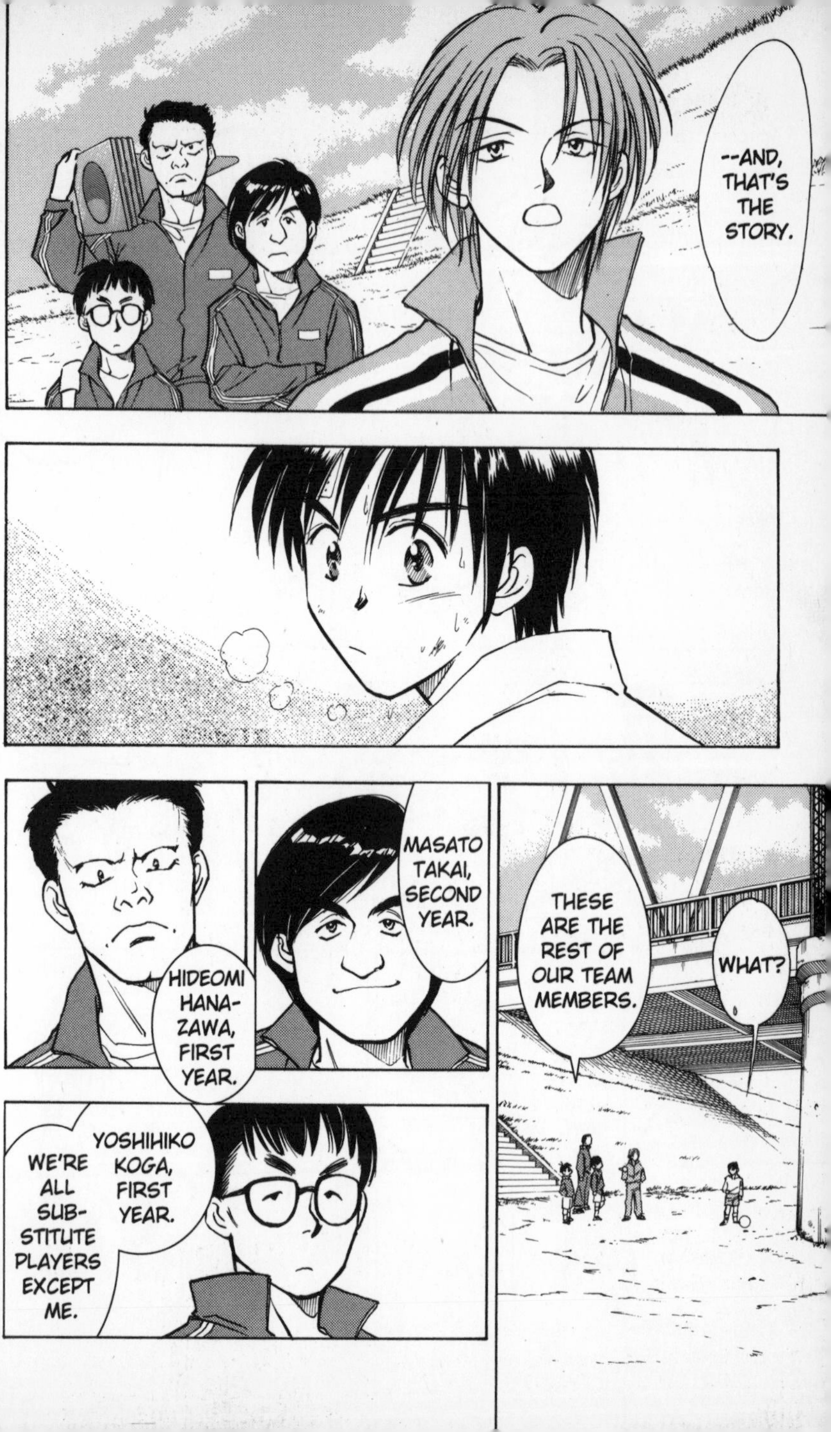
--AND, THAT'S THE STORY.
WHAT?
THESE ARE THE REST OF OUR TEAM MEMBERS.
MASATO TAKAI, SECOND YEAR.
HIDEOMI HANA-ZAWA, FIRST YEAR.
YOSHIHIKO KOGA, FIRST YEAR.
WE'RE ALL SUB-STITUTE PLAYERS EXCEPT ME.

READ THIS WAY

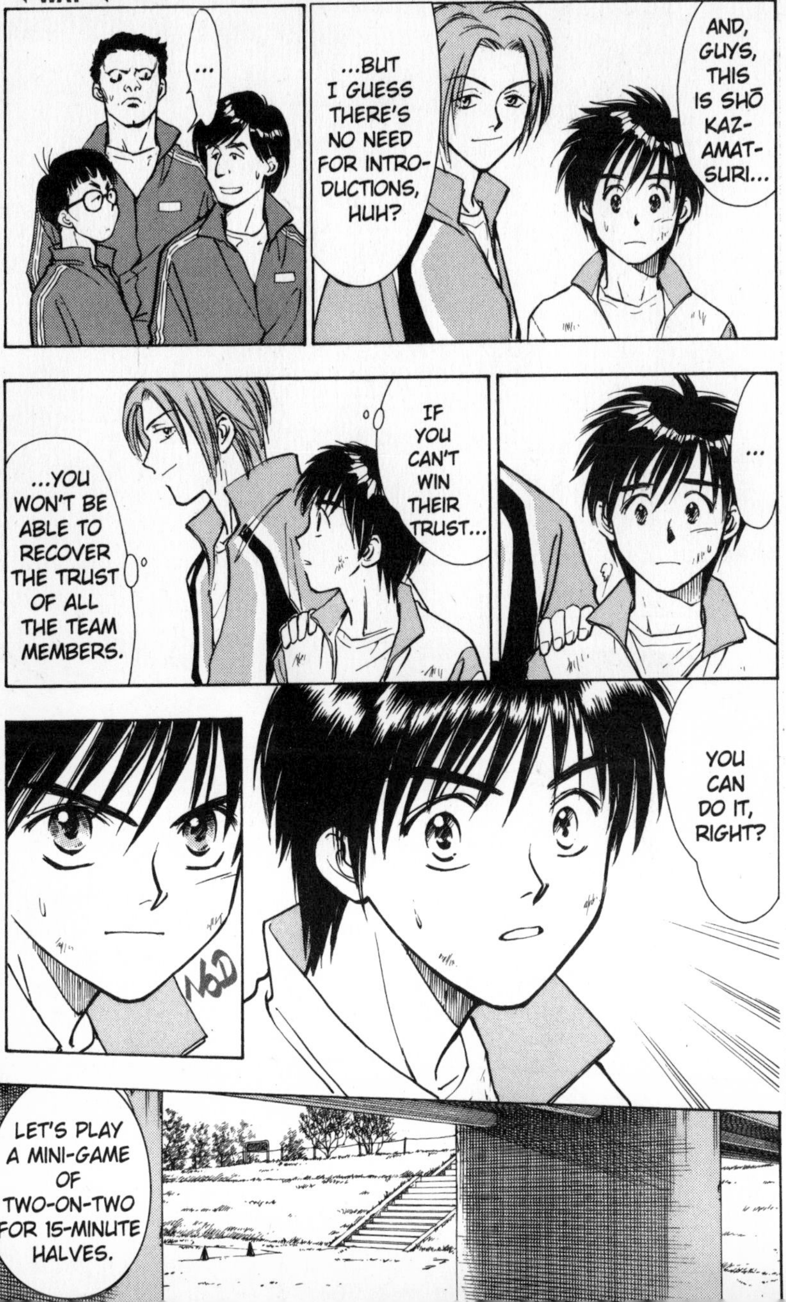
AND, GUYS, THIS IS SHŌ KAZAMATSURI...
...BUT I GUESS THERE'S NO NEED FOR INTRODUCTIONS, HUH?
...
...
IF YOU CAN'T WIN THEIR TRUST...
...YOU WON'T BE ABLE TO RECOVER THE TRUST OF ALL THE TEAM MEMBERS.
YOU CAN DO IT, RIGHT?
LET'S PLAY A MINI-GAME OF TWO-ON-TWO FOR 15-MINUTE HALVES.

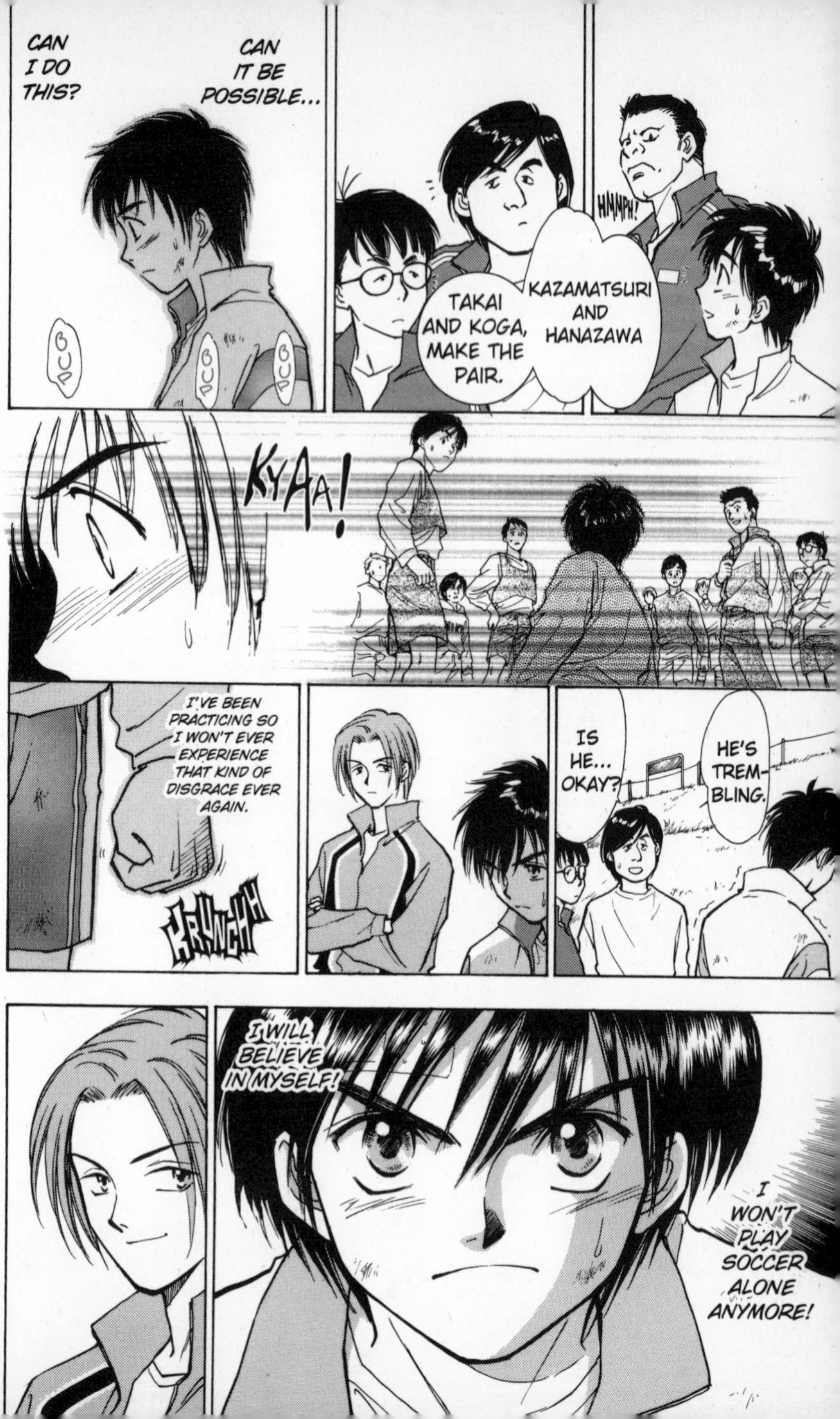

HMMPH!
KAZAMATSURI AND HANAZAWA
CAN IT BE POSSIBLE...
TAKAI AND KOGA, MAKE THE PAIR.
CAN I DO THIS?
BUP
BUP
BUP
KYAA!
HE'S TREM-BLING.
IS HE... OKAY?
I'VE BEEN PRACTICING SO I WON'T EVER EXPERIENCE THAT KIND OF DISGRACE EVER AGAIN.
KRUNCH
I WON'T PLAY SOCCER ALONE ANYMORE!
I WILL BELIEVE IN MYSELF!

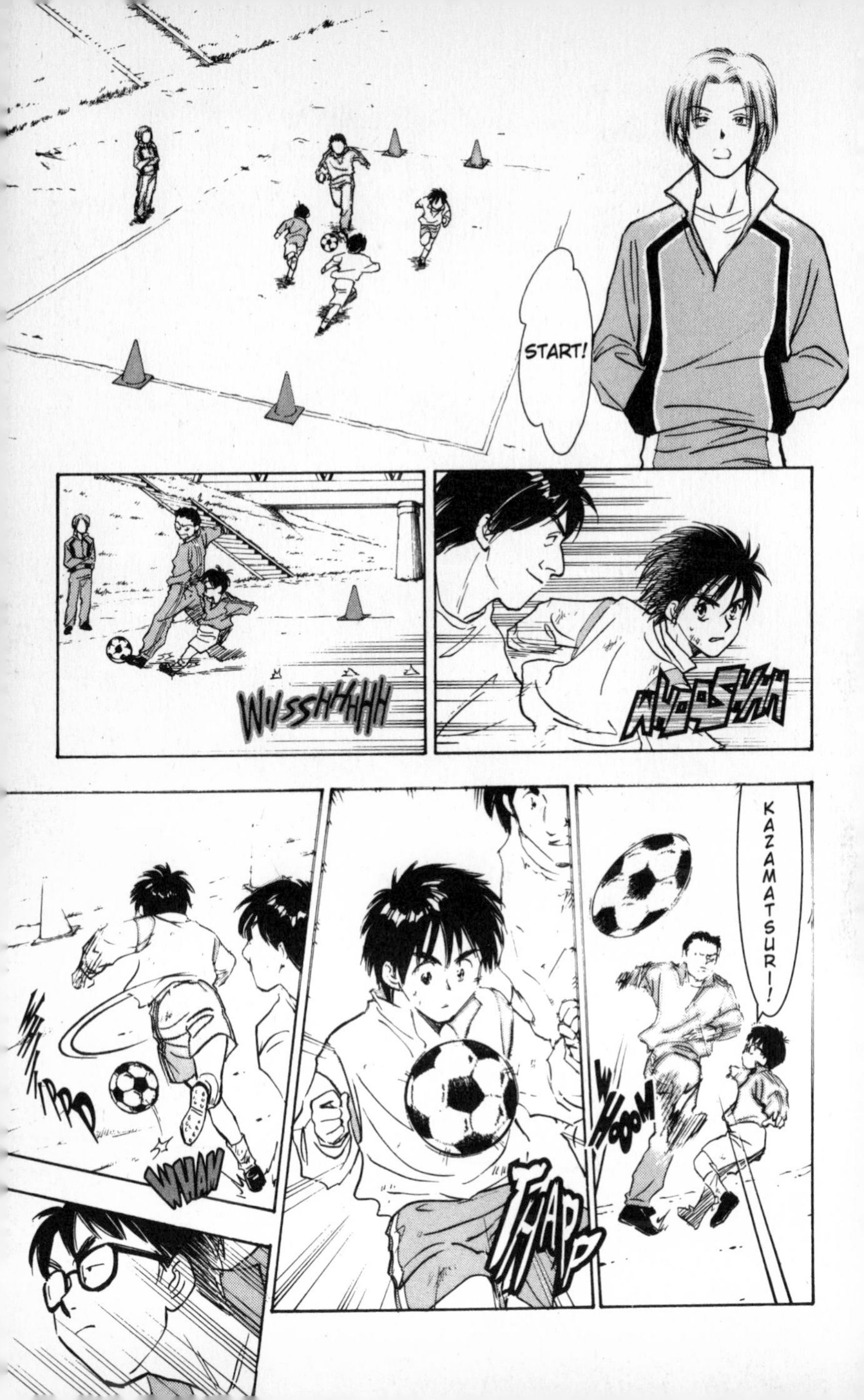
START!
WHISSHHHHH
KAZAMATSURI!
WHOOOM
THAPP
WHAM

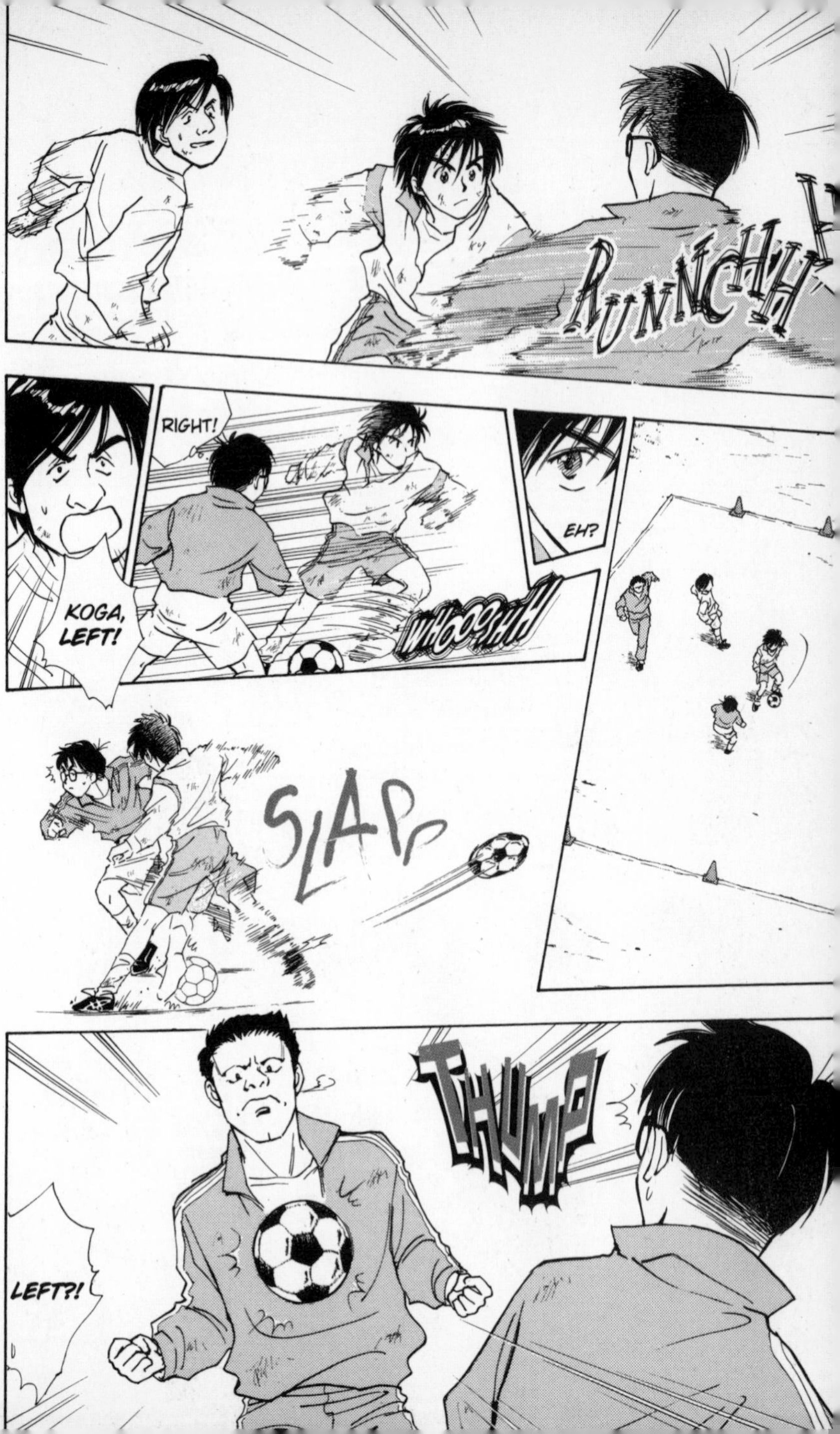
RUNNCHHH
EH?
RIGHT!
KOGA, LEFT!
SLAP
THUMP
LEFT?!

READ THIS WAY

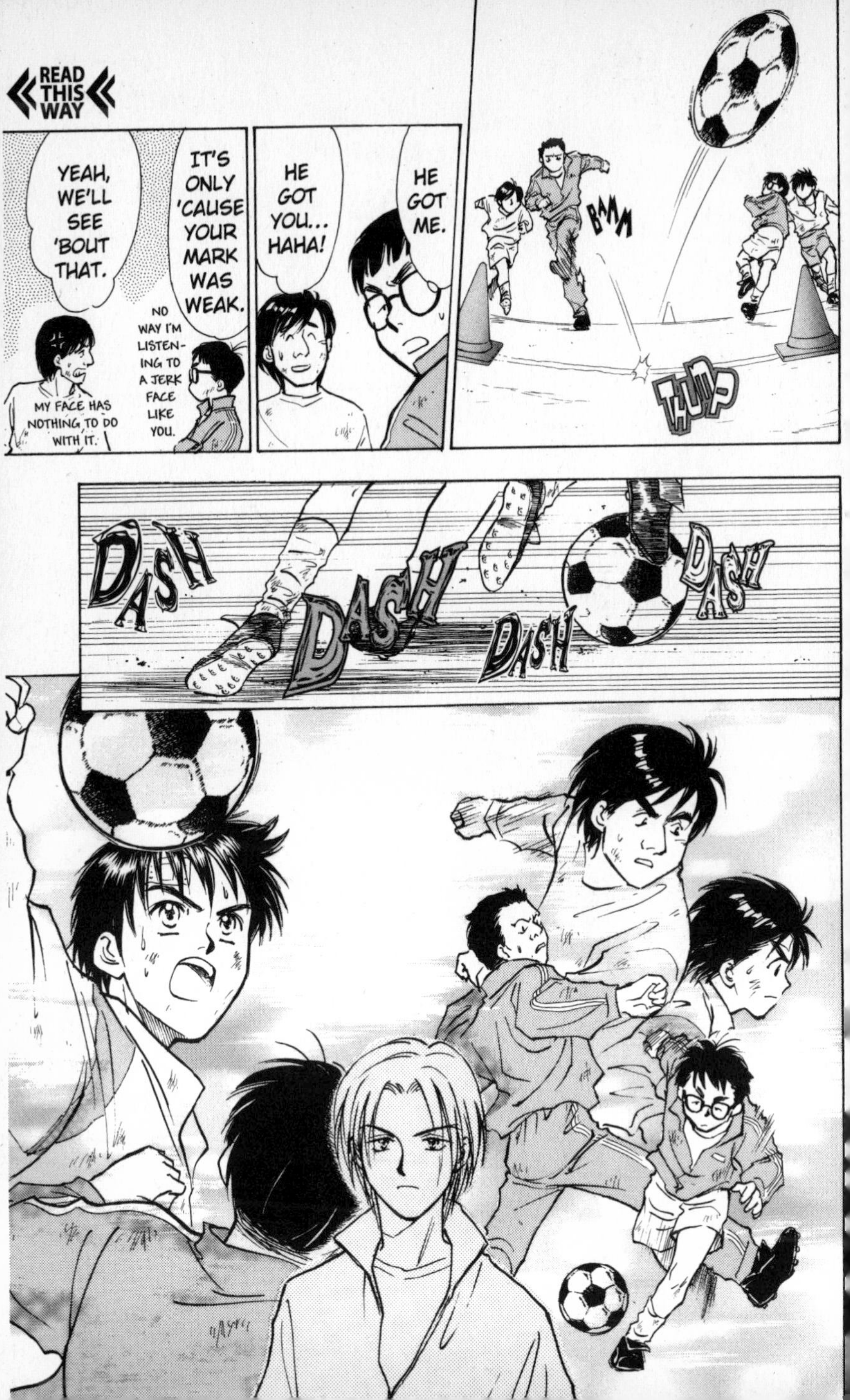
BAMM
THUMP
HE GOT ME.
HE GOT YOU... HAHA!
IT'S ONLY 'CAUSE YOUR MARK WAS WEAK.
YEAH, WE'LL SEE 'BOUT THAT.
NO WAY I'M LISTEN-ING TO A JERK FACE LIKE YOU.
MY FACE HAS NOTHING TO DO WITH IT.
DASH
DASH
DASH
DASH

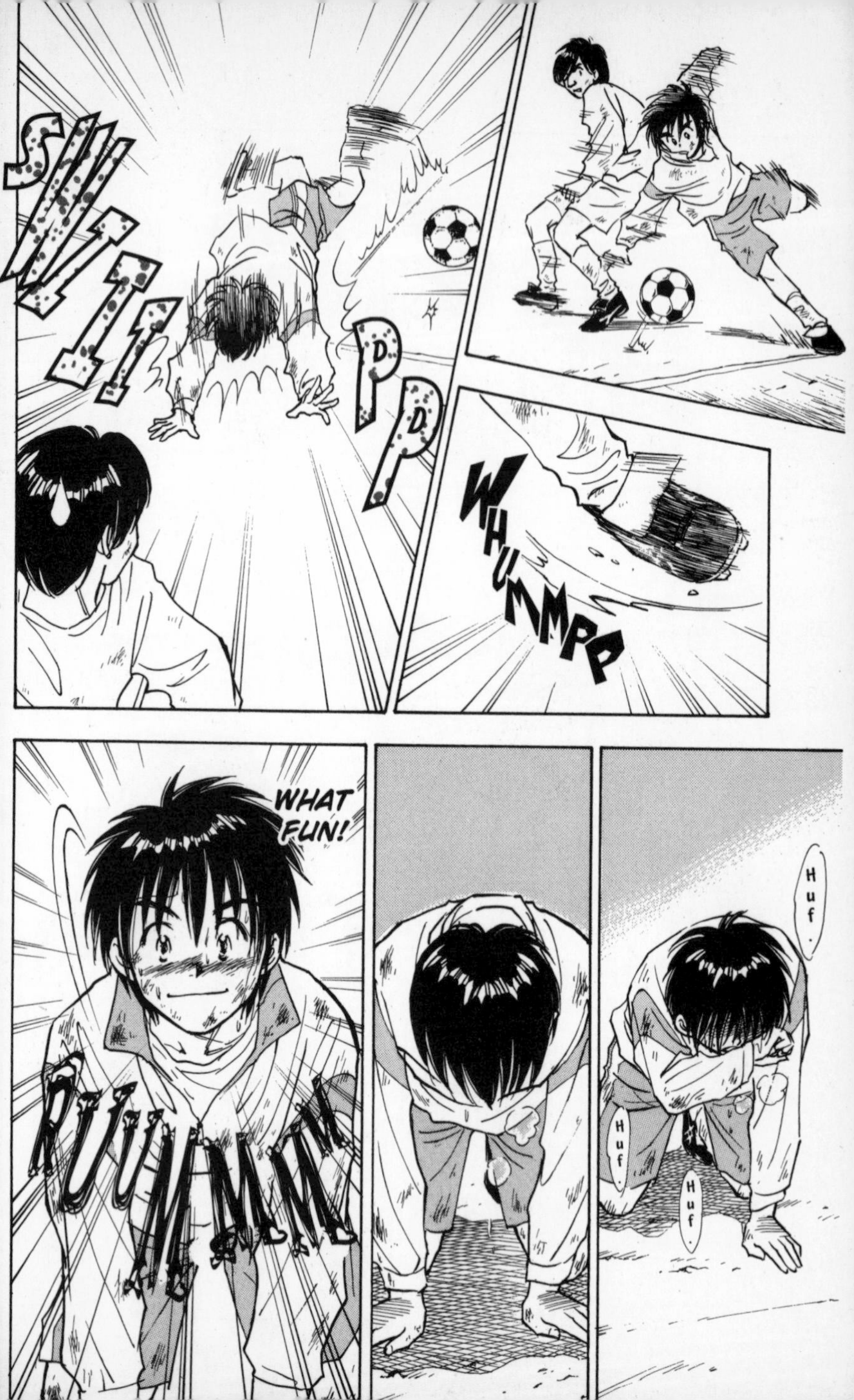

WHUMMPP
SWIIPP
Huf.
Huf.
Huf.
WHAT FUN!
RUUMMM

READ THIS WAY

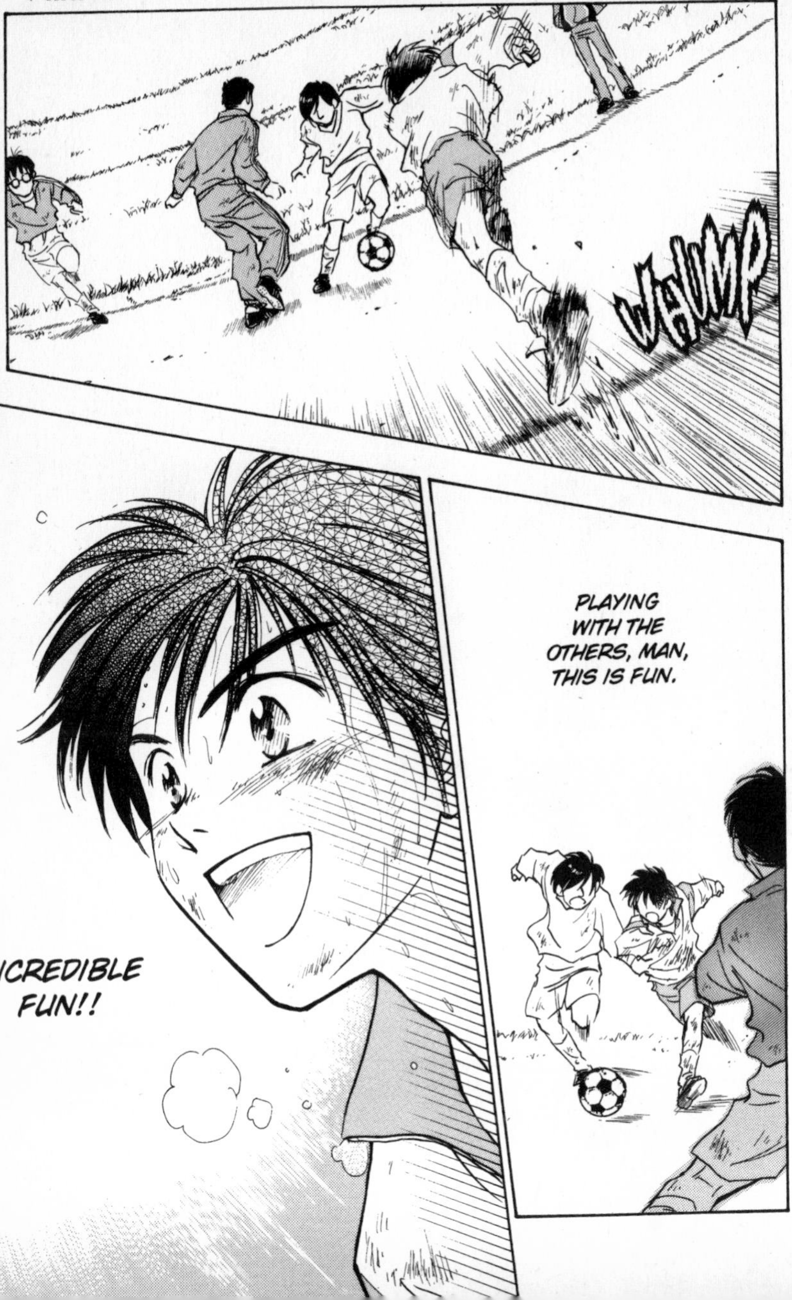
WHUMP
PLAYING WITH THE OTHERS, MAN, THIS IS FUN.
INCREDIBLE FUN!!

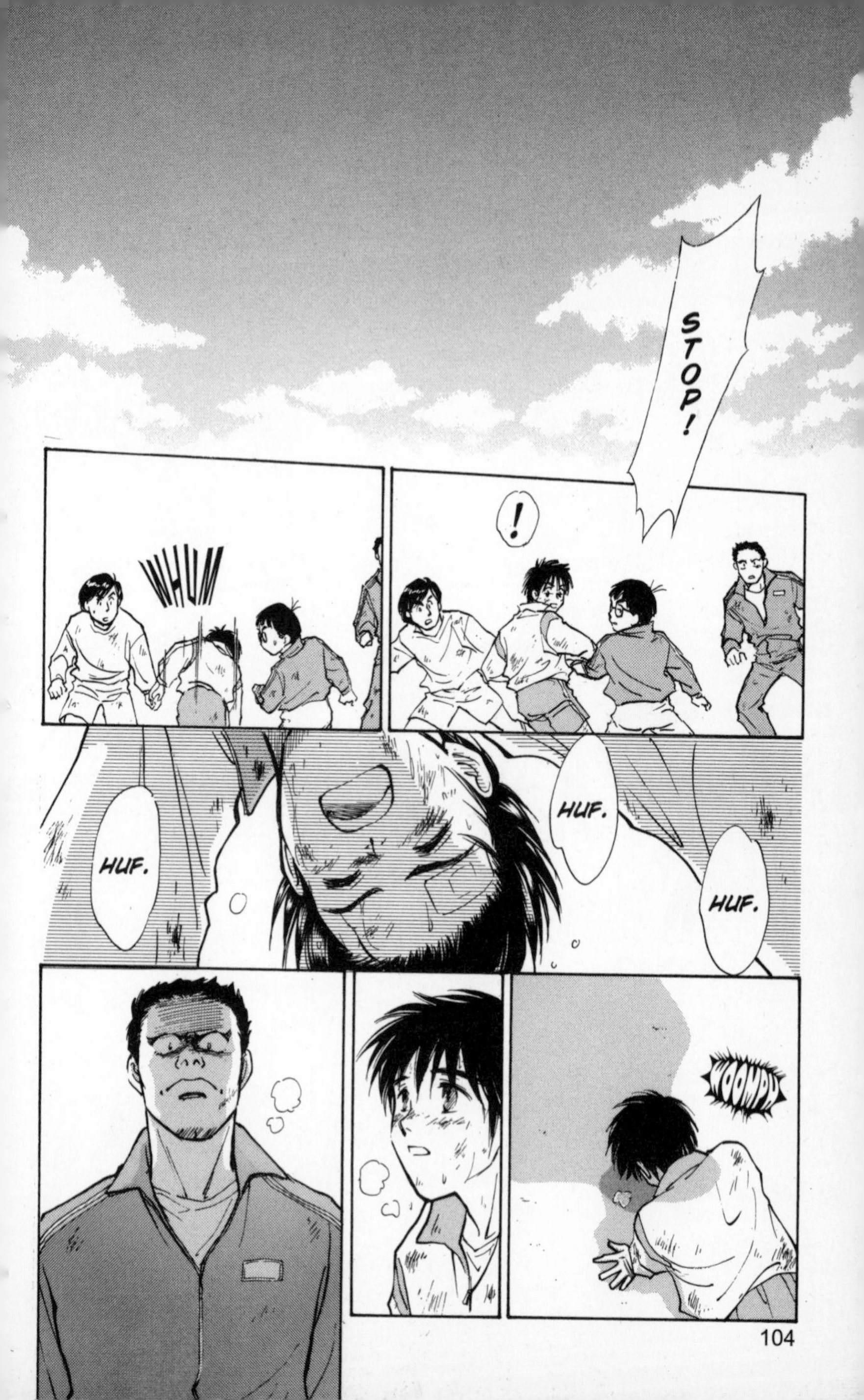
STOP!
!
WHUM
HUF.
HUF.
HUF.
WOOMPH

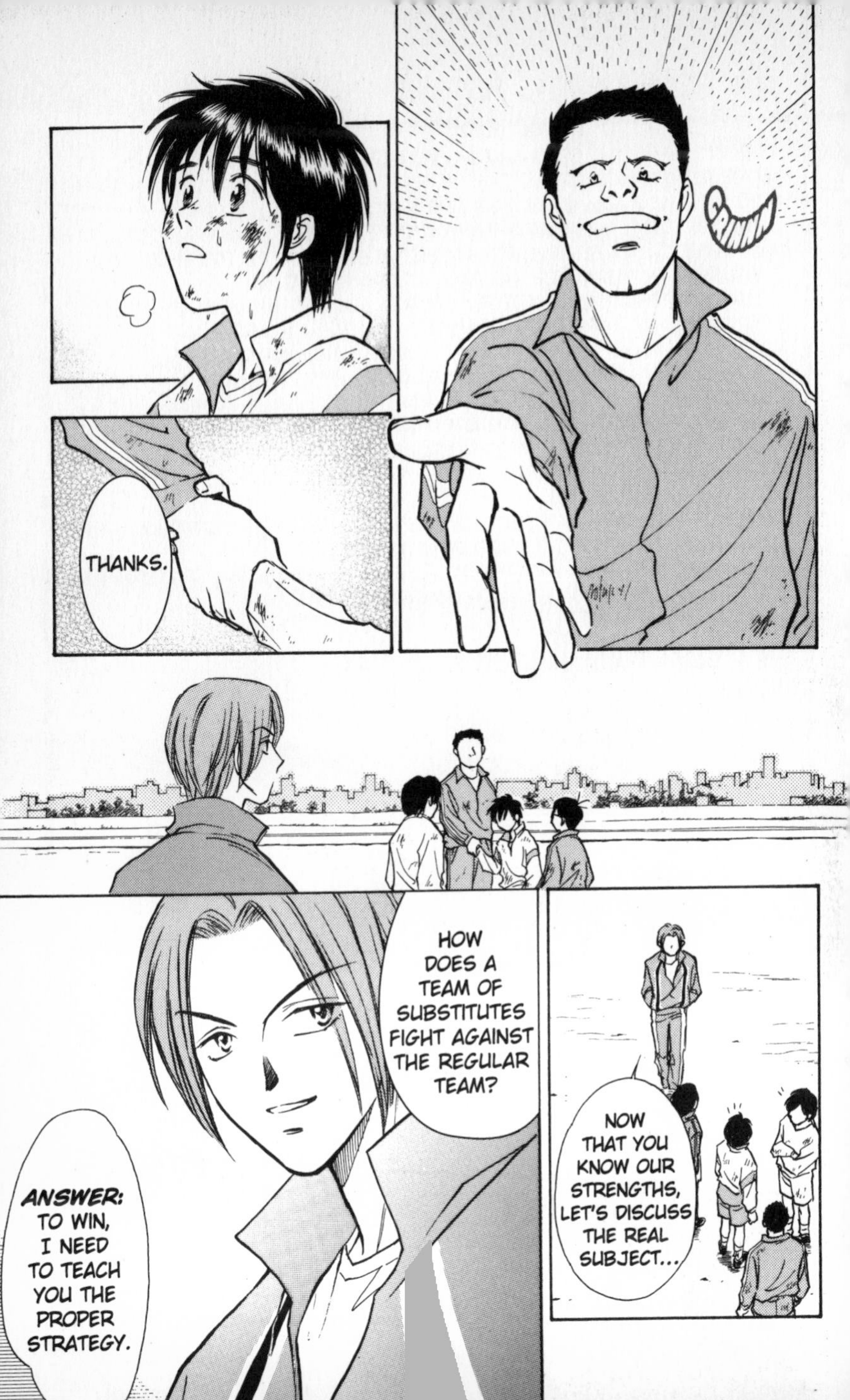
THANKS.
NOW THAT YOU KNOW OUR STRENGTHS, LET'S DISCUSS THE REAL SUBJECT...
HOW DOES A TEAM OF SUBSTITUTES FIGHT AGAINST THE REGULAR TEAM?
ANSWER: TO WIN, I NEED TO TEACH YOU THE PROPER STRATEGY.

ROLE OF THE FORWARDS

IN THE PAST, THE FORWARD'S (FW) BIGGEST RESPONSIBILITY WAS TO SCORE POINTS. NOWADAYS, THE FW MUST NOT ONLY SCORE POINTS BUT ALSO BECOME A CHANCE MAKER FOR A PASS.

THE FW MUST, MOST IMPORTANTLY, DEFEND WELL. THE FW MUST NOT ONLY HAVE THE OFFENSIVE POWER BUT ALSO NEEDS TO PRESSURE THE OPPONENTS BY PURSUING THE BALL AT THE FRONTLINE.

IN THE PRESENT TIME, THE FW CANNOT SUCCEED UNLESS HE/SHE HAS EVERY SKILL REQUIRED FOR PLAYING SOCCER, SUCH AS MAKING GOALS, DOING POST-PLAY, PERFORMING A CHANCE-MAKE, AND DEFENDING.

IN THE PAST, THE BEST SOCCER PLAYERS WERE POSITIONED AS MIDDLE FIELDERS (MF) AND THEY TOOK THE ROLE OF THE GAME-MAKER. RECENTLY, THE GOOD PLAYERS ARE PLACED AS FWS AROUND THE WORLD. DESPITE THIS, JAPANESE SOCCER TEAMS STILL TEND TO PLACE THEIR BEST PLAYERS AS MFS, AND THAT MIGHT BE THE REASON WHY WE LACK STRIKERS IN OUR TEAMS.

PEOPLE WHO HAD WATCHED THE FRENCH WORLD CUP PROBABLY KNOW HOW GREAT A PLAYER THE WORLD'S FWS ARE.

ANYHOW, WHEN YOU WATCH SOCCER GAMES, PLEASE PAY ATTENTION TO OTHER PLAYS BESIDES THE SCORING DONE BY FWS.

--TATSUYA WATANABE *(WINNING RUN)*

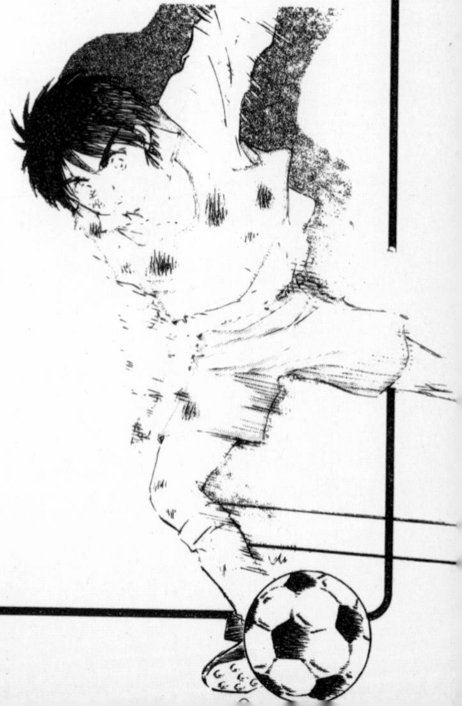

STAGE.4 FOR TOMORROW

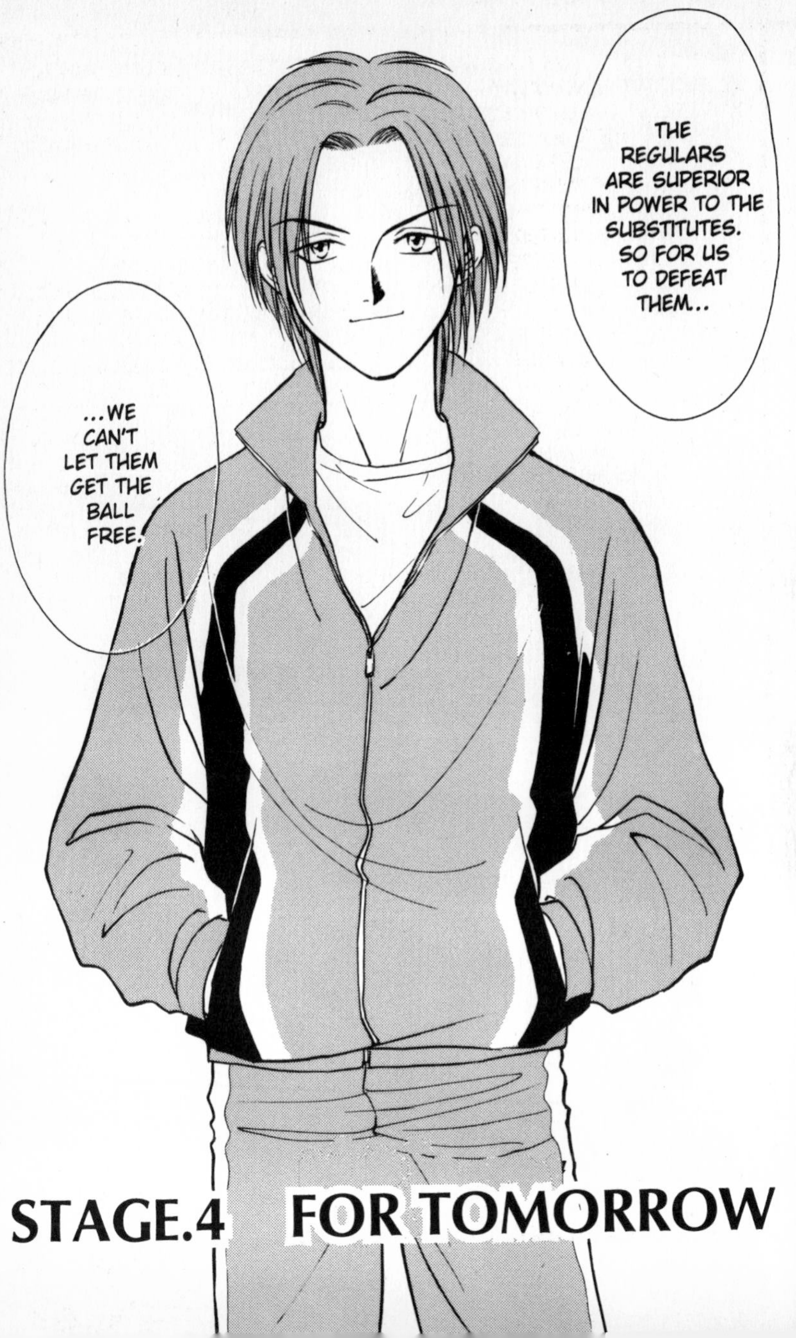
THE REGULARS ARE SUPERIOR IN POWER TO THE SUBSTITUTES. SO FOR US TO DEFEAT THEM...
...WE CAN'T LET THEM GET THE BALL FREE.

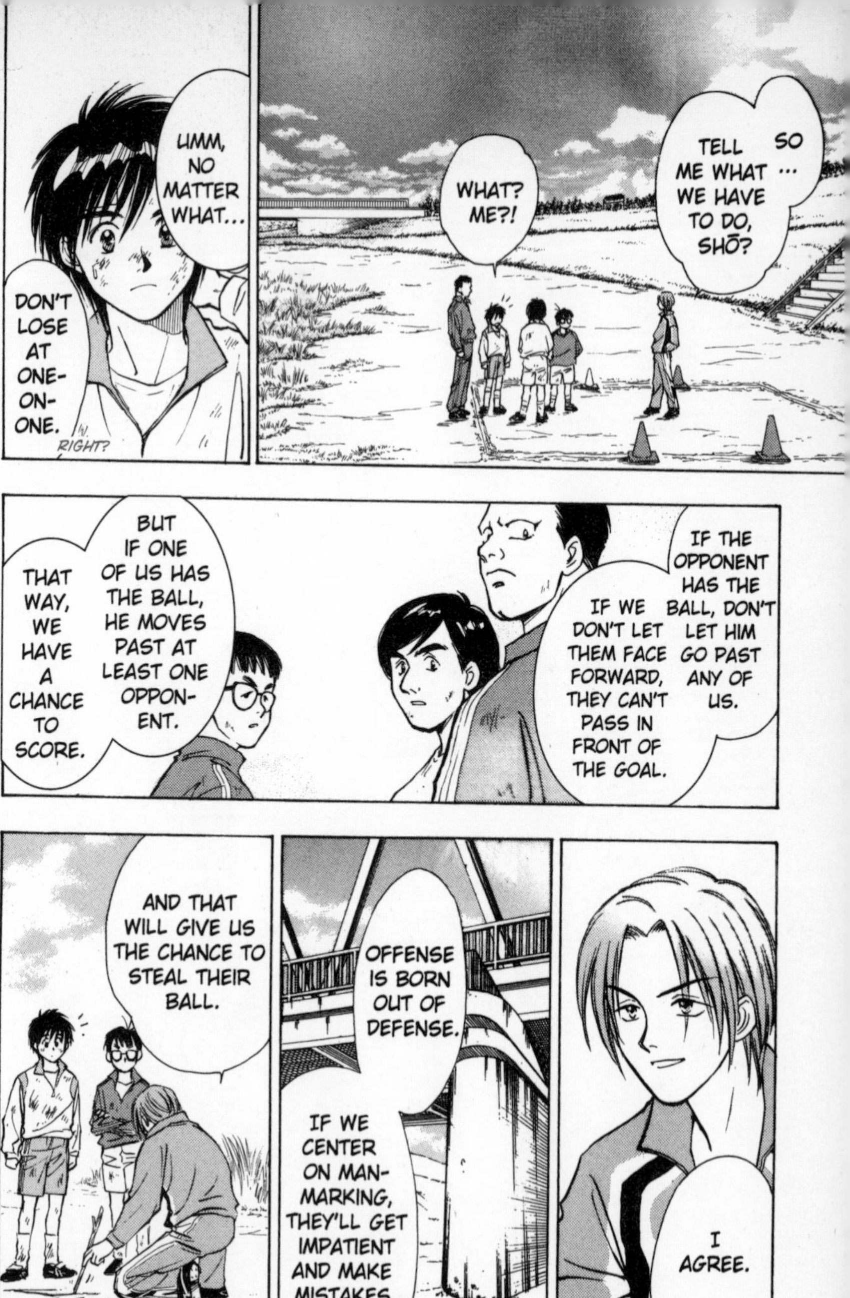
SO... TELL ME WHAT WE HAVE TO DO, SHŌ?
WHAT? ME?!
UMM, NO MATTER WHAT...
DON'T LOSE AT ONE-ON-ONE.
RIGHT?
IF THE OPPONENT HAS THE BALL, DON'T LET HIM GO PAST ANY OF US.
IF WE DON'T LET THEM FACE FORWARD, THEY CAN'T PASS IN FRONT OF THE GOAL.
BUT IF ONE OF US HAS THE BALL, HE MOVES PAST AT LEAST ONE OPPONENT.
THAT WAY, WE HAVE A CHANCE TO SCORE.
I AGREE.
OFFENSE IS BORN OUT OF DEFENSE.
IF WE CENTER ON MAN-MARKING, THEY'LL GET IMPATIENT AND MAKE MISTAKES.
AND THAT WILL GIVE US THE CHANCE TO STEAL THEIR BALL.
SKRITCHHH

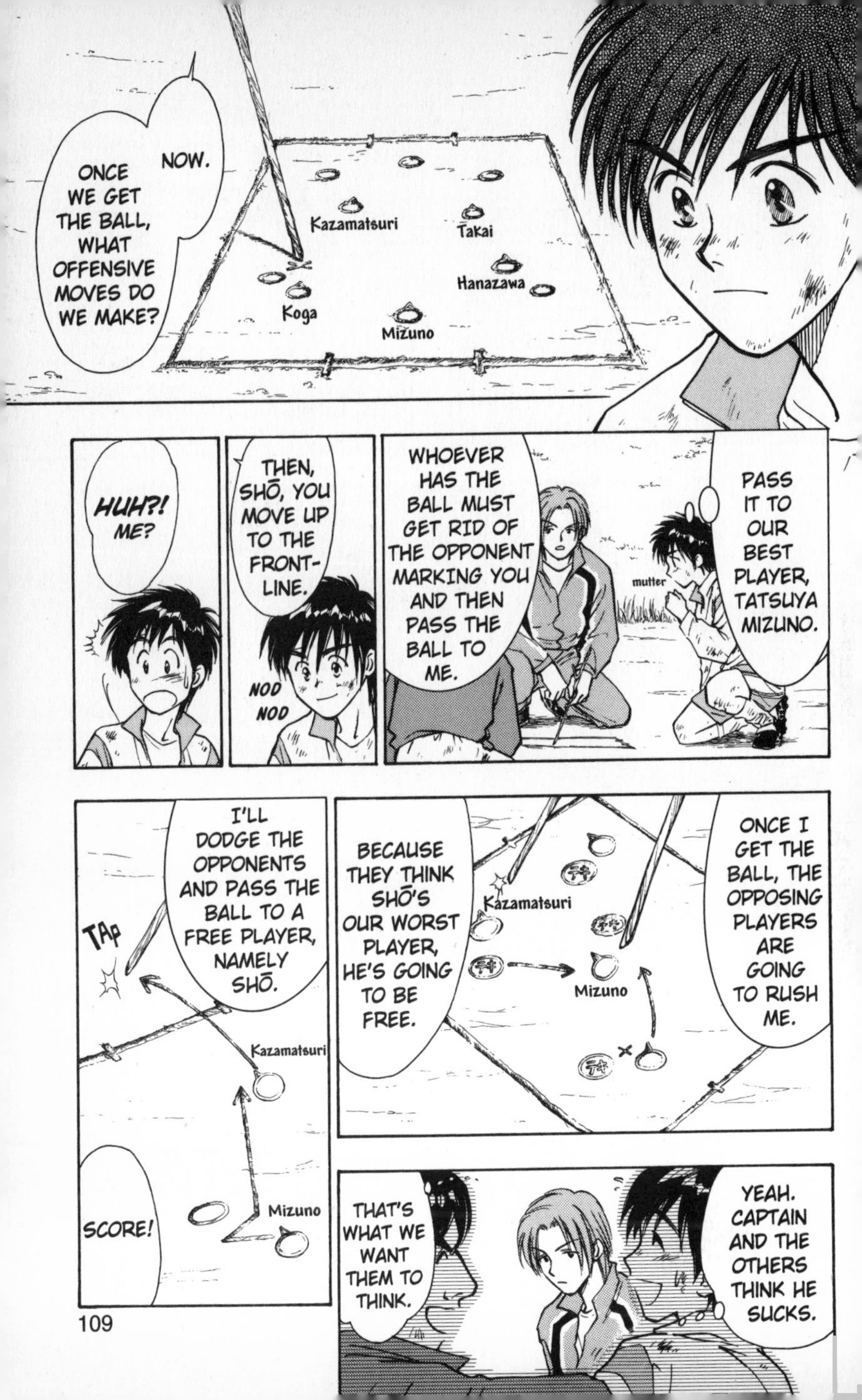
NOW.
ONCE WE GET THE BALL, WHAT OFFENSIVE MOVES DO WE MAKE?
Kazamatsuri
Takai
Hanazawa
Koga
Mizuno
PASS IT TO OUR BEST PLAYER, TATSUYA MIZUNO.
mutter
WHOEVER HAS THE BALL MUST GET RID OF THE OPPONENT MARKING YOU AND THEN PASS THE BALL TO ME.
THEN, SHŌ, YOU MOVE UP TO THE FRONT-LINE.
NOD NOD
HUH?! ME?
ONCE I GET THE BALL, THE OPPOSING PLAYERS ARE GOING TO RUSH ME.
BECAUSE THEY THINK SHŌ'S OUR WORST PLAYER, HE'S GOING TO BE FREE.
Kazamatsuri
Mizuno
YEAH. CAPTAIN AND THE OTHERS THINK HE SUCKS.
THAT'S WHAT WE WANT THEM TO THINK.
I'LL DODGE THE OPPONENTS AND PASS THE BALL TO A FREE PLAYER, NAMELY SHŌ.
TAP
Kazamatsuri
Mizuno
SCORE!

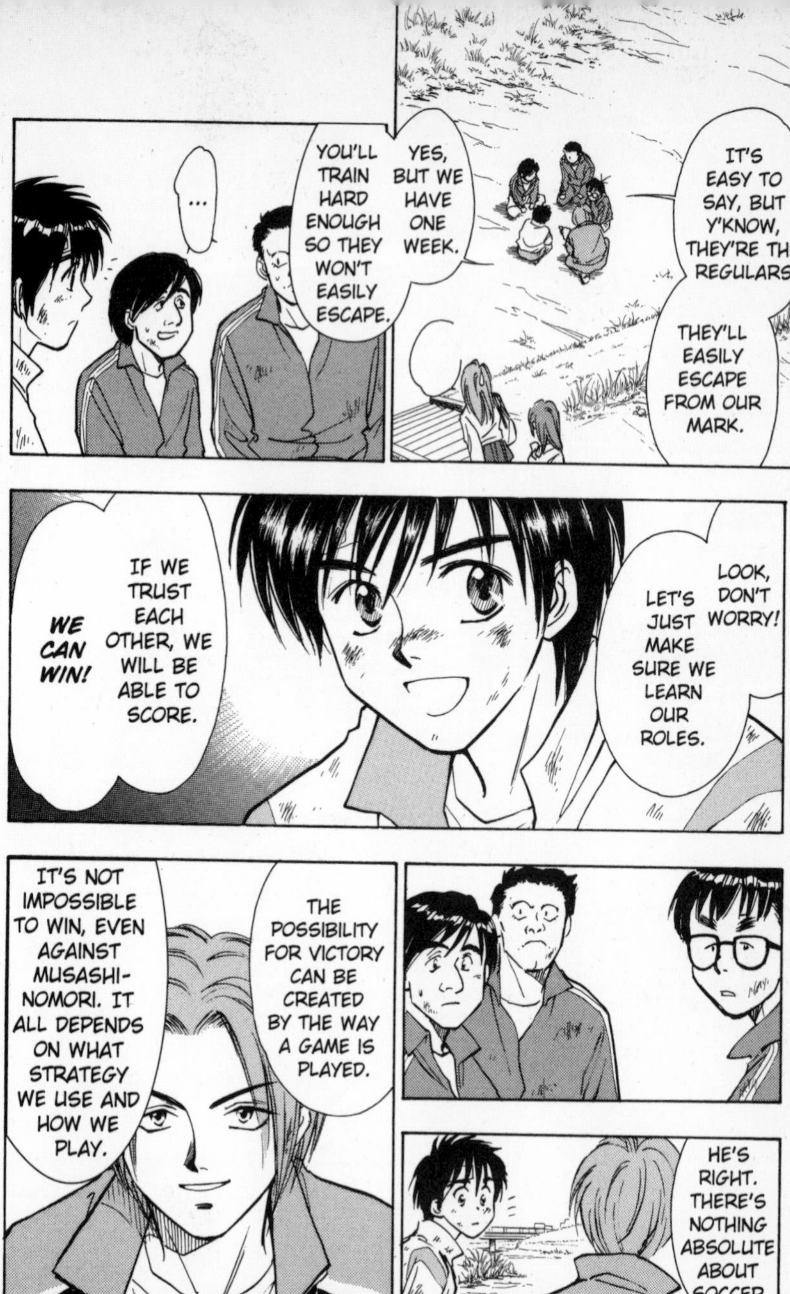
IT'S EASY TO SAY, BUT Y'KNOW, THEY'RE THE REGULARS.
THEY'LL EASILY ESCAPE FROM OUR MARK.
YES, BUT WE HAVE ONE WEEK.
YOU'LL TRAIN HARD ENOUGH SO THEY WON'T EASILY ESCAPE.
...
LOOK, DON'T WORRY!
LET'S JUST MAKE SURE WE LEARN OUR ROLES.
IF WE TRUST EACH OTHER, WE WILL BE ABLE TO SCORE.
WE CAN WIN!
HE'S RIGHT. THERE'S NOTHING ABSOLUTE ABOUT SOCCER.
THE POSSIBILITY FOR VICTORY CAN BE CREATED BY THE WAY A GAME IS PLAYED.
IT'S NOT IMPOSSIBLE TO WIN, EVEN AGAINST MUSASHI-NOMORI. IT ALL DEPENDS ON WHAT STRATEGY WE USE AND HOW WE PLAY.

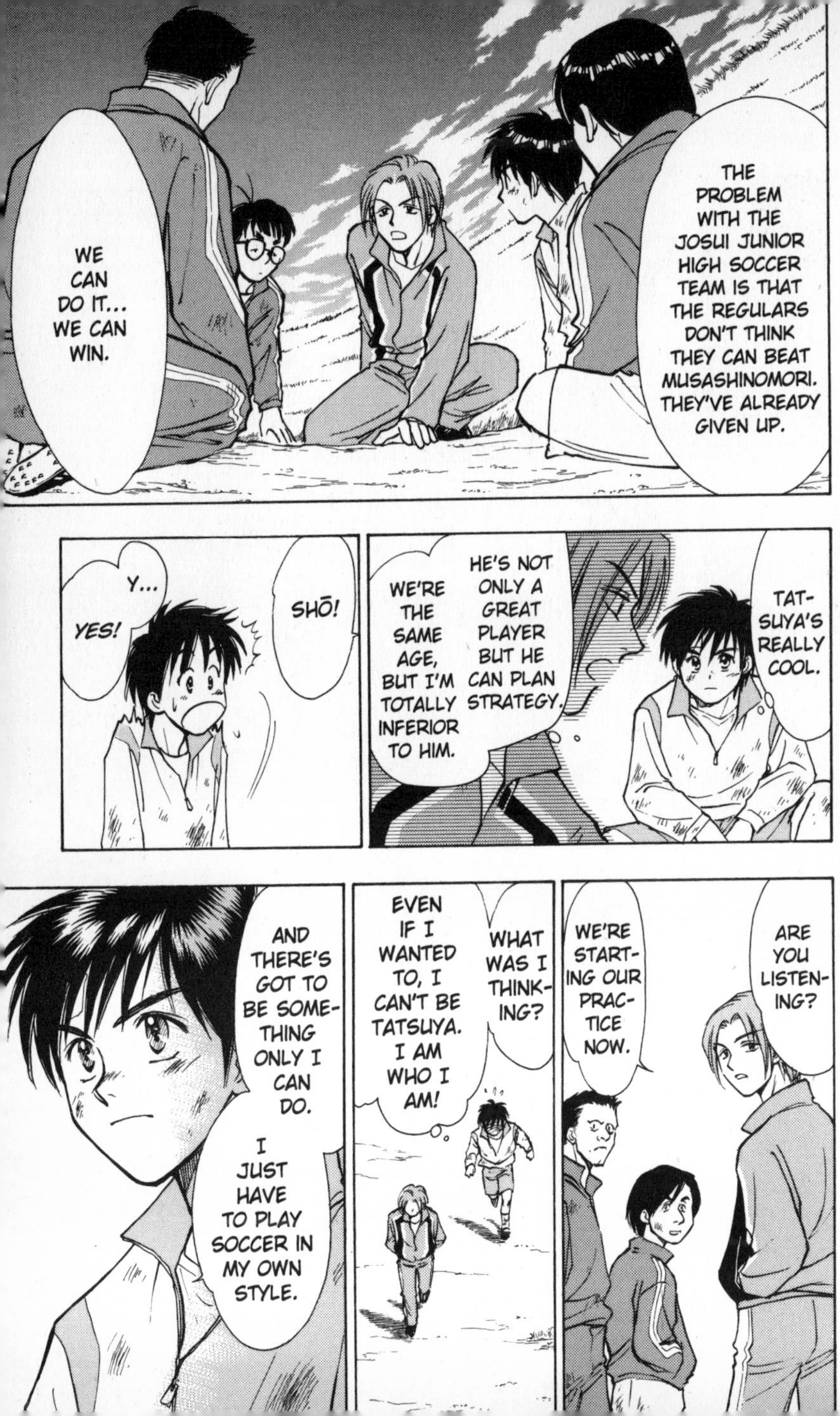
THE PROBLEM WITH THE JOSUI JUNIOR HIGH SOCCER TEAM IS THAT THE REGULARS DON'T THINK THEY CAN BEAT MUSASHINOMORI. THEY'VE ALREADY GIVEN UP.
WE CAN DO IT... WE CAN WIN.
TAT-SUYA'S REALLY COOL.
HE'S NOT ONLY A GREAT PLAYER BUT HE CAN PLAN STRATEGY.
WE'RE THE SAME AGE, BUT I'M TOTALLY INFERIOR TO HIM.
SHŌ!
Y... YES!
ARE YOU LISTEN-ING?
WE'RE START-ING OUR PRAC-TICE NOW.
WHAT WAS I THINK-ING?
EVEN IF I WANTED TO, I CAN'T BE TATSUYA. I AM WHO I AM!
AND THERE'S GOT TO BE SOME-THING ONLY I CAN DO.
I JUST HAVE TO PLAY SOCCER IN MY OWN STYLE.

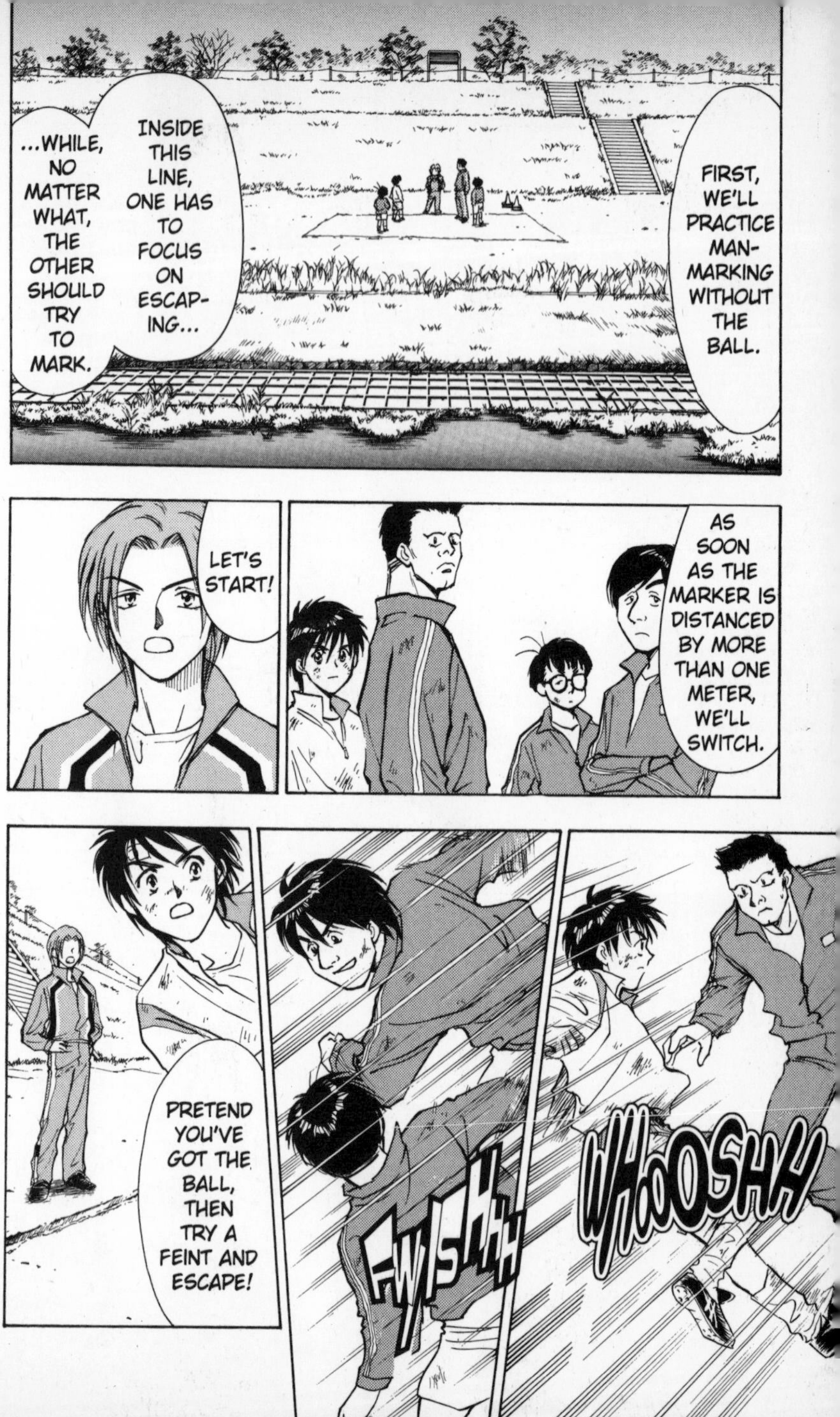
FIRST, WE'LL PRACTICE MAN-MARKING WITHOUT THE BALL.
INSIDE THIS LINE, ONE HAS TO FOCUS ON ESCAPING...
...WHILE, NO MATTER WHAT, THE OTHER SHOULD TRY TO MARK.
AS SOON AS THE MARKER IS DISTANCED BY MORE THAN ONE METER, WE'LL SWITCH.
LET'S START!
WHOOSHH
FWISHHH
PRETEND YOU'VE GOT THE BALL, THEN TRY A FEINT AND ESCAPE!

READ THIS WAY

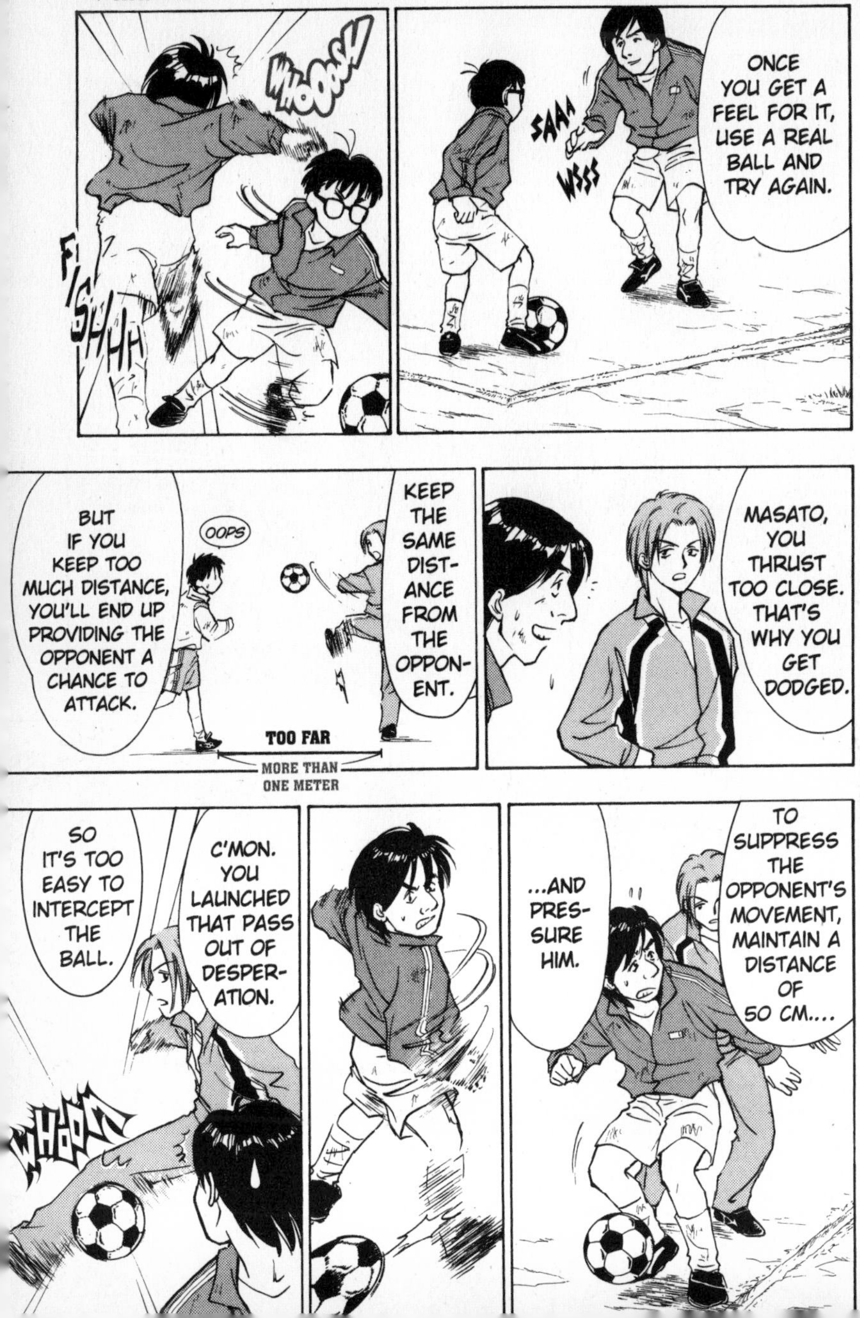
ONCE YOU GET A FEEL FOR IT, USE A REAL BALL AND TRY AGAIN.
SAAA
WSSS
WHOOOSH
FISHHH
MASATO, YOU THRUST TOO CLOSE. THAT'S WHY YOU GET DODGED.
KEEP THE SAME DIST-ANCE FROM THE OPPON-ENT.
OOPS
BUT IF YOU KEEP TOO MUCH DISTANCE, YOU'LL END UP PROVIDING THE OPPONENT A CHANCE TO ATTACK.
TOO FAR
MORE THAN ONE METER
TO SUPPRESS THE OPPONENT'S MOVEMENT, MAINTAIN A DISTANCE OF 50 CM....
...AND PRES-SURE HIM.
C'MON. YOU LAUNCHED THAT PASS OUT OF DESPER-ATION.
SO IT'S TOO EASY TO INTERCEPT THE BALL.
WHOOS

READ THIS WAY

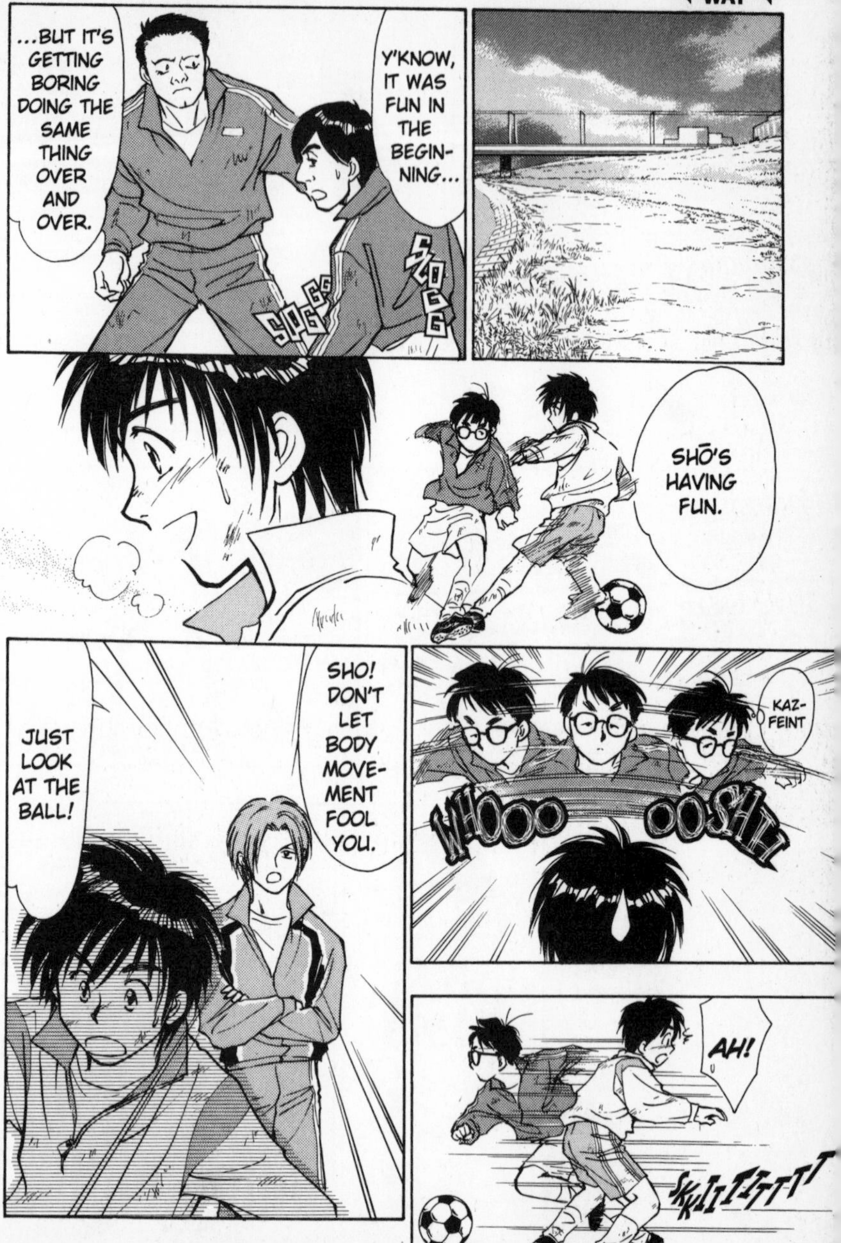
Y'KNOW, IT WAS FUN IN THE BEGIN-NING...
...BUT IT'S GETTING BORING DOING THE SAME THING OVER AND OVER.
SHŌ'S HAVING FUN.
KAZ-FEINT
AH!
SHO! DON'T LET BODY MOVE-MENT FOOL YOU.
JUST LOOK AT THE BALL!

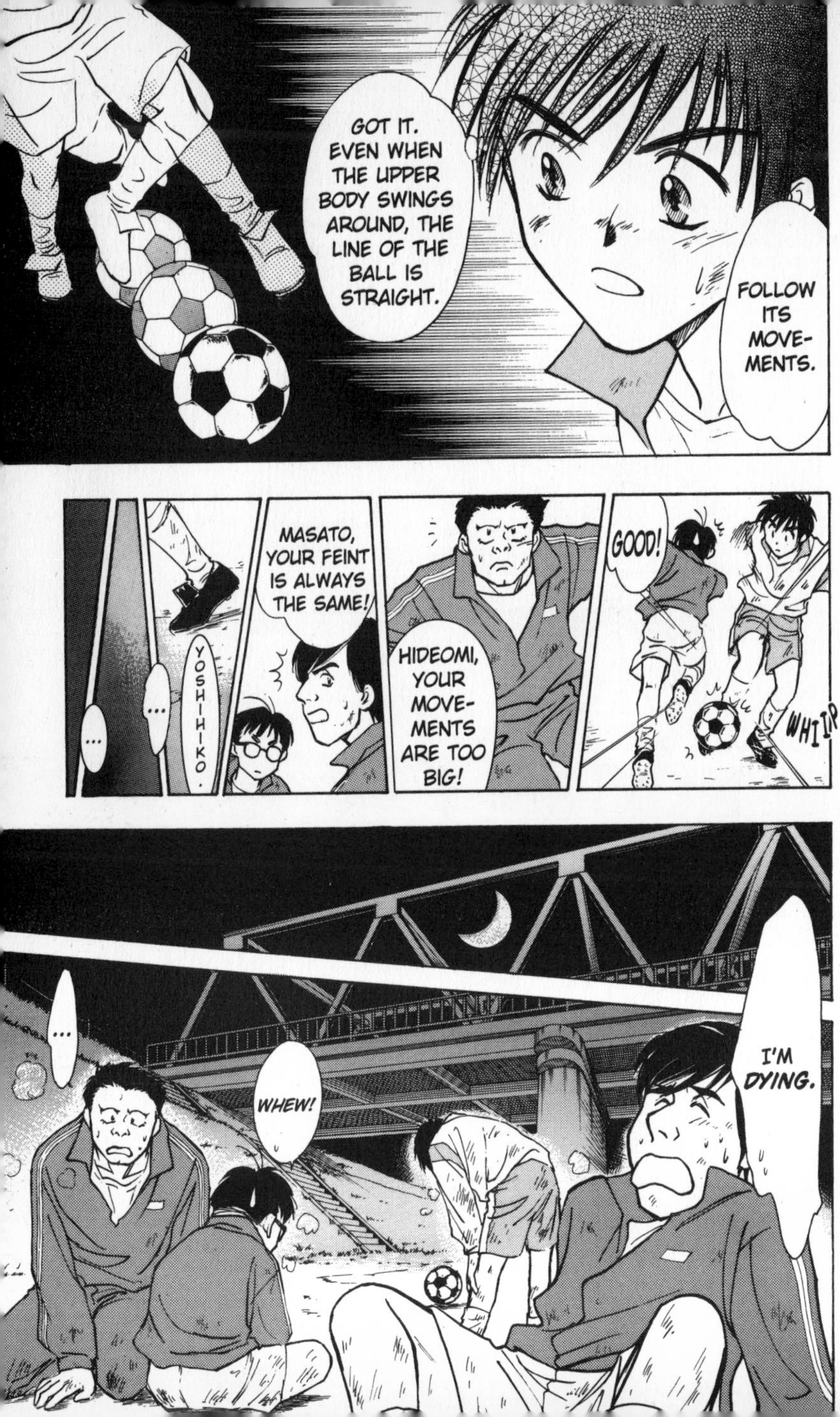
FOLLOW ITS MOVE-MENTS.
GOT IT. EVEN WHEN THE UPPER BODY SWINGS AROUND, THE LINE OF THE BALL IS STRAIGHT.
GOOD!
WHIIIP
HIDEOMI, YOUR MOVE-MENTS ARE TOO BIG!
MASATO, YOUR FEINT IS ALWAYS THE SAME!
YOSHIHIKO.
...
...
I'M DYING.
WHEW!
...

READ THIS WAY

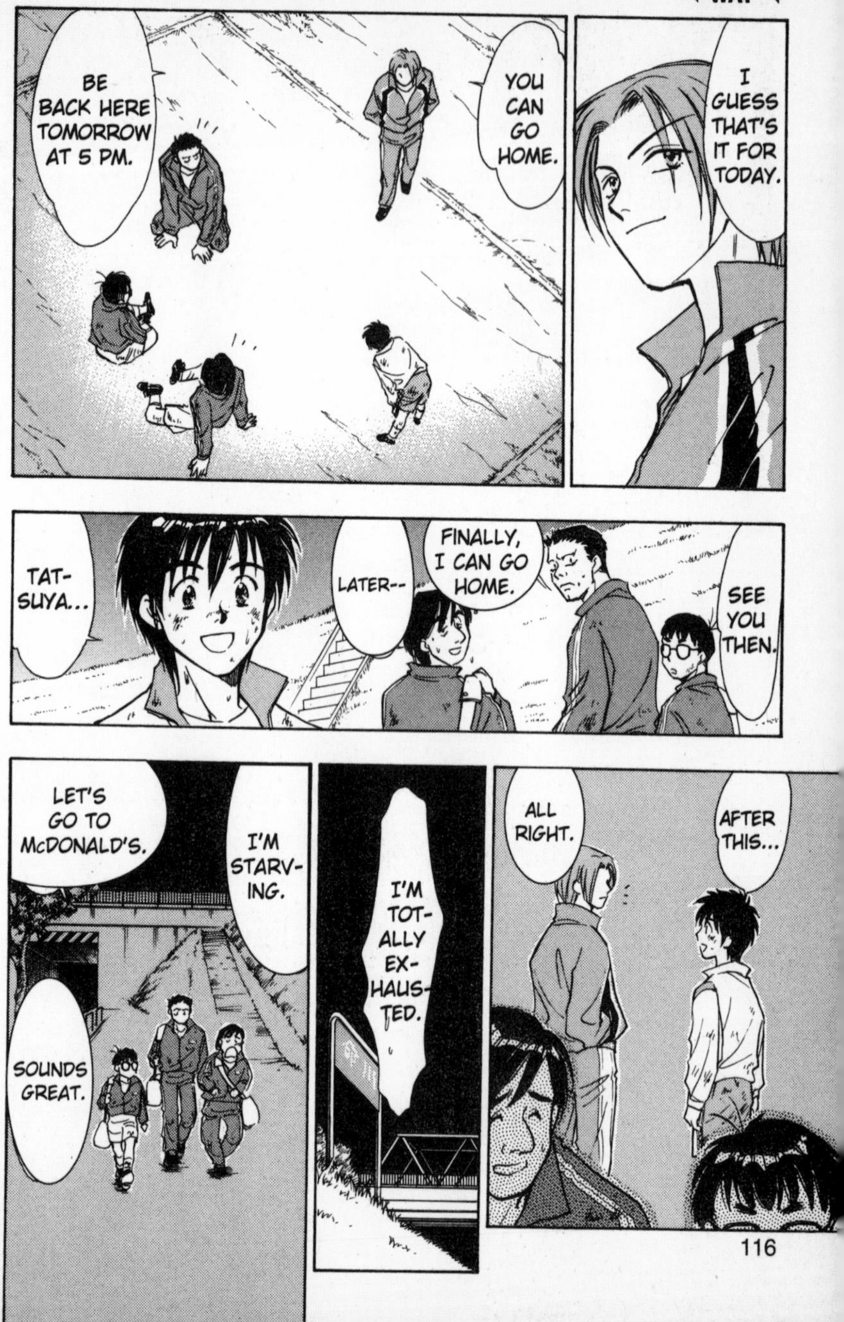
I GUESS THAT'S IT FOR TODAY.
YOU CAN GO HOME.
BE BACK HERE TOMORROW AT 5 PM.
SEE YOU THEN.
FINALLY, I CAN GO HOME.
LATER--
TAT-SUYA...
AFTER THIS...
ALL RIGHT.
I'M TOT-ALLY EX-HAUS-TED.
I'M STARV-ING.
LET'S GO TO McDONALD'S.
SOUNDS GREAT.

READ THIS WAY

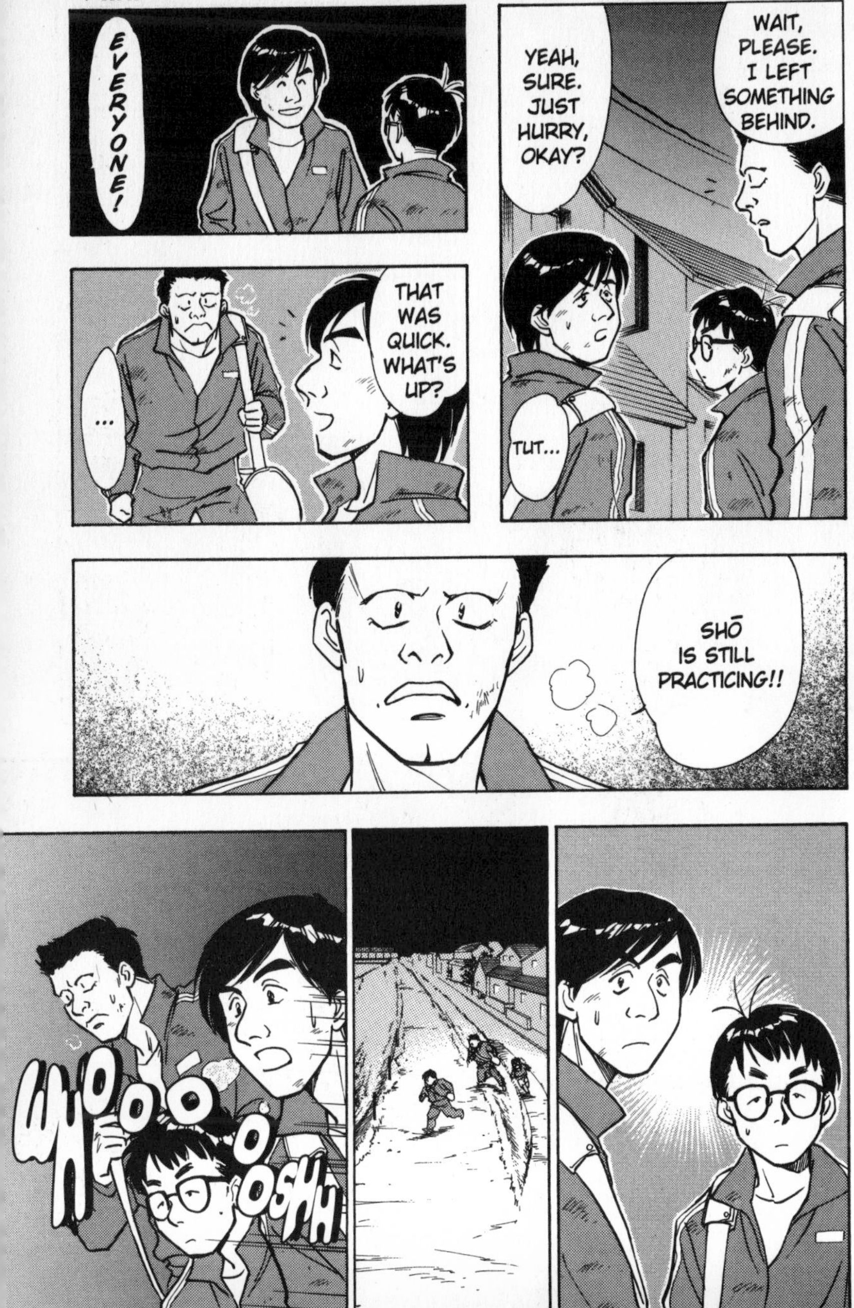
WAIT, PLEASE. I LEFT SOMETHING BEHIND.
YEAH, SURE. JUST HURRY, OKAY?
TUT...
EVERYONE!
THAT WAS QUICK. WHAT'S UP?
...
SHŌ IS STILL PRACTICING!!
WHOOOOOSHH

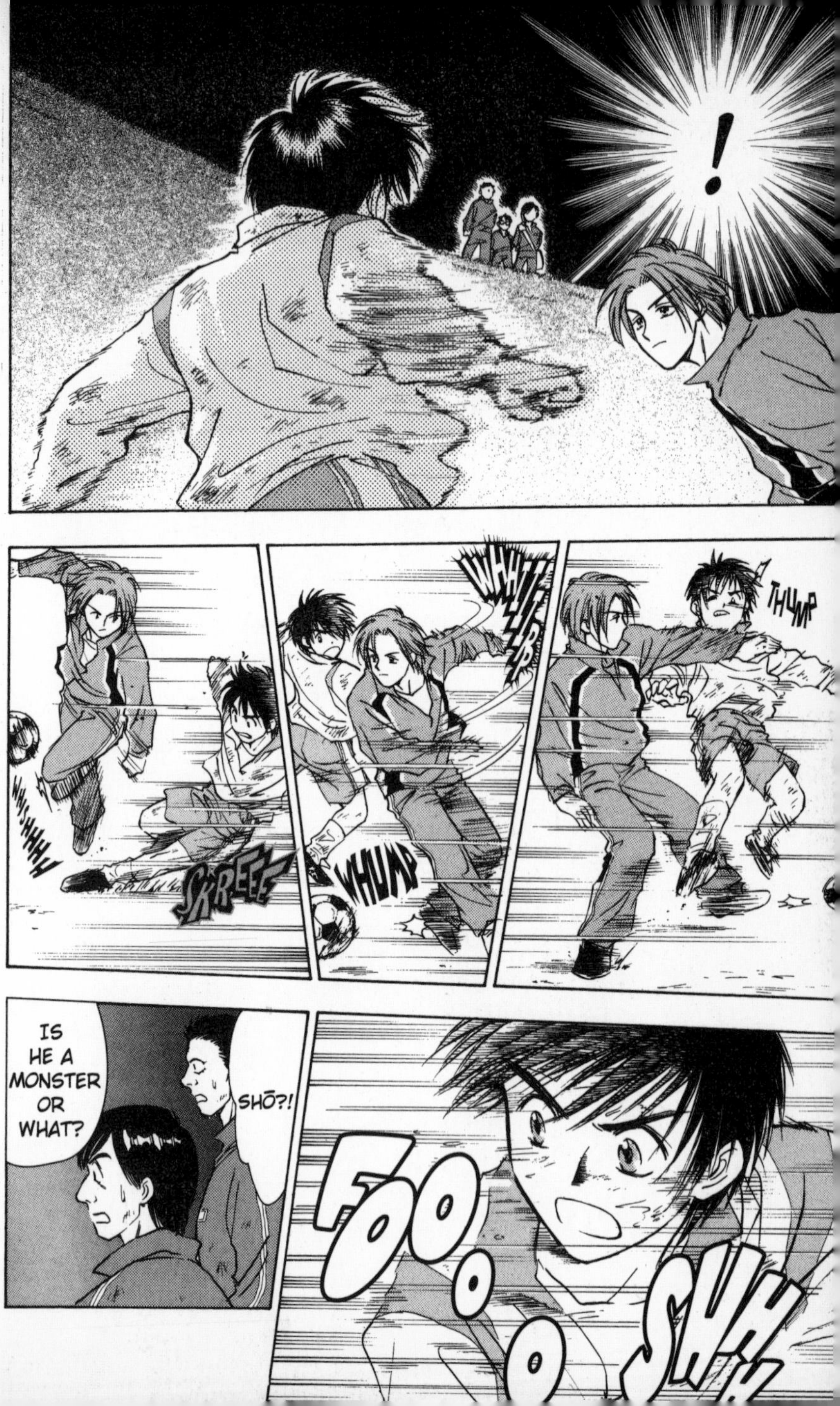
!
THUMP
WHUMP
SKREEE
WHISHHH
FOOOOO
SHH
SHŌ?!
IS HE A MONSTER OR WHAT?

READ THIS WAY

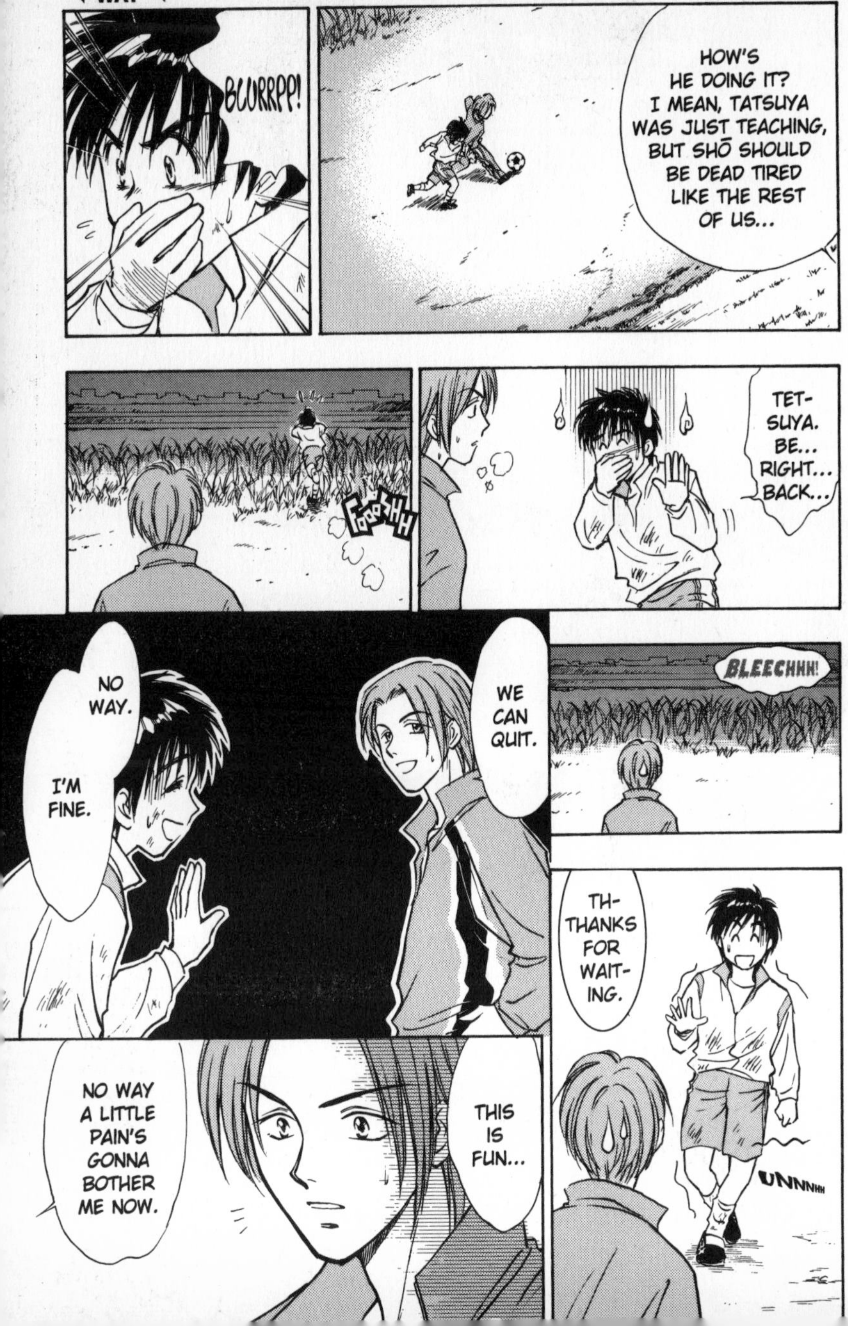
HOW'S HE DOING IT? I MEAN, TATSUYA WAS JUST TEACHING, BUT SHŌ SHOULD BE DEAD TIRED LIKE THE REST OF US...
BLURRPP!
TET-SUYA. BE... RIGHT... BACK...
FOOOSHH
BLEECHHH!
TH-THANKS FOR WAIT-ING.
UNNNHH
WE CAN QUIT.
NO WAY.
I'M FINE.
THIS IS FUN...
NO WAY A LITTLE PAIN'S GONNA BOTHER ME NOW.

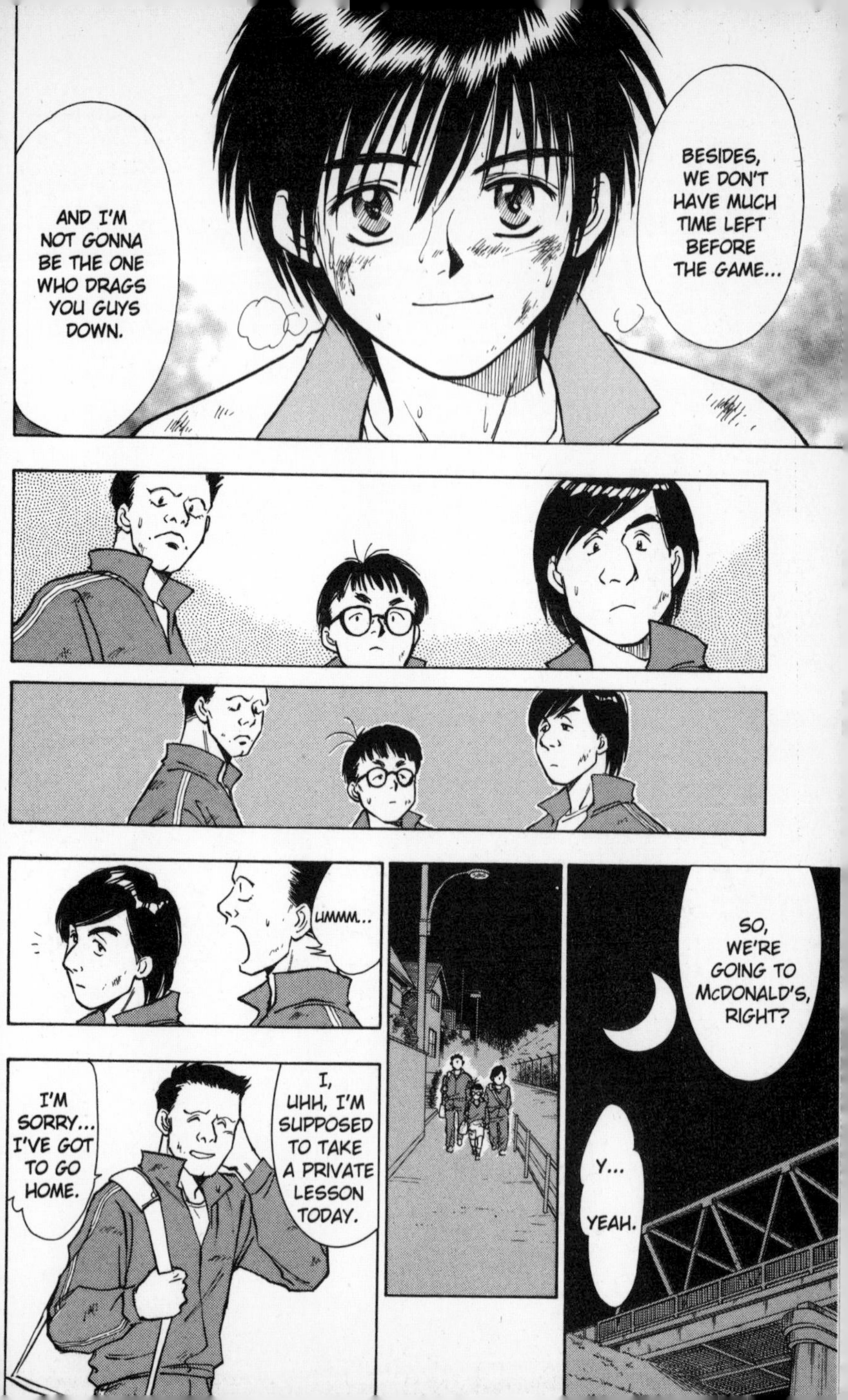
BESIDES, WE DON'T HAVE MUCH TIME LEFT BEFORE THE GAME...
AND I'M NOT GONNA BE THE ONE WHO DRAGS YOU GUYS DOWN.
SO, WE'RE GOING TO McDONALD'S, RIGHT?
Y... YEAH.
UMMM...
I, UHH, I'M SUPPOSED TO TAKE A PRIVATE LESSON TODAY.
I'M SORRY... I'VE GOT TO GO HOME.

READ THIS WAY

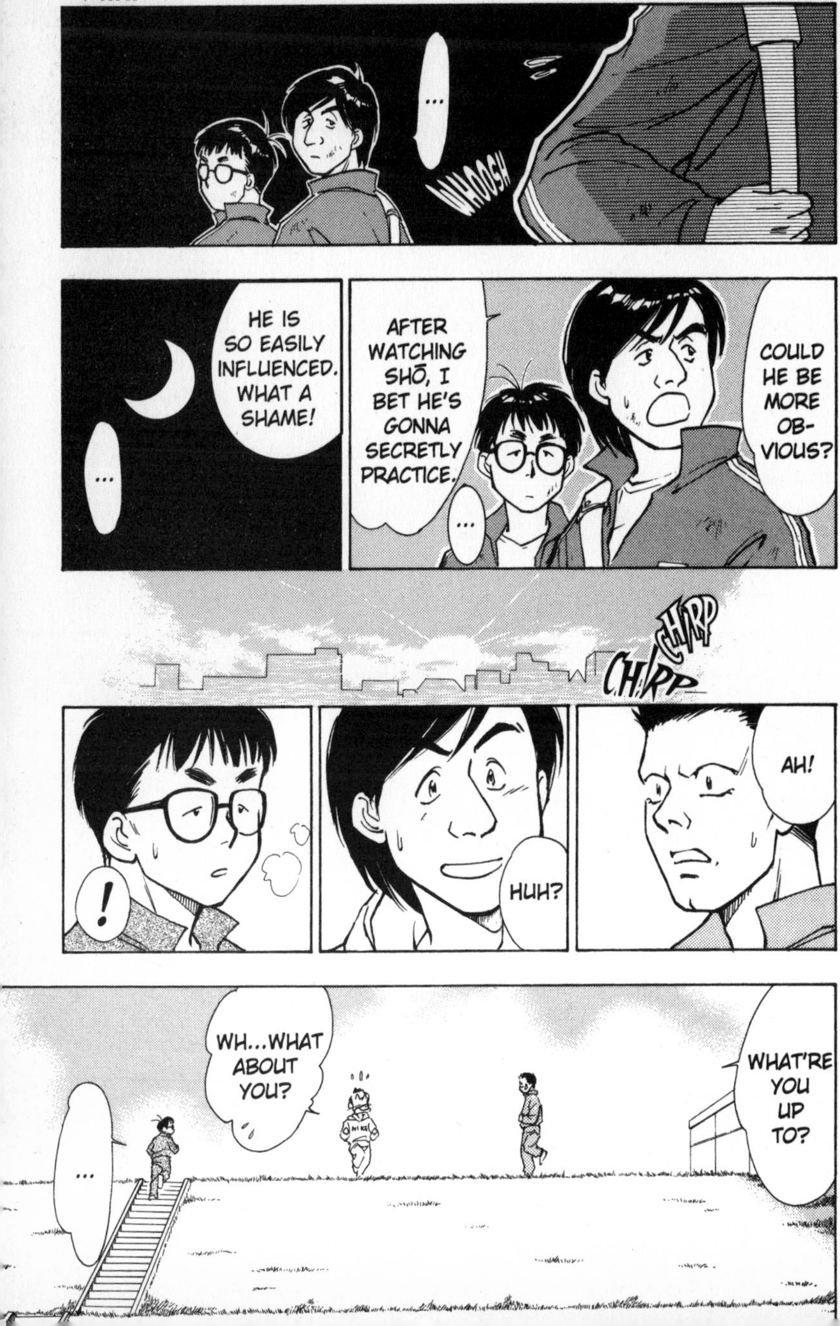

WHOOSH
...
COULD HE BE MORE OB-VIOUS?
AFTER WATCHING SHŌ, I BET HE'S GONNA SECRETLY PRACTICE.
...
HE IS SO EASILY INFLUENCED. WHAT A SHAME!
...
CHIRP
CHIRP
AH!
HUH?
!
WHAT'RE YOU UP TO?
WH...WHAT ABOUT YOU?
...

READ THIS WAY

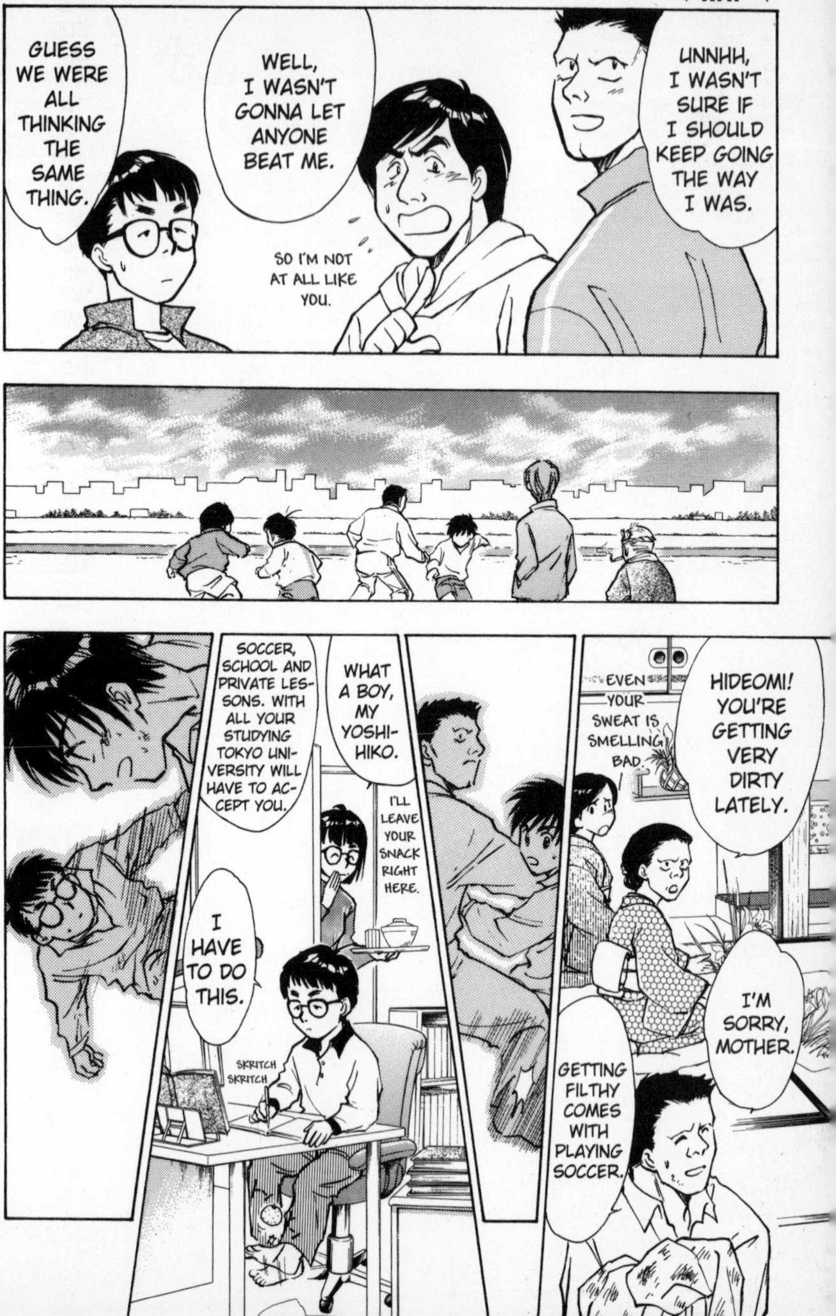
UNNHH, I WASN'T SURE IF I SHOULD KEEP GOING THE WAY I WAS.
WELL, I WASN'T GONNA LET ANYONE BEAT ME.
SO I'M NOT AT ALL LIKE YOU.
GUESS WE WERE ALL THINKING THE SAME THING.
HIDEOMI! YOU'RE GETTING VERY DIRTY LATELY.
EVEN YOUR SWEAT IS SMELLING BAD.
I'M SORRY, MOTHER.
GETTING FILTHY COMES WITH PLAYING SOCCER.
WHAT A BOY, MY YOSHI-HIKO.
SOCCER, SCHOOL AND PRIVATE LES-SONS. WITH ALL YOUR STUDYING TOKYO UNI-VERSITY WILL HAVE TO AC-CEPT YOU.
I'LL LEAVE YOUR SNACK RIGHT HERE.
I HAVE TO DO THIS.
SKRITCH SKRITCH

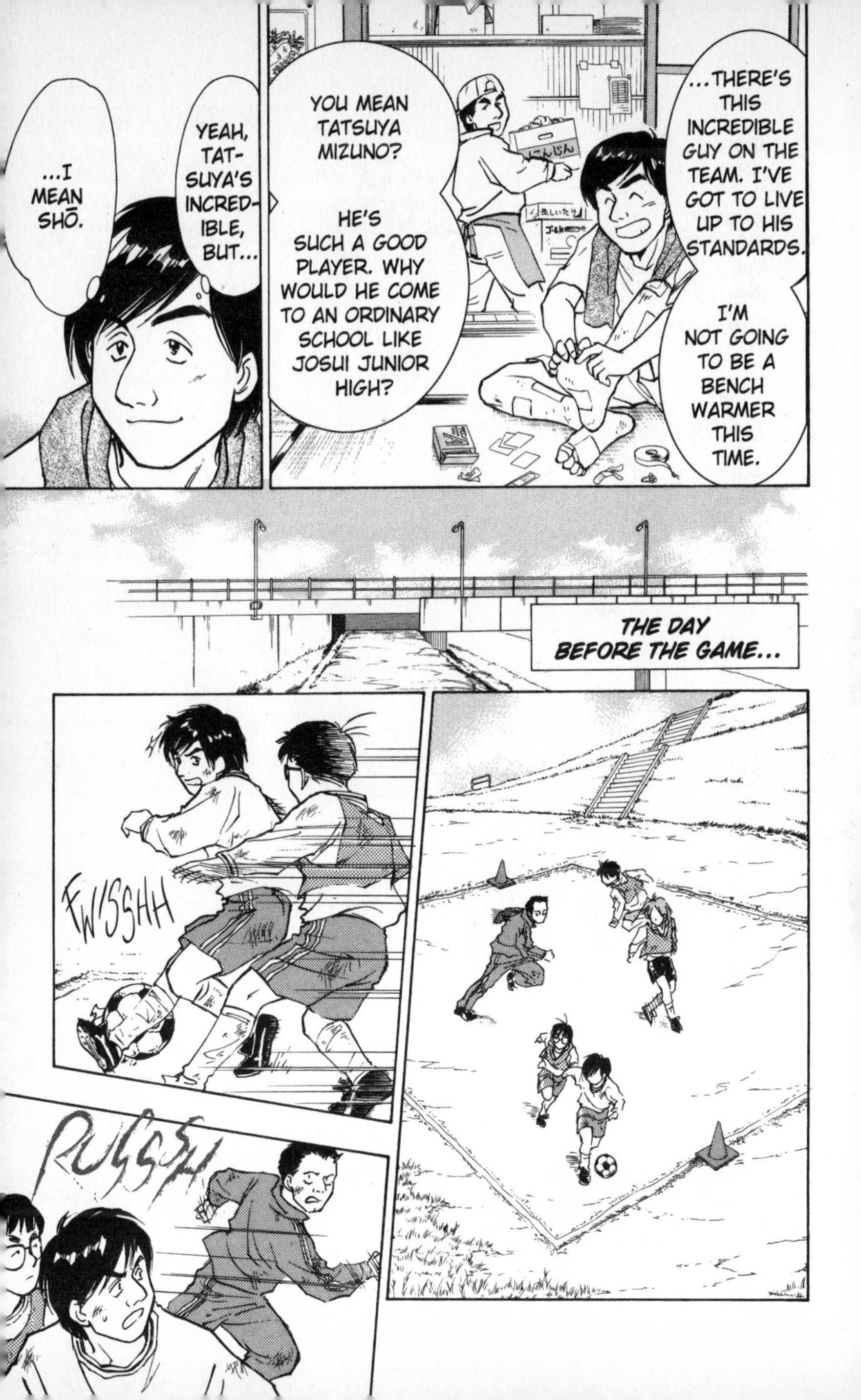
...THERE'S THIS INCREDIBLE GUY ON THE TEAM. I'VE GOT TO LIVE UP TO HIS STANDARDS.
I'M NOT GOING TO BE A BENCH WARMER THIS TIME.
YOU MEAN TATSUYA MIZUNO?
HE'S SUCH A GOOD PLAYER. WHY WOULD HE COME TO AN ORDINARY SCHOOL LIKE JOSUI JUNIOR HIGH?
YEAH, TAT-SUYA'S INCRED-IBLE, BUT...
...I MEAN SHŌ.
THE DAY BEFORE THE GAME...
FWISSHH
RUSSH

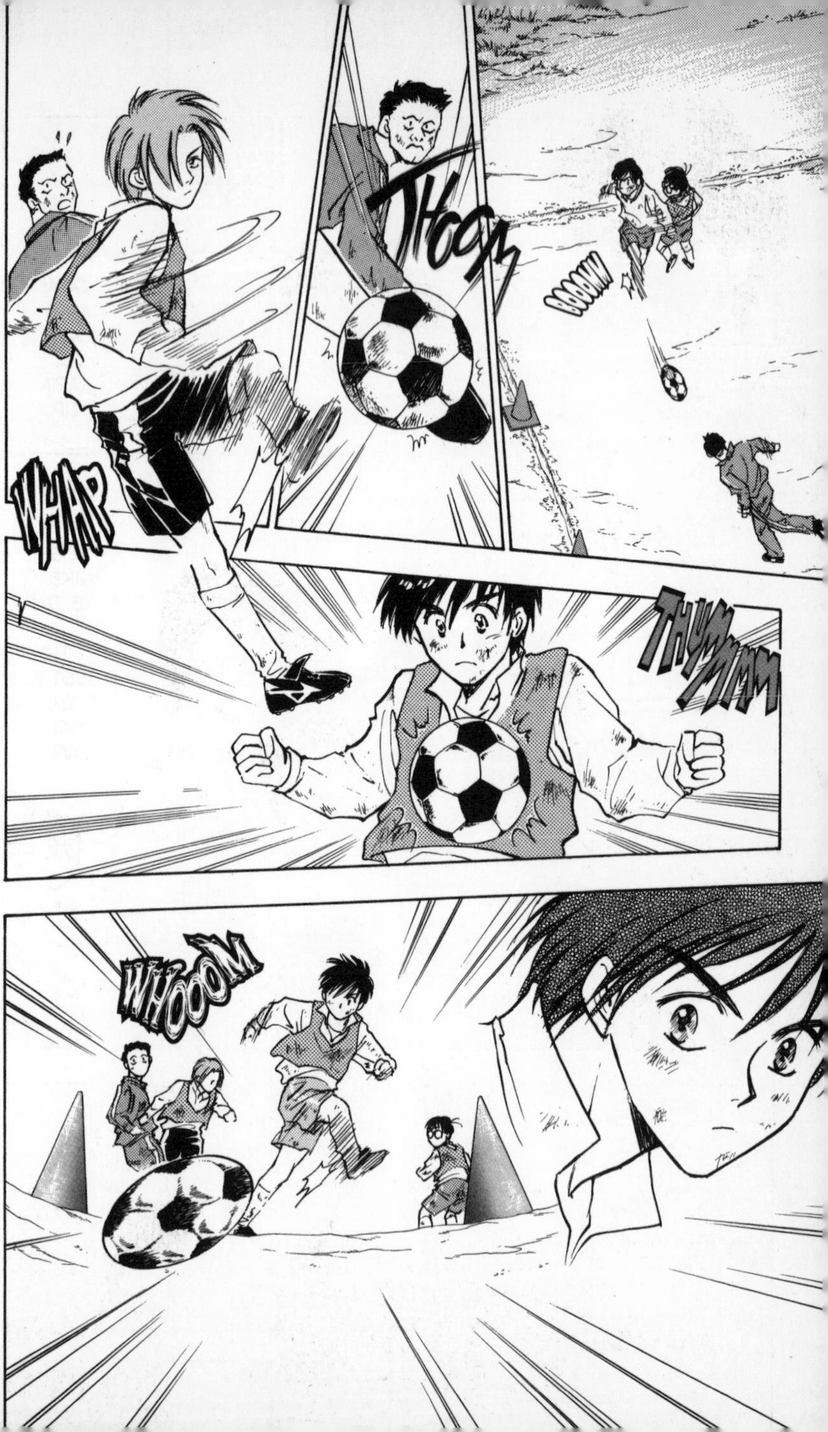
THOOM
BOOOM
WHAP
THUMMMM
WHOOOM

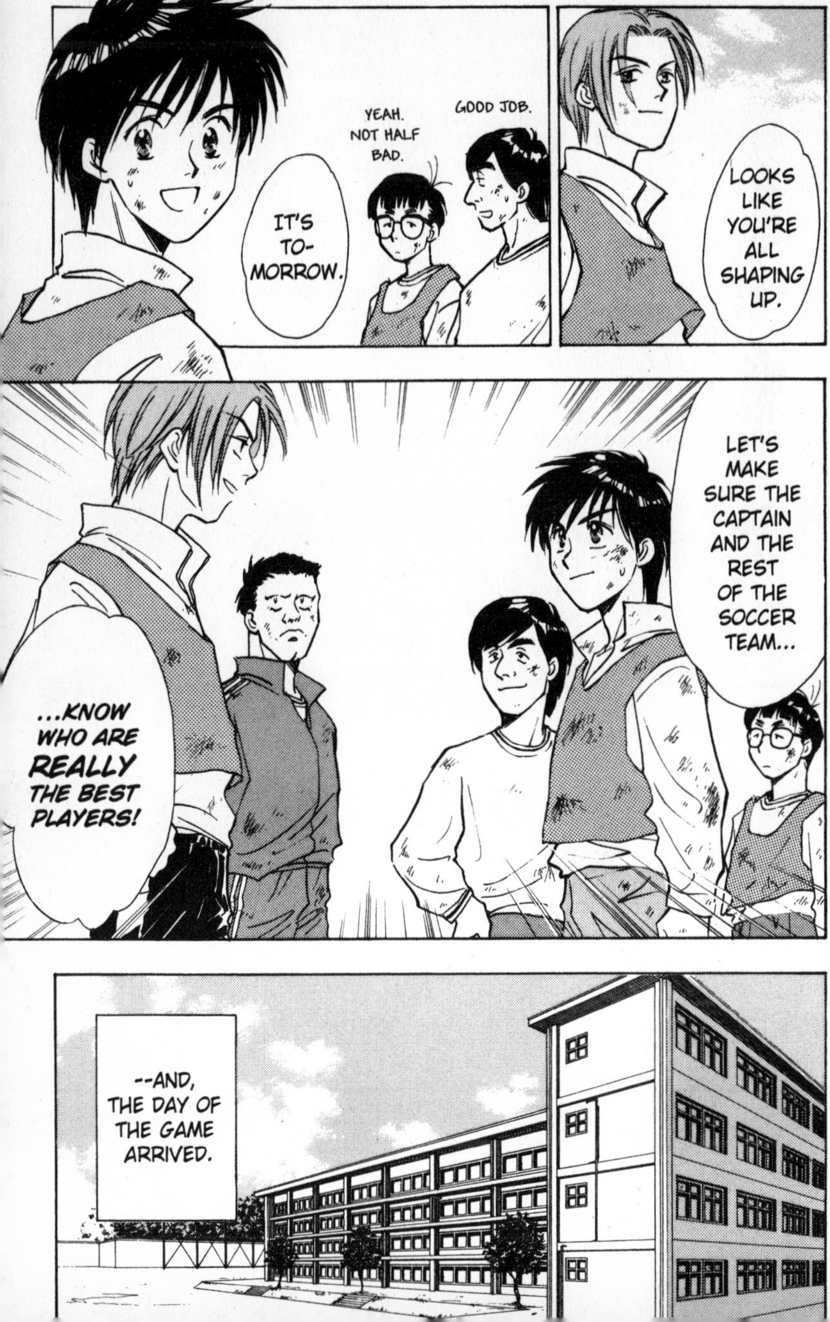
LOOKS LIKE YOU'RE ALL SHAPING UP.
GOOD JOB.
YEAH. NOT HALF BAD.
IT'S TO-MORROW.
LET'S MAKE SURE THE CAPTAIN AND THE REST OF THE SOCCER TEAM...
...KNOW WHO ARE REALLY THE BEST PLAYERS!
--AND, THE DAY OF THE GAME ARRIVED.

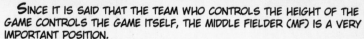

THE ROLE OF THE MIDDLE FIELDER

SINCE IT IS SAID THAT THE TEAM WHO CONTROLS THE HEIGHT OF THE GAME CONTROLS THE GAME ITSELF, THE MIDDLE FIELDER (MF) IS A VERY IMPORTANT POSITION.

THE MF RECEIVES THE BALL FROM THE DEFENDER (DF) WHO STEALS THE BALL FROM THE OPPONENTS. THE MF THEN SETS UP THE GAME AND SENDS THE FORWARDS (FW) THE LAST-PASS. THAT REPRESENTS THE MF'S ROLE.

HOWEVER, JUST LIKE THE FW, THE MF NOWADAYS IS REQUIRED TO HAVE MULTIPLE SKILLS. ALONG WITH STAMINA, HE/SHE MUST NOT ONLY HAVE A GOOD SENSE FOR A PASS, BUT ALSO MUST HAVE THE SKILL TO SHOOT AND DEFEND. THAT'S PRETTY MUCH EVERY SKILL REQUIRED TO PLAY SOCCER.

IN ADDITION, IF AN MF IS ALSO A BORANCH, THEN HE/SHE MUST NOT ONLY COOPERATE WITH THE DF BUT ALSO THINK ABOUT THE BALANCE BETWEEN OFFENSE AND DEFENSE. IT'S A POSITION THAT DEMANDS A KEEN STRATEGIC EYE AND AN ABILITY TO READ THE FLOW OF EACH GAME. BORANCH NOT ONLY USES HIS/HER BODY, BUT ALSO HIS/HER MIND A LOT MORE THAN OTHER POSITIONS DO.

IF AN MF IS AN OFFENSIVE MF, HIS/HER ABILITY HOLDS AN IMPORTANT KEY FOR THE TEAM'S OFFENSIVE MOVES. HE/SHE WILL BE MARKED THOROUGHLY BY THE OPPOSING DF, AND YET MUST CREATE A DECISIVE MOMENT AND, SEIZING THAT CHANCE, HE/SHE MUST SHOOT.

IT IS NOT AN OVERSTATEMENT TO SAY THAT THE ABILITY OF THE MF DETERMINES THE TEAM'S VICTORY OR DEFEAT.
I MUST SAY, THE PLAYER, MIZUNO, IS PERFECTLY SUITED AS AN MF.

--TATSUYA WATANABE (WINNING RUN)

STAGE.5 WEIGHT OF THE DREAM

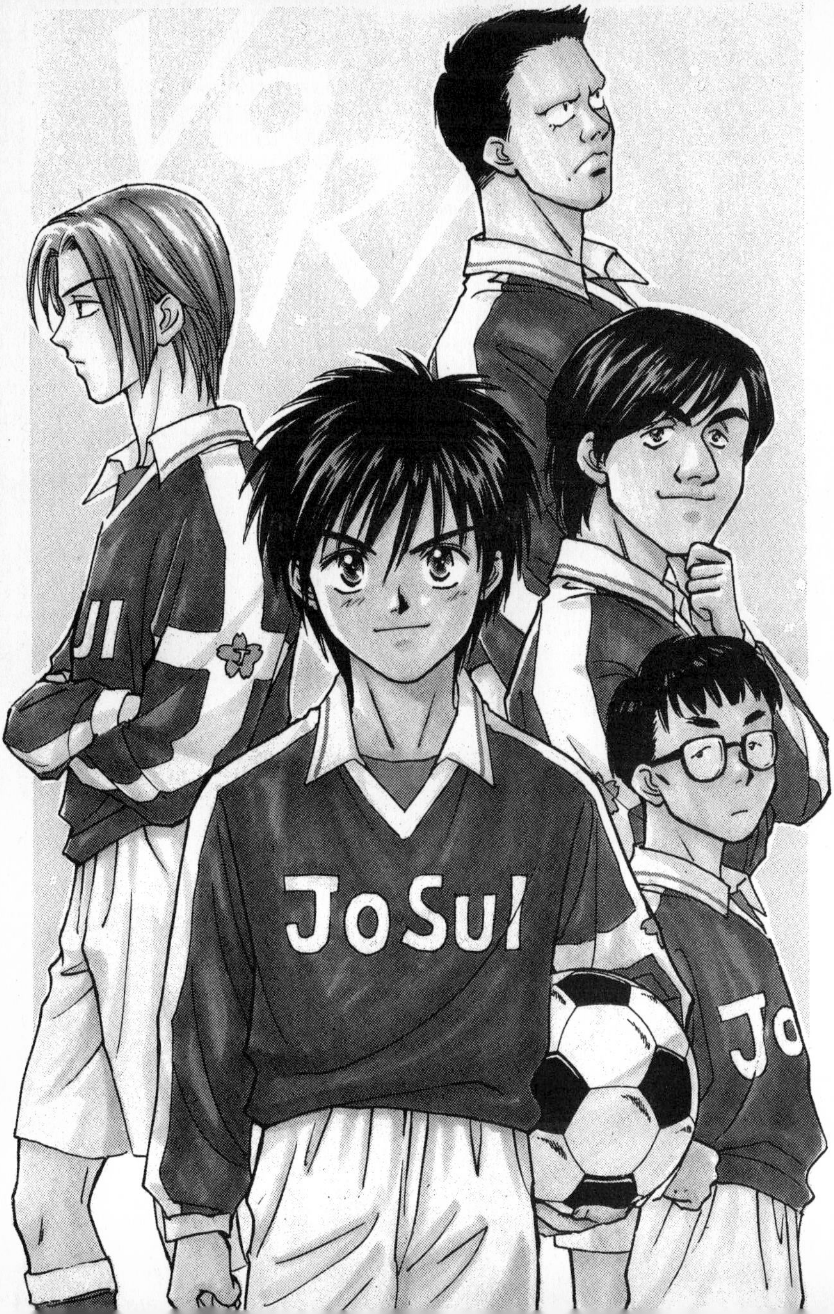
JoSui

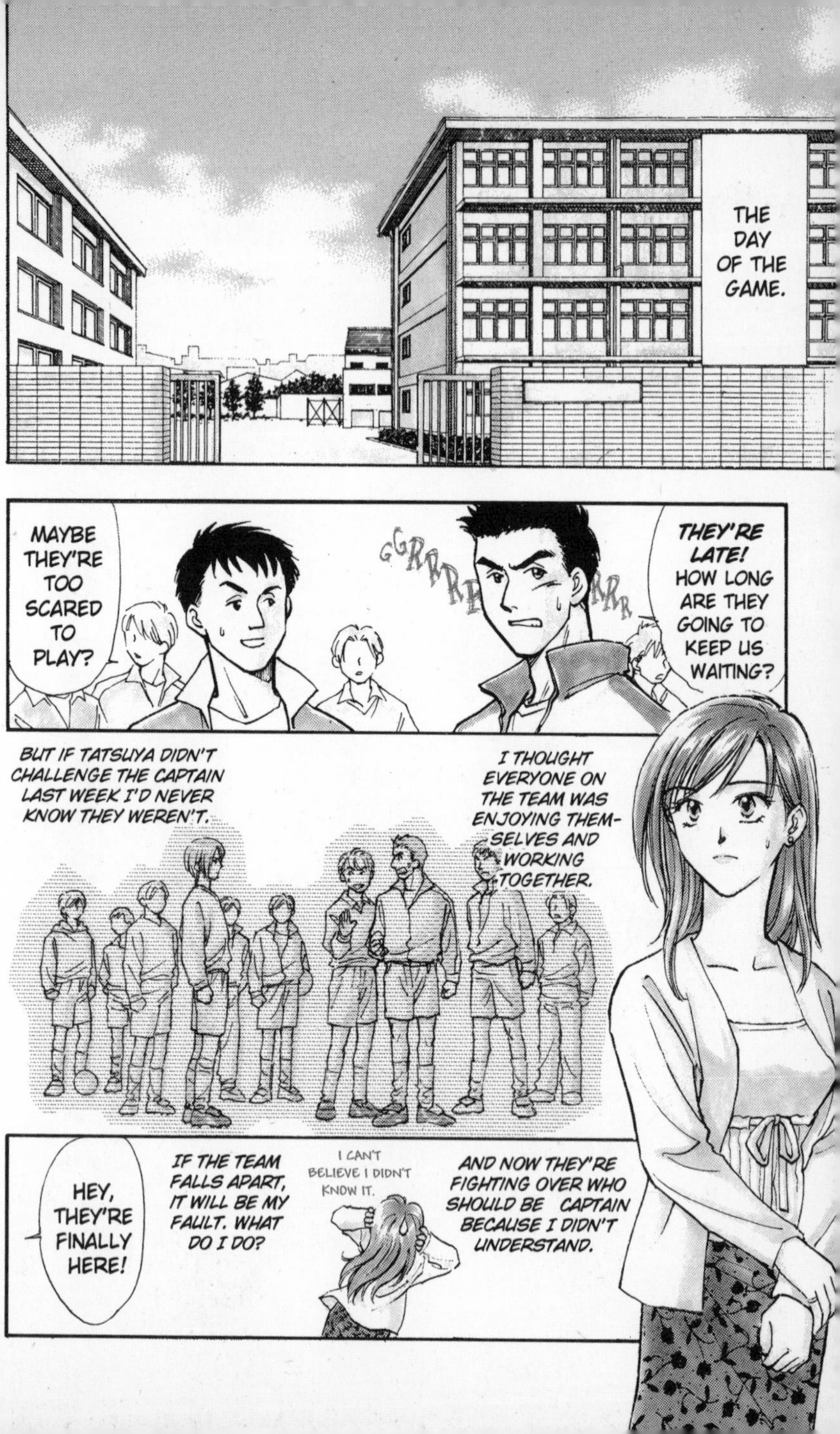
THE DAY OF THE GAME.
THEY'RE LATE! HOW LONG ARE THEY GOING TO KEEP US WAITING?
GGRRRRRRRR
MAYBE THEY'RE TOO SCARED TO PLAY?
I THOUGHT EVERYONE ON THE TEAM WAS ENJOYING THEM-SELVES AND WORKING TOGETHER.
BUT IF TATSUYA DIDN'T CHALLENGE THE CAPTAIN LAST WEEK I'D NEVER KNOW THEY WEREN'T.
AND NOW THEY'RE FIGHTING OVER WHO SHOULD BE CAPTAIN BECAUSE I DIDN'T UNDERSTAND.
I CAN'T BELIEVE I DIDN'T KNOW IT.
IF THE TEAM FALLS APART, IT WILL BE MY FAULT. WHAT DO I DO?
HEY, THEY'RE FINALLY HERE!

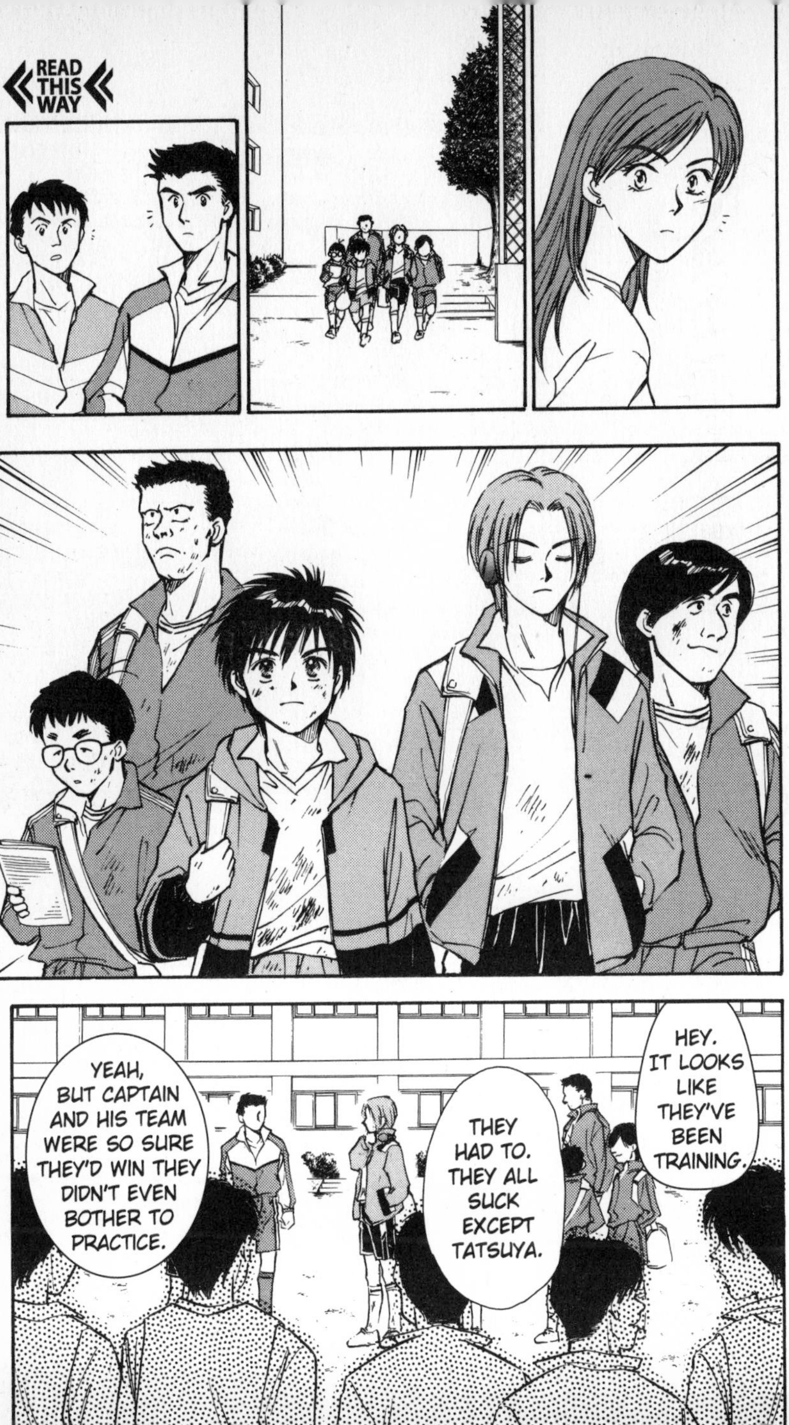
READ THIS WAY
HEY. IT LOOKS LIKE THEY'VE BEEN TRAINING.
THEY HAD TO. THEY ALL SUCK EXCEPT TATSUYA.
YEAH, BUT CAPTAIN AND HIS TEAM WERE SO SURE THEY'D WIN THEY DIDN'T EVEN BOTHER TO PRACTICE.

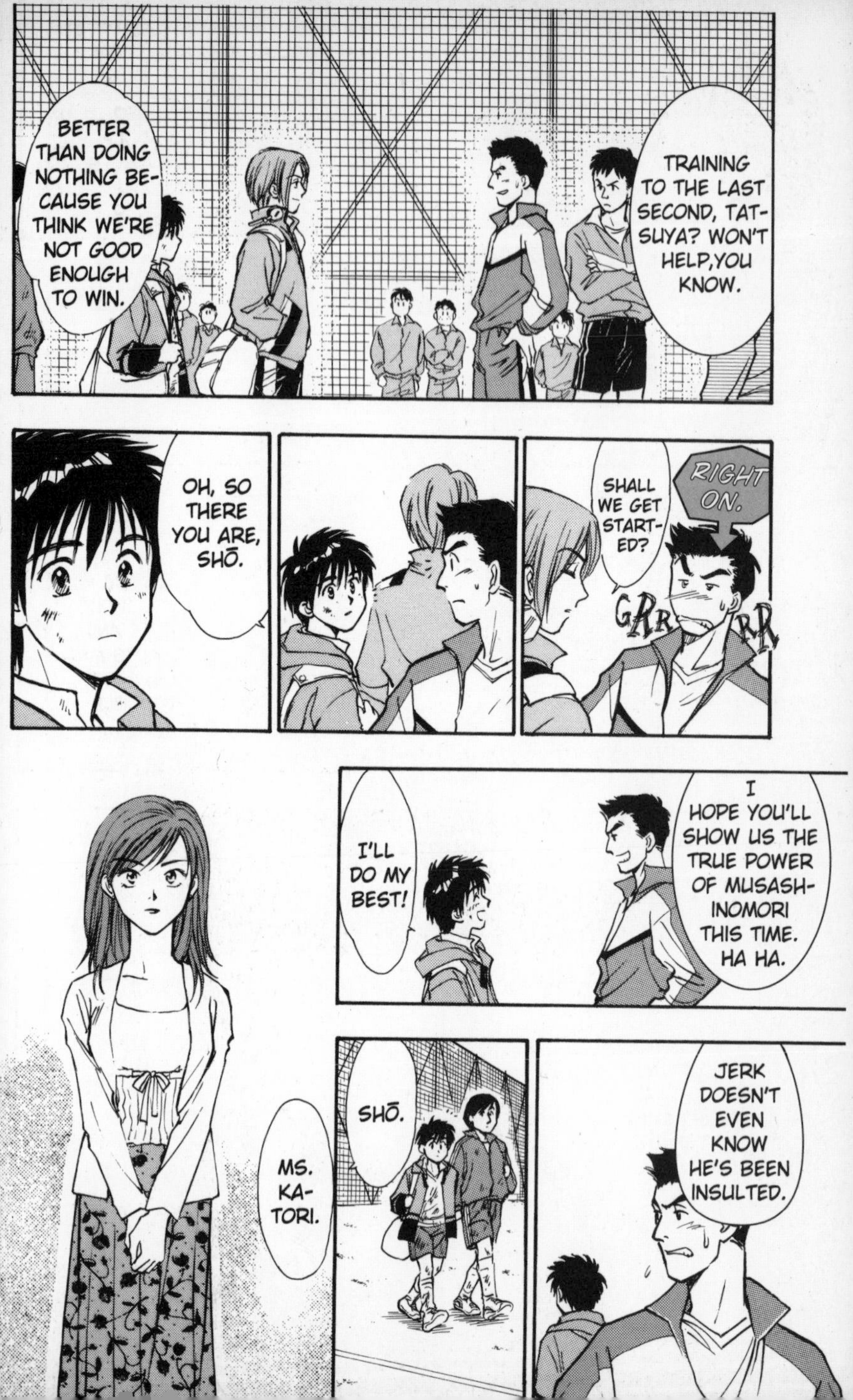
TRAINING TO THE LAST SECOND, TATSUYA? WON'T HELP,YOU KNOW.
BETTER THAN DOING NOTHING BECAUSE YOU THINK WE'RE NOT GOOD ENOUGH TO WIN.
RIGHT ON.
SHALL WE GET STARTED?
GRRRR
OH, SO THERE YOU ARE, SHŌ.
I HOPE YOU'LL SHOW US THE TRUE POWER OF MUSASHINOMORI THIS TIME. HA HA.
I'LL DO MY BEST!
JERK DOESN'T EVEN KNOW HE'S BEEN INSULTED.
SHŌ.
MS. KATORI.

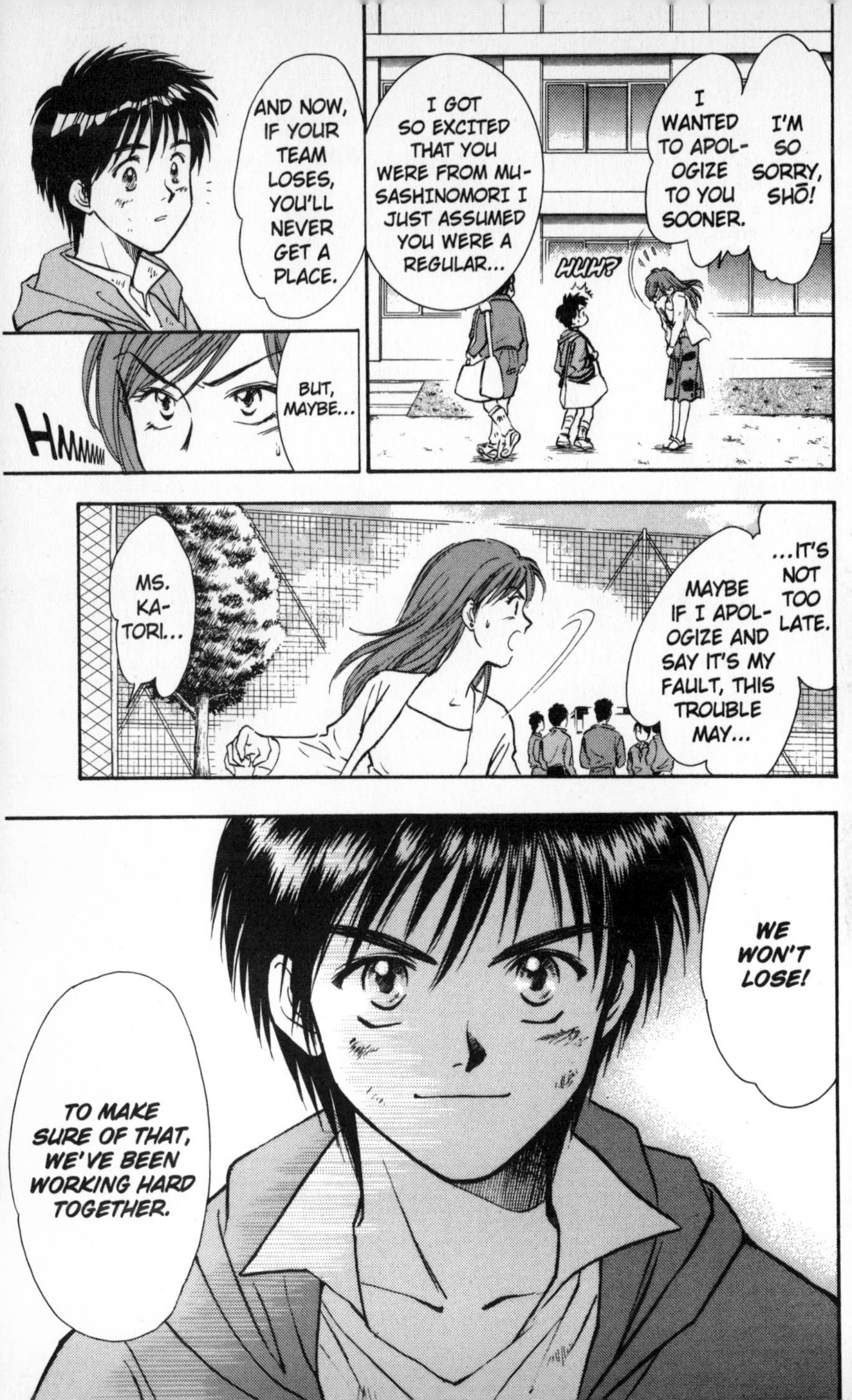
I'M SO SORRY, SHŌ!
I WANTED TO APOLOGIZE TO YOU SOONER.
HUH?
I GOT SO EXCITED THAT YOU WERE FROM MUSASHINOMORI I JUST ASSUMED YOU WERE A REGULAR...
AND NOW, IF YOUR TEAM LOSES, YOU'LL NEVER GET A PLACE.
BUT, MAYBE...
HMMMMM
...IT'S NOT TOO LATE.
MAYBE IF I APOLOGIZE AND SAY IT'S MY FAULT, THIS TROUBLE MAY...
MS. KATORI...
WE WON'T LOSE!
TO MAKE SURE OF THAT, WE'VE BEEN WORKING HARD TOGETHER.

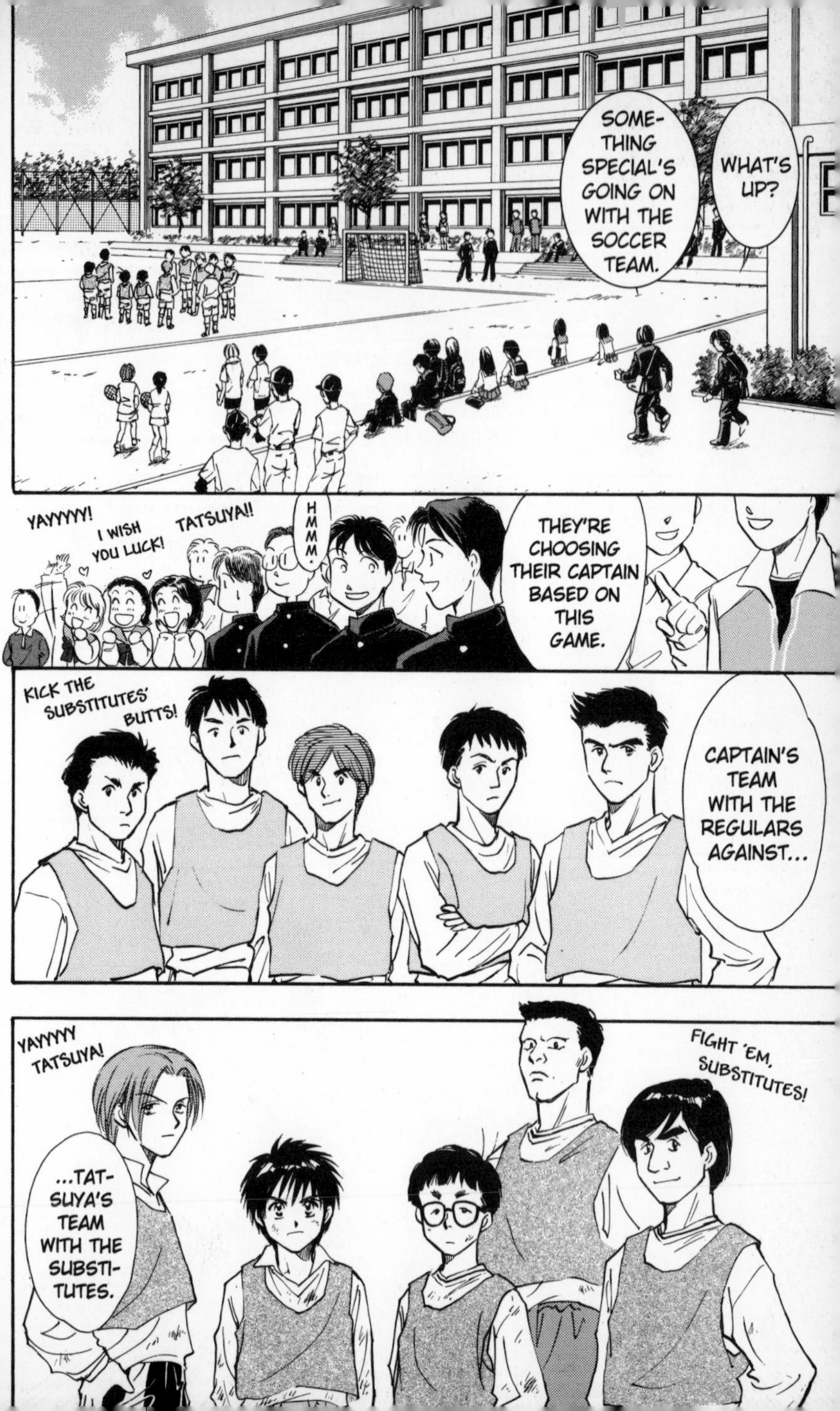
WHAT'S UP?
SOMETHING SPECIAL'S GOING ON WITH THE SOCCER TEAM.
THEY'RE CHOOSING THEIR CAPTAIN BASED ON THIS GAME.
HMMM.
TATSUYA!!
I WISH YOU LUCK!
YAYYYYY!
CAPTAIN'S TEAM WITH THE REGULARS AGAINST...
KICK THE SUBSTITUTES' BUTTS!
FIGHT 'EM, SUBSTITUTES!
YAYYYYY TATSUYA!
...TATSUYA'S TEAM WITH THE SUBSTITUTES.

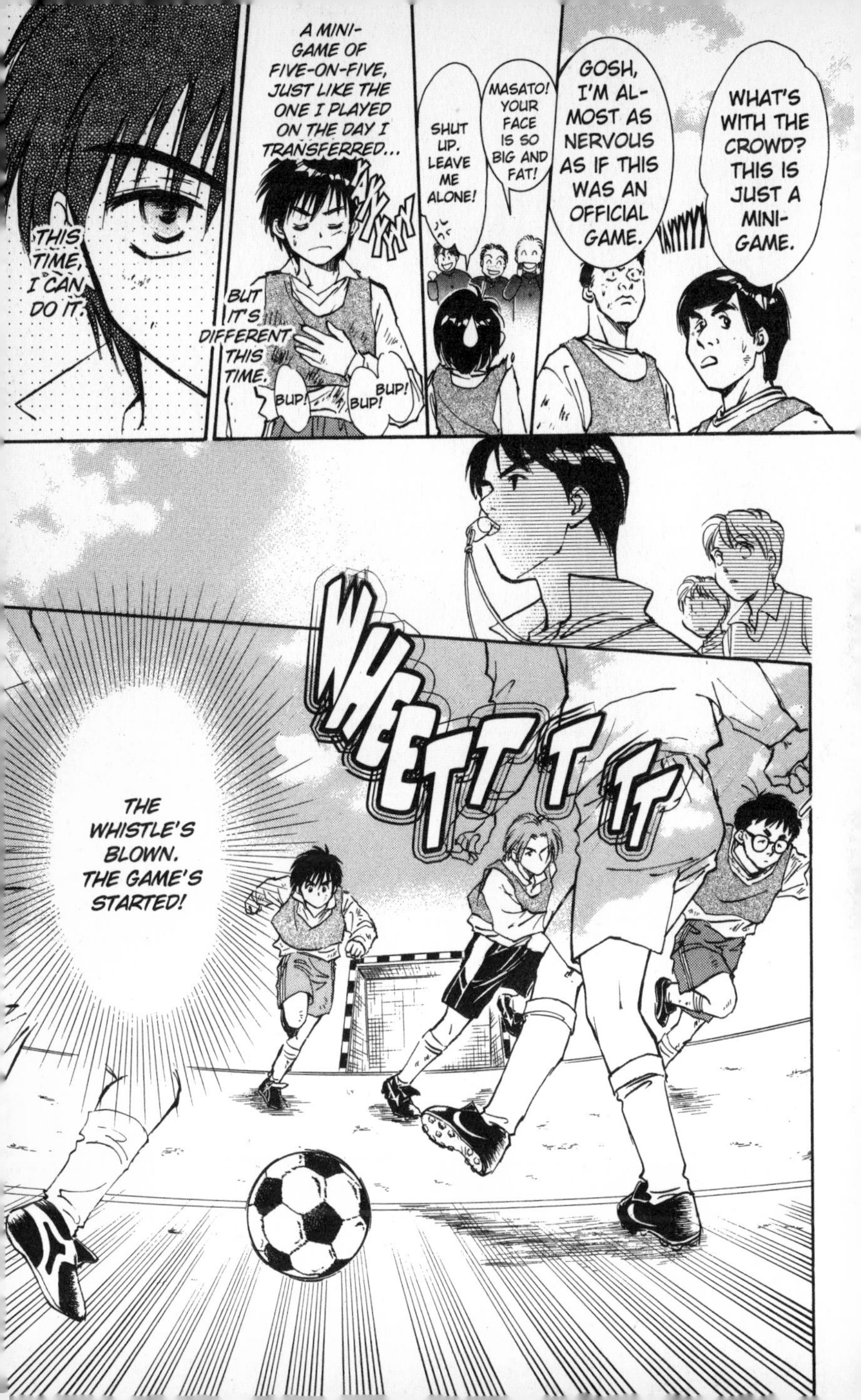
WHAT'S WITH THE CROWD? THIS IS JUST A MINI-GAME.
GOSH, I'M ALMOST AS NERVOUS AS IF THIS WAS AN OFFICIAL GAME.
MASATO! YOUR FACE IS SO BIG AND FAT!
SHUT UP. LEAVE ME ALONE!
A MINI-GAME OF FIVE-ON-FIVE, JUST LIKE THE ONE I PLAYED ON THE DAY I TRANSFERRED...
BUT IT'S DIFFERENT THIS TIME.
BUP! BUP! BUP!
THIS TIME, I CAN DO IT.
WHEETT T TT
THE WHISTLE'S BLOWN. THE GAME'S STARTED!

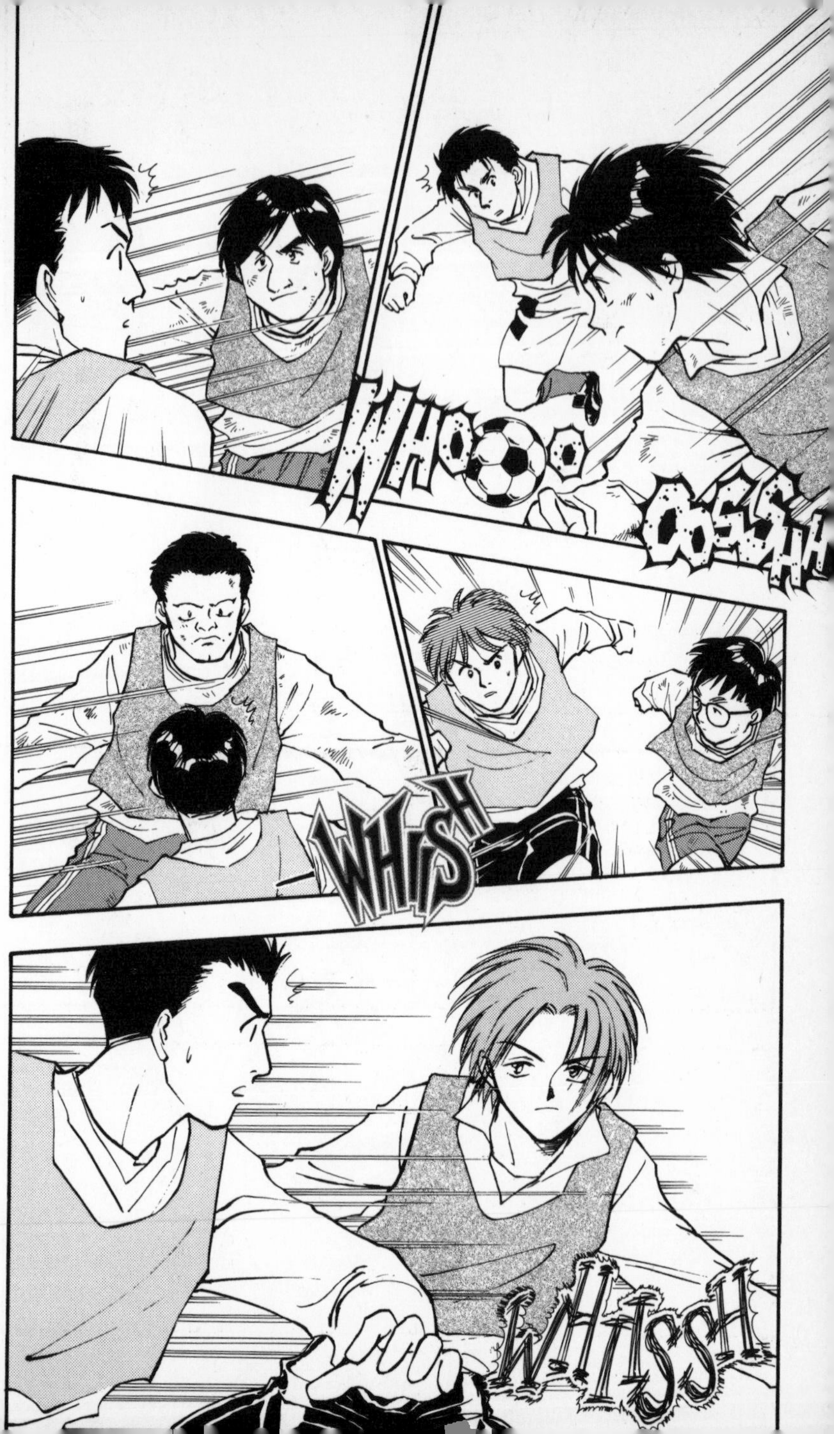
WHOO
OOSSHA
WHISH
WHISSH

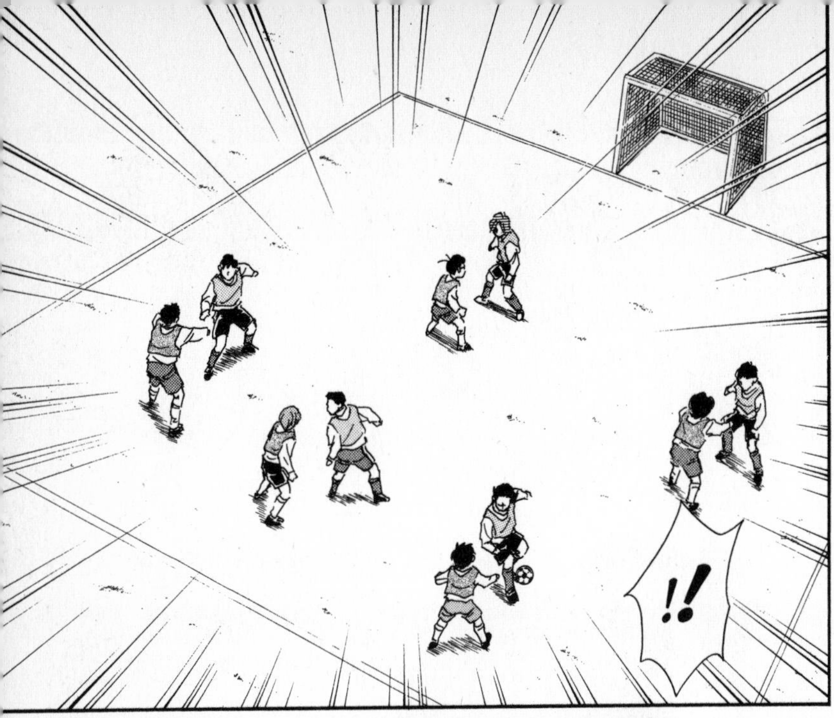
!!

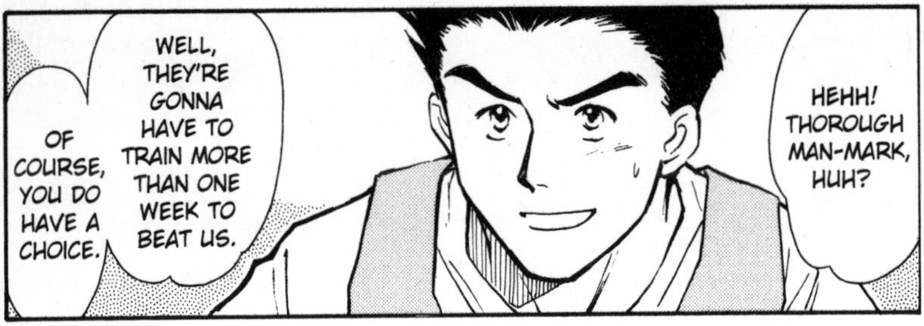
HEHH! THOROUGH MAN-MARK, HUH?
WELL, THEY'RE GONNA HAVE TO TRAIN MORE THAN ONE WEEK TO BEAT US.
OF COURSE, YOU DO HAVE A CHOICE.

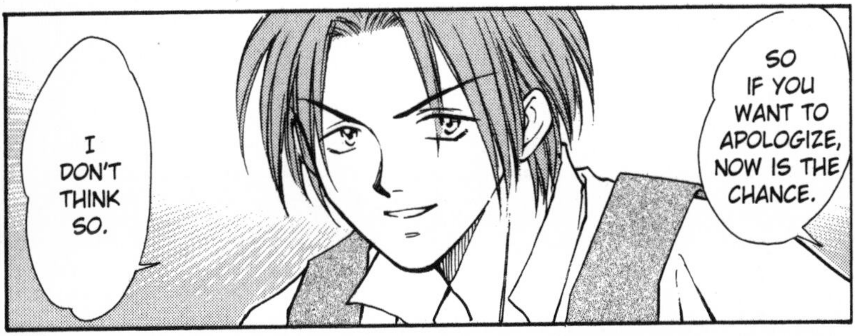
SO IF YOU WANT TO APOLOGIZE, NOW IS THE CHANCE.
I DON'T THINK SO.

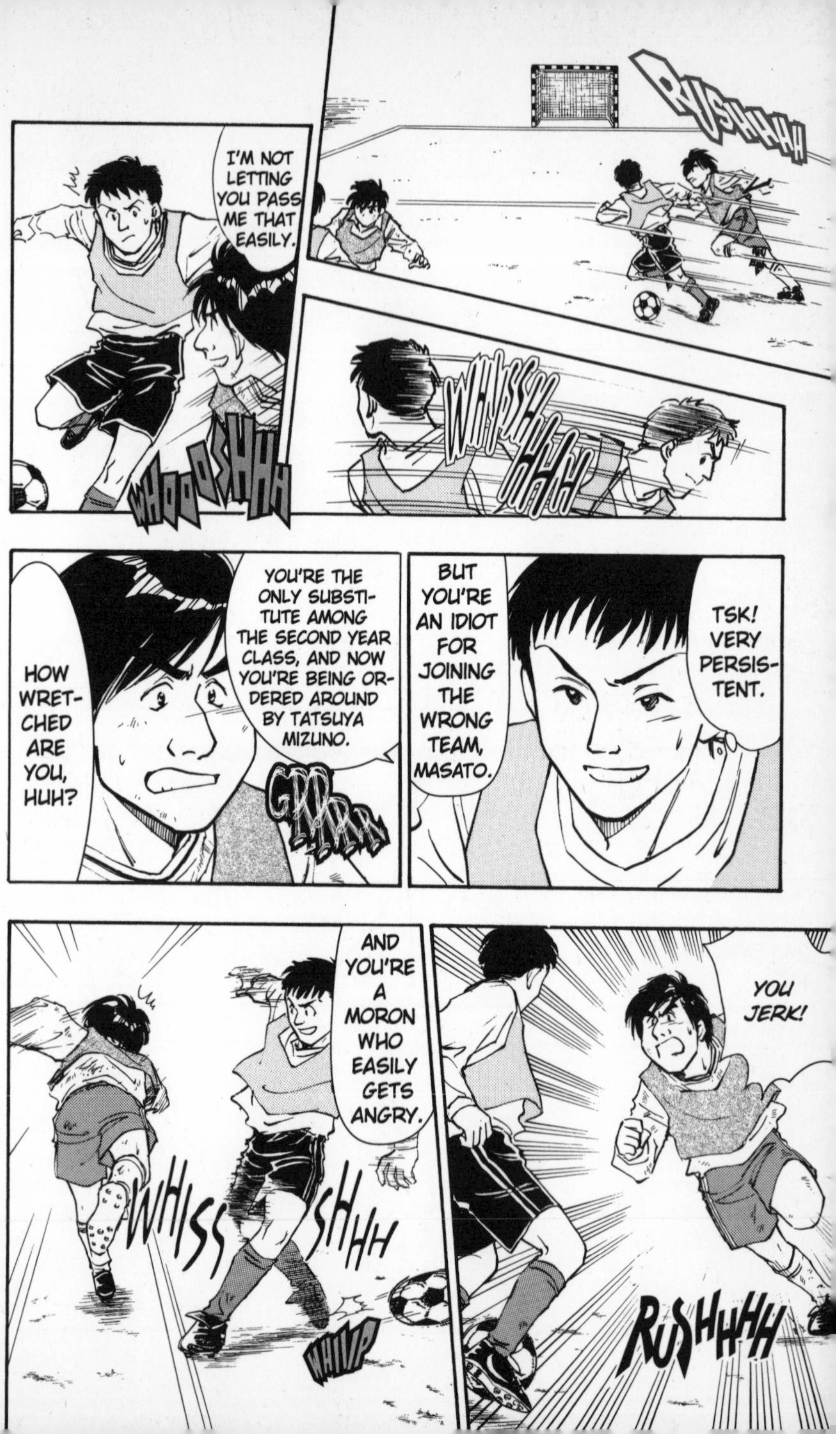
RUSHHHH
I'M NOT LETTING YOU PASS ME THAT EASILY.
WHOOOSHHH
TSK! VERY PERSISTENT.
BUT YOU'RE AN IDIOT FOR JOINING THE WRONG TEAM, MASATO.
YOU'RE THE ONLY SUBSTITUTE AMONG THE SECOND YEAR CLASS, AND NOW YOU'RE BEING ORDERED AROUND BY TATSUYA MIZUNO.
HOW WRETCHED ARE YOU, HUH?
YOU JERK!
RUSHHHH
AND YOU'RE A MORON WHO EASILY GETS ANGRY.
WHISS SHHH

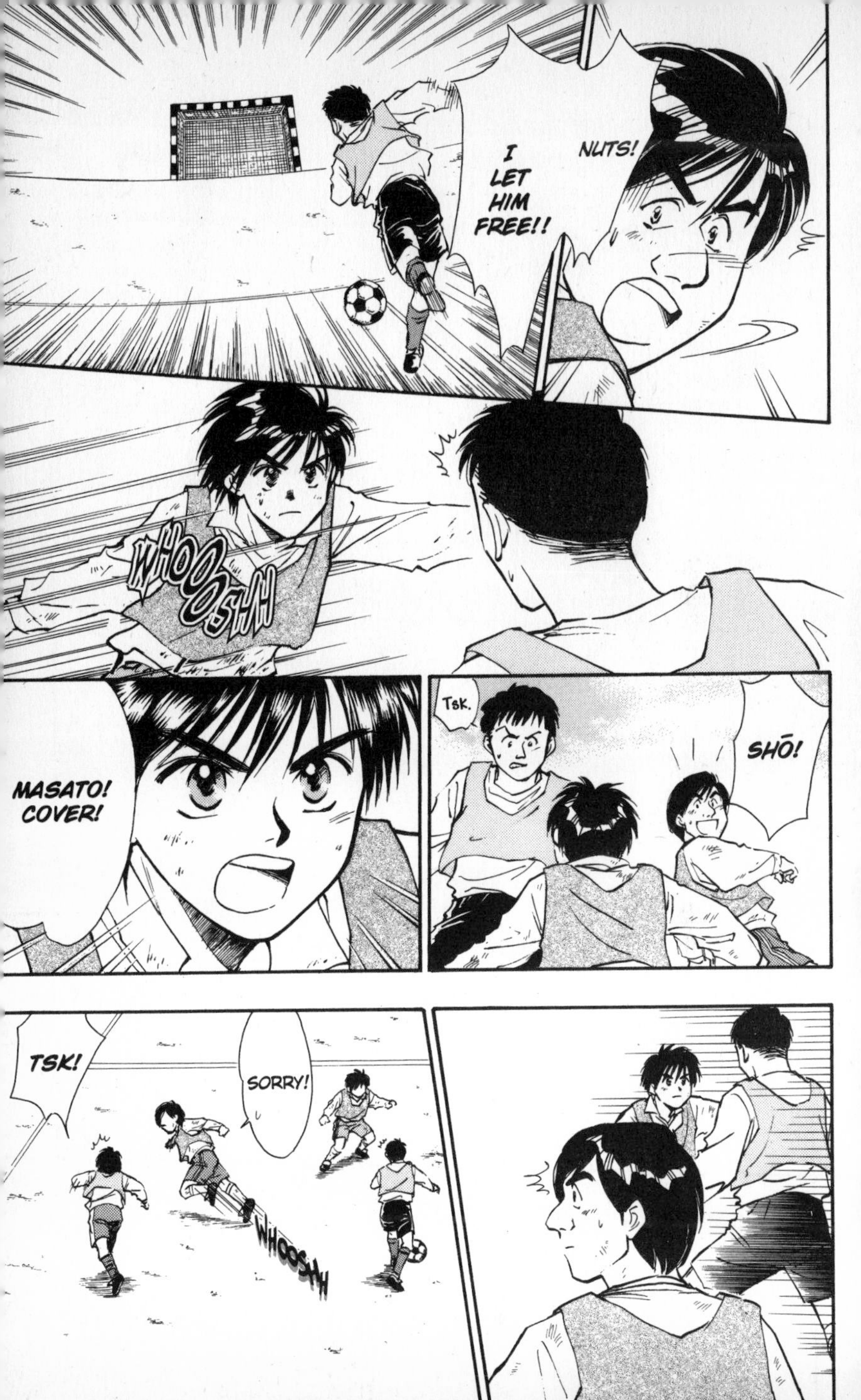
NUTS!
I LET HIM FREE!!
WHOOSHH
SHŌ!
Tsk.
MASATO! COVER!
SORRY!
TSK!
WHOOSHH

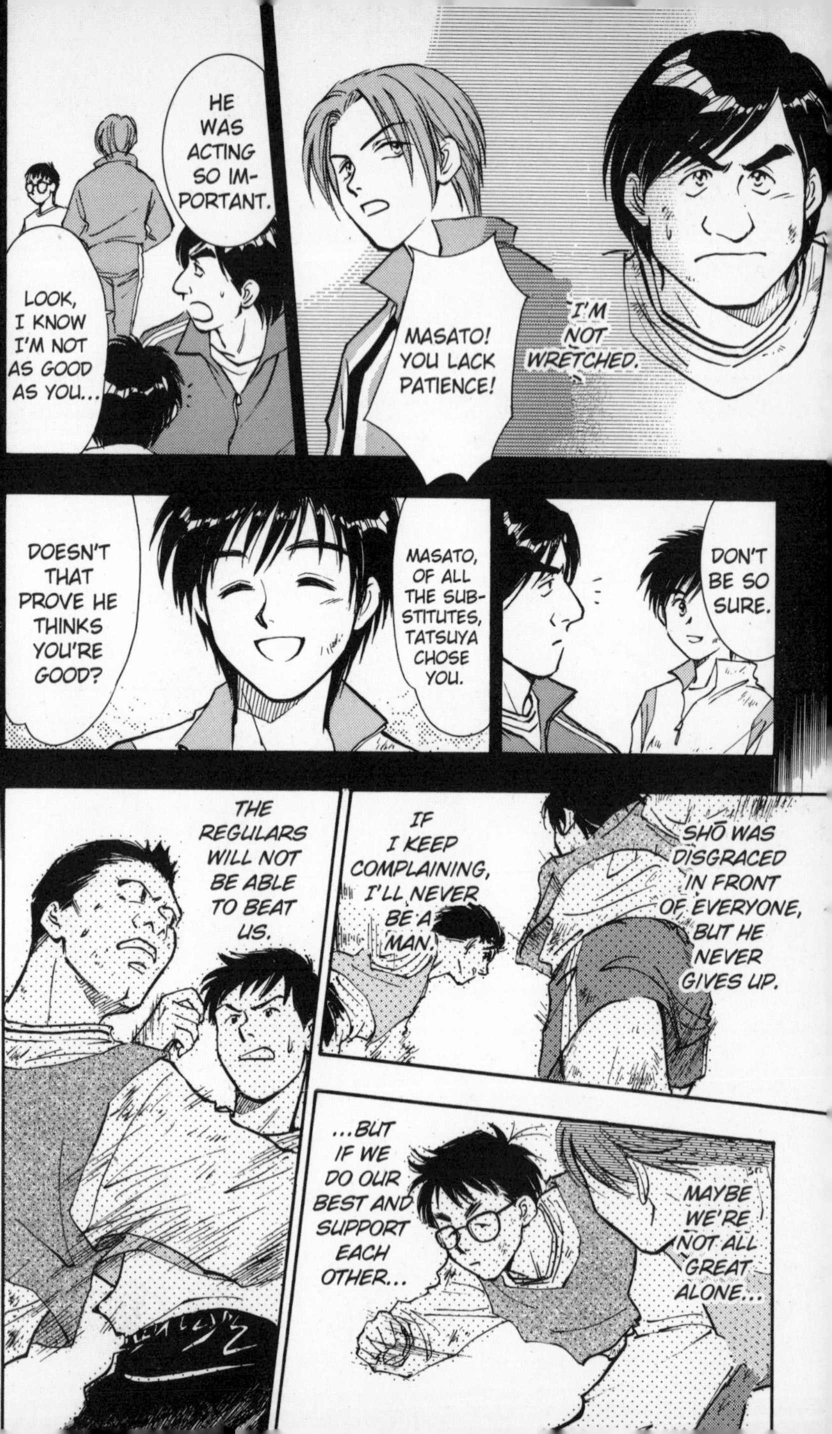
I'M NOT WRETCHED.
MASATO! YOU LACK PATIENCE!
HE WAS ACTING SO IMPORTANT.
LOOK, I KNOW I'M NOT AS GOOD AS YOU...
DON'T BE SO SURE.
MASATO, OF ALL THE SUBSTITUTES, TATSUYA CHOSE YOU.
DOESN'T THAT PROVE HE THINKS YOU'RE GOOD?
SHO WAS DISGRACED IN FRONT OF EVERYONE, BUT HE NEVER GIVES UP.
IF I KEEP COMPLAINING, I'LL NEVER BE A MAN.
MAYBE WE'RE NOT ALL GREAT ALONE...
...BUT IF WE DO OUR BEST AND SUPPORT EACH OTHER...
THE REGULARS WILL NOT BE ABLE TO BEAT US.

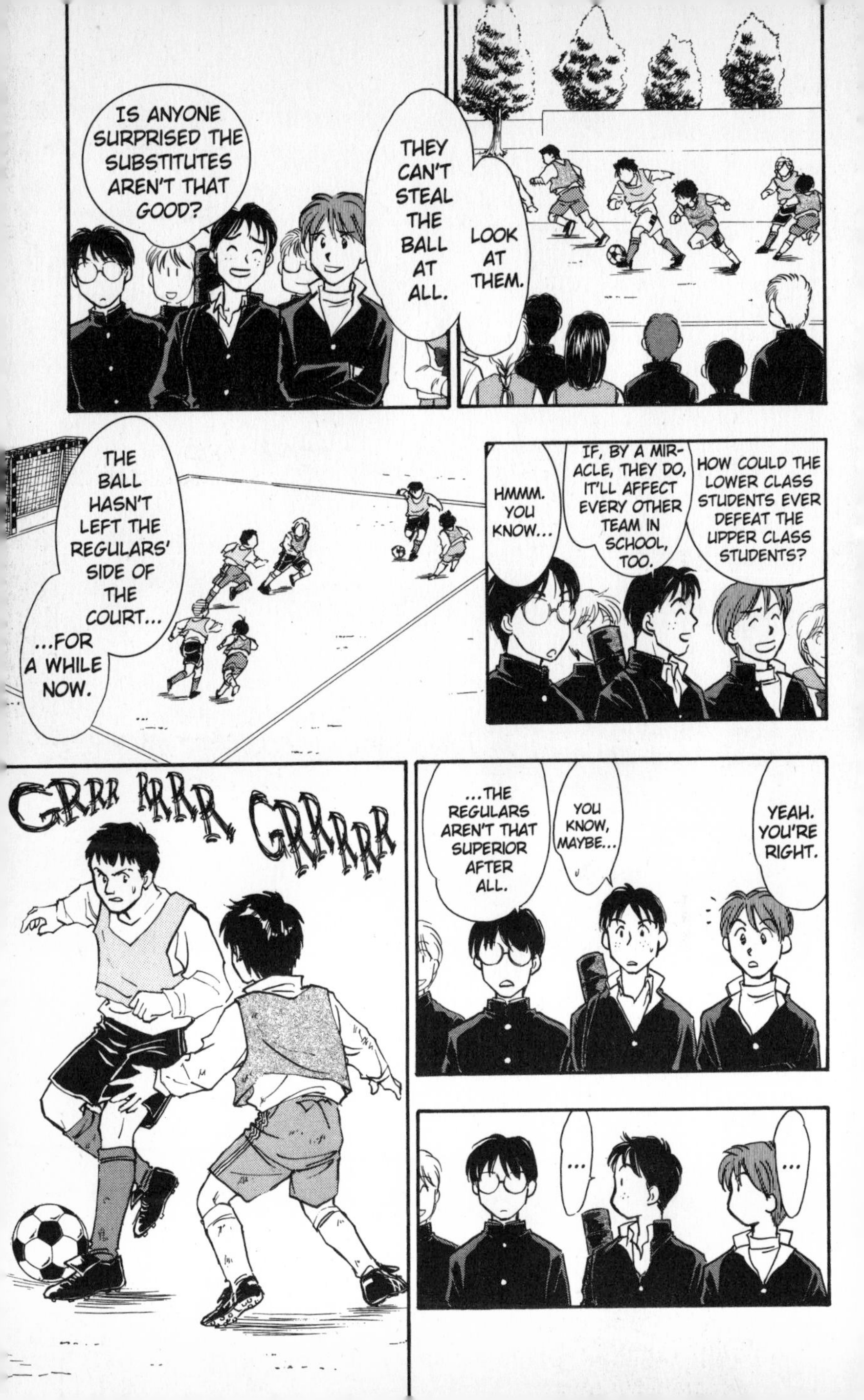
LOOK AT THEM.
THEY CAN'T STEAL THE BALL AT ALL.
IS ANYONE SURPRISED THE SUBSTITUTES AREN'T THAT GOOD?
HOW COULD THE LOWER CLASS STUDENTS EVER DEFEAT THE UPPER CLASS STUDENTS?
IF, BY A MIR-ACLE, THEY DO, IT'LL AFFECT EVERY OTHER TEAM IN SCHOOL, TOO.
HMMM. YOU KNOW...
THE BALL HASN'T LEFT THE REGULARS' SIDE OF THE COURT...
...FOR A WHILE NOW.
YEAH. YOU'RE RIGHT.
YOU KNOW, MAYBE...
...THE REGULARS AREN'T THAT SUPERIOR AFTER ALL.
...
...
GRRR RRRR GRRRRR

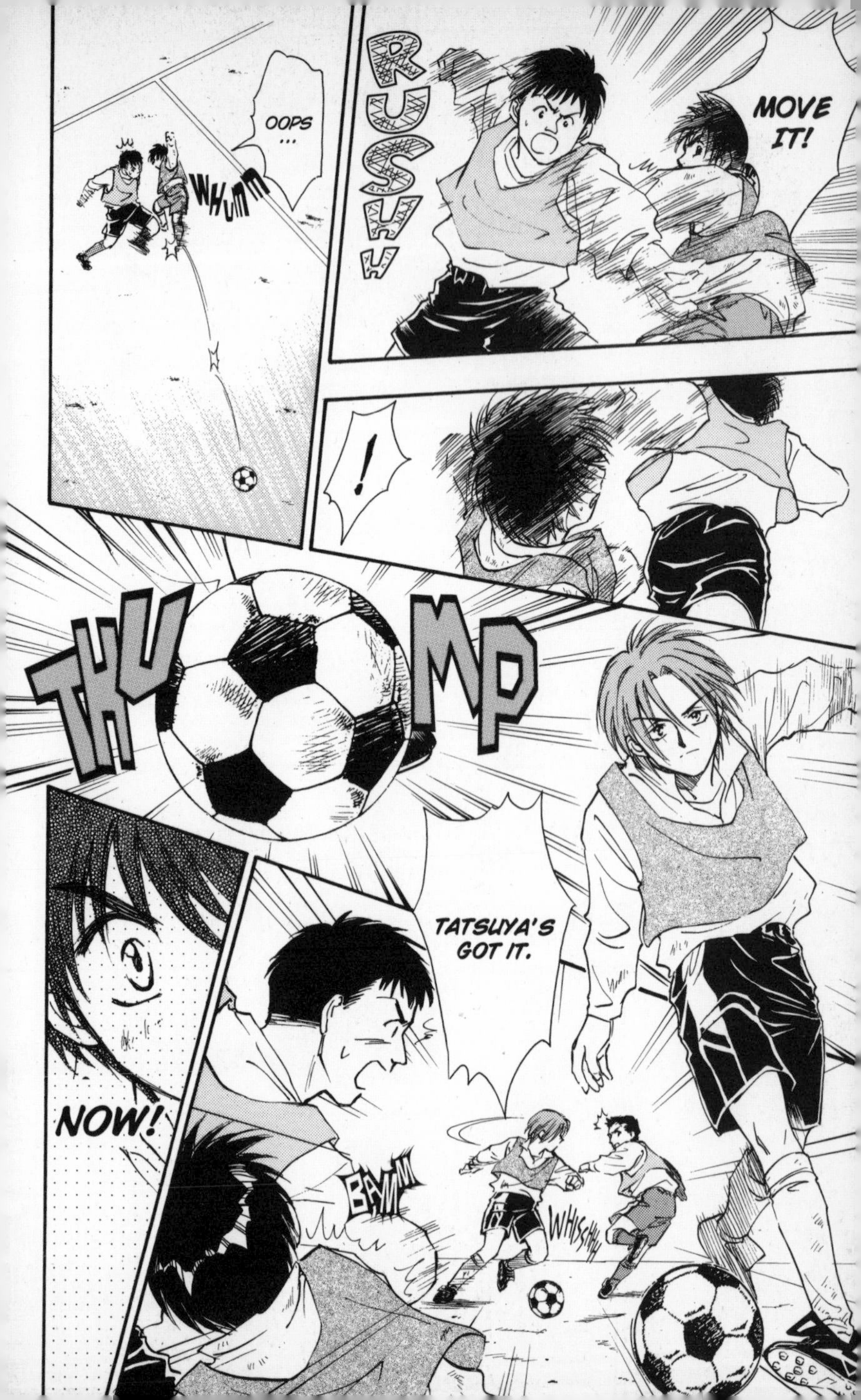
RUSHH!
MOVE IT!
!
OOPS ...
WHUMP
THUMP
TATSUYA'S GOT IT.
NOW!
BAMM
WHISHH

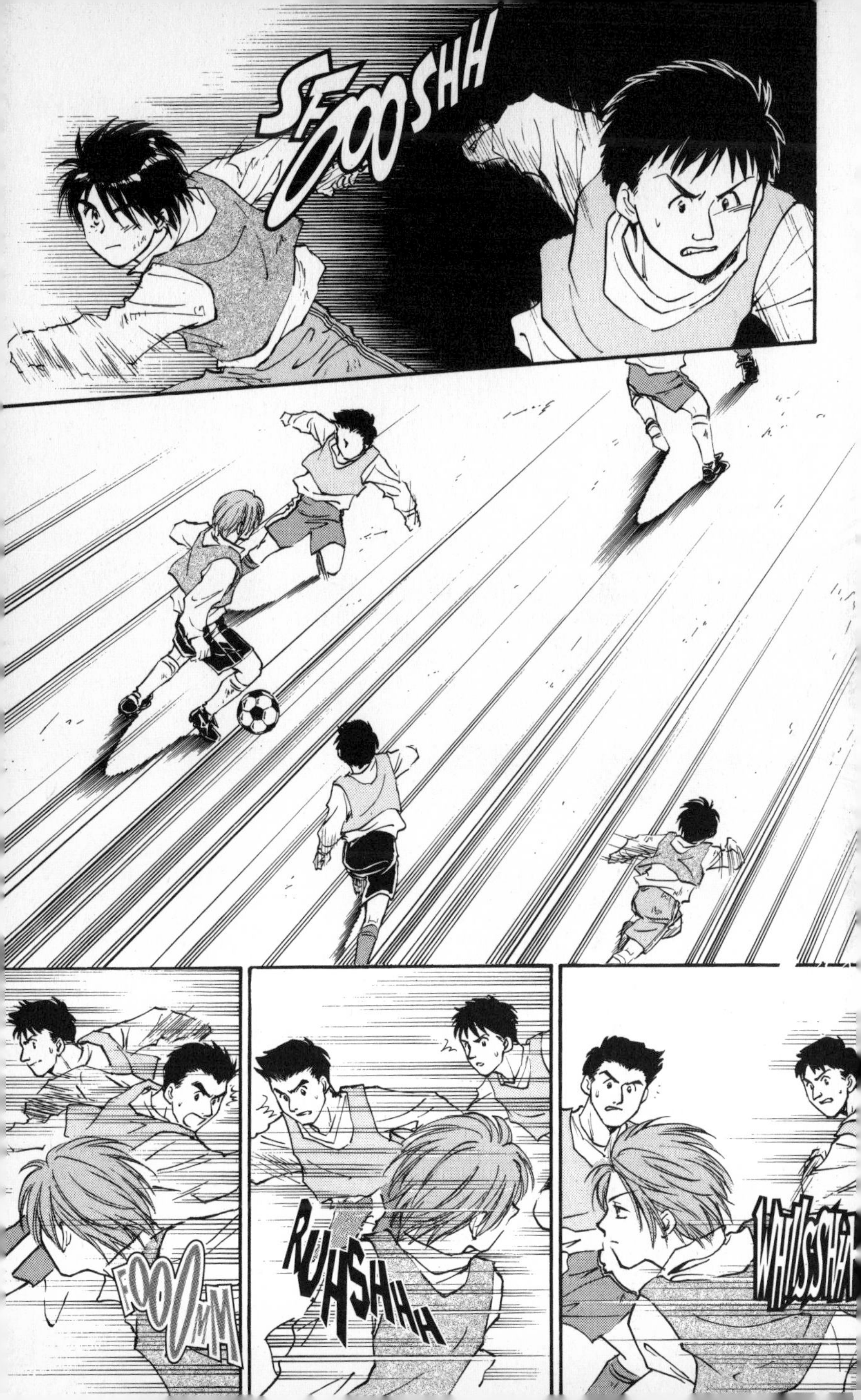
SFOOSHH
WHUSSHA
RUHSHHH
FOOOMM

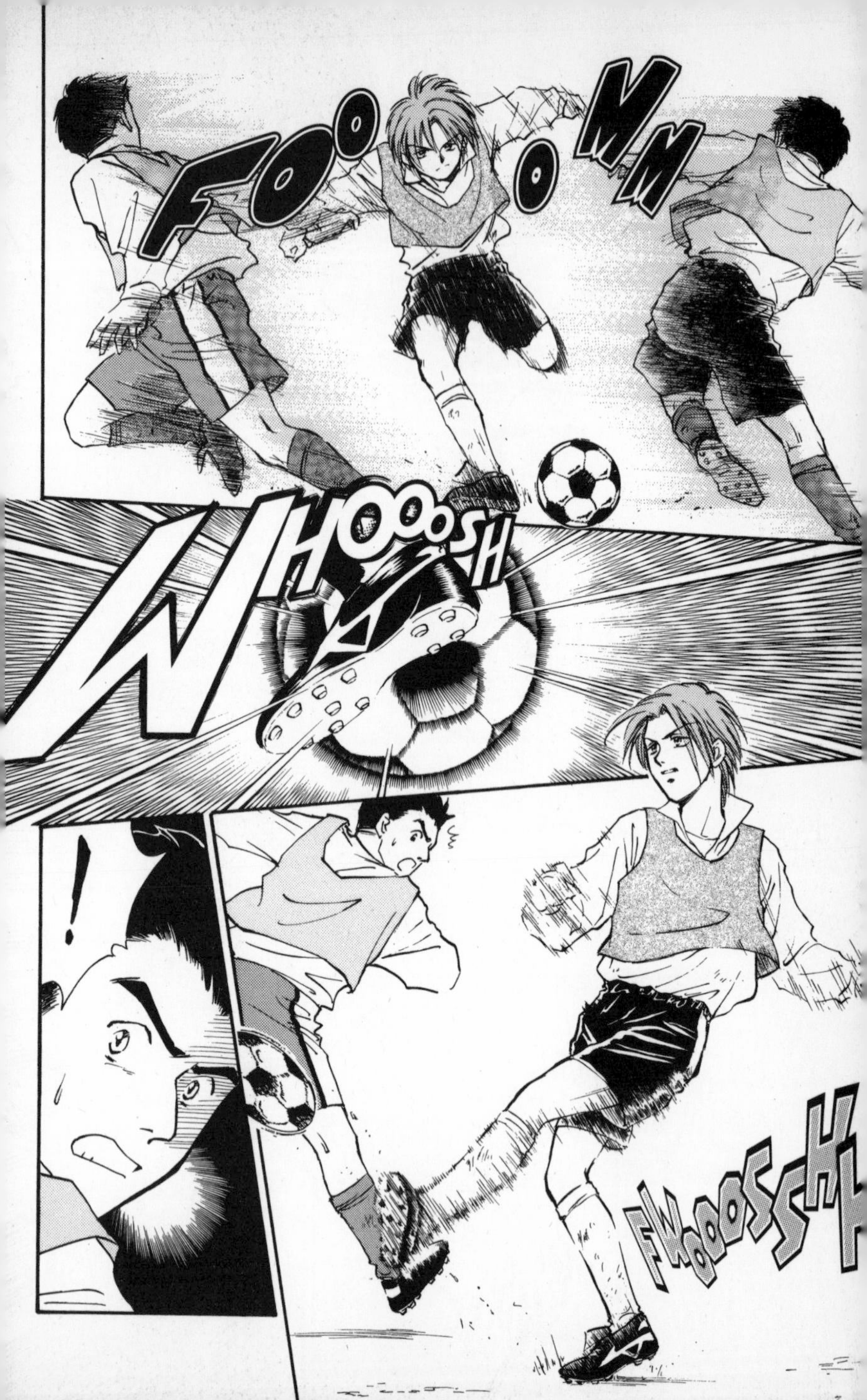
FOOOMM
WHOOOSH
FWOOOSH
!

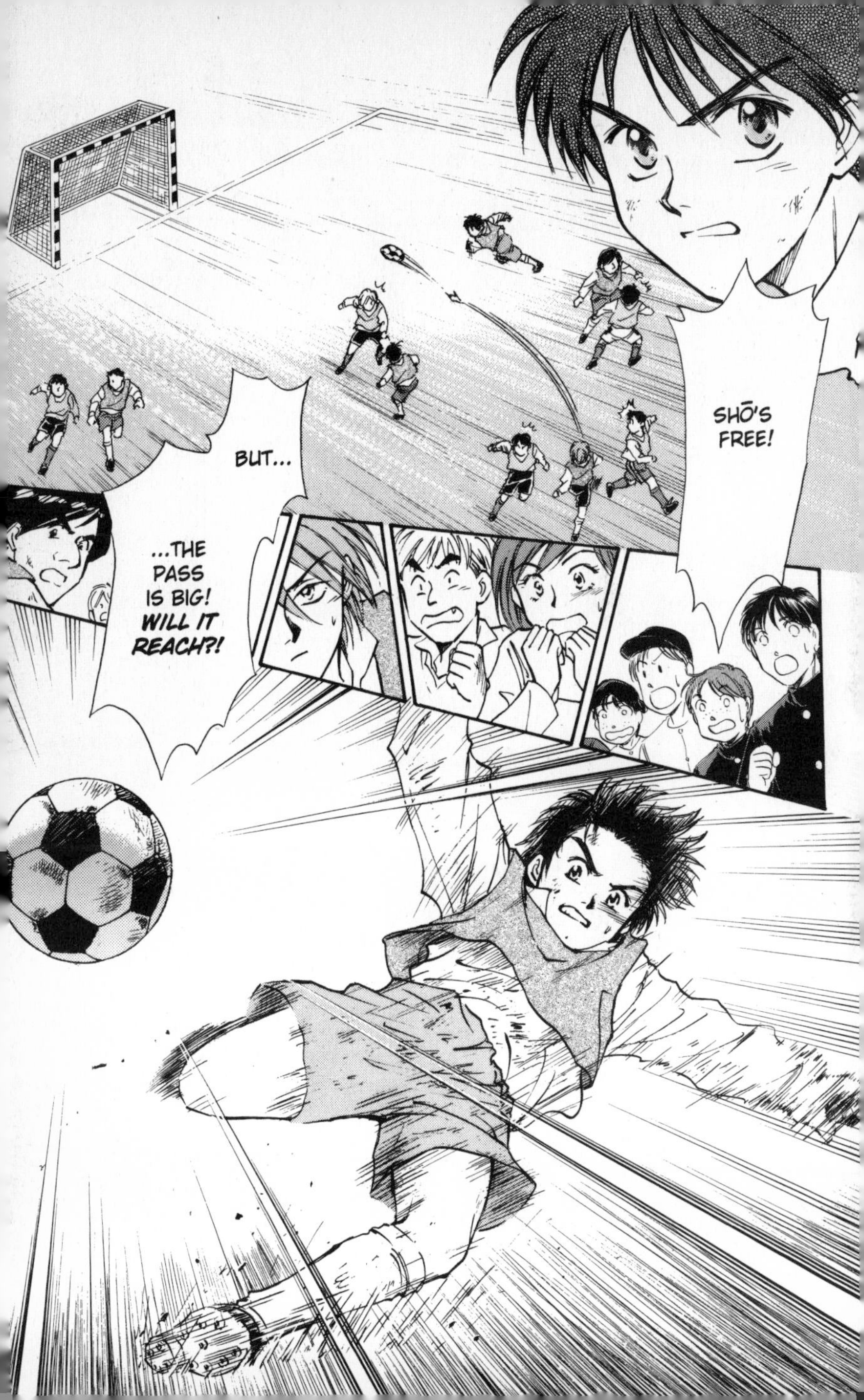
SHŌ'S FREE!
BUT...
...THE PASS IS BIG! *WILL IT REACH?!*

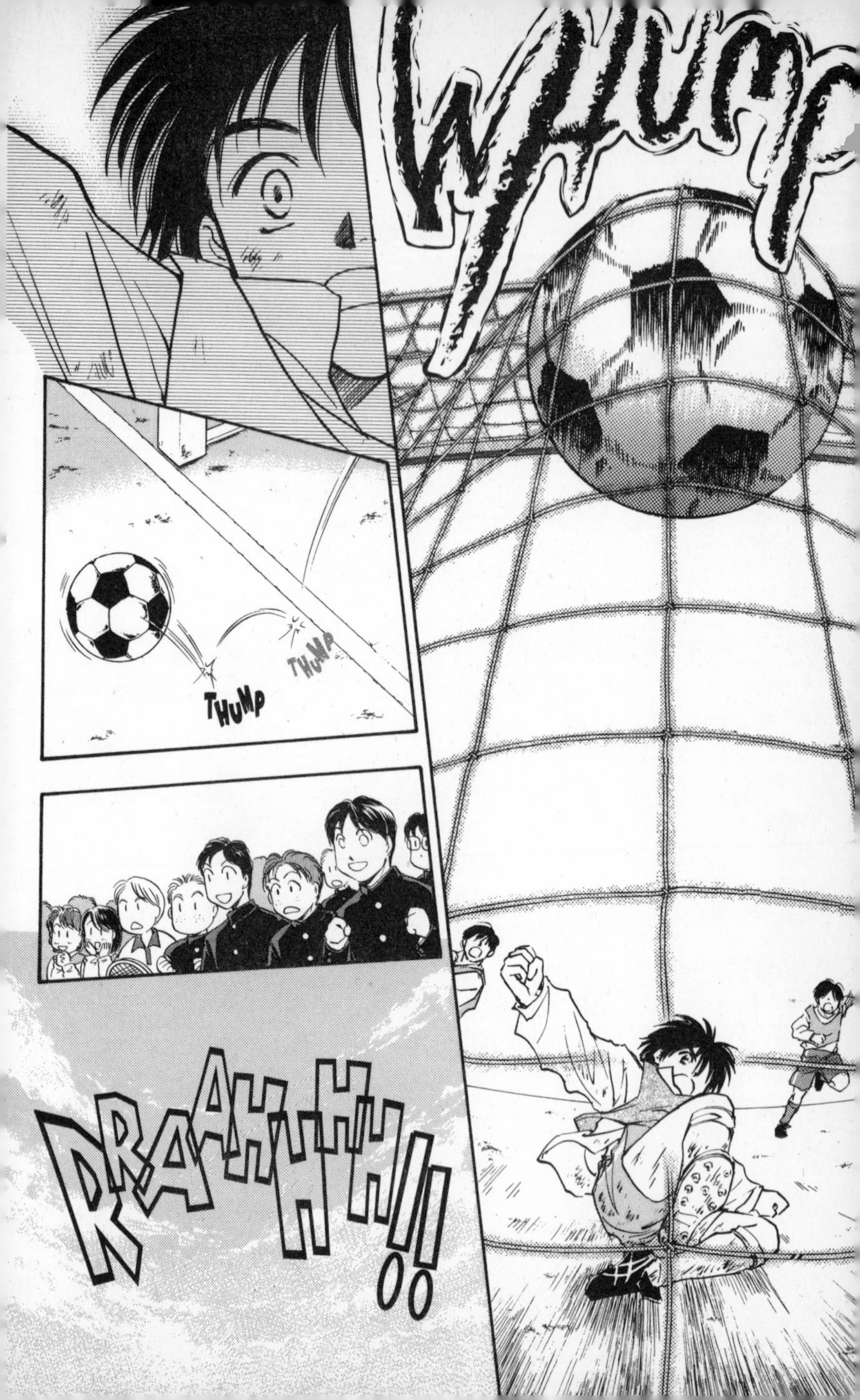
THUMP
THUMP
RAAHHHH!!

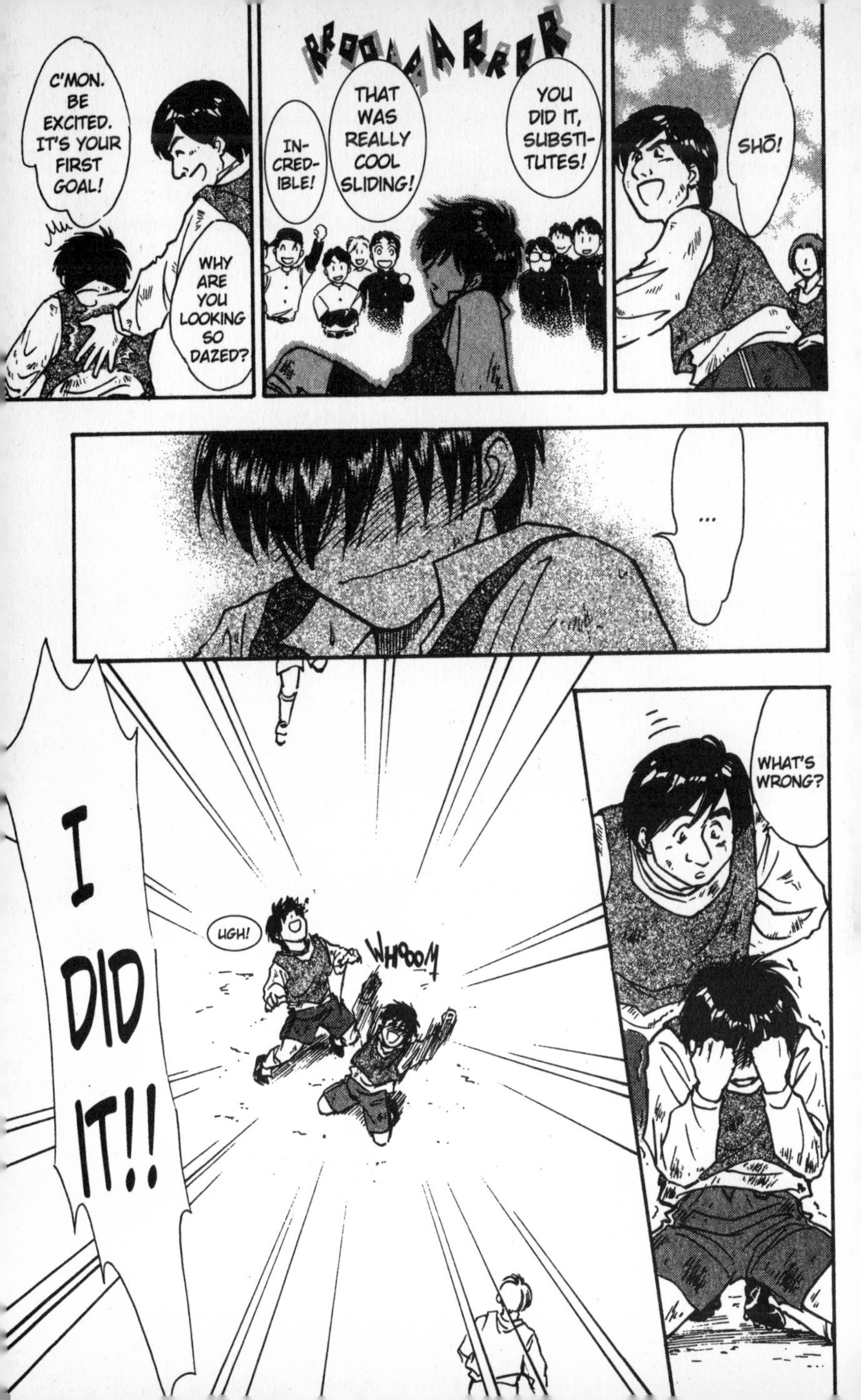
SHŌ!
RROOAARRRR
YOU DID IT, SUBSTITUTES!
THAT WAS REALLY COOL SLIDING!
IN-CREDIBLE!
C'MON. BE EXCITED. IT'S YOUR FIRST GOAL!
WHY ARE YOU LOOKING SO DAZED?
...
WHAT'S WRONG?
I DID IT!!
UGH!
WHOOM

●ROLE OF THE DEFENDERS ●

THE DEFENDER (DF) IS LITERALLY A PLAYER WHO DEFENDS. THE DF IS POSITIONED FURTHEST IN THE REAR, AND HIS/HER PRIMARY JOB IS TO DEFEND AGAINST THE OPPONENT'S OFFENSE.

TO DEFEND AGAINST THE FOREIGN PLAYERS, IT IS ESSENTIAL TO HAVE A LARGE-SIZED PLAYER WHO CAN HANDLE TOUGH COLLISIONS. BUT SOCCER NOWADAYS REQUIRES THE DF TO HAVE BOTH SPEED AND HEIGHT ON TOP OF IT.

BESIDES, EVEN THE DF CANNOT FOCUS ON DEFENSE ALONE. THE MOMENT THE BALL IS STOLEN FROM THE OPPONENT, THE OFFENSE STARTS. THAT MEANS A GOOD SENSE FOR PASSING WITH THE ABILITY TO PERFORM LONG-KICKS IS CRUCIAL.

IN ADDITION, THE PLAYERS POSITIONED ON BOTH SIDE-BACKS WILL BECOME THE STARTING POINT OF THE OFFENSE, AND AS THE OFFENSE DRIVES THE BALL FORWARD, THE PLAYER MUST ACCURATELY DO THE CENTERING. AND OF COURSE, HE/SHE MUST BE ABLE TO SHOOT.

ANOTHER ROLE OF THE DF IS TO ACHIEVE HEADSHOTS, USING HIS/HER HEIGHT, ESPECIALLY DURING A SET-PLAY SUCH AS A CORNER-KICK, AFTER POSITIONING HIMSELF/HERSELF IN FRONT OF THE GOAL.

--TATSUYA WATANABE (*WINNING RUN*)

SKKSSH

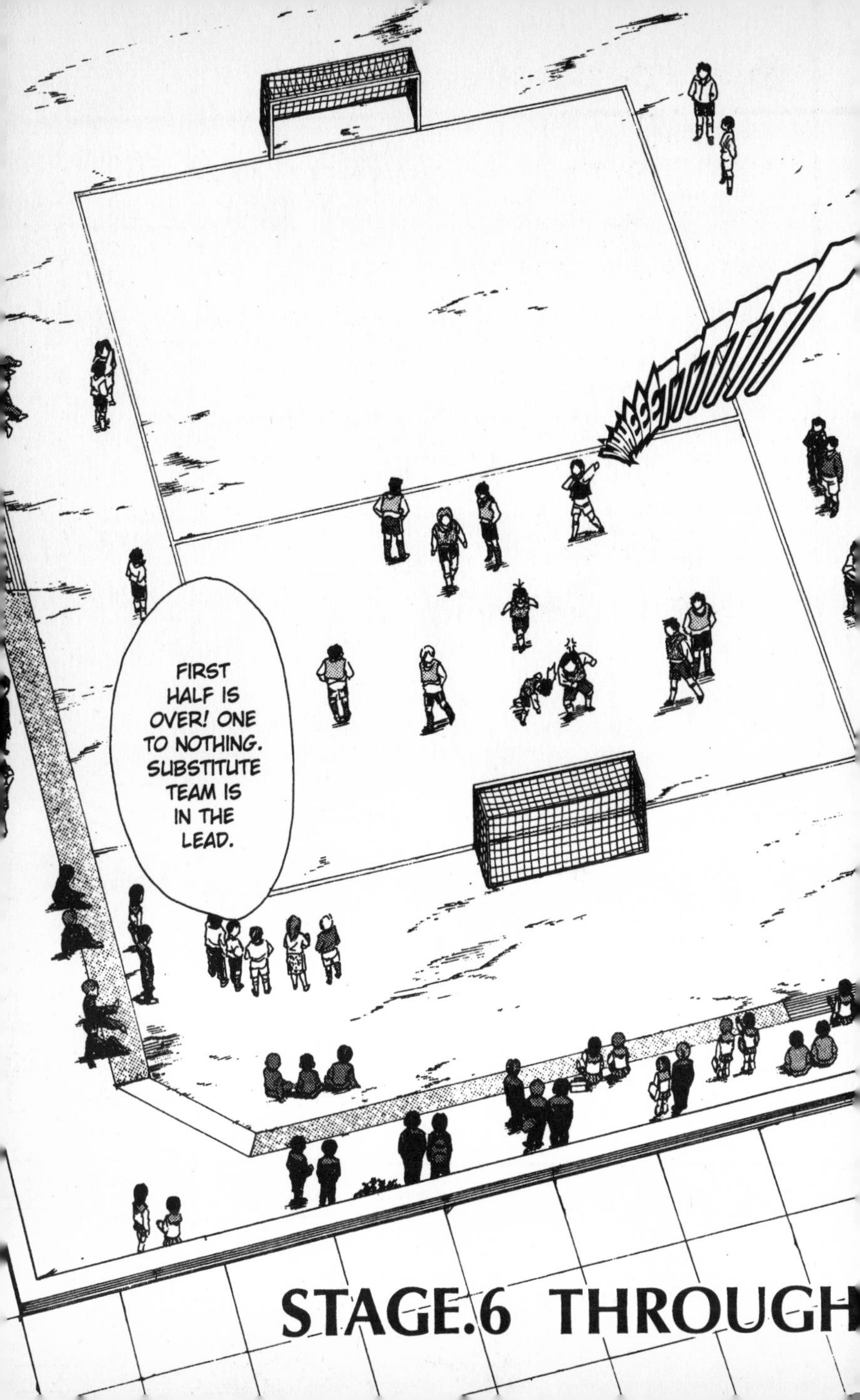
FIRST HALF IS OVER! ONE TO NOTHING. SUBSTITUTE TEAM IS IN THE LEAD.

STAGE.6 THROUGH

READ THIS WAY

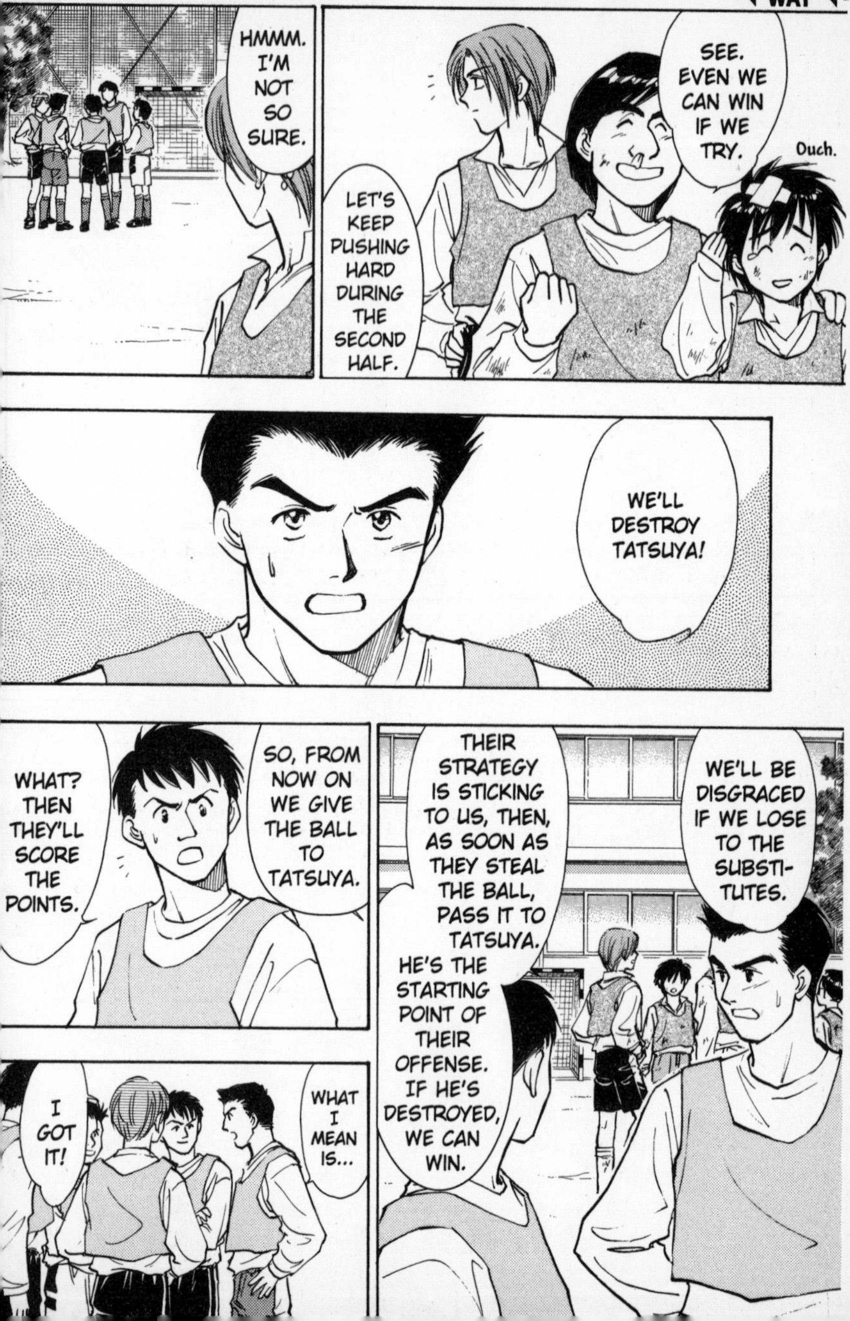
SEE. EVEN WE CAN WIN IF WE TRY.
Ouch.
LET'S KEEP PUSHING HARD DURING THE SECOND HALF.
HMMM. I'M NOT SO SURE.
WE'LL DESTROY TATSUYA!
WE'LL BE DISGRACED IF WE LOSE TO THE SUBSTI-TUTES.
THEIR STRATEGY IS STICKING TO US, THEN, AS SOON AS THEY STEAL THE BALL, PASS IT TO TATSUYA.
HE'S THE STARTING POINT OF THEIR OFFENSE. IF HE'S DESTROYED, WE CAN WIN.
SO, FROM NOW ON WE GIVE THE BALL TO TATSUYA.
WHAT? THEN THEY'LL SCORE THE POINTS.
WHAT I MEAN IS...
I GOT IT!

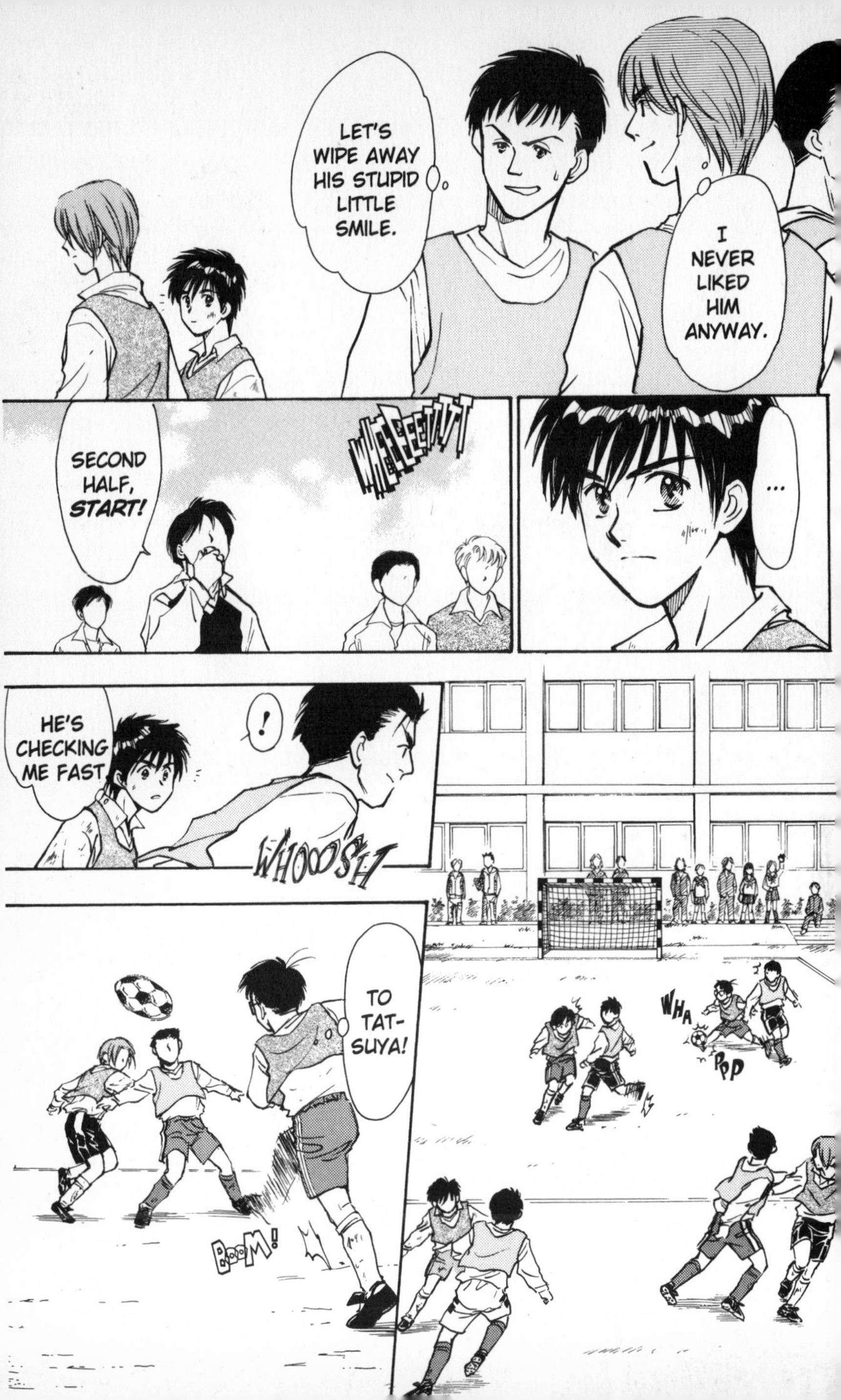
I NEVER LIKED HIM ANYWAY.
LET'S WIPE AWAY HIS STUPID LITTLE SMILE.
...
WHEEEETTTT
SECOND HALF, START!
!
HE'S CHECKING ME FAST
WHOOOSH
WHAPPP
TO TAT-SUYA!
BOOOM!

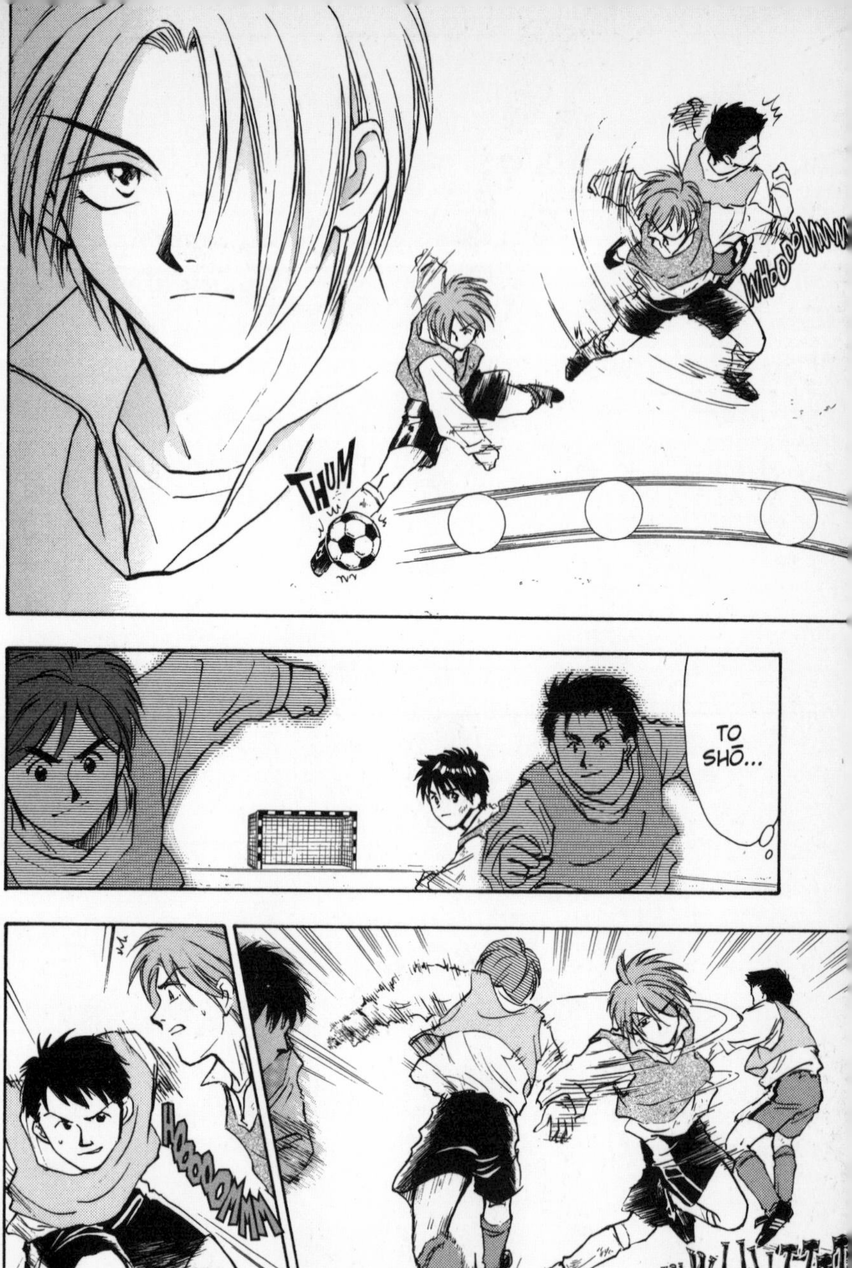
WHOOOMMM
THUM
TO SHŌ...
FWIIIITTTT
HOOOOOMMM

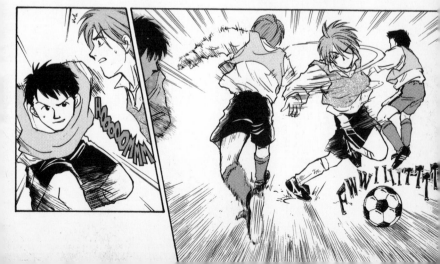

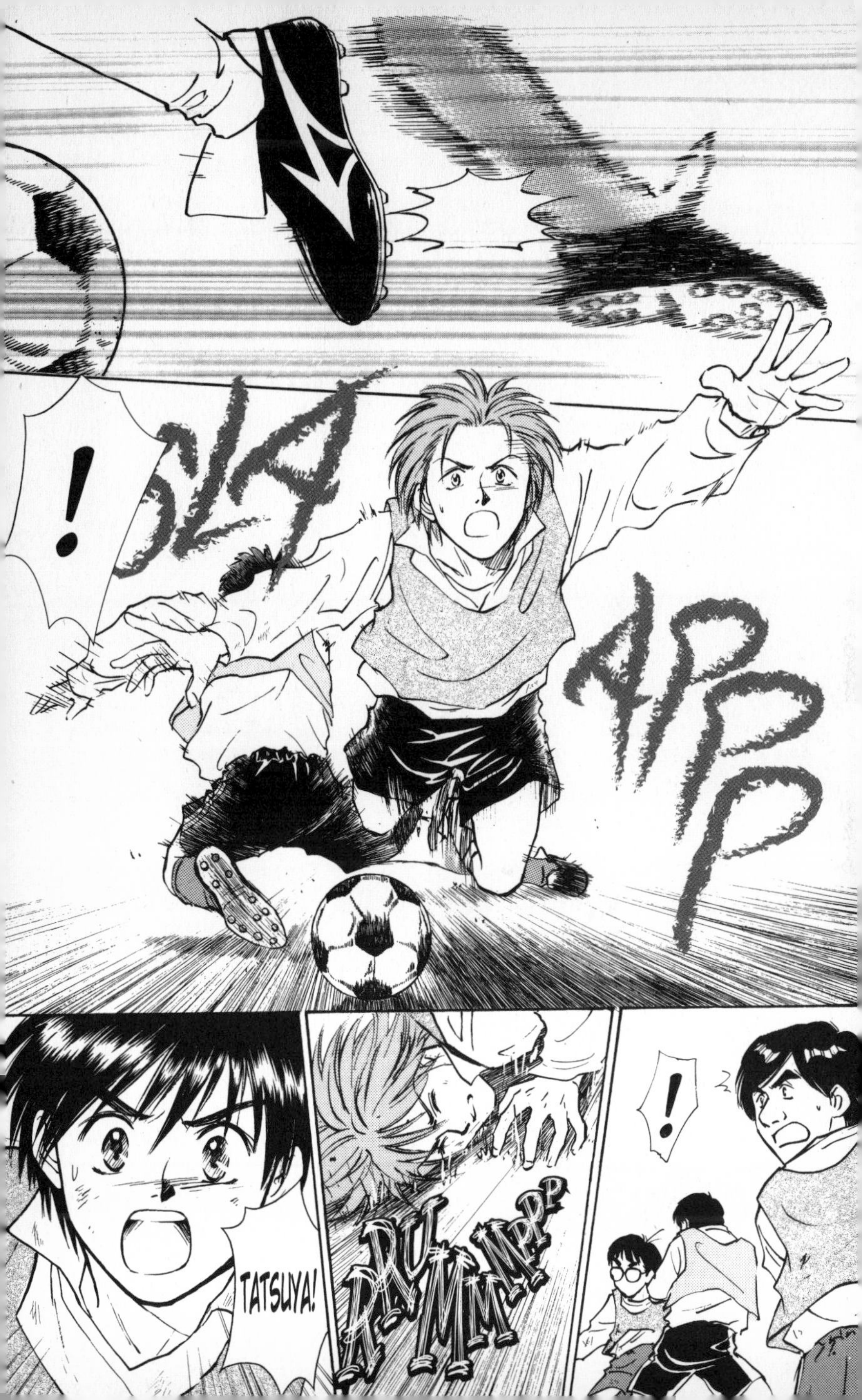
!
!
TATSUYA!

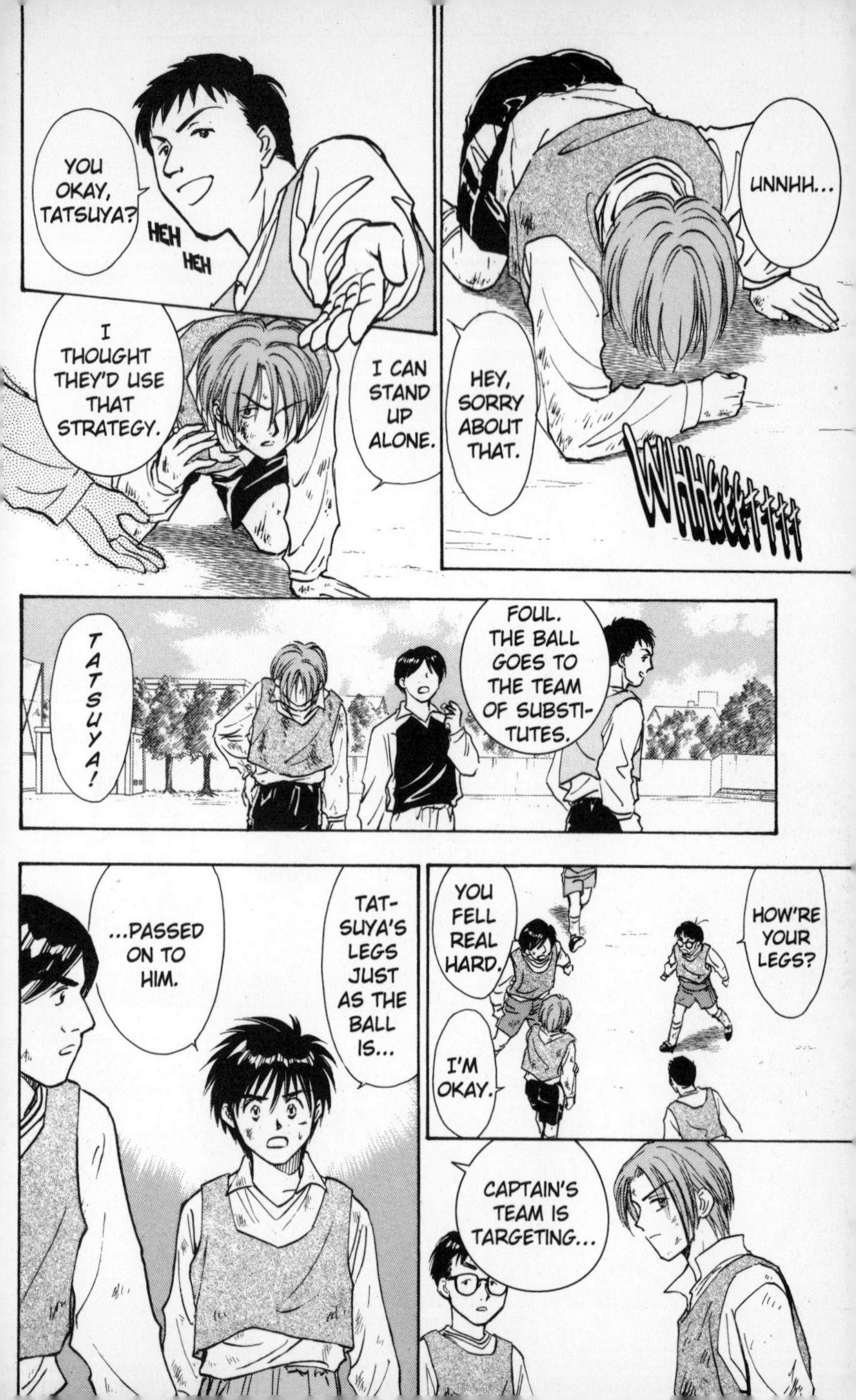
UNNHH...
HEY, SORRY ABOUT THAT.
YOU OKAY, TATSUYA?
HEH HEH
I CAN STAND UP ALONE.
I THOUGHT THEY'D USE THAT STRATEGY.
FOUL. THE BALL GOES TO THE TEAM OF SUBSTITUTES.
TATSUYA!
HOW'RE YOUR LEGS?
YOU FELL REAL HARD.
I'M OKAY.
CAPTAIN'S TEAM IS TARGETING...
TATSUYA'S LEGS JUST AS THE BALL IS...
...PASSED ON TO HIM.

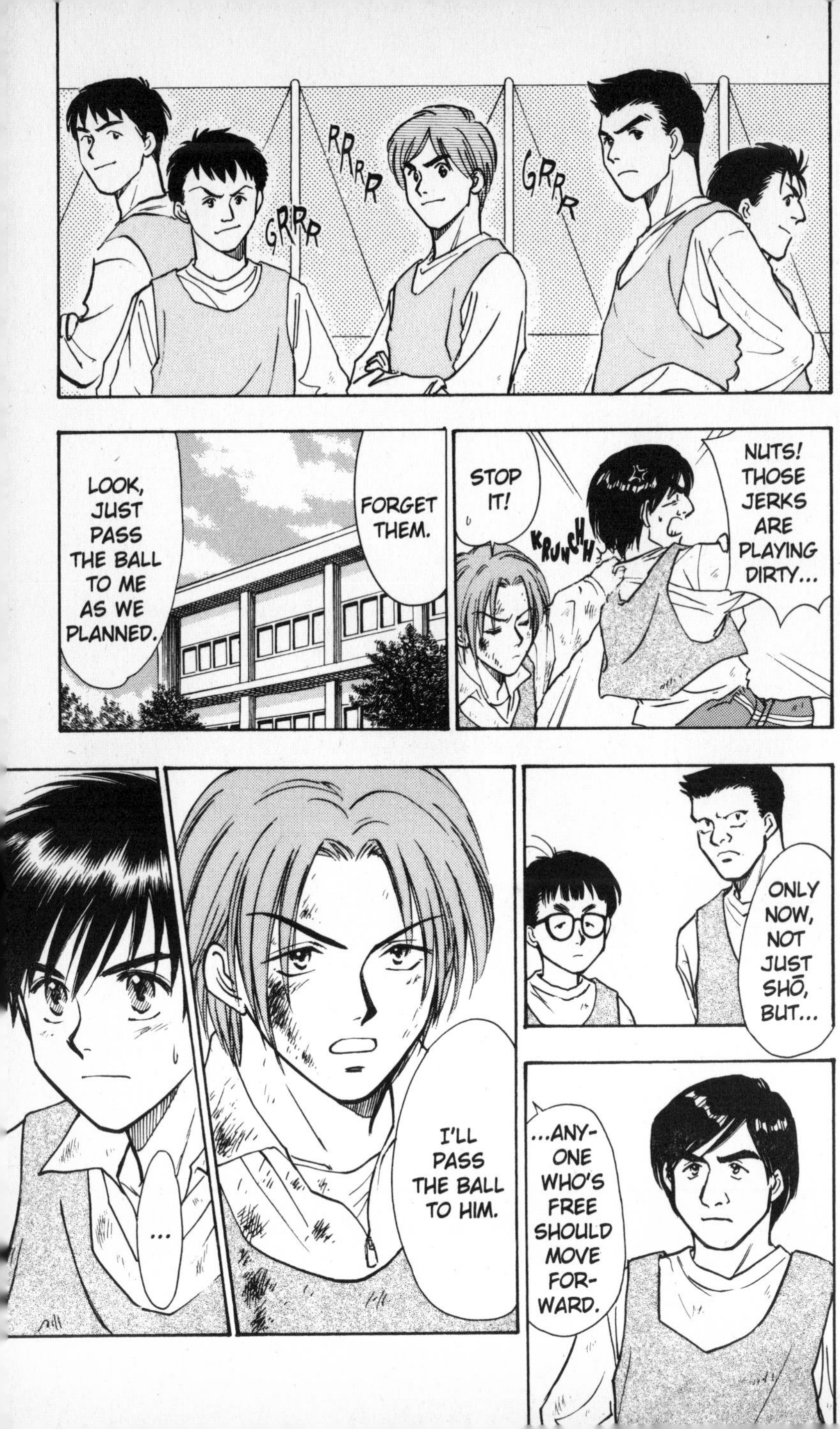
GRRR
RRRRR
GRRRR
NUTS! THOSE JERKS ARE PLAYING DIRTY...
KRUNCHH
STOP IT!
FORGET THEM.
LOOK, JUST PASS THE BALL TO ME AS WE PLANNED.
ONLY NOW, NOT JUST SHŌ, BUT...
...ANYONE WHO'S FREE SHOULD MOVE FORWARD.
I'LL PASS THE BALL TO HIM.
...

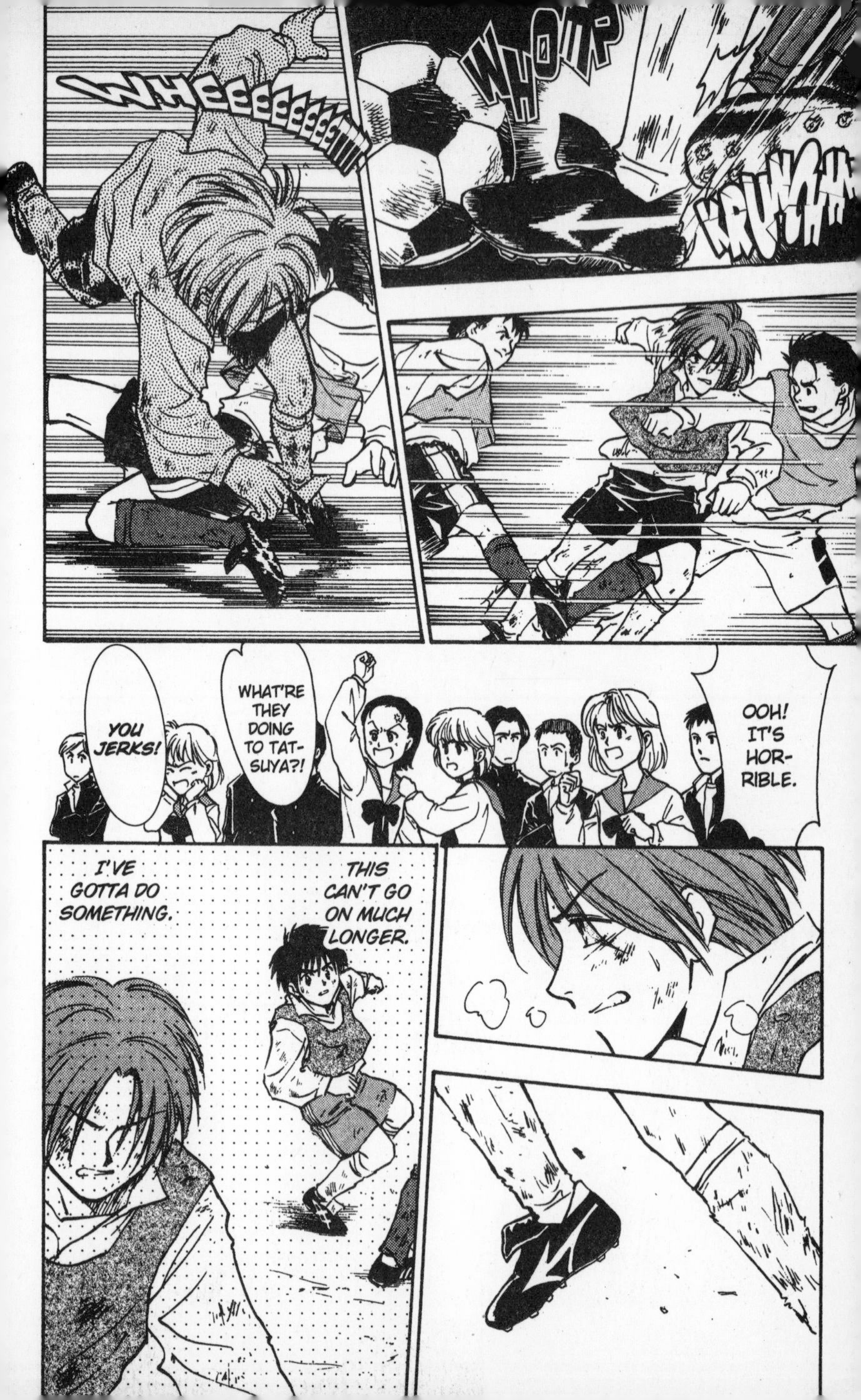
WHOOTP
KRUNCH
WHEEEEEEEEEEE
OOH! IT'S HORRIBLE.
WHAT'RE THEY DOING TO TATSUYA?!
YOU JERKS!
THIS CAN'T GO ON MUCH LONGER.
I'VE GOTTA DO SOMETHING.

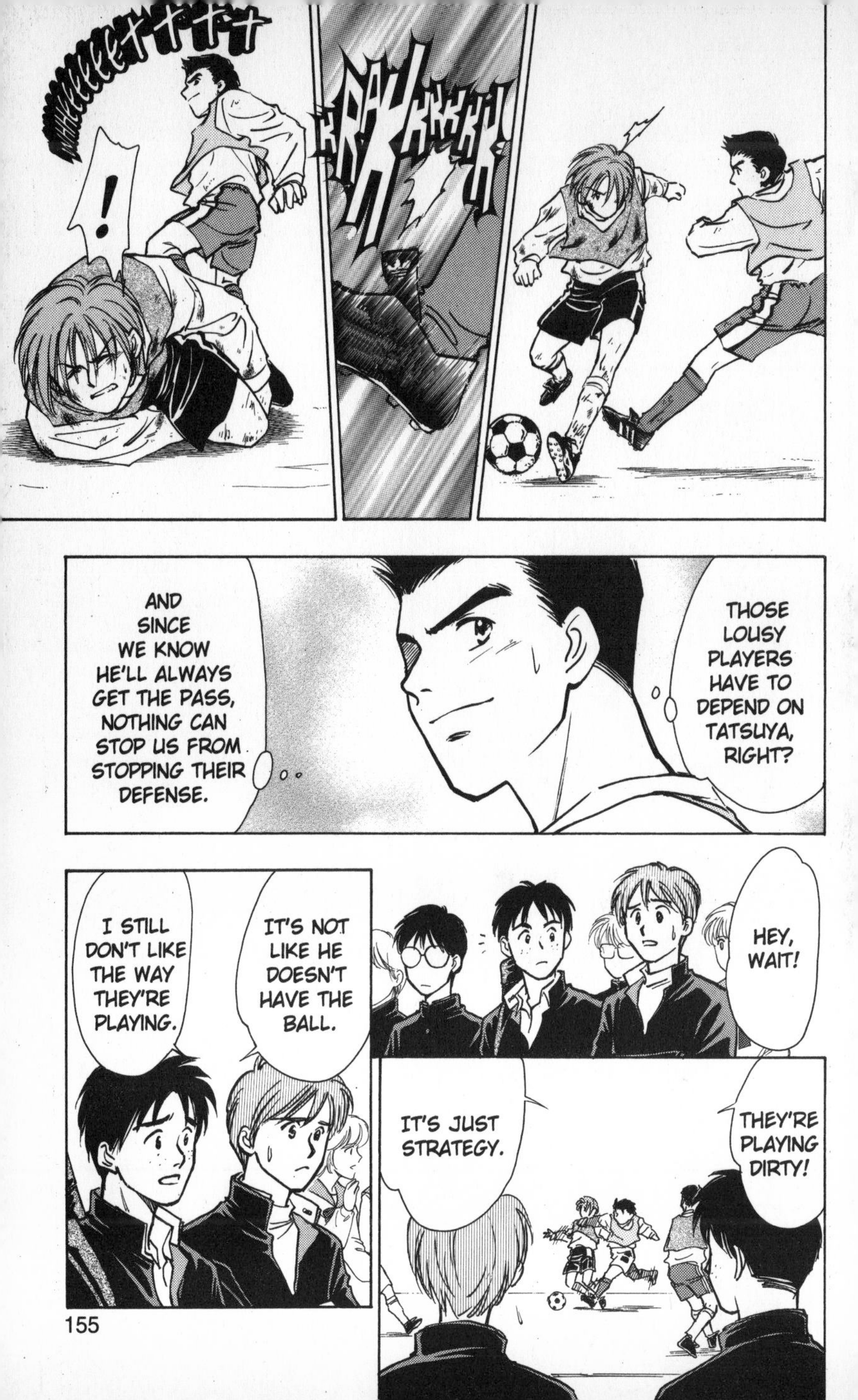
!
THOSE LOUSY PLAYERS HAVE TO DEPEND ON TATSUYA, RIGHT?
AND SINCE WE KNOW HE'LL ALWAYS GET THE PASS, NOTHING CAN STOP US FROM STOPPING THEIR DEFENSE.
HEY, WAIT!
THEY'RE PLAYING DIRTY!
IT'S JUST STRATEGY.
IT'S NOT LIKE HE DOESN'T HAVE THE BALL.
I STILL DON'T LIKE THE WAY THEY'RE PLAYING.

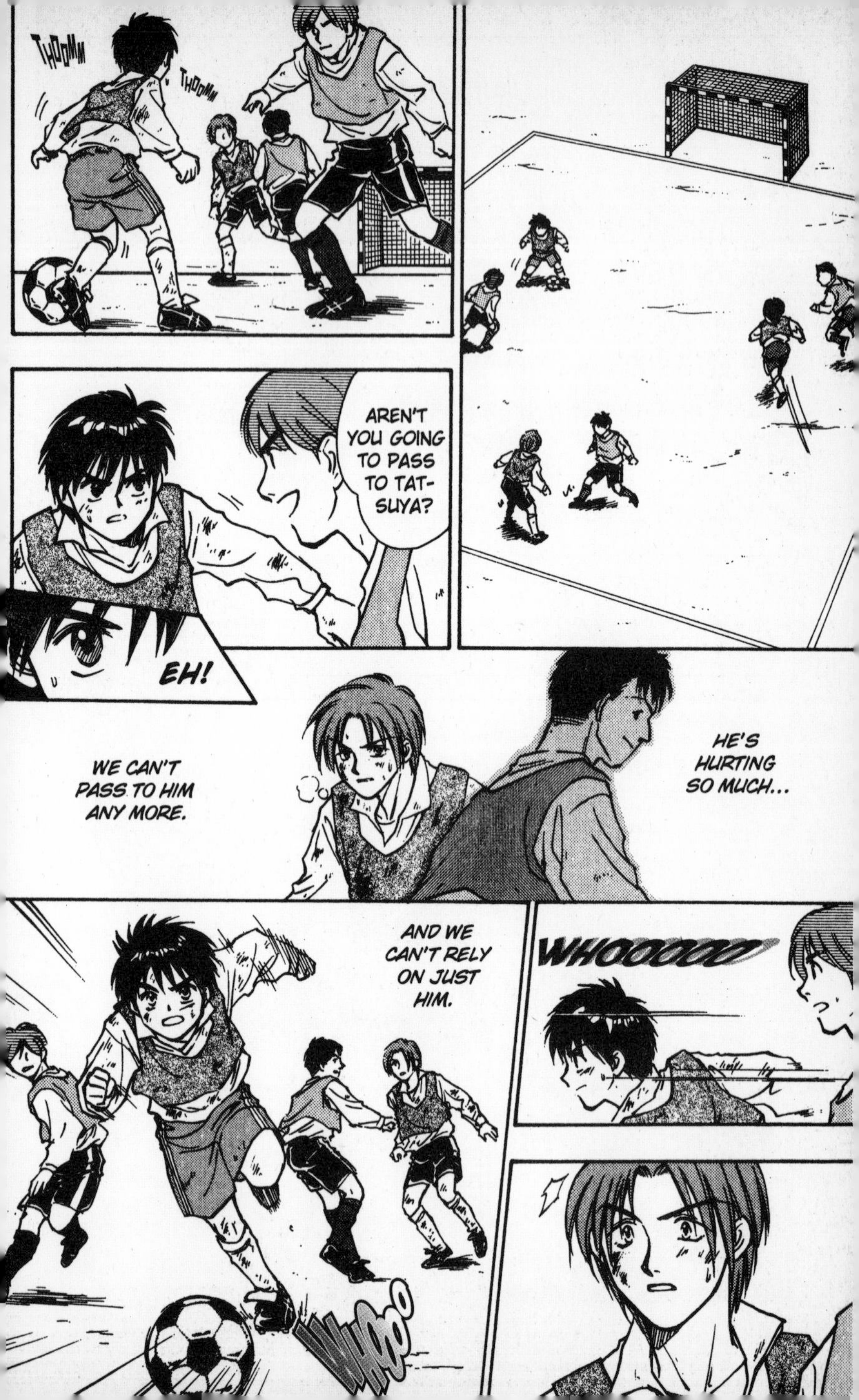

THOOMM
THOOMM
AREN'T YOU GOING TO PASS TO TAT-SUYA?
EH!
HE'S HURTING SO MUCH...
WE CAN'T PASS TO HIM ANY MORE.
WHOOOOOO
AND WE CAN'T RELY ON JUST HIM.

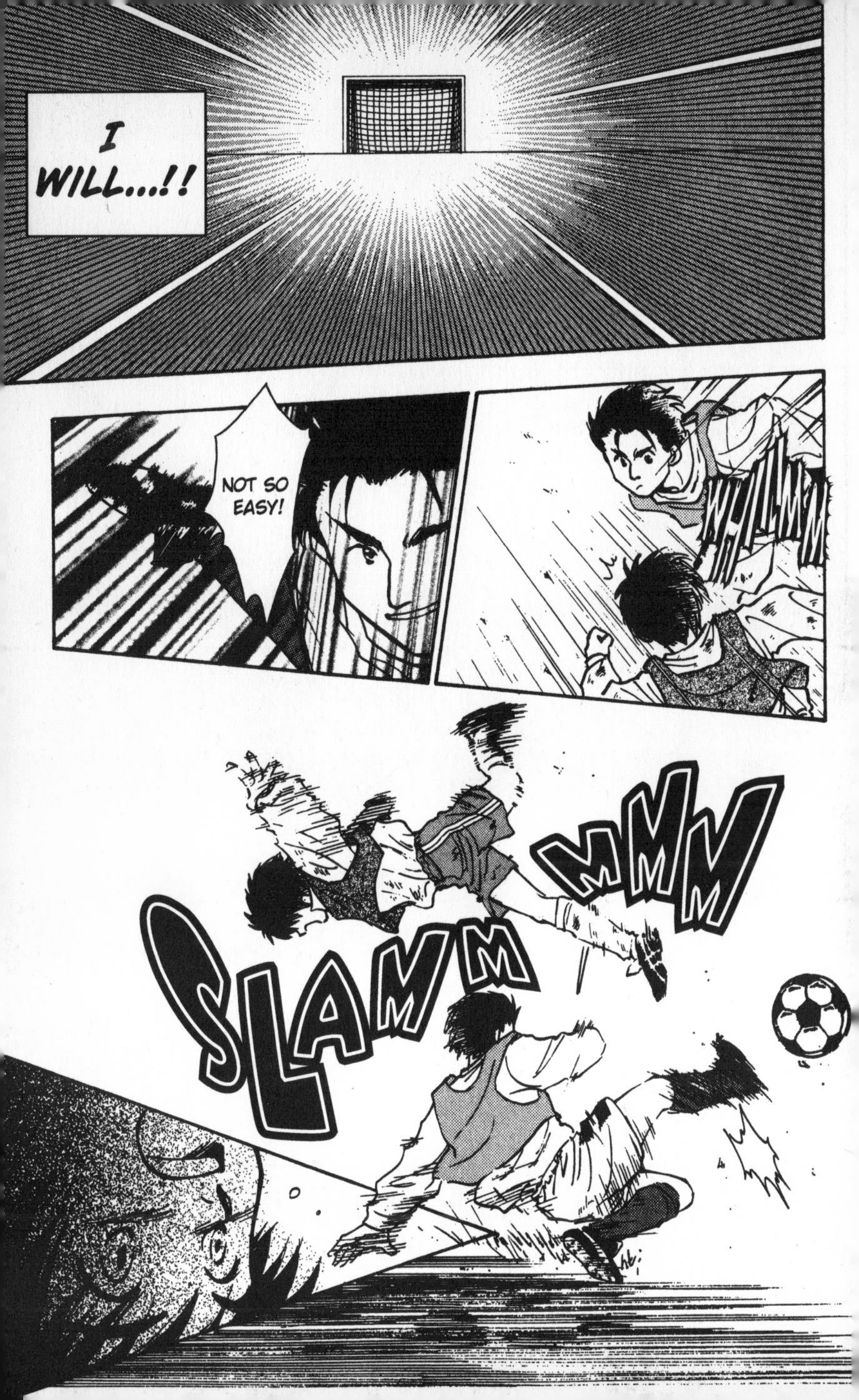

I WILL...!!
NOT SO EASY!
WHAMMM
SLAMM
MMM

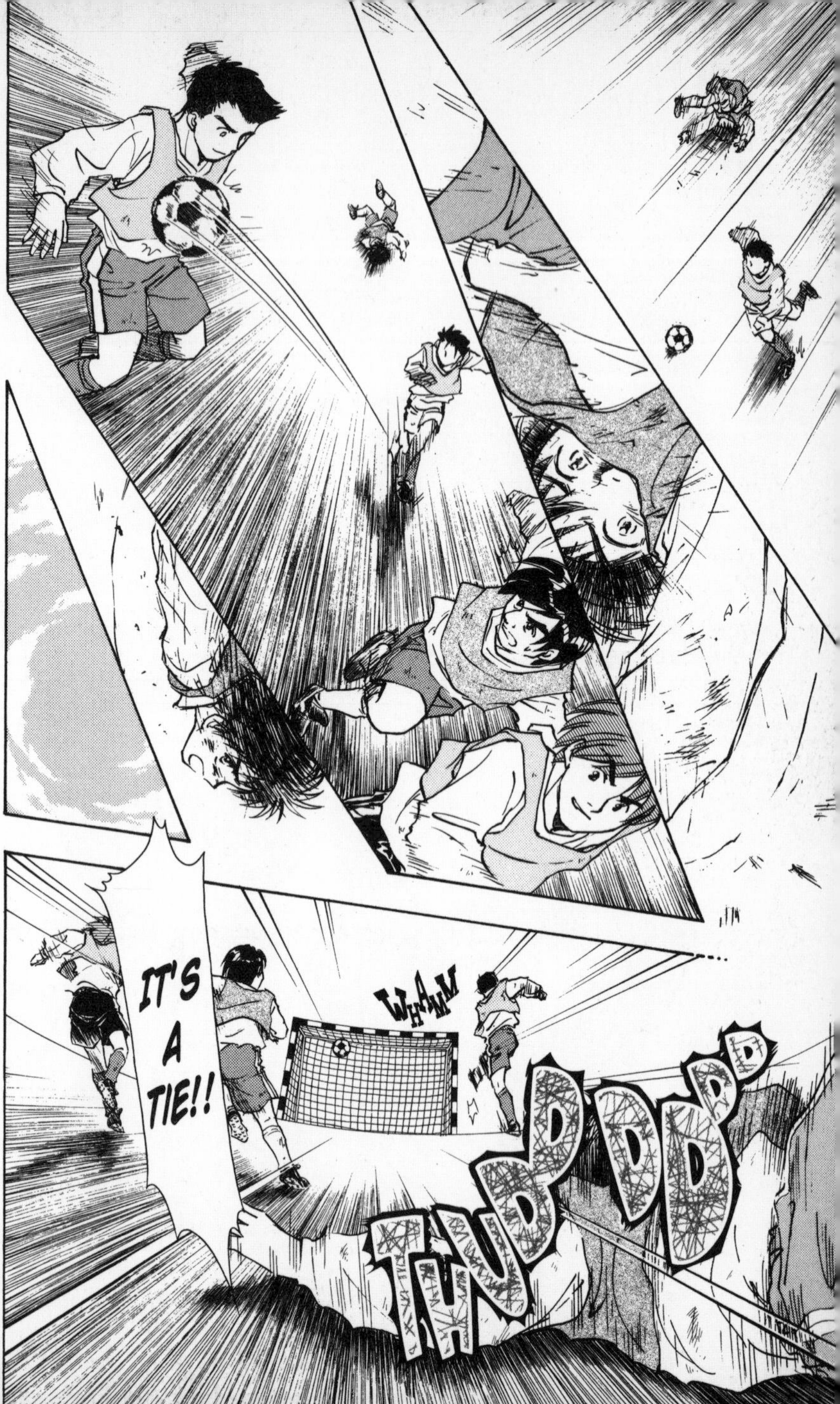
WHAMM
IT'S A TIE!!
THUD DDD

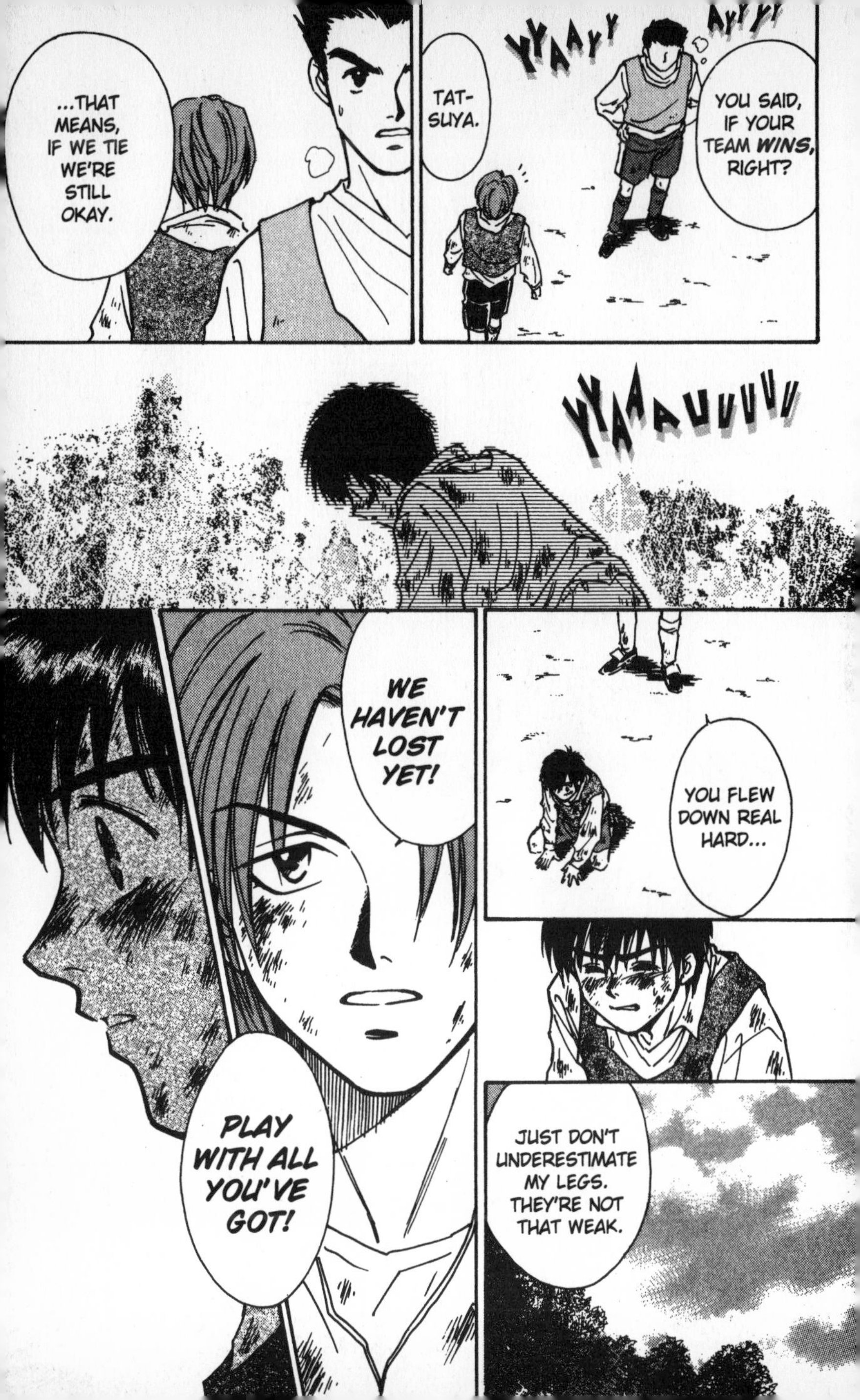
YYAAYY AYYYY
YOU SAID, IF YOUR TEAM WINS, RIGHT?
TAT-SUYA.
...THAT MEANS, IF WE TIE WE'RE STILL OKAY.
YYAAAUUUUU
YOU FLEW DOWN REAL HARD...
JUST DON'T UNDERESTIMATE MY LEGS. THEY'RE NOT THAT WEAK.
WE HAVEN'T LOST YET!
PLAY WITH ALL YOU'VE GOT!

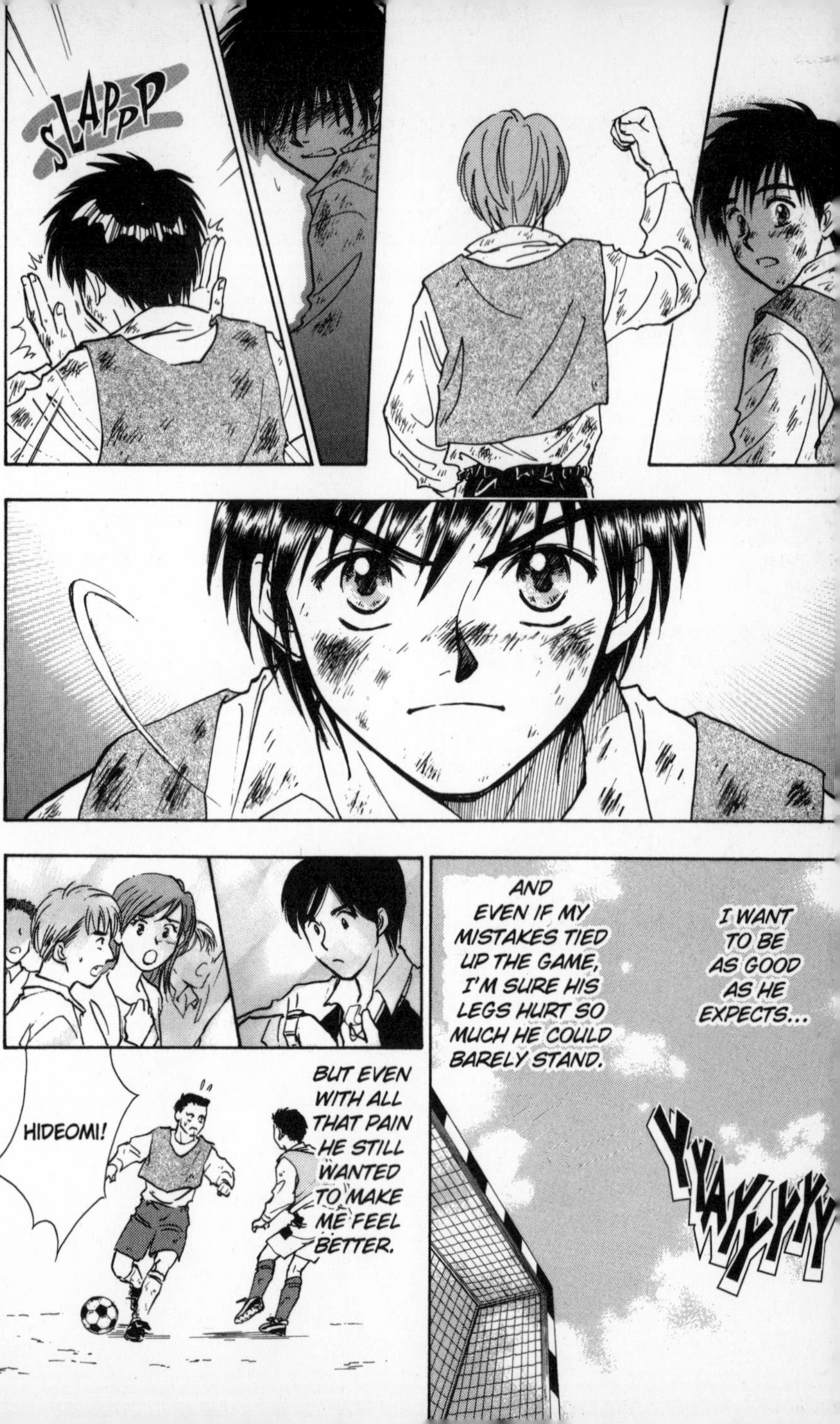
SLAPPP
I WANT TO BE AS GOOD AS HE EXPECTS...
AND EVEN IF MY MISTAKES TIED UP THE GAME, I'M SURE HIS LEGS HURT SO MUCH HE COULD BARELY STAND.
YYAYYYY
BUT EVEN WITH ALL THAT PAIN HE STILL WANTED TO MAKE ME FEEL BETTER.
HIDEOMI!

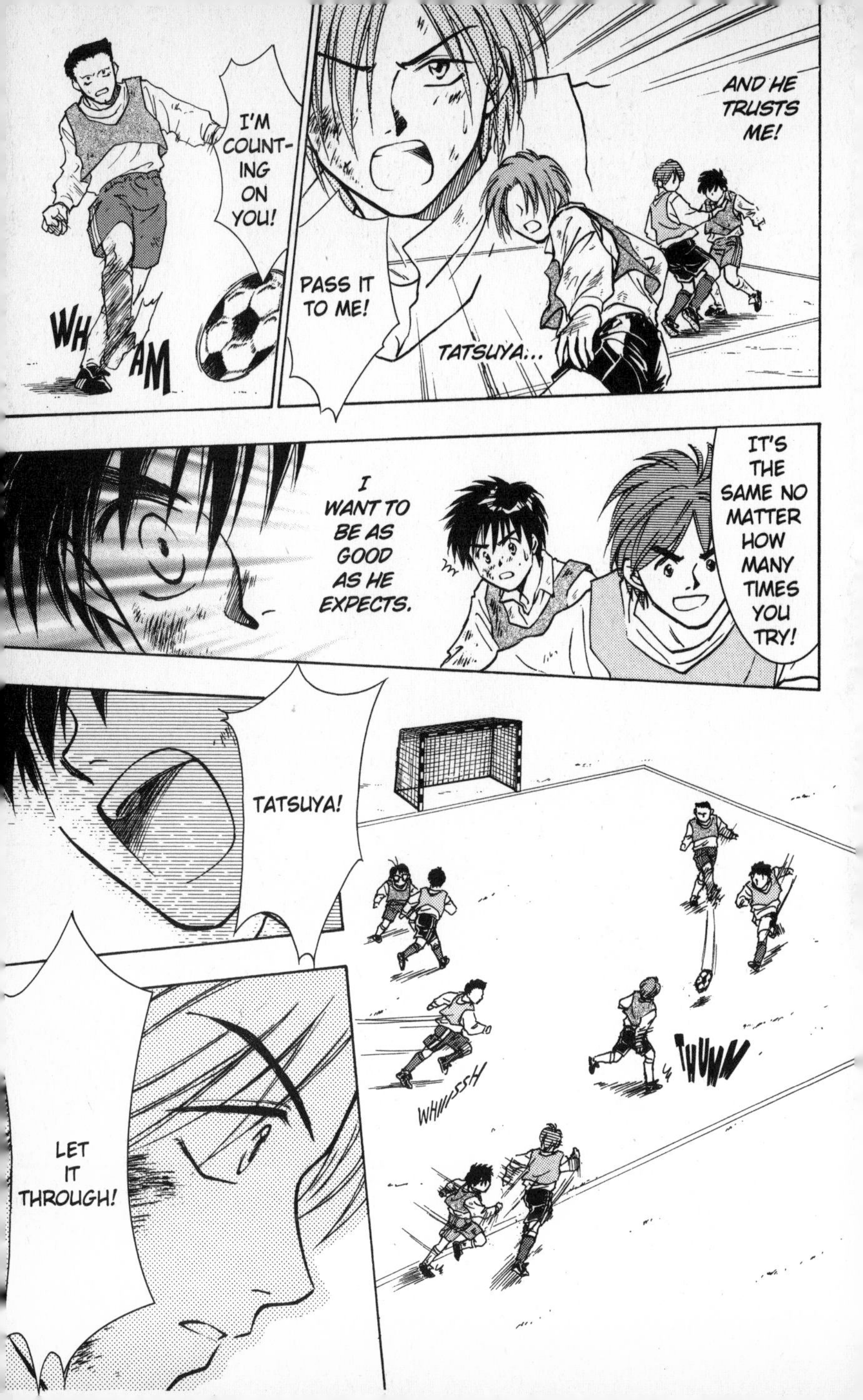
AND HE TRUSTS ME!
PASS IT TO ME!
TATSUYA...
I'M COUNTING ON YOU!
WHAM
IT'S THE SAME NO MATTER HOW MANY TIMES YOU TRY!
I WANT TO BE AS GOOD AS HE EXPECTS.
THUMM
WHIIISSH
TATSUYA!
LET IT THROUGH!

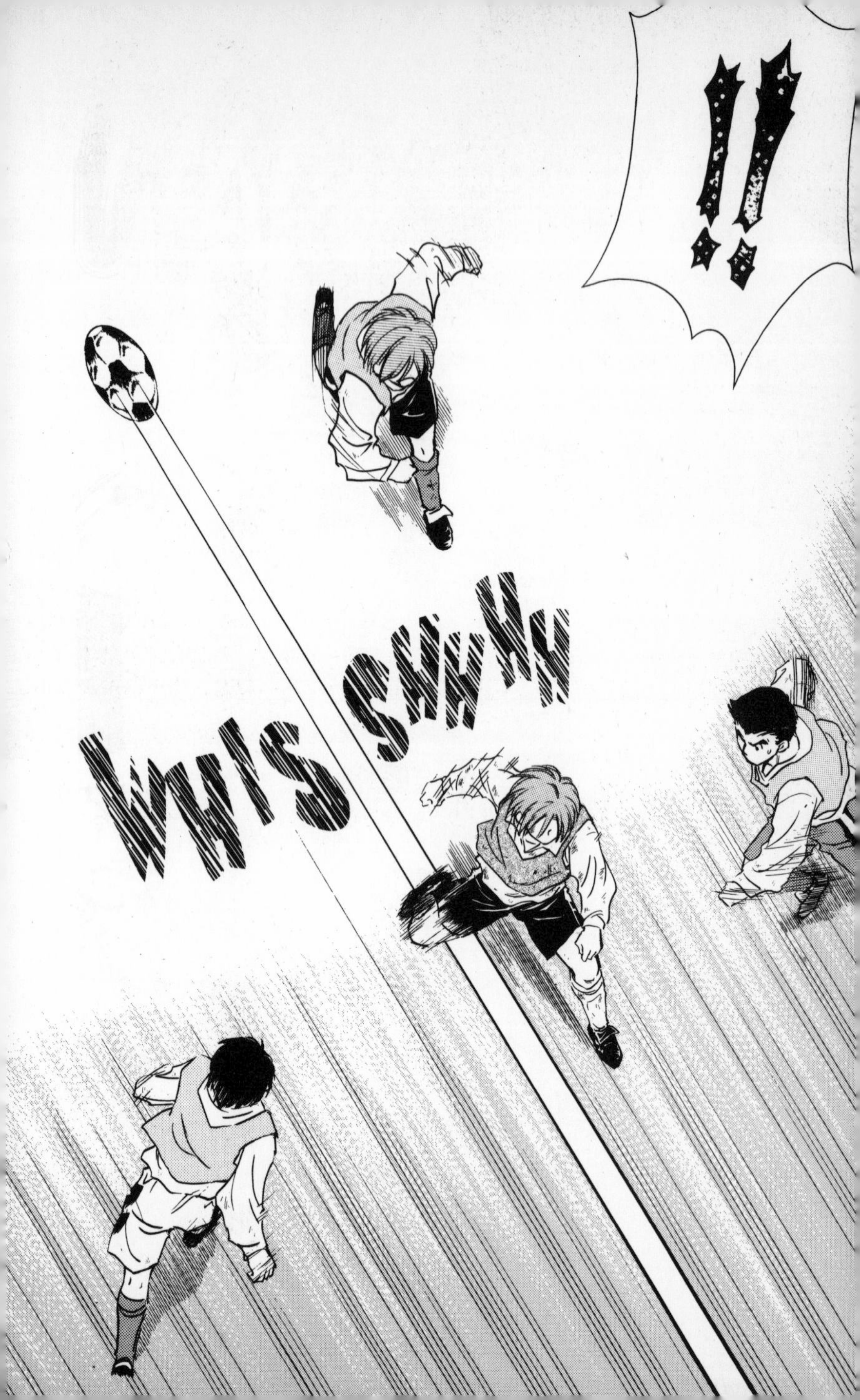
!!
WHISSHHH

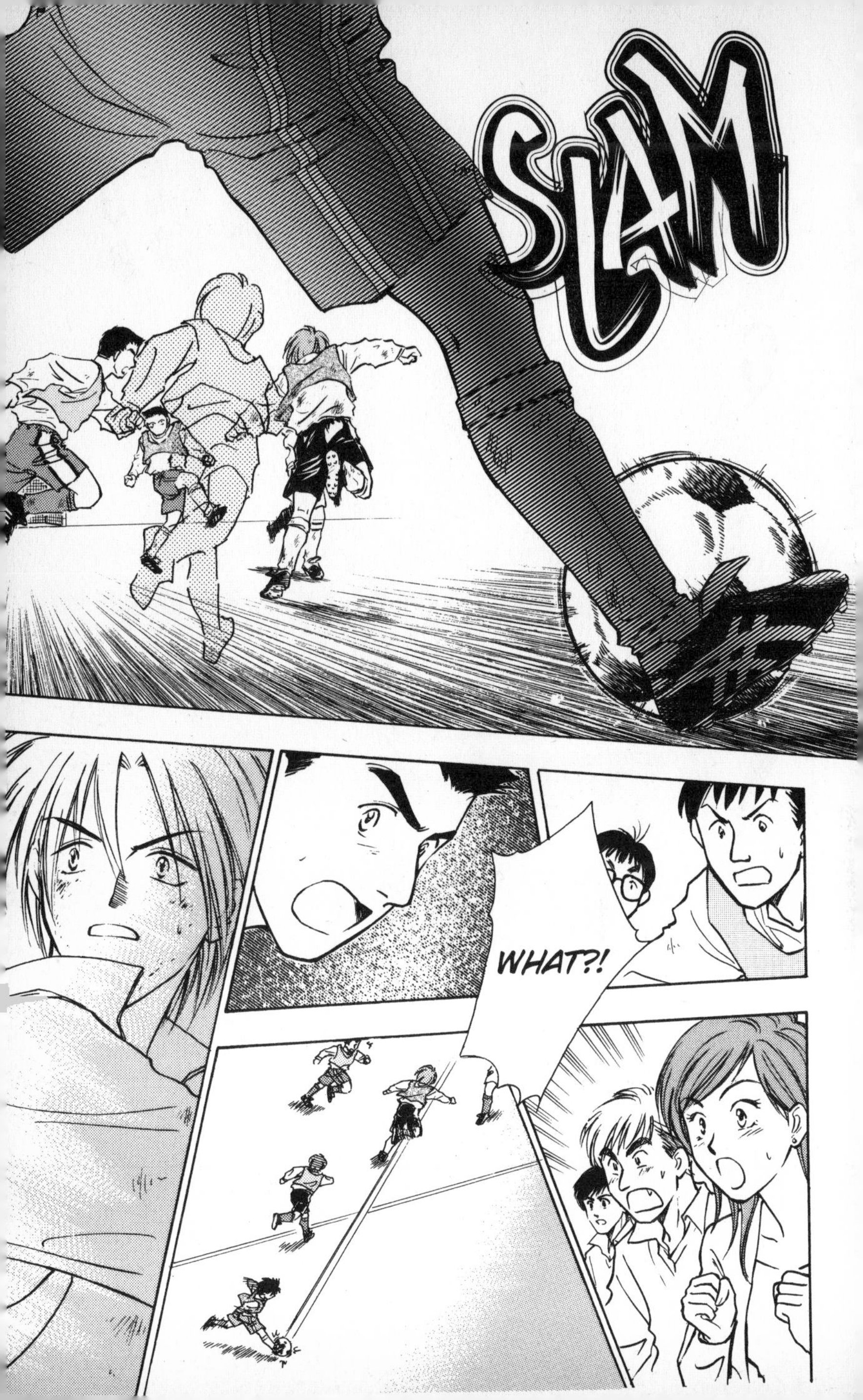
SLAM
WHAT?!

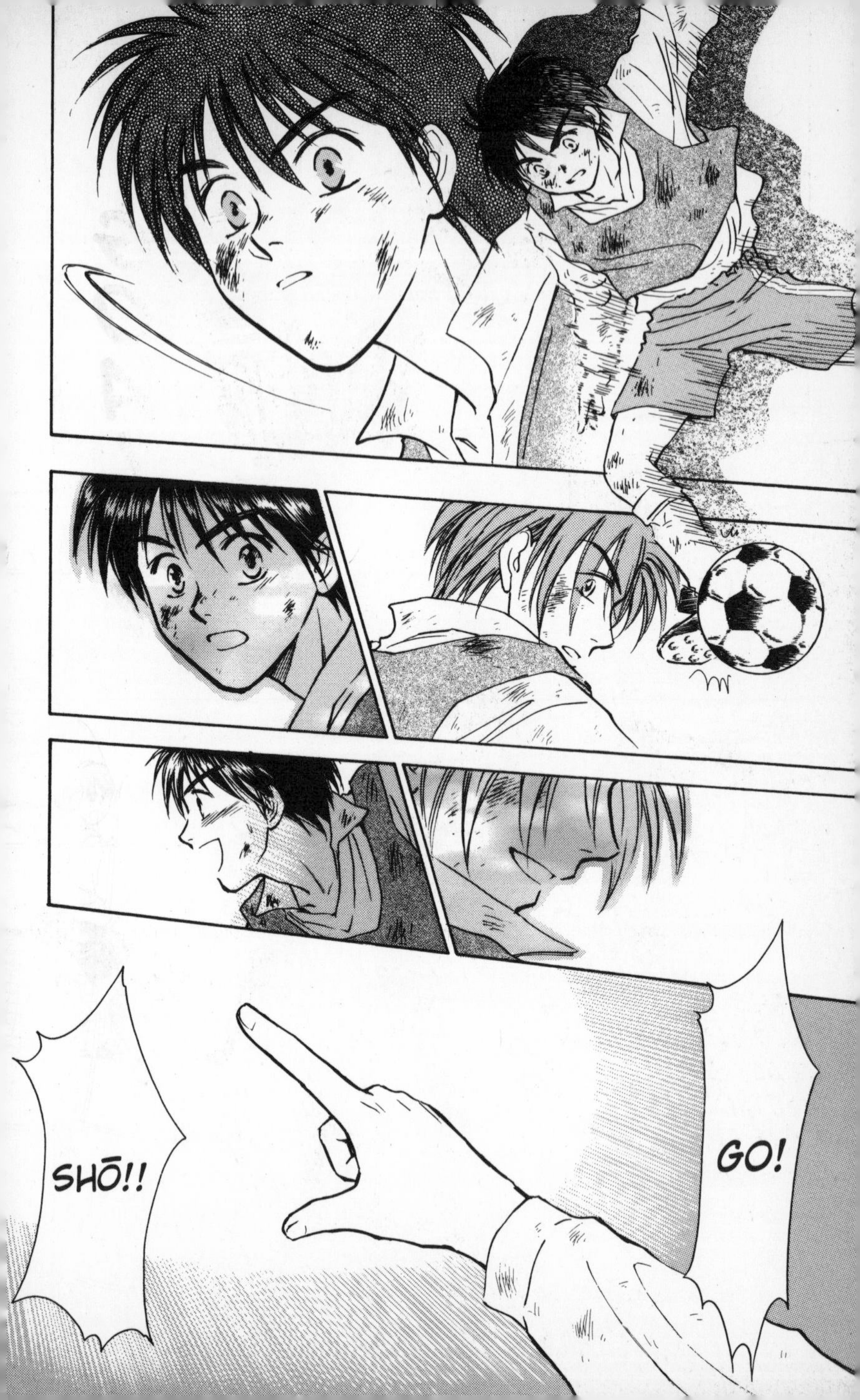
GO!
SHŌ!!

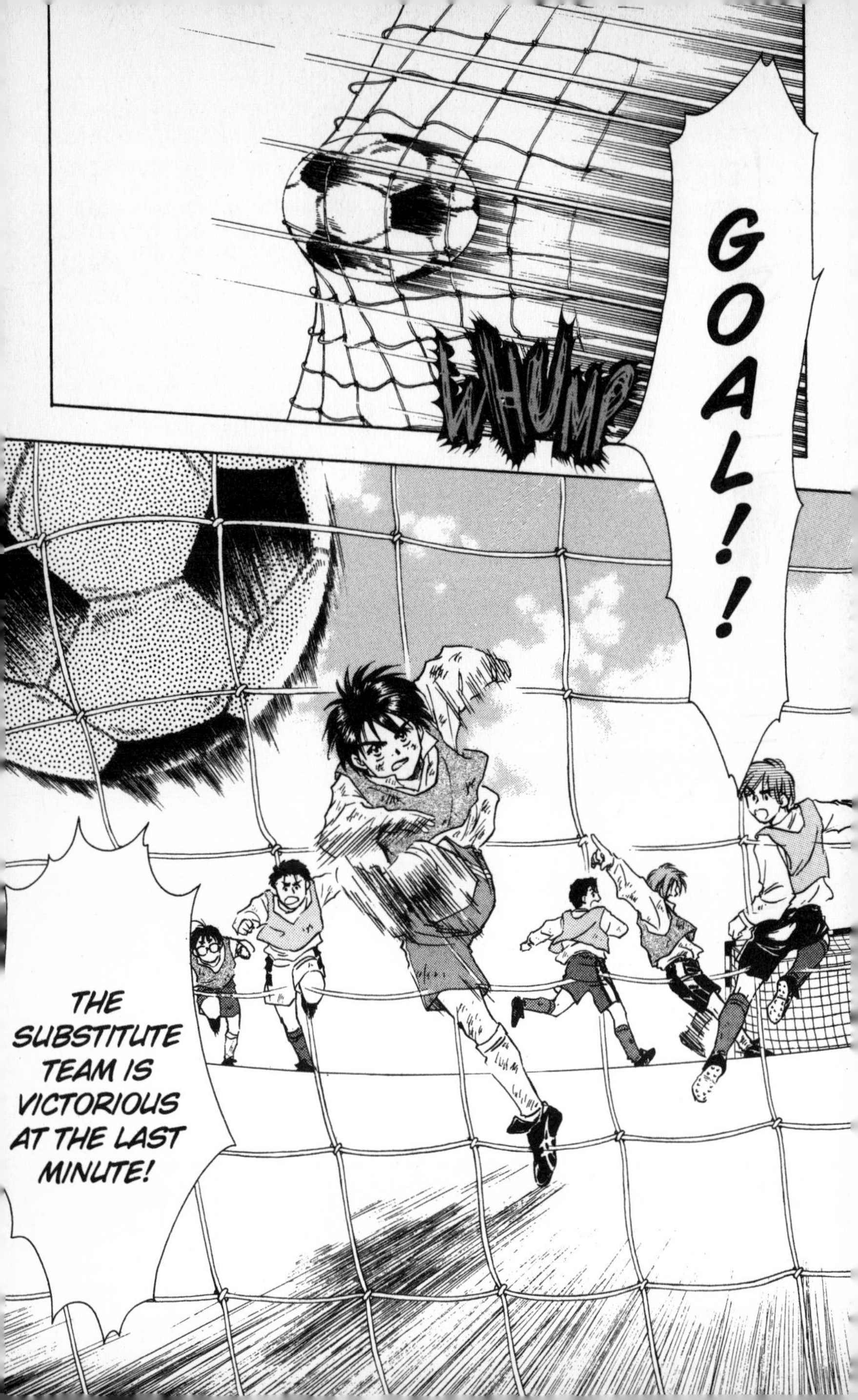
WHUMP
GOAL!!!
THE SUBSTITUTE TEAM IS VICTORIOUS AT THE LAST MINUTE!

THROUGH-PASS

THERE'S NOTHING AS EXHILARATING TO A TEAM AS A SUCCESSFULLY PERFORMED THROUGH-PASS. AND, THERE'S NOTHING AS SHOCKING TO THE OPPOSING TEAM.

THE THROUGH-PASS IS ACHIEVED BY AIMING RIGHT BETWEEN THE OPPOSING PLAYERS AND SENDING THE BALL TO THE OPEN SPACE BEHIND THEM. WHEN SUCH A PASS IS SUCCESSFUL, THERE'S A STRONG CHANCE FOR A RECEIVING PLAYER TO FACE THE GOALKEEPER (GK) ONE-ON-ONE. YOU MIGHT HAVE HEARD THE TERM KILLER-PASS. IT REFERS TO A PASS THAT ESTABLISHES A DECISIVE MOMENT, AND A THROUGH-PASS CAN EFFECTIVELY ACHIEVE IT.

IN ADDITION, A PASS, WHERE A PLAYER PRETENDS TO RECEIVE THE BALL, BUT INSTEAD, WITHOUT TOUCHING IT, LETS IT PASS ON TO ANOTHER PLAYER POSITIONED BEYOND, IS ALSO CALLED A THROUGH-PASS. THIS PASS CAN ONLY BE ACHIEVED BY KNOWING WHERE YOUR TEAM MEMBERS ARE POSITIONED. WHEN SUCCESSFUL, IT FEINTS THE OPPOSING PLAYERS AND CAN LEAD TO A BIG OPPORTUNITY.

AMONG THE VARIOUS FORMS OF PASSES, THROUGH-PASS IS ONE OF THE ARTFUL ONES. A WHILE BACK, THERE WAS NO ONE BETTER THAN JEKO TO PERFORM THAT PASS. CURRENTLY, AMONG THE JAPANESE REPRESENTATIVES, PLAYERS MINAMI AND NAKATA ARE GOOD AT IT.

NONETHELESS, IT IS NOWADAYS BECOMING MORE AND MORE DIFFICULT TO SUCCEED PASSING THE BALL THROUGH...

--TATSUYA WATANABE (*WINNING RUN*)

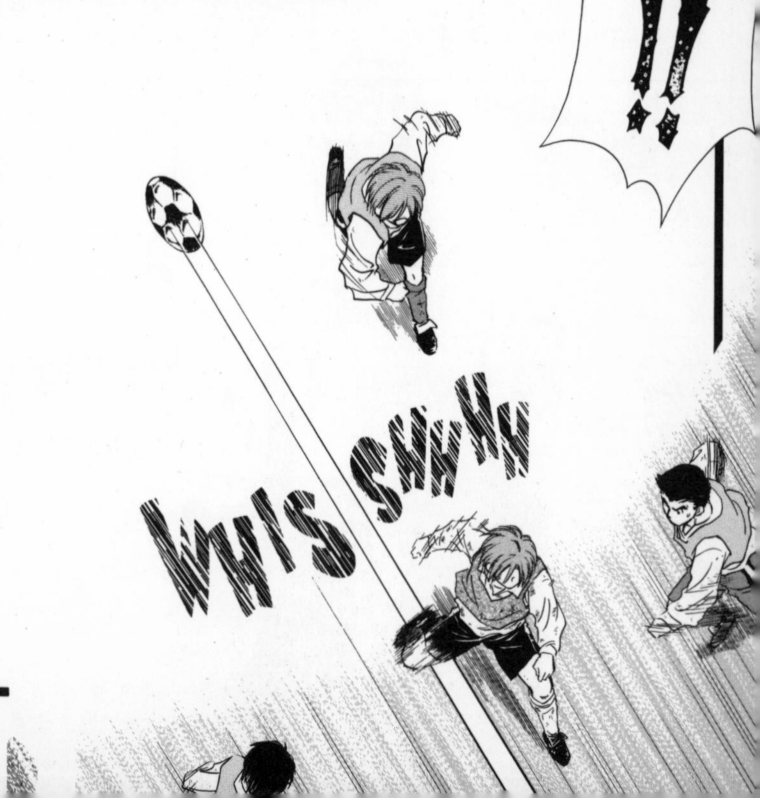
!!
WHISSHHH

STAGE.7 REFLECTIONS OF EACH OTHER

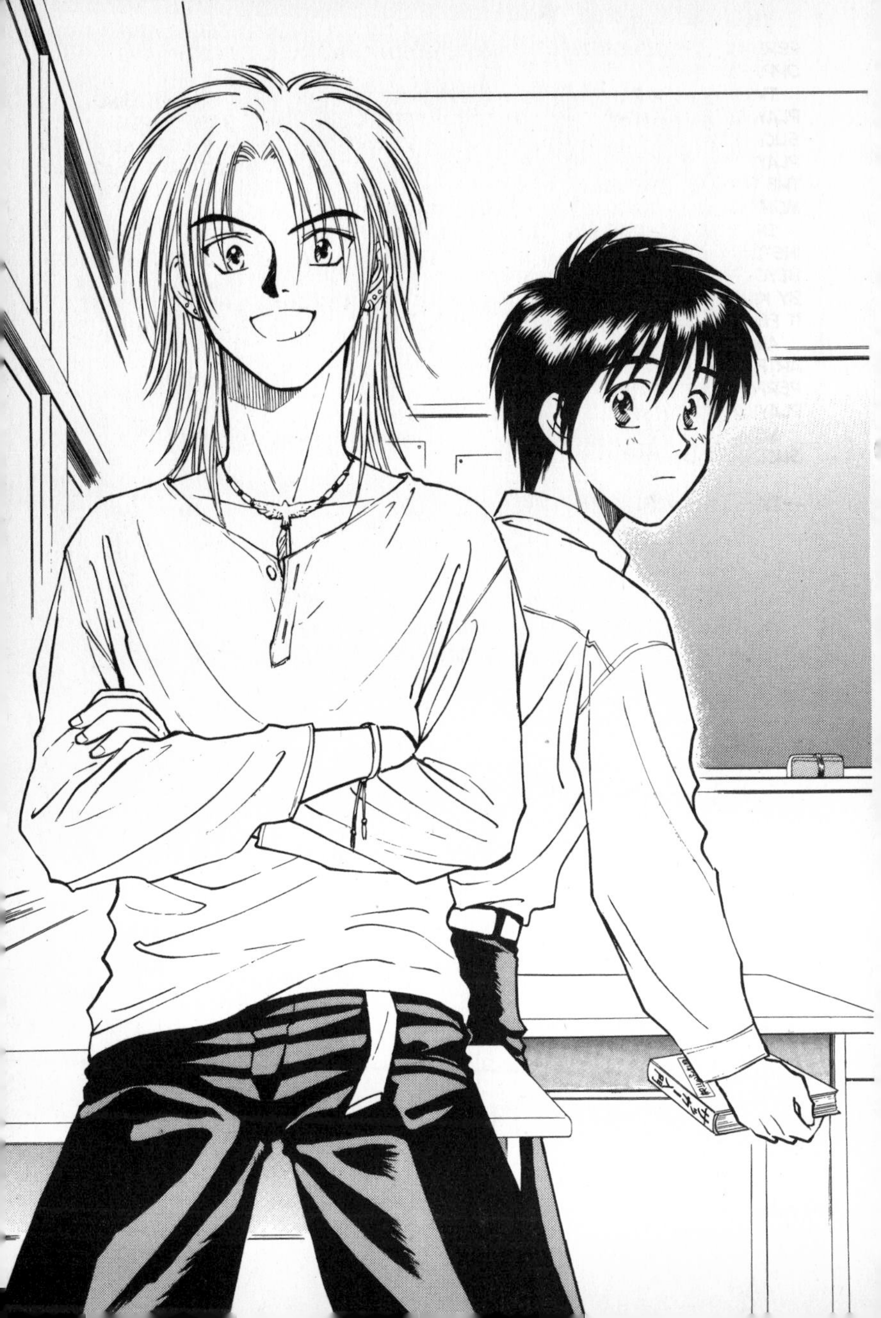

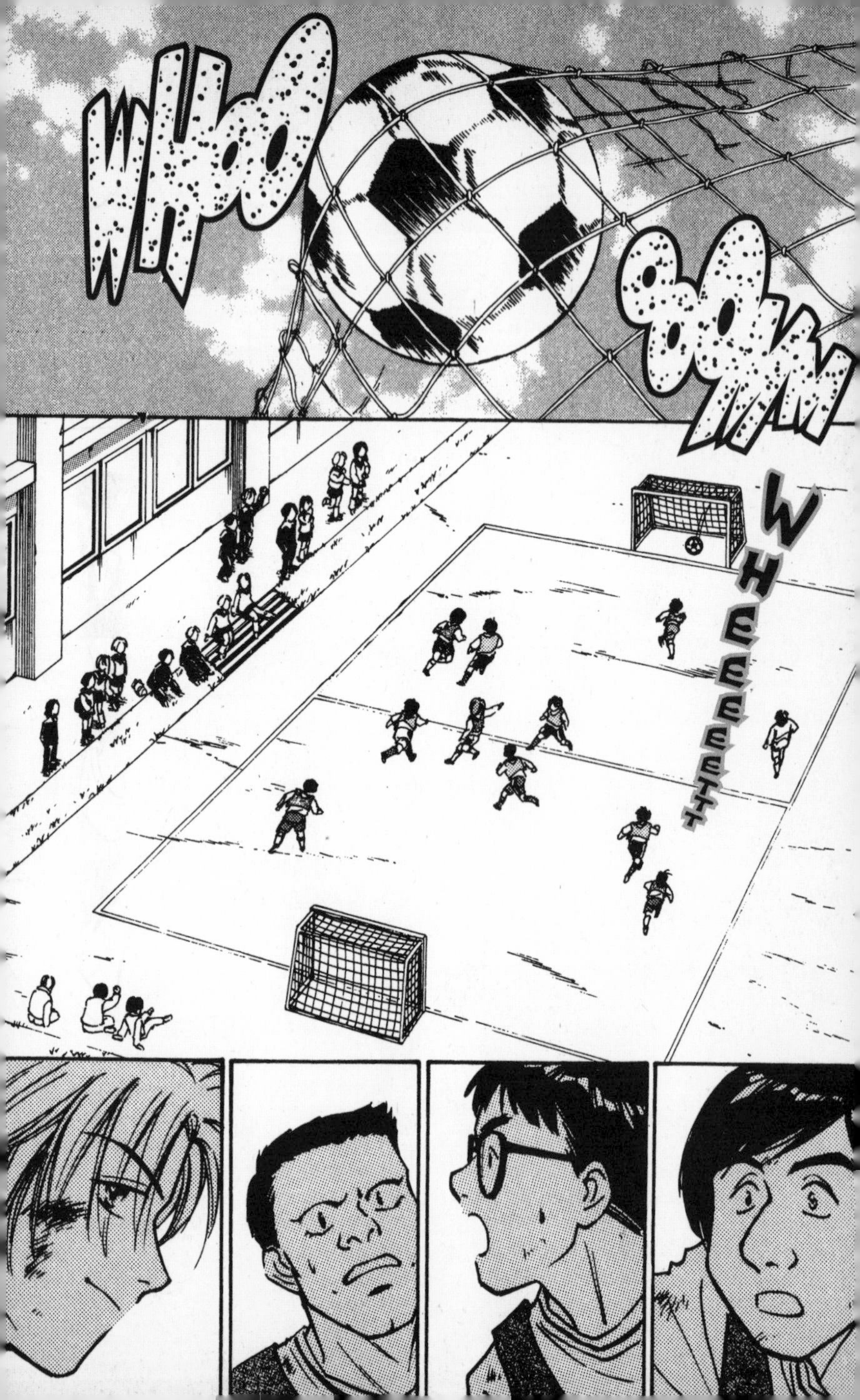
WHO
OOM
WHEEEETT

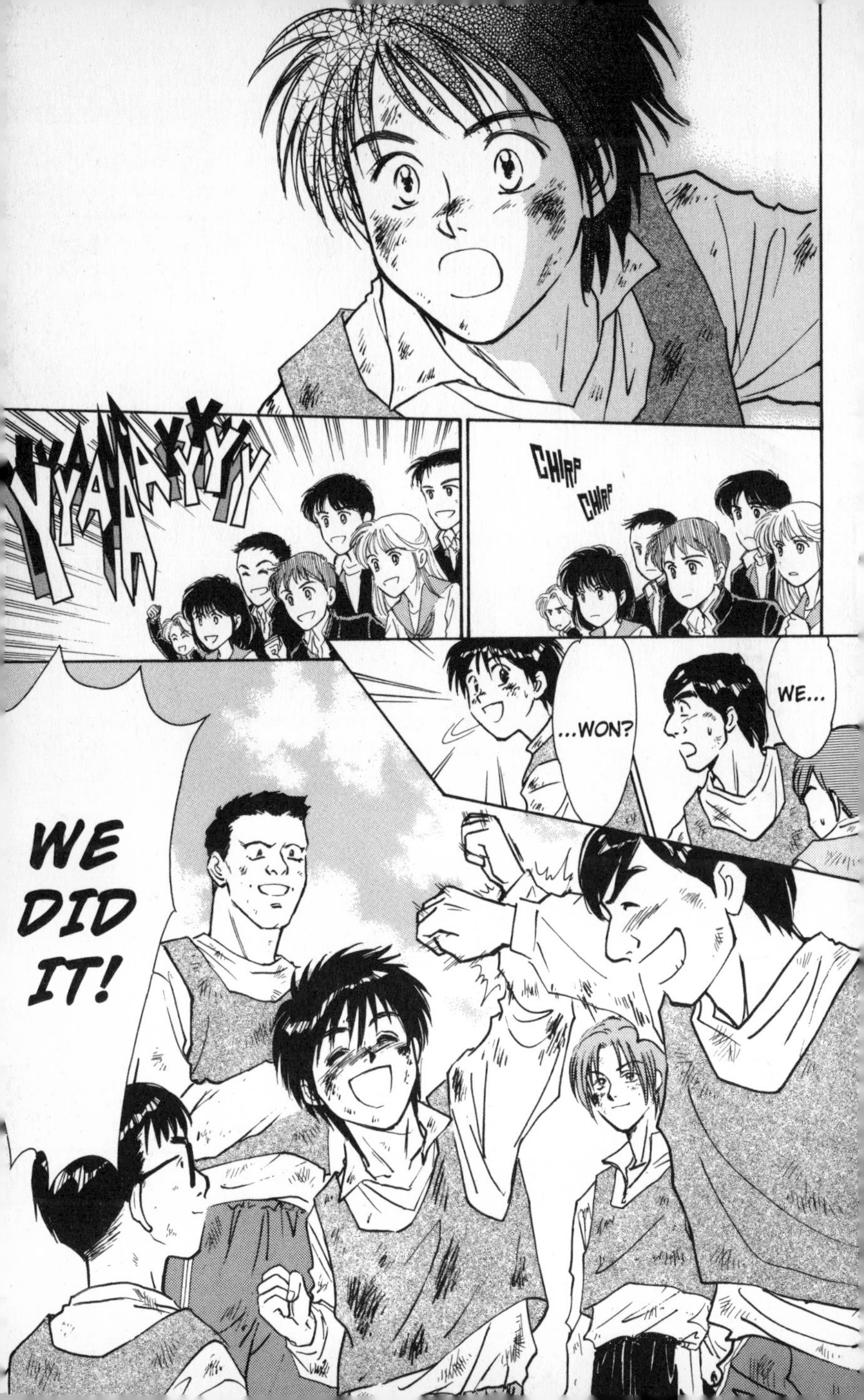
CHIRP
CHIRP
YAAAYYYY
WE...
...WON?
WE DID IT!

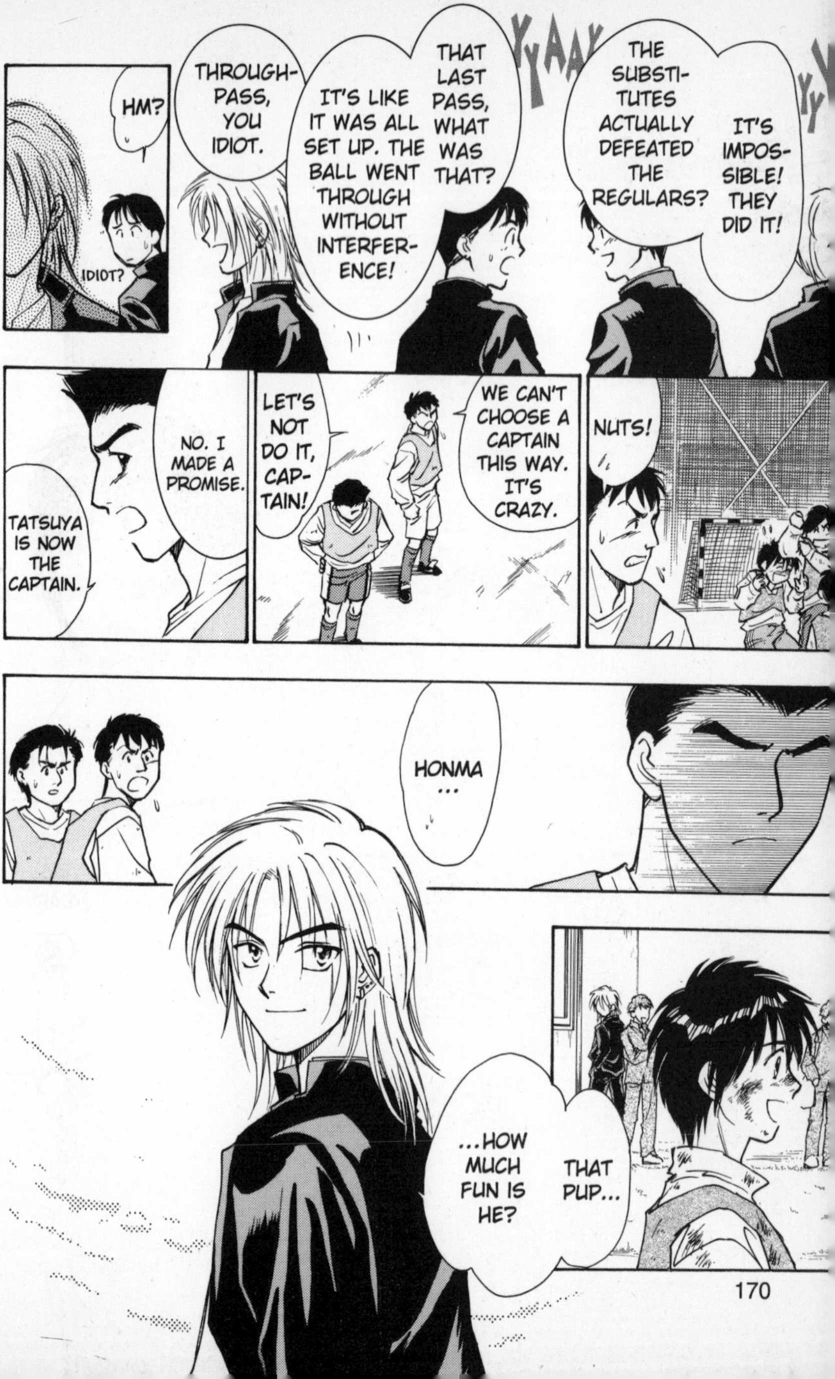
YYAAY
IT'S IMPOSSIBLE! THEY DID IT!
THE SUBSTITUTES ACTUALLY DEFEATED THE REGULARS?
THAT LAST PASS, WHAT WAS THAT?
IT'S LIKE IT WAS ALL SET UP. THE BALL WENT THROUGH WITHOUT INTERFERENCE!
THROUGH-PASS, YOU IDIOT.
HM?
IDIOT?
NUTS!
WE CAN'T CHOOSE A CAPTAIN THIS WAY. IT'S CRAZY.
LET'S NOT DO IT, CAPTAIN!
NO. I MADE A PROMISE.
TATSUYA IS NOW THE CAPTAIN.
HONMA ...
THAT PUP...
...HOW MUCH FUN IS HE?

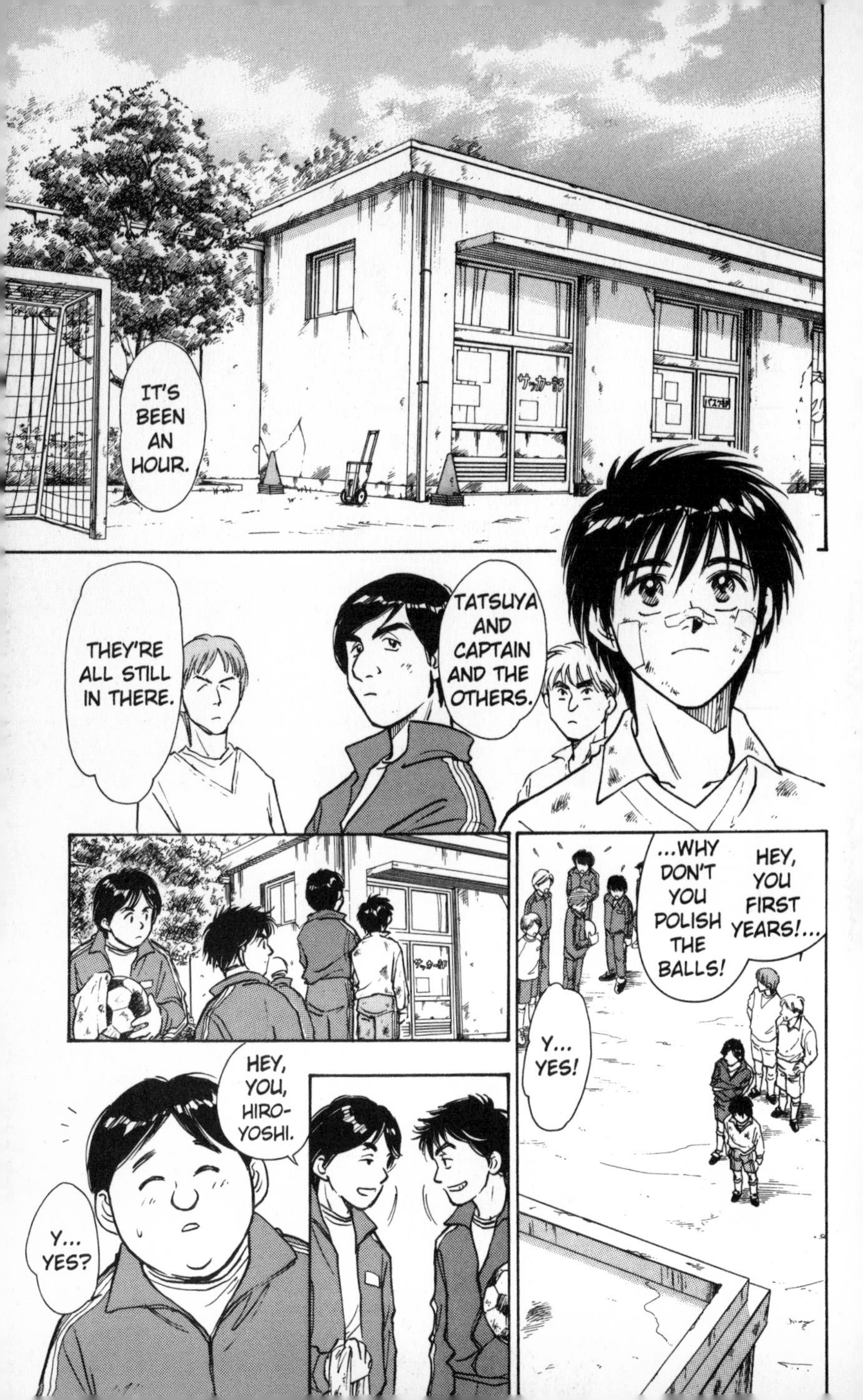
IT'S BEEN AN HOUR.
TATSUYA AND CAPTAIN AND THE OTHERS.
THEY'RE ALL STILL IN THERE.
HEY, YOU FIRST YEARS!...
...WHY DON'T YOU POLISH THE BALLS!
Y... YES!
HEY, YOU, HIRO-YOSHI.
Y... YES?

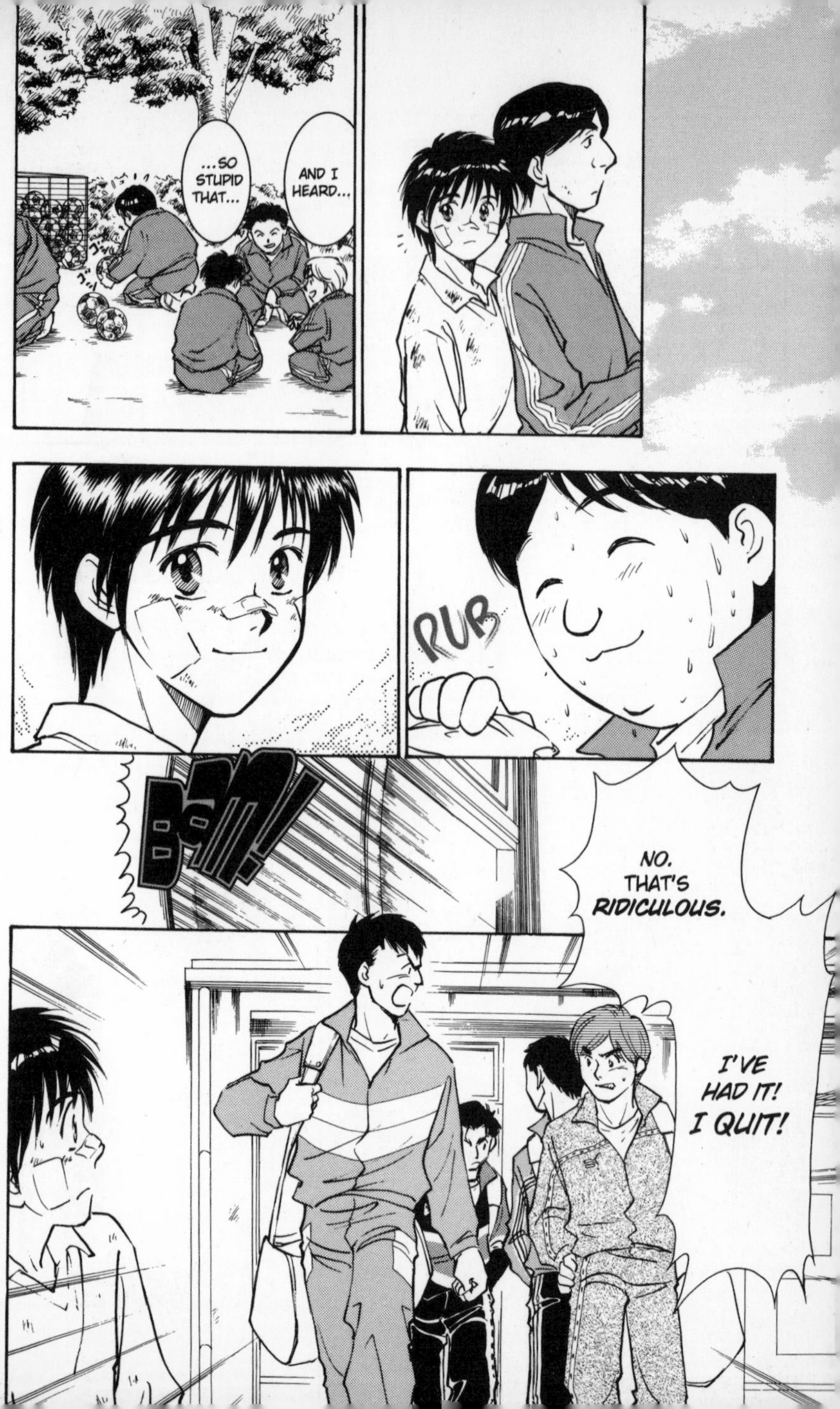
AND I HEARD...
...SO STUPID THAT...
RUB
BAM!!
NO. THAT'S RIDICULOUS.
I'VE HAD IT! I QUIT!

READ THIS WAY

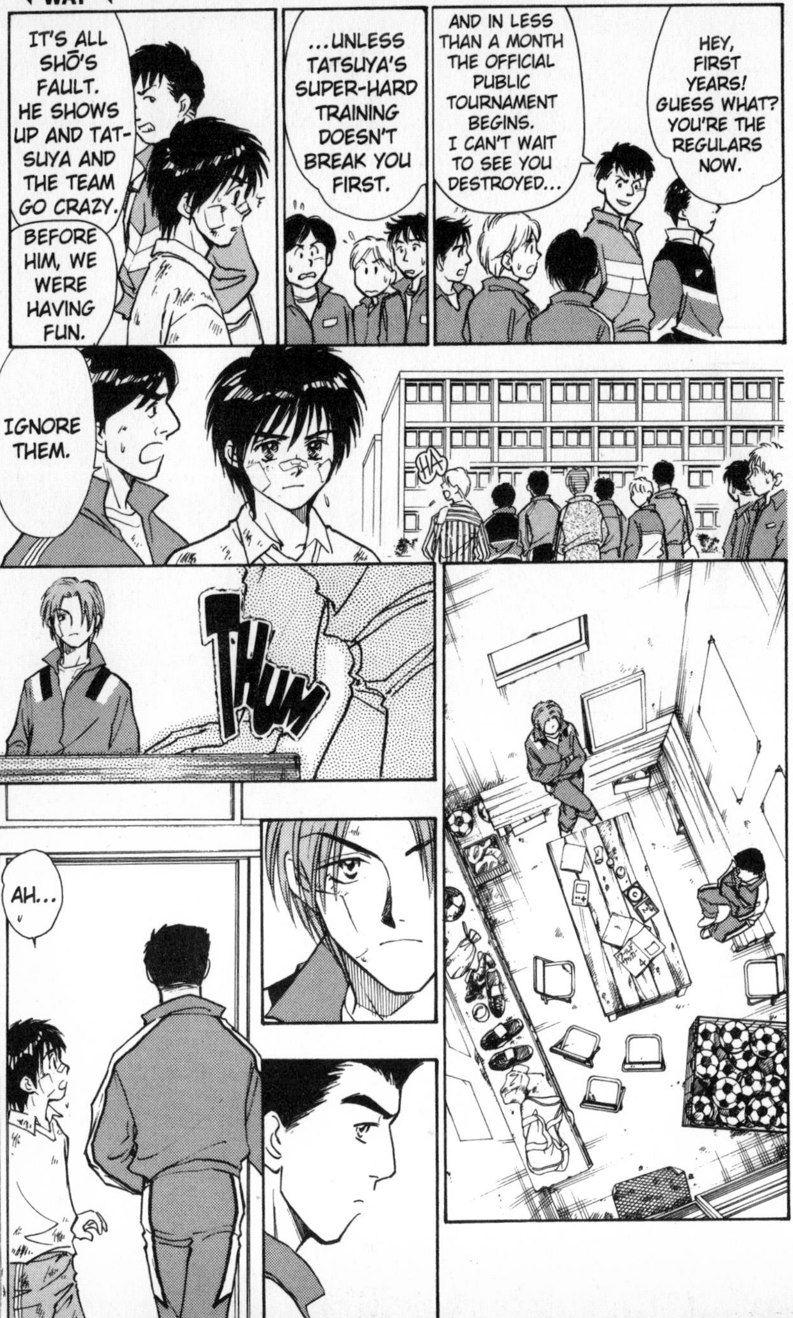

HEY, FIRST YEARS! GUESS WHAT? YOU'RE THE REGULARS NOW.
AND IN LESS THAN A MONTH THE OFFICIAL PUBLIC TOURNAMENT BEGINS. I CAN'T WAIT TO SEE YOU DESTROYED...
...UNLESS TATSUYA'S SUPER-HARD TRAINING DOESN'T BREAK YOU FIRST.
IT'S ALL SHŌ'S FAULT. HE SHOWS UP AND TAT-SUYA AND THE TEAM GO CRAZY.
BEFORE HIM, WE WERE HAVING FUN.
HA
IGNORE THEM.
THUM
AH...

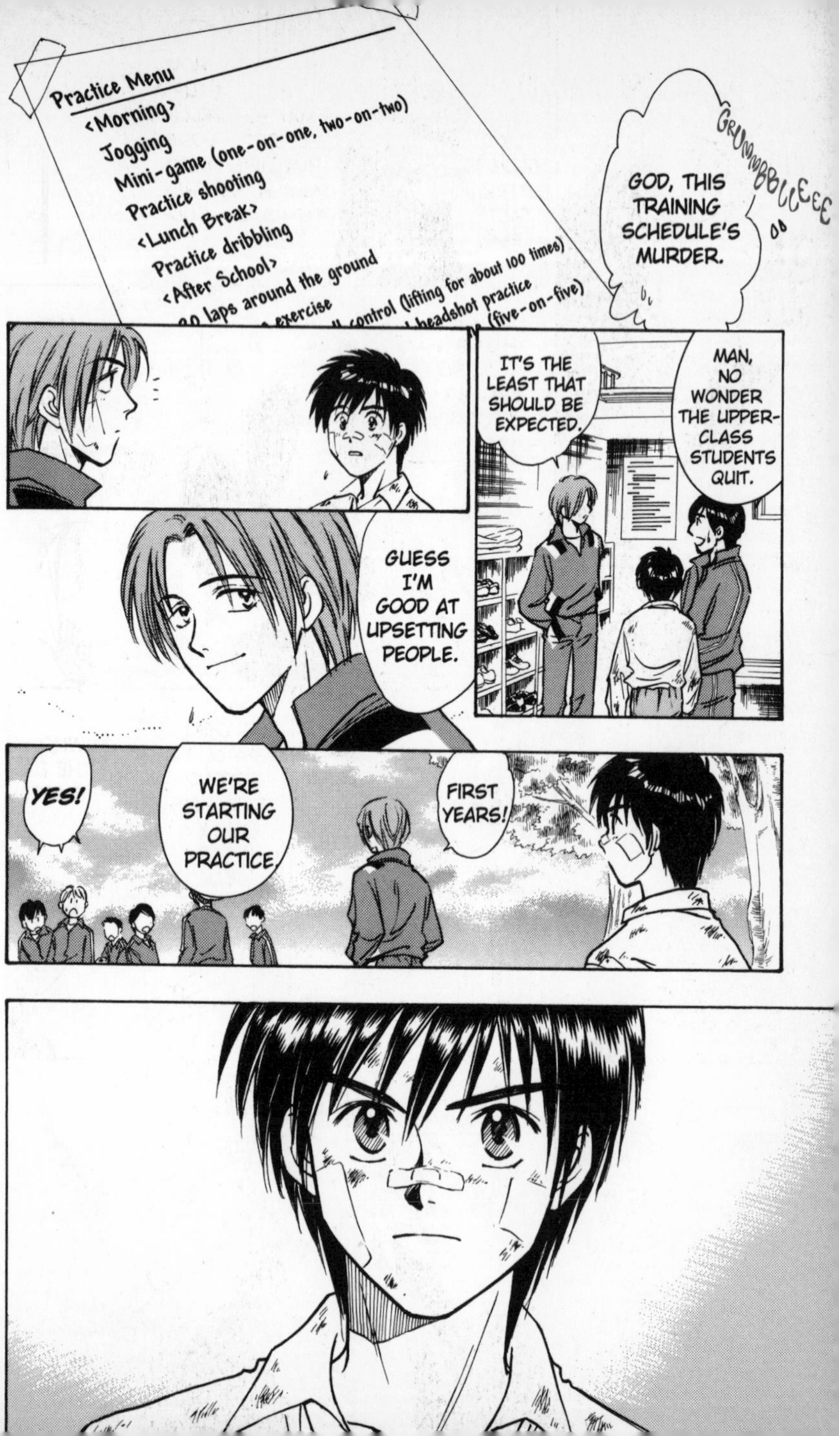
GRUMMBBLLEEE
GOD, THIS TRAINING SCHEDULE'S MURDER.
Practice Menu
<Morning>
Jogging
Mini-game (one-on-one, two-on-two)
Practice shooting
<Lunch Break>
Practice dribbling
<After School>
laps around the ground
exercise
control (lifting for about 100 times)
headshot practice
(five-on-five)
MAN, NO WONDER THE UPPER-CLASS STUDENTS QUIT.
IT'S THE LEAST THAT SHOULD BE EXPECTED.
GUESS I'M GOOD AT UPSETTING PEOPLE.
FIRST YEARS!
WE'RE STARTING OUR PRACTICE.
YES!

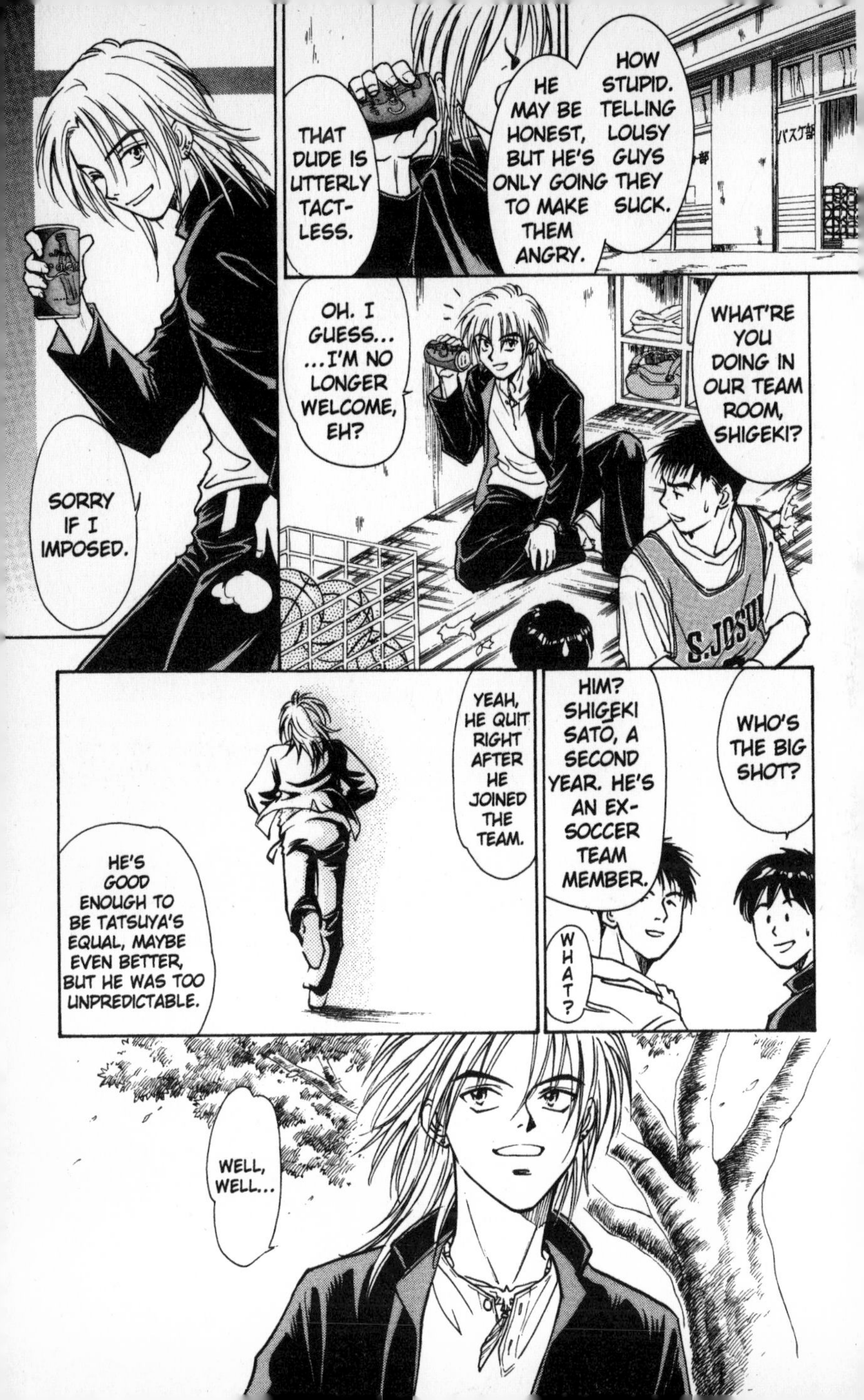
HOW STUPID. TELLING LOUSY GUYS THEY SUCK.
HE MAY BE HONEST, BUT HE'S ONLY GOING TO MAKE THEM ANGRY.
THAT DUDE IS UTTERLY TACT-LESS.
WHAT'RE YOU DOING IN OUR TEAM ROOM, SHIGEKI?
OH. I GUESS... ...I'M NO LONGER WELCOME, EH?
SORRY IF I IMPOSED.
WHO'S THE BIG SHOT?
HIM? SHIGEKI SATO, A SECOND YEAR. HE'S AN EX-SOCCER TEAM MEMBER.
WHAT?
YEAH, HE QUIT RIGHT AFTER HE JOINED THE TEAM.
HE'S GOOD ENOUGH TO BE TATSUYA'S EQUAL, MAYBE EVEN BETTER, BUT HE WAS TOO UNPREDICTABLE.
WELL, WELL...

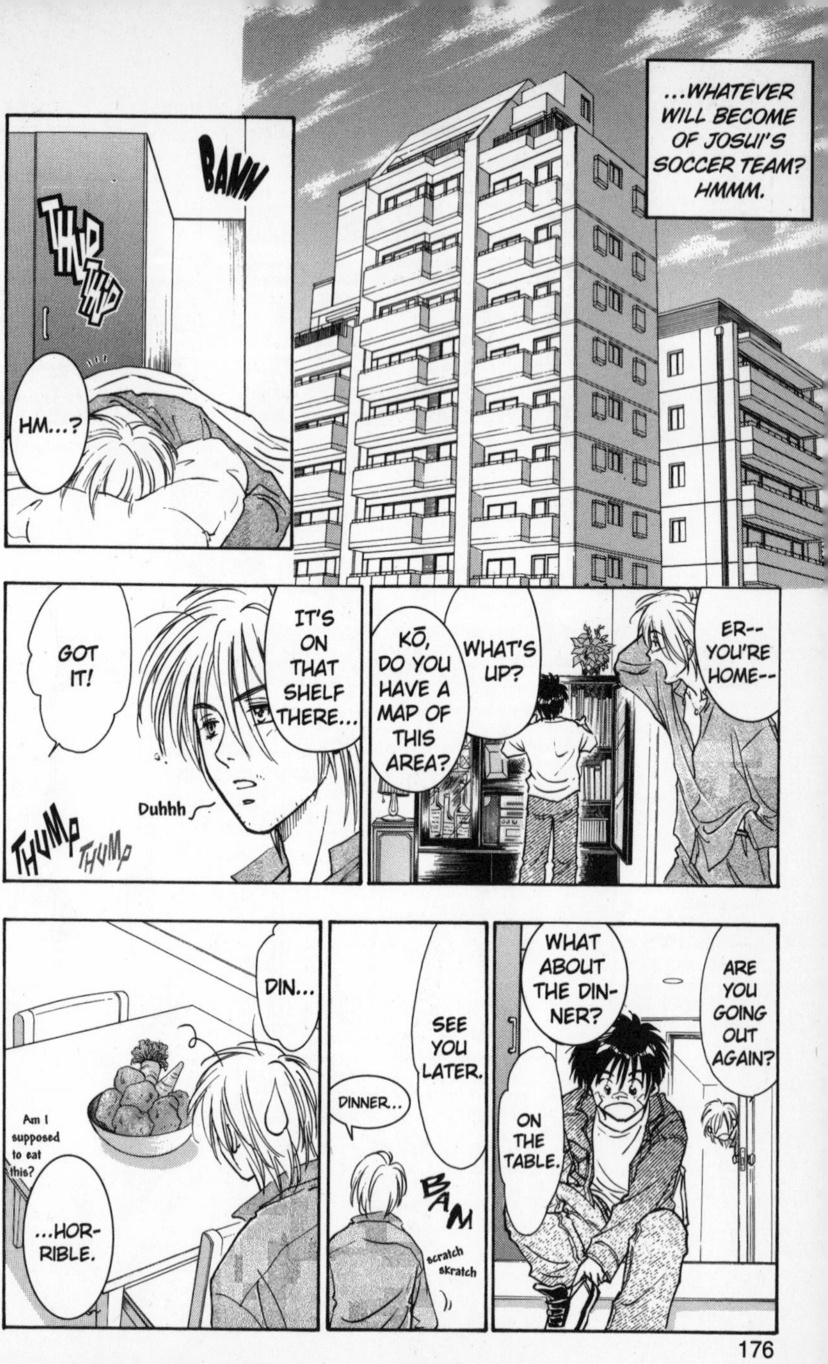
...WHATEVER WILL BECOME OF JOSUI'S SOCCER TEAM? HMMM.
BAMN
THUD THUD
HM...?
ER-- YOU'RE HOME--
WHAT'S UP?
KŌ, DO YOU HAVE A MAP OF THIS AREA?
IT'S ON THAT SHELF THERE...
GOT IT!
Duhhh
THUMP THUMP
ARE YOU GOING OUT AGAIN?
WHAT ABOUT THE DIN-NER?
ON THE TABLE.
SEE YOU LATER.
DINNER...
BAM
scratch skratch
DIN...
Am I supposed to eat this?
...HOR-RIBLE.

READ THIS WAY

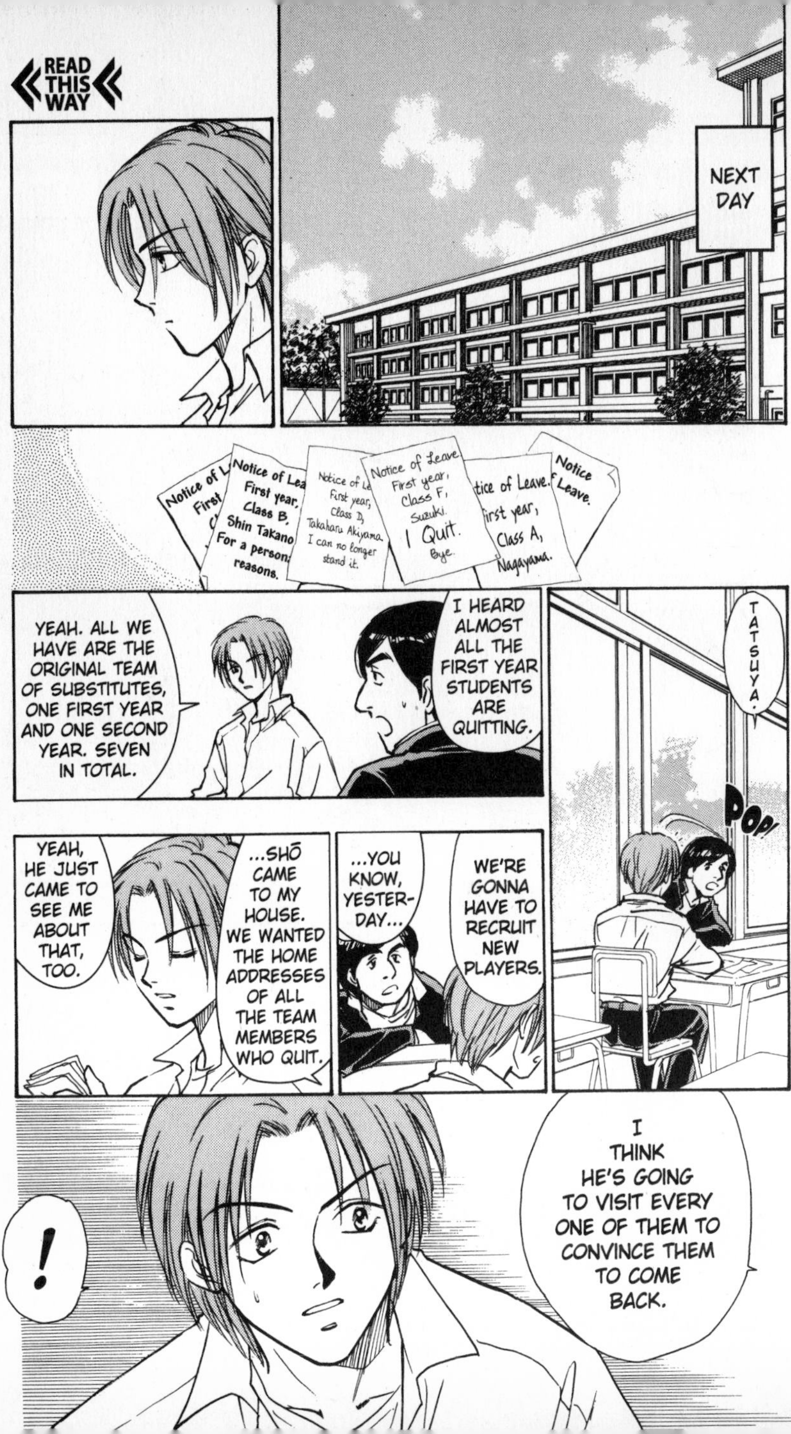
NEXT DAY
Notice Leave.
Notice of Leave. First year, Class A, Nagayama.
Notice of Leave. First year, Class F, Suzuki. I Quit. Bye.
Notice of Le First year, Class D, Takaharu Akiyama. I can no longer stand it.
Notice of Lea First year, Class B, Shin Takano For a person reasons.
Notice of L First
TATSUYA.
POP!
I HEARD ALMOST ALL THE FIRST YEAR STUDENTS ARE QUITTING.
YEAH. ALL WE HAVE ARE THE ORIGINAL TEAM OF SUBSTITUTES, ONE FIRST YEAR AND ONE SECOND YEAR. SEVEN IN TOTAL.
WE'RE GONNA HAVE TO RECRUIT NEW PLAYERS.
...YOU KNOW, YESTER-DAY...
...SHŌ CAME TO MY HOUSE. WE WANTED THE HOME ADDRESSES OF ALL THE TEAM MEMBERS WHO QUIT.
YEAH, HE JUST CAME TO SEE ME ABOUT THAT, TOO.
I THINK HE'S GOING TO VISIT EVERY ONE OF THEM TO CONVINCE THEM TO COME BACK.
!

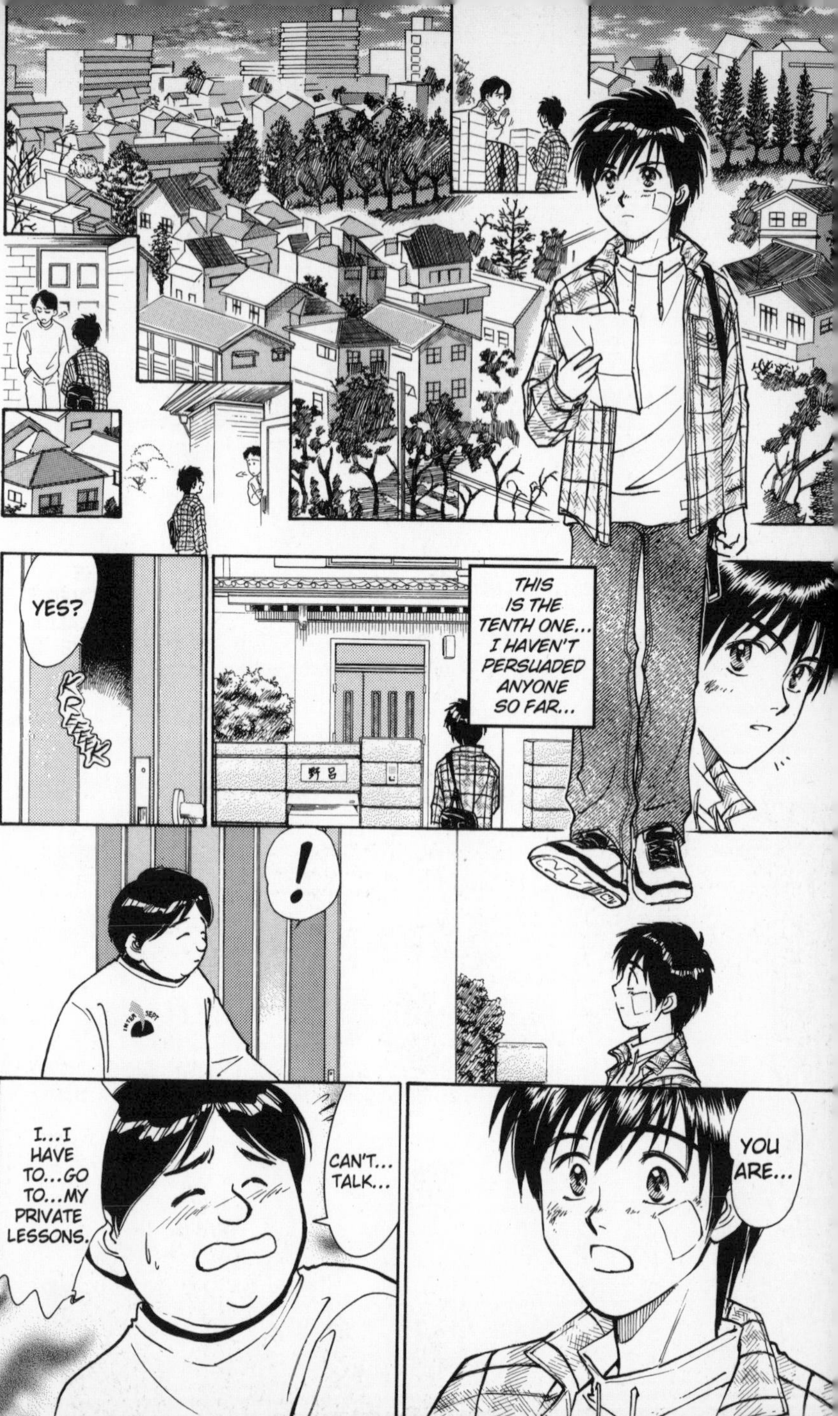
THIS IS THE TENTH ONE... I HAVEN'T PERSUADED ANYONE SO FAR...
野呂
YES?
KREEEEK
!
YOU ARE...
CAN'T... TALK...
I...I HAVE TO...GO TO...MY PRIVATE LESSONS.

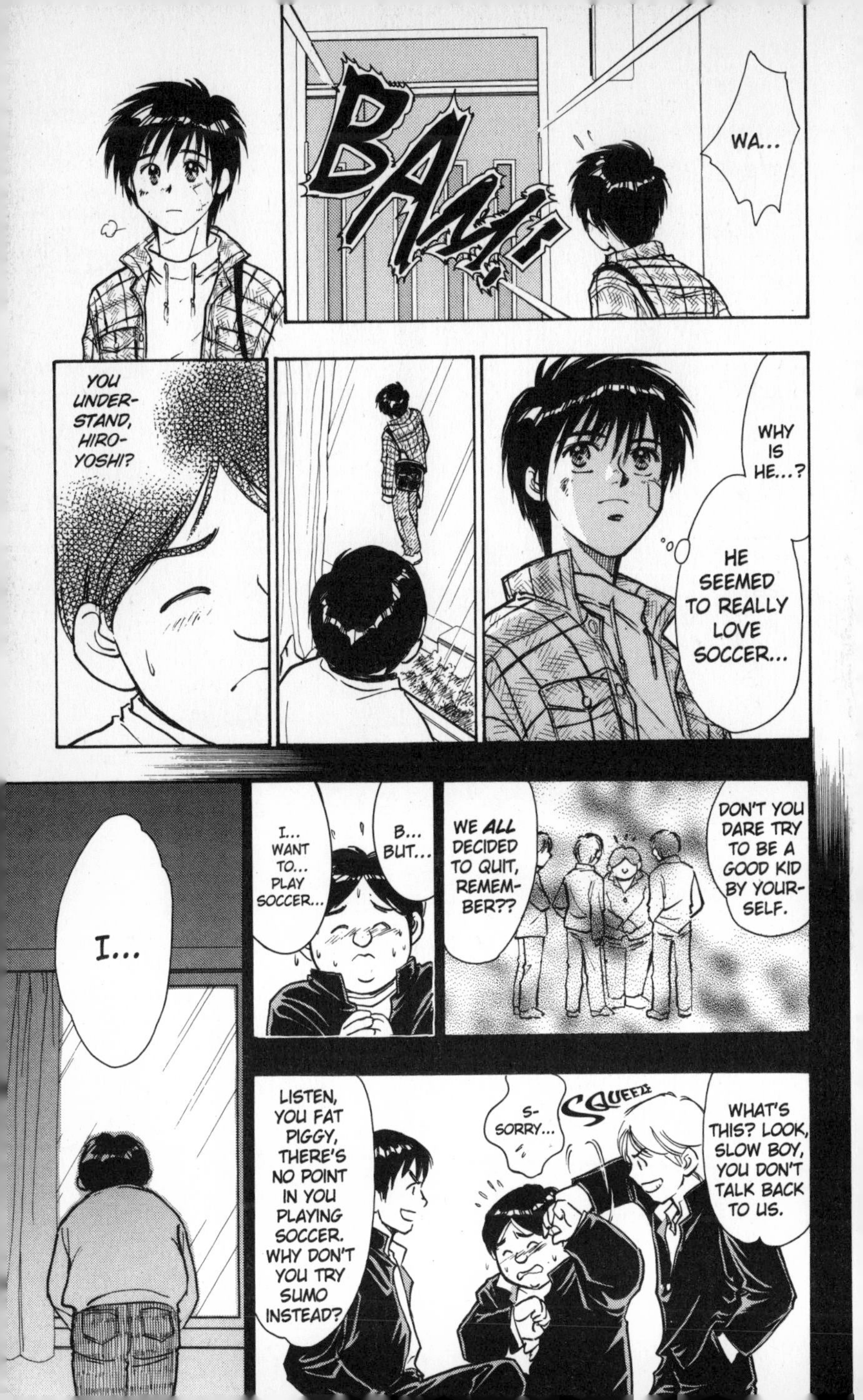
WA...
BAM!
WHY IS HE...?
HE SEEMED TO REALLY LOVE SOCCER...
YOU UNDERSTAND, HIRO-YOSHI?
DON'T YOU DARE TRY TO BE A GOOD KID BY YOUR-SELF.
WE ALL DECIDED TO QUIT, REMEMBER??
B... BUT...
I... WANT TO... PLAY SOCCER...
WHAT'S THIS? LOOK, SLOW BOY, YOU DON'T TALK BACK TO US.
SQUEEE
S-SORRY...
LISTEN, YOU FAT PIGGY, THERE'S NO POINT IN YOU PLAYING SOCCER. WHY DON'T YOU TRY SUMO INSTEAD?
I...

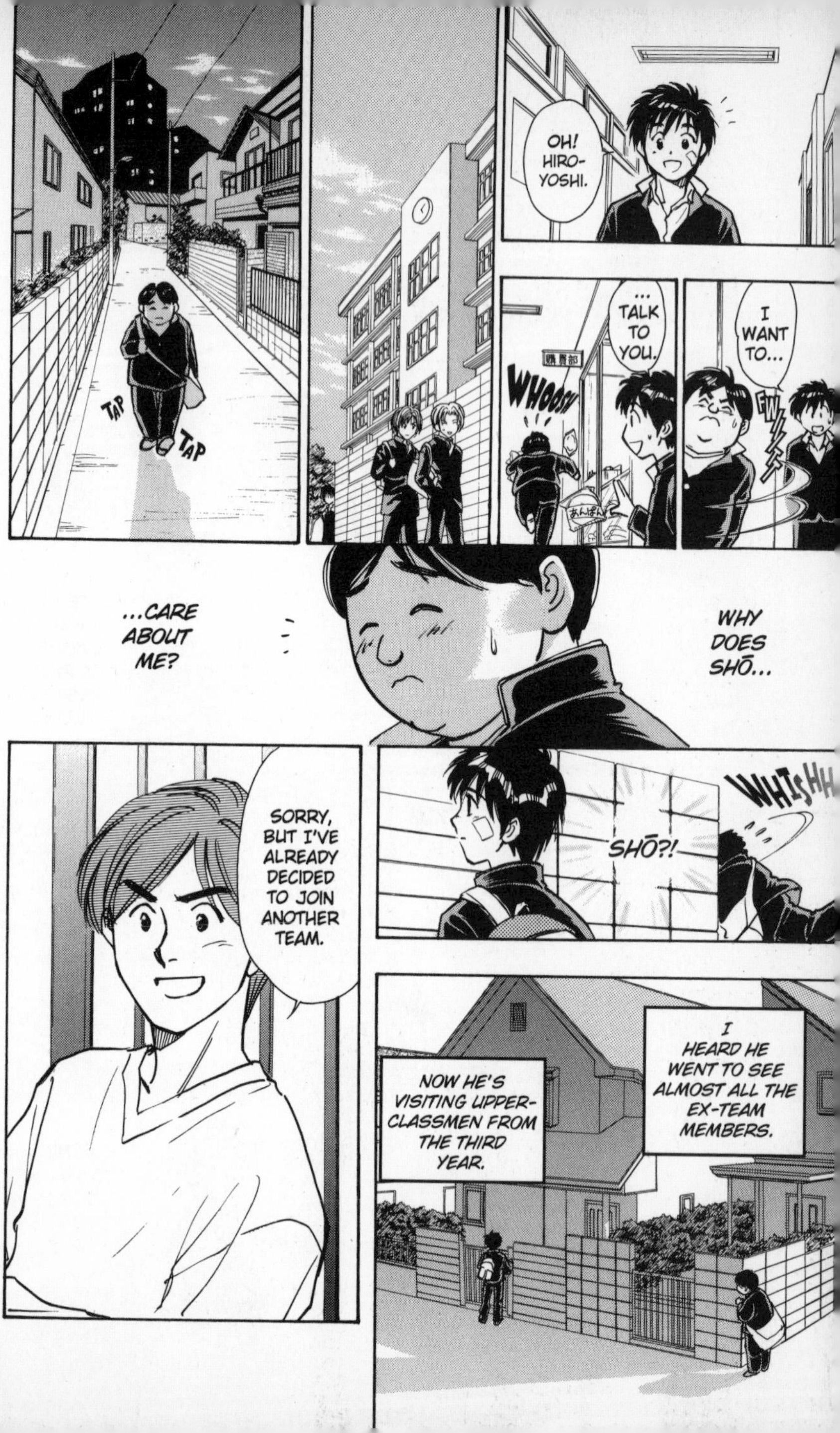
OH! HIRO-YOSHI.
I WANT TO...
... TALK TO YOU.
WHOOSH
TAP
TAP
WHY DOES SHŌ...
...CARE ABOUT ME?
WHISHH
SHŌ?!
I HEARD HE WENT TO SEE ALMOST ALL THE EX-TEAM MEMBERS.
NOW HE'S VISITING UPPER-CLASSMEN FROM THE THIRD YEAR.
SORRY, BUT I'VE ALREADY DECIDED TO JOIN ANOTHER TEAM.

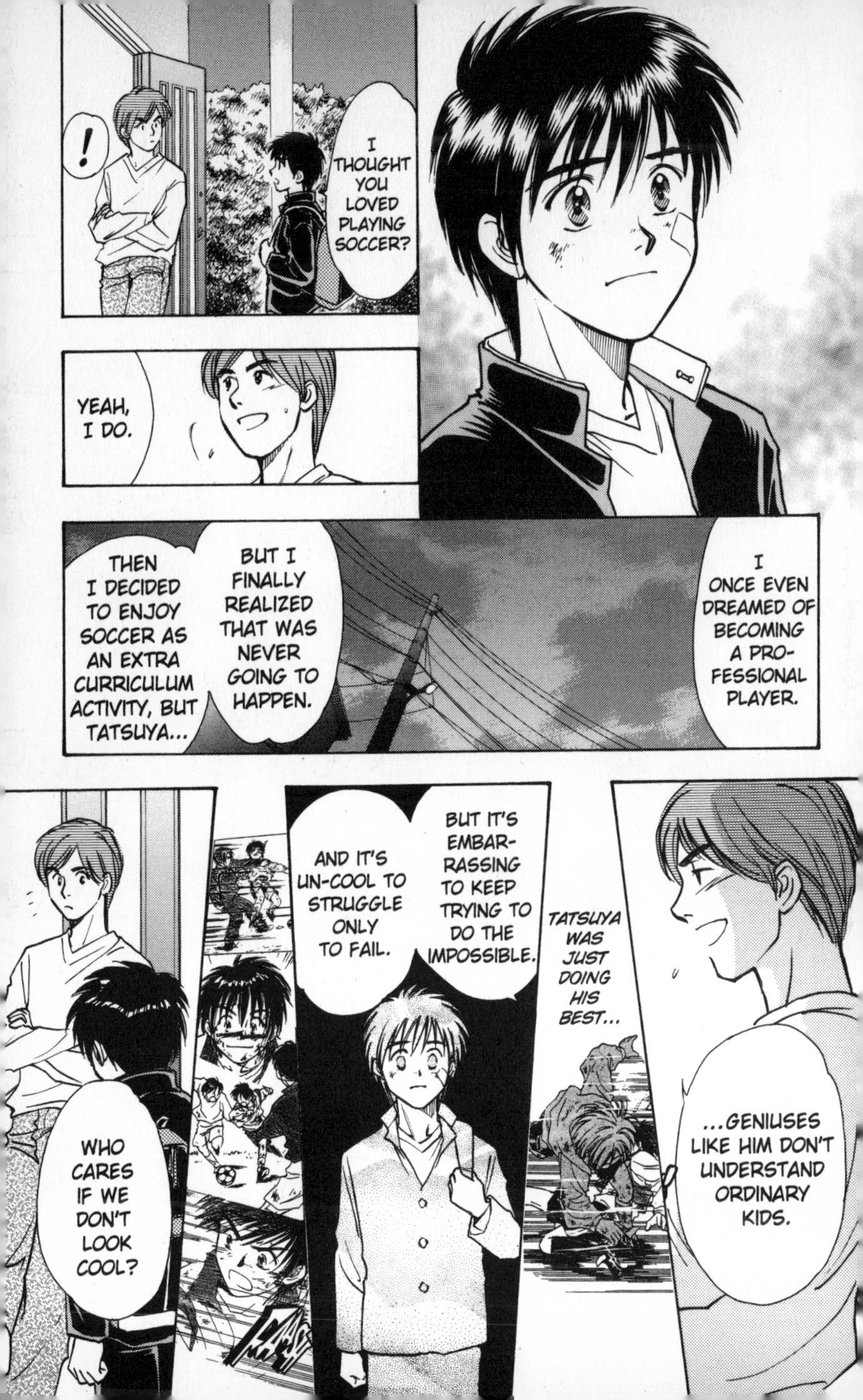
!
I THOUGHT YOU LOVED PLAYING SOCCER?
YEAH, I DO.
I ONCE EVEN DREAMED OF BECOMING A PRO-FESSIONAL PLAYER.
BUT I FINALLY REALIZED THAT WAS NEVER GOING TO HAPPEN.
THEN I DECIDED TO ENJOY SOCCER AS AN EXTRA CURRICULUM ACTIVITY, BUT TATSUYA...
...GENIUSES LIKE HIM DON'T UNDERSTAND ORDINARY KIDS.
TATSUYA WAS JUST DOING HIS BEST...
BUT IT'S EMBAR-RASSING TO KEEP TRYING TO DO THE IMPOSSIBLE.
AND IT'S UN-COOL TO STRUGGLE ONLY TO FAIL.
WHO CARES IF WE DON'T LOOK COOL?

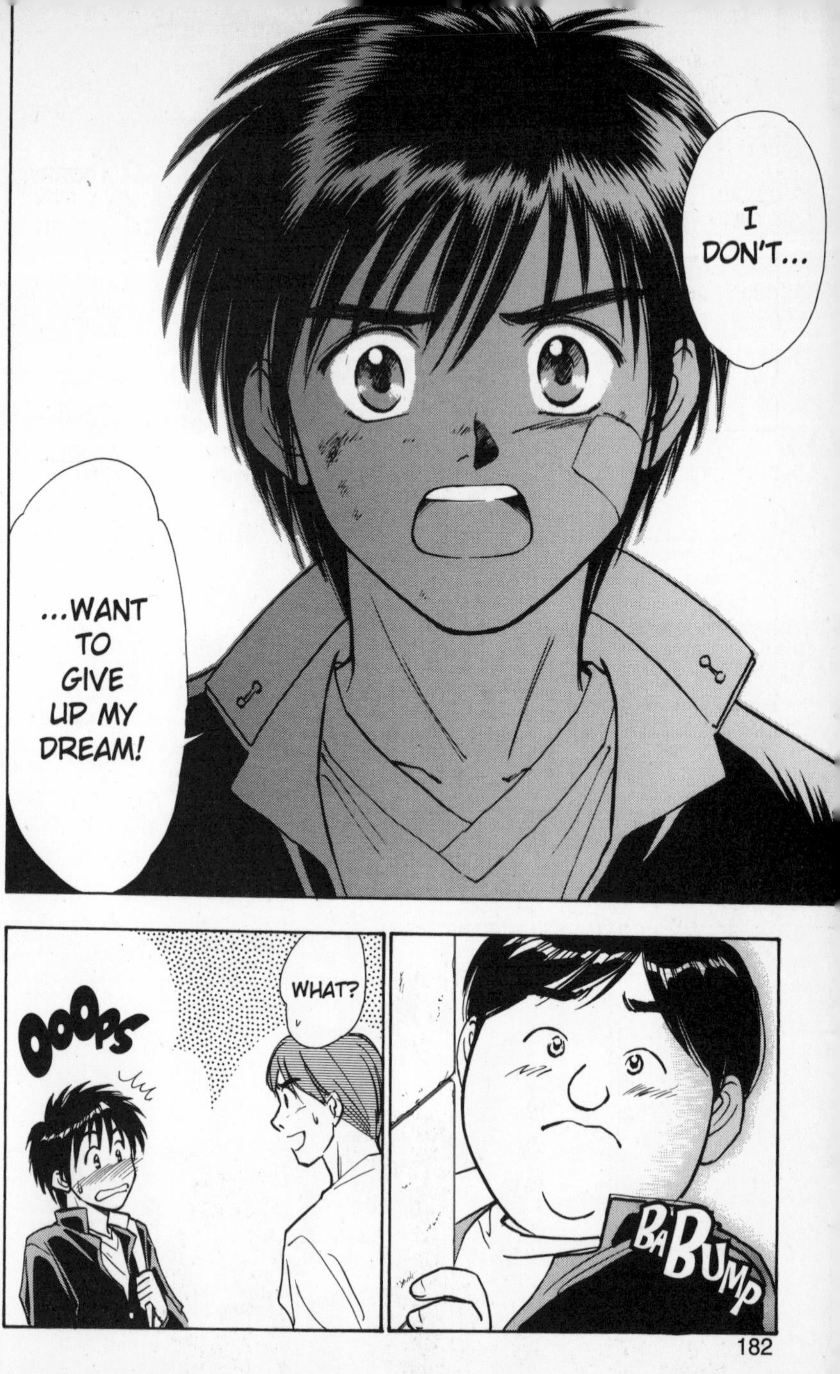
I DON'T...
...WANT TO GIVE UP MY DREAM!
BA BUMP
WHAT?
OOOPS

READ THIS WAY

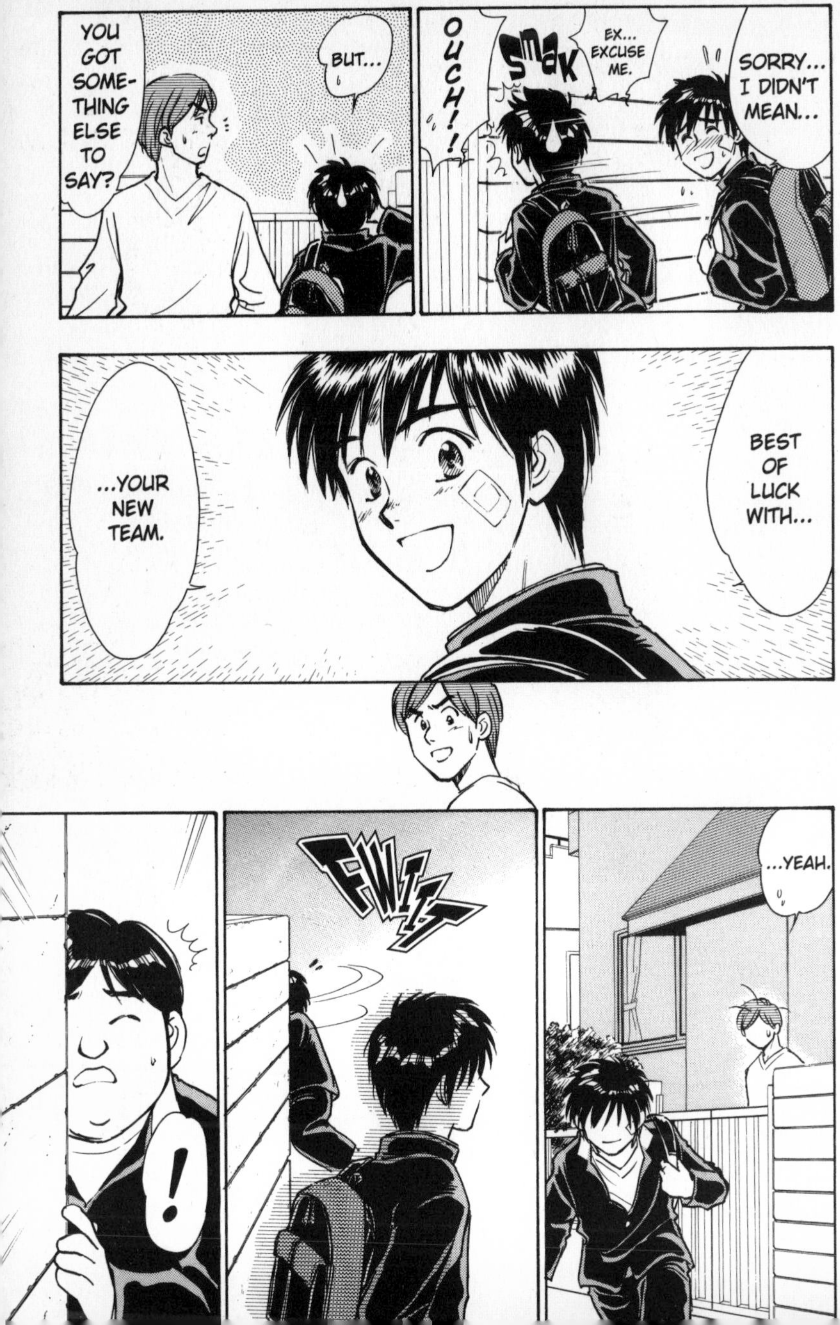
SORRY... I DIDN'T MEAN...
EX... EXCUSE ME.
SMAK
OUCH!!
BUT...
YOU GOT SOME-THING ELSE TO SAY?
BEST OF LUCK WITH...
...YOUR NEW TEAM.
...YEAH.
FWIT
!

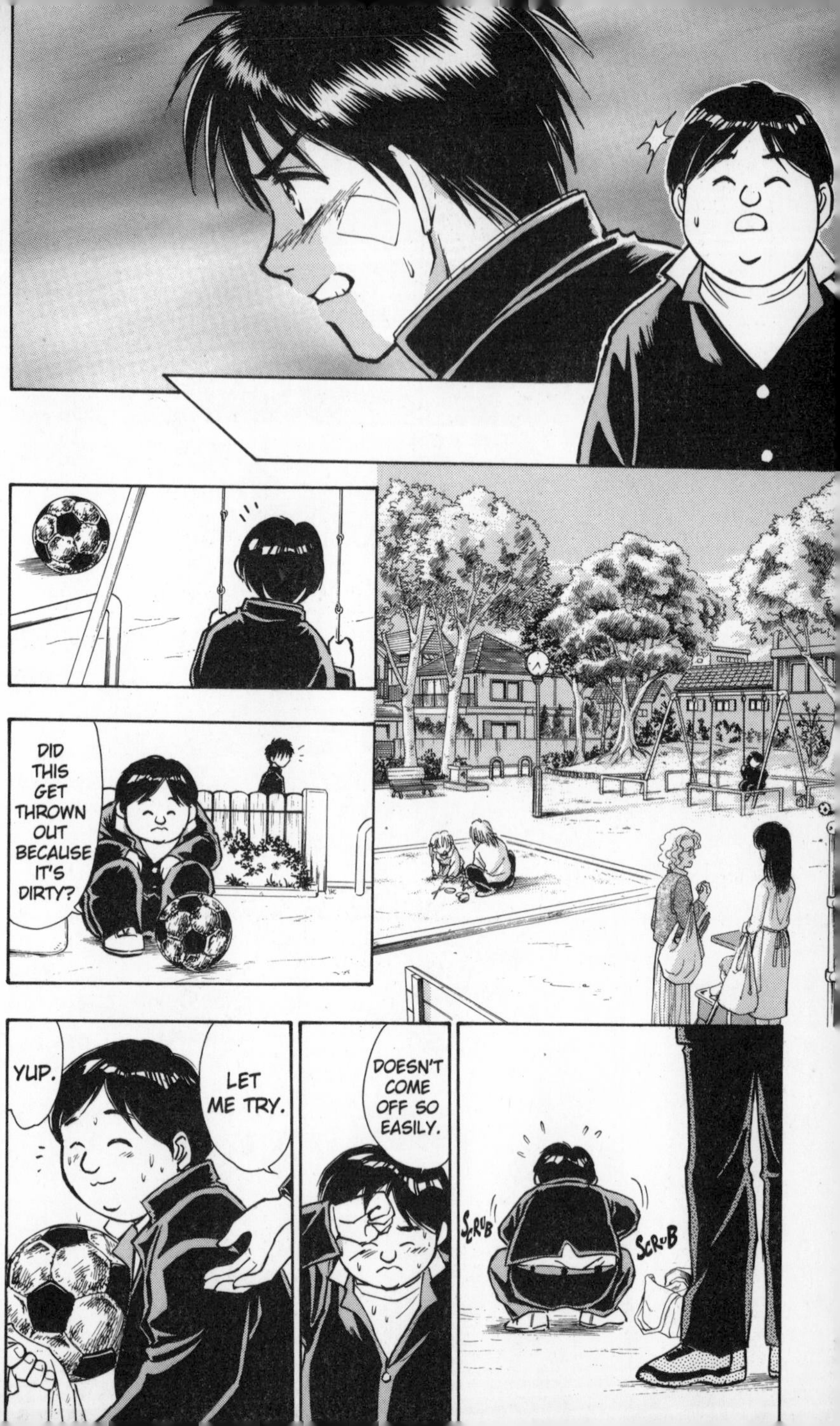
DID THIS GET THROWN OUT BECAUSE IT'S DIRTY?
YUP.
LET ME TRY.
DOESN'T COME OFF SO EASILY.
SCRUB
SCRUB

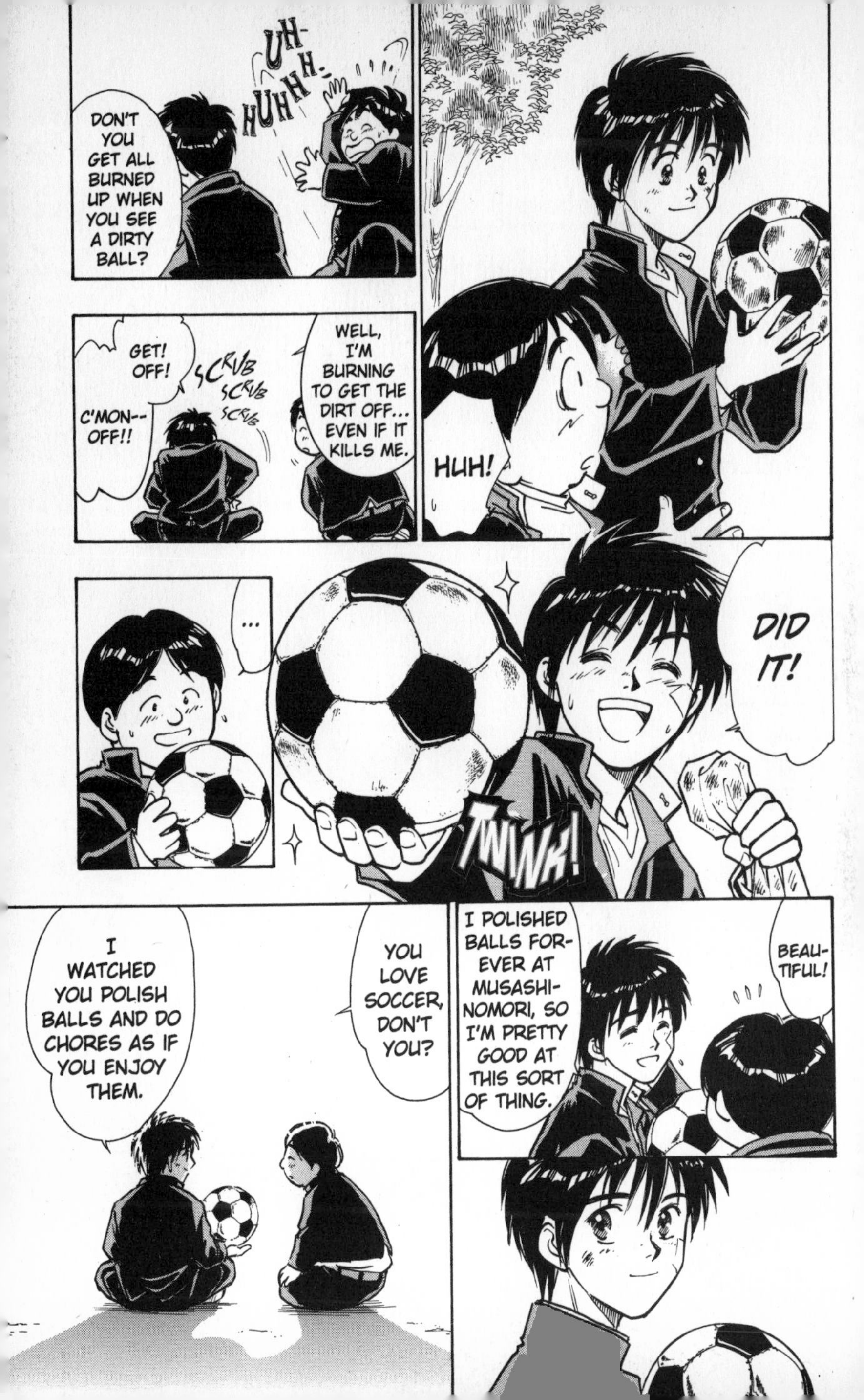
HUH!
UH-HUHH.
DON'T YOU GET ALL BURNED UP WHEN YOU SEE A DIRTY BALL?
WELL, I'M BURNING TO GET THE DIRT OFF... EVEN IF IT KILLS ME.
SCRUB SCRUB SCRUB
GET! OFF!
C'MON-- OFF!!
DID IT!
TWINK!
...
BEAU-TIFUL!
I POLISHED BALLS FOR-EVER AT MUSASHI-NOMORI, SO I'M PRETTY GOOD AT THIS SORT OF THING.
YOU LOVE SOCCER, DON'T YOU?
I WATCHED YOU POLISH BALLS AND DO CHORES AS IF YOU ENJOY THEM.

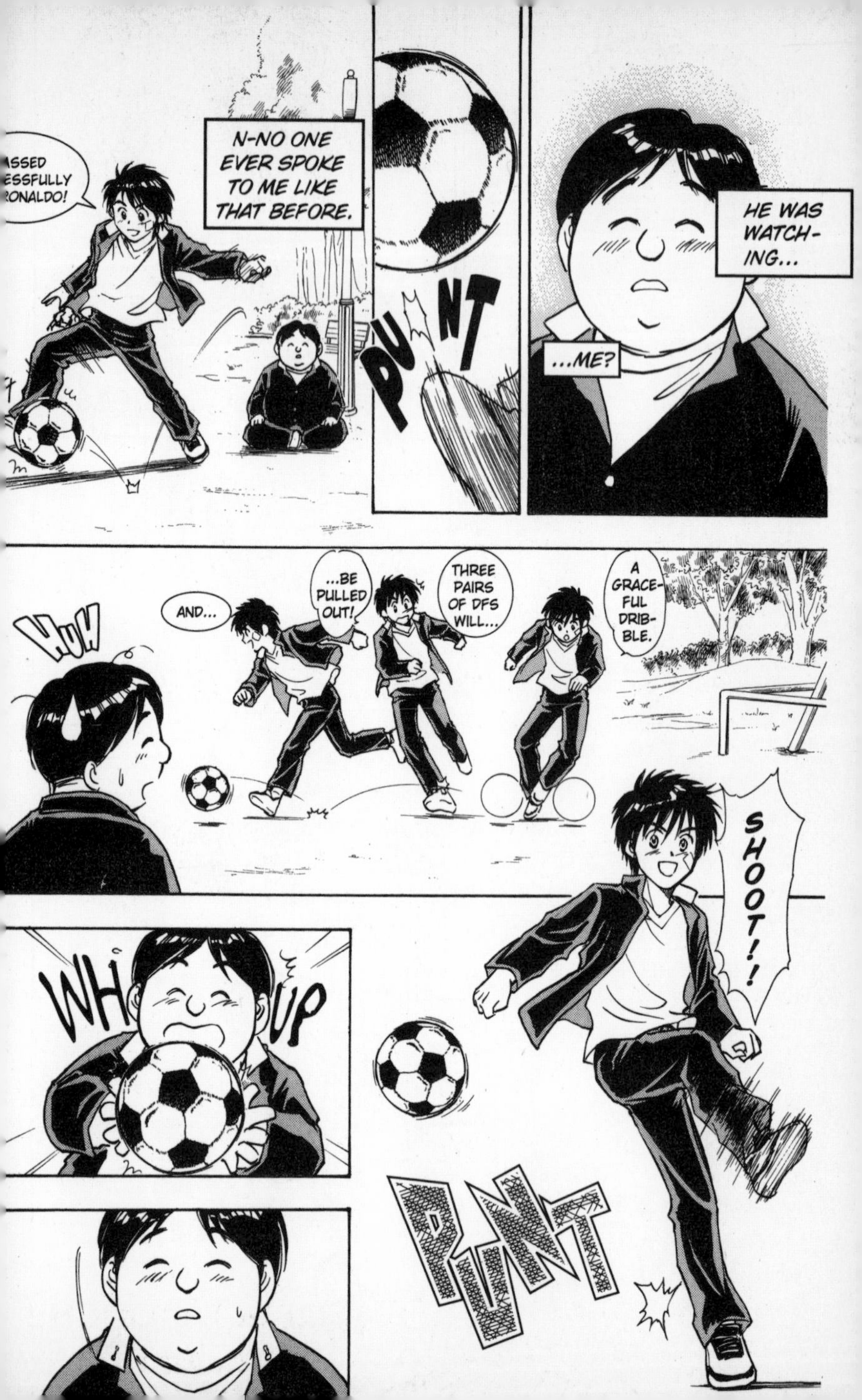
HE WAS WATCHING...
...ME?
PUNT
N-NO ONE EVER SPOKE TO ME LIKE THAT BEFORE.
ASSED ESSFULLY RONALDO!
A GRACEFUL DRIBBLE.
THREE PAIRS OF DFS WILL...
...BE PULLED OUT!
AND...
HUH
SHOOT!!
PUNT
WHUP

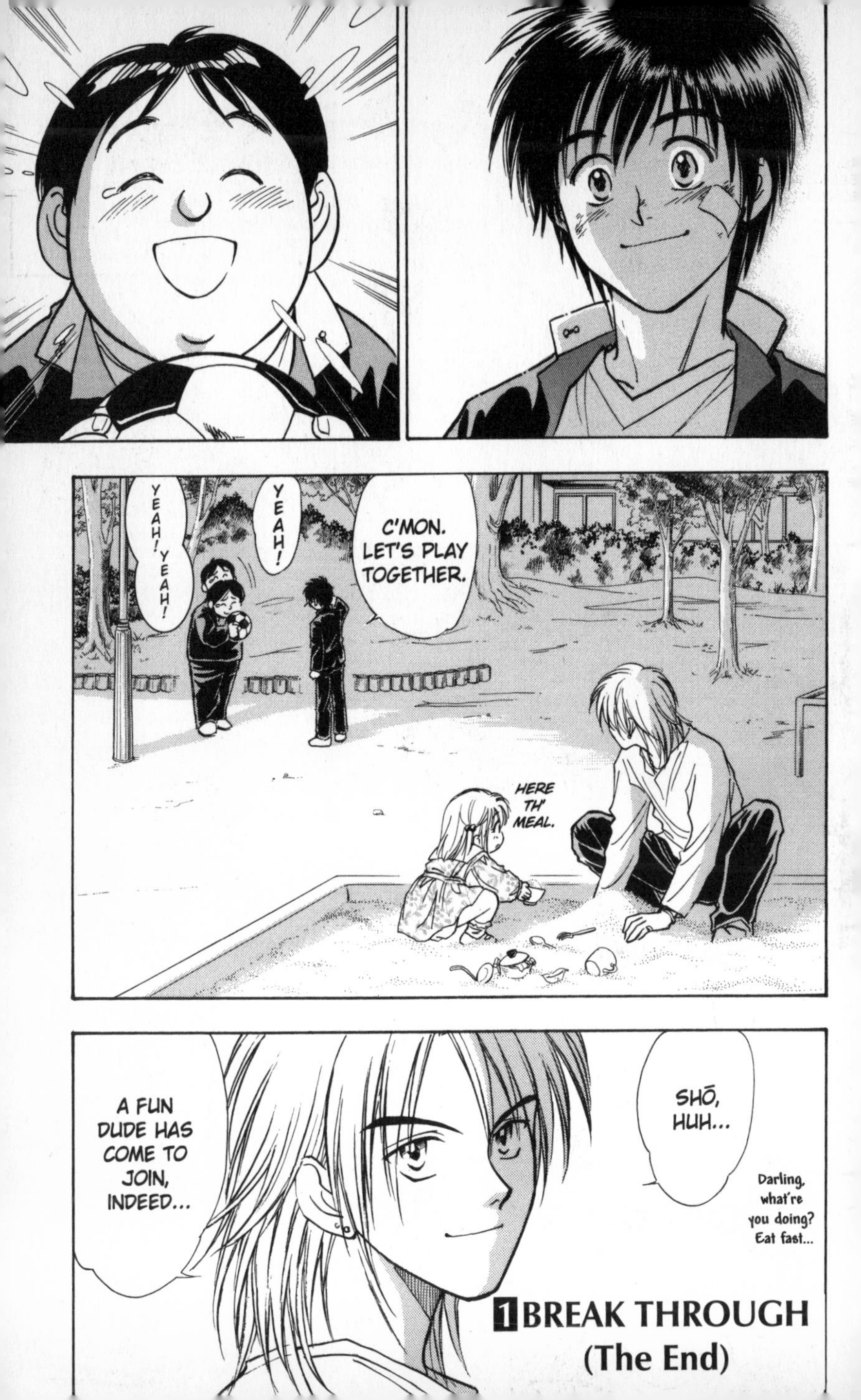
C'MON. LET'S PLAY TOGETHER.
YEAH!
YEAH! YEAH! YEAH!
HERE TH' MEAL.
SHŌ, HUH...
Darling, what're you doing? Eat fast...
A FUN DUDE HAS COME TO JOIN, INDEED...
1 BREAK THROUGH
(The End)

DAI SUKE NOTE

WE RECEIVED A LOT OF FAN LETTERS REQUESTING PROFILE INFORMATION OF THE MAIN CHARACTERS. SO, HERE THEY ARE.

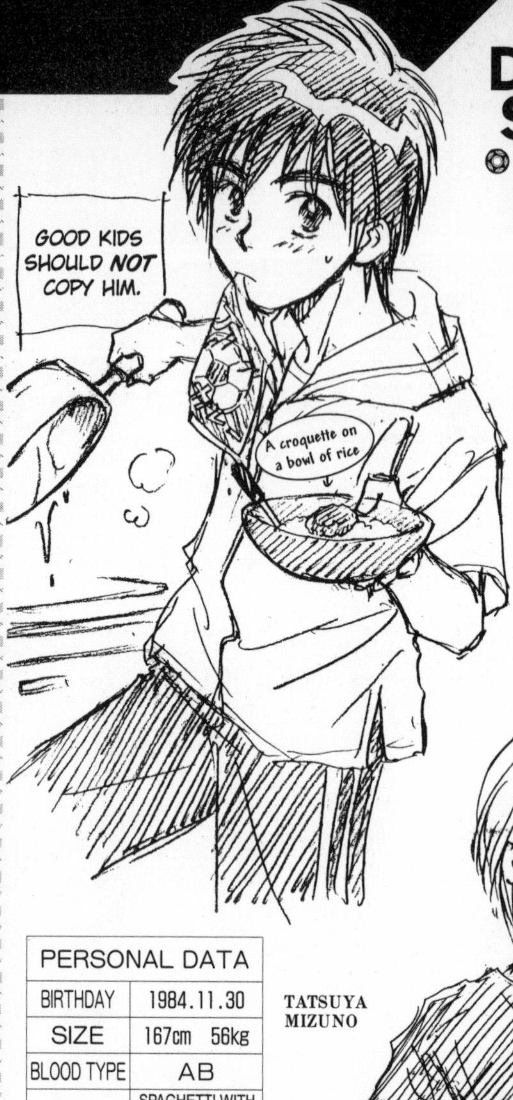
GOOD KIDS SHOULD **NOT** COPY HIM.
A croquette on a bowl of rice

SHŌ KAZAMATSURI

PERSONAL DATA	
BIRTHDAY	1984.5.10
SIZE	146cm 40kg
BLOOD TYPE	A
FAVORITE FOOD	CURRY RICE, DRY FRIED CHICKEN, KIT KAT.
WHAT HE DISLIKES	SEA CUCUMBERS
HOBBY & SPECIAL SKILLS	SOCCER. ABILITY TO SLEEP ANYWHERE.

TATSUYA MIZUNO

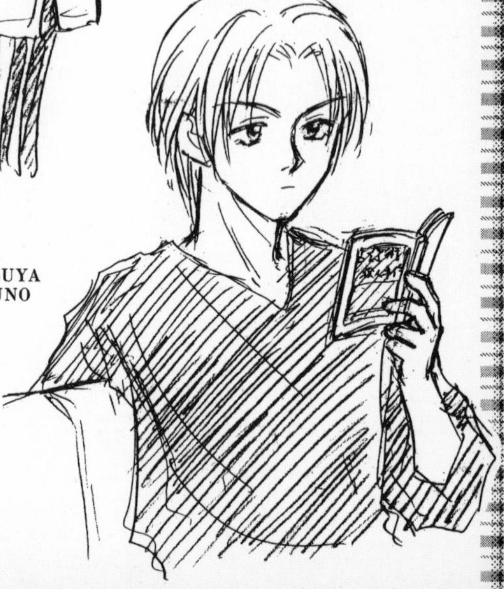

PERSONAL DATA	
BIRTHDAY	1984.11.30
SIZE	167cm 56kg
BLOOD TYPE	AB
FAVORITE FOOD	SPAGHETTI WITH SPICY FISH ROE, LAYERED CHEESE CAKE.
WHAT HE DISLIKES	NATTO, A FERMENTED STICKY SOY BEAN.
HOBBY & SPECIAL SKILLS	PLAYING WITH DOGS. MAKING PEOPLE UPSET.

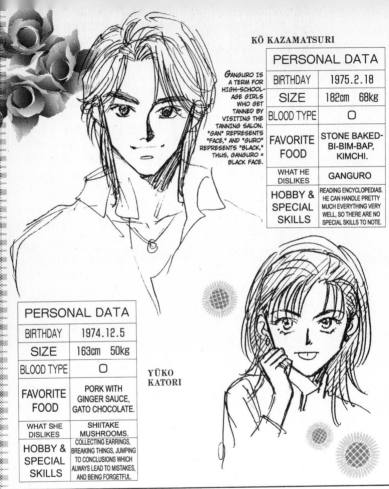

KŌ KAZAMATSURI

PERSONAL DATA	
BIRTHDAY	1975.2.18
SIZE	182cm 68kg
BLOOD TYPE	O
FAVORITE FOOD	STONE BAKED-BI-BIM-BAP, KIMCHI.
WHAT HE DISLIKES	GANGURO
HOBBY & SPECIAL SKILLS	READING ENCYCLOPEDIAS. HE CAN HANDLE PRETTY MUCH EVERYTHING VERY WELL, SO THERE ARE NO SPECIAL SKILLS TO NOTE.

Ganguro is a term for high-school-age girls who get tanned by visiting the tanning salon. "Gan" represents "face," and "guro" represents "black," thus, ganguro = black face.

YŪKO KATORI

PERSONAL DATA	
BIRTHDAY	1974.12.5
SIZE	163cm 50kg
BLOOD TYPE	O
FAVORITE FOOD	PORK WITH GINGER SAUCE, GATO CHOCOLATE.
WHAT SHE DISLIKES	SHIITAKE MUSHROOMS.
HOBBY & SPECIAL SKILLS	COLLECTING EARRINGS, BREAKING THINGS, JUMPING TO CONCLUSIONS WHICH ALWAYS LEAD TO MISTAKES, AND BEING FORGETFUL.

● **EXTRA: HERE ARE THE ANSWERS TO ADDITIONAL QUESTIONS:**

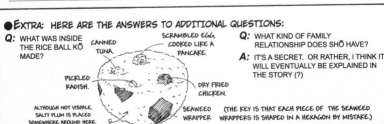

Q: WHAT WAS INSIDE THE RICE BALL KŌ MADE?

CANNED TUNA.
SCRAMBLED EGG, COOKED LIKE A PANCAKE.
PICKLED RADISH.
DRY FRIED CHICKEN.
ALTHOUGH NOT VISIBLE, SALTY PLUM IS PLACED SOMEWHERE AROUND HERE.
SEAWEED WRAPPER

(THE KEY IS THAT EACH PIECE OF THE SEAWEED WRAPPERS IS SHAPED IN A HEXAGON BY MISTAKE.)

Q: WHAT KIND OF FAMILY RELATIONSHIP DOES SHŌ HAVE?

A: IT'S A SECRET. OR RATHER, I THINK IT WILL EVENTUALLY BE EXPLAINED IN THE STORY (?)

Small Whistle! Theatre!!

Manga by Seki, Assistant S

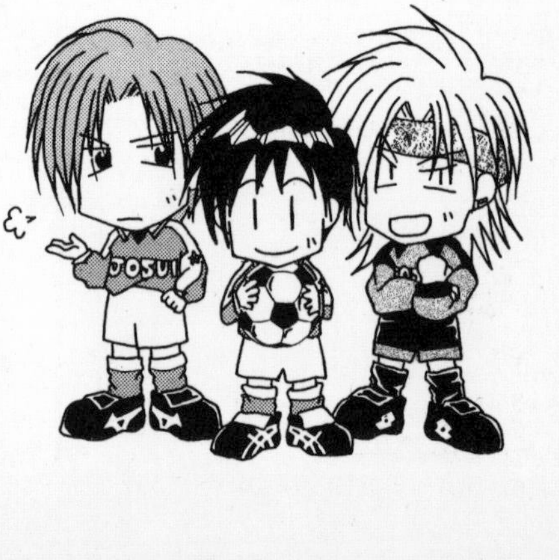

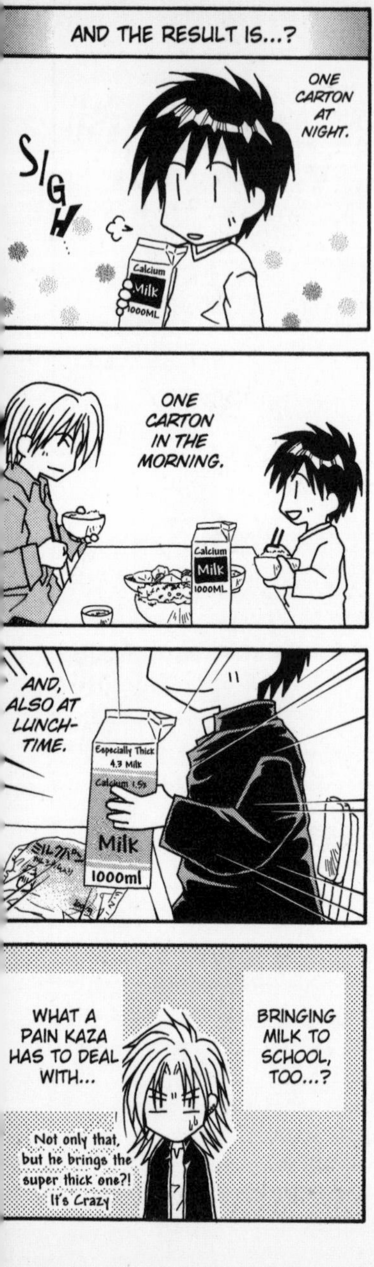
AND THE RESULT IS...?
ONE CARTON AT NIGHT.
SIGH...
Calcium Milk 1000ML
ONE CARTON IN THE MORNING.
Calcium Milk 1000ML
AND, ALSO AT LUNCH-TIME.
Especially Thick 4.3 Milk
Milk 1000ml
BRINGING MILK TO SCHOOL, TOO...?
WHAT A PAIN KAZA HAS TO DEAL WITH...
Not only that, but he brings the super thick one?! It's Crazy

MORE BEAUTIFUL THAN ANYONE ELSE...
SPLASH
SPLASH
ALL RIGHT! I GOTTA DO THAT...
STARE
AHHH
I'M BEAUTIFUL AGAIN TODAY.

TO BE CONTINUED IN VOLUME TWO... MAYBE...

The Four Kings of Josui Junior High.
Morinaga
Takai
Koga
Hanazawa
Mizuno
10
Art by Assistant NXY

Thanks for the nice comic strip! (Daisuke Higuchi)

Next in Whistle!

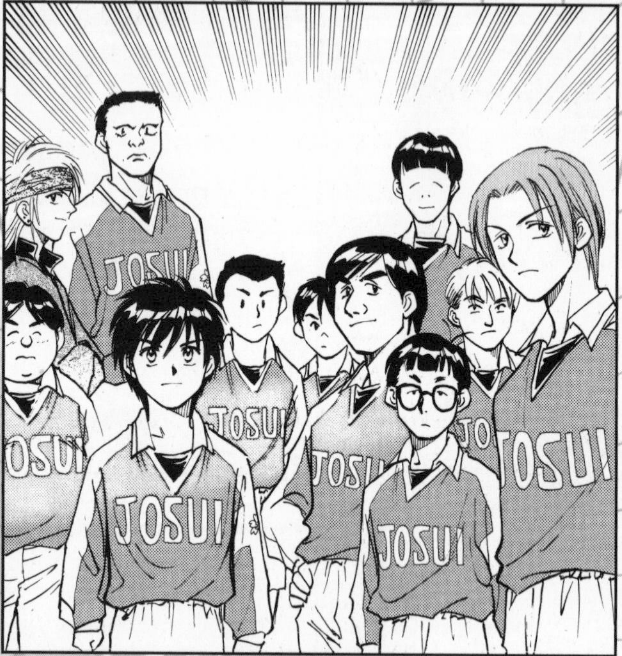
JOSUI
JOSUI
JOSUI
JOSUI

ON YOUR MARKS

Shô and his pals finally number 11 and that means they're ready for high-kicking, goal-to-goal soccer action. Unfortunately, team Josui's first game is against super elite Musashinomori private school. Shô's crew may have boundless pluck and enthusiasm but do they have the talent to compete with the reigning champions from last season? Maybe not… but they have a secret weapon by the name of Tatsuya Mizuno. Not only is Tatsuya the best player on Josui's squad, but he's also the son of the coach from Musashinomori!! Soccer action and familial complications all in the next volume of **Whistle!**

Available November 2004!

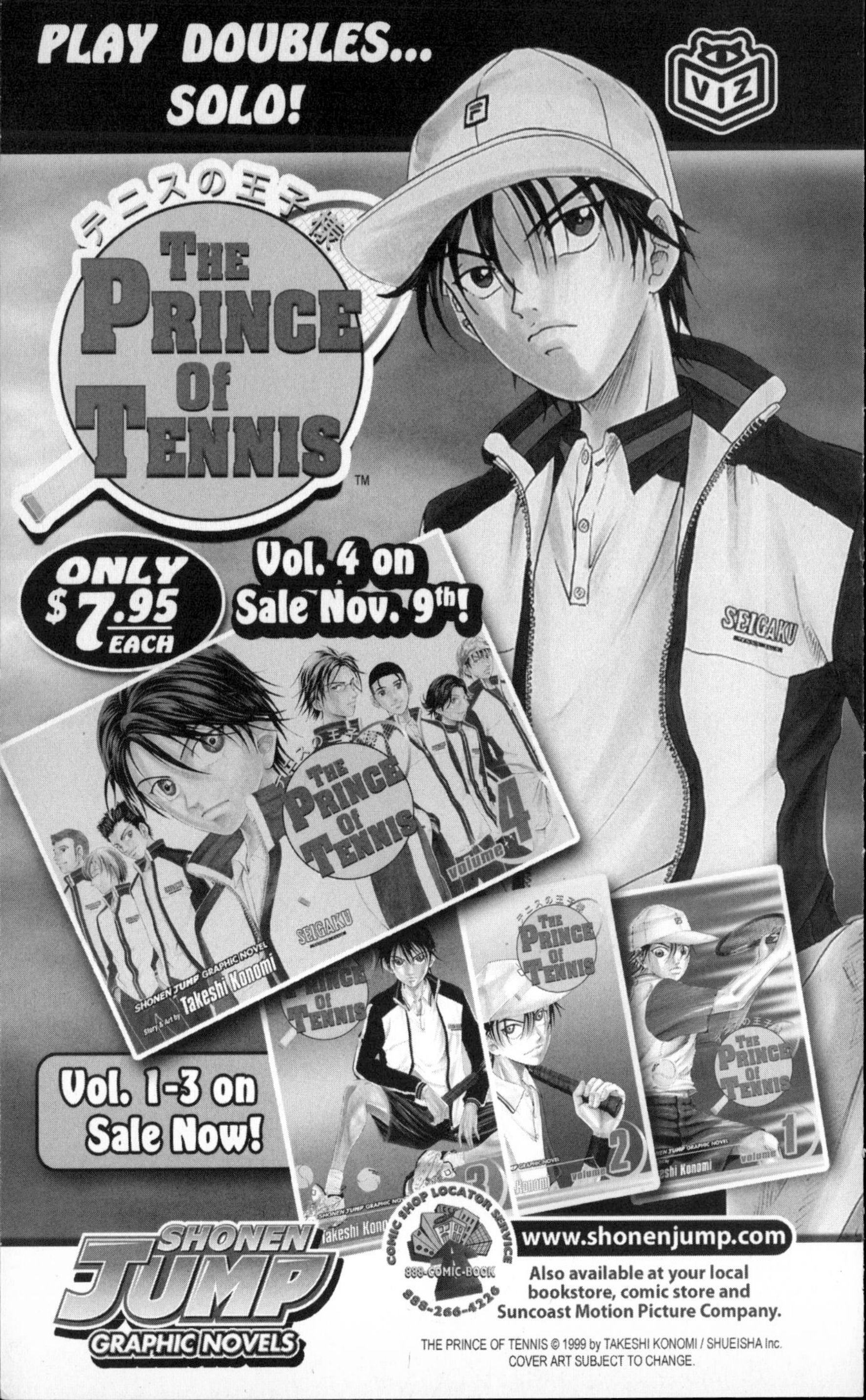

PLAY DOUBLES...
SOLO!
VIZ
テニスの王子様
THE PRINCE OF TENNIS™
ONLY $7.95 EACH
Vol. 4 on Sale Nov. 9th!
Vol. 1-3 on Sale Now!
SHONEN JUMP GRAPHIC NOVELS
COMIC SHOP LOCATOR SERVICE
888-COMIC-BOOK
888-266-4226
www.shonenjump.com
Also available at your local bookstore, comic store and Suncoast Motion Picture Company.
THE PRINCE OF TENNIS © 1999 by TAKESHI KONOMI / SHUEISHA Inc.
COVER ART SUBJECT TO CHANGE.

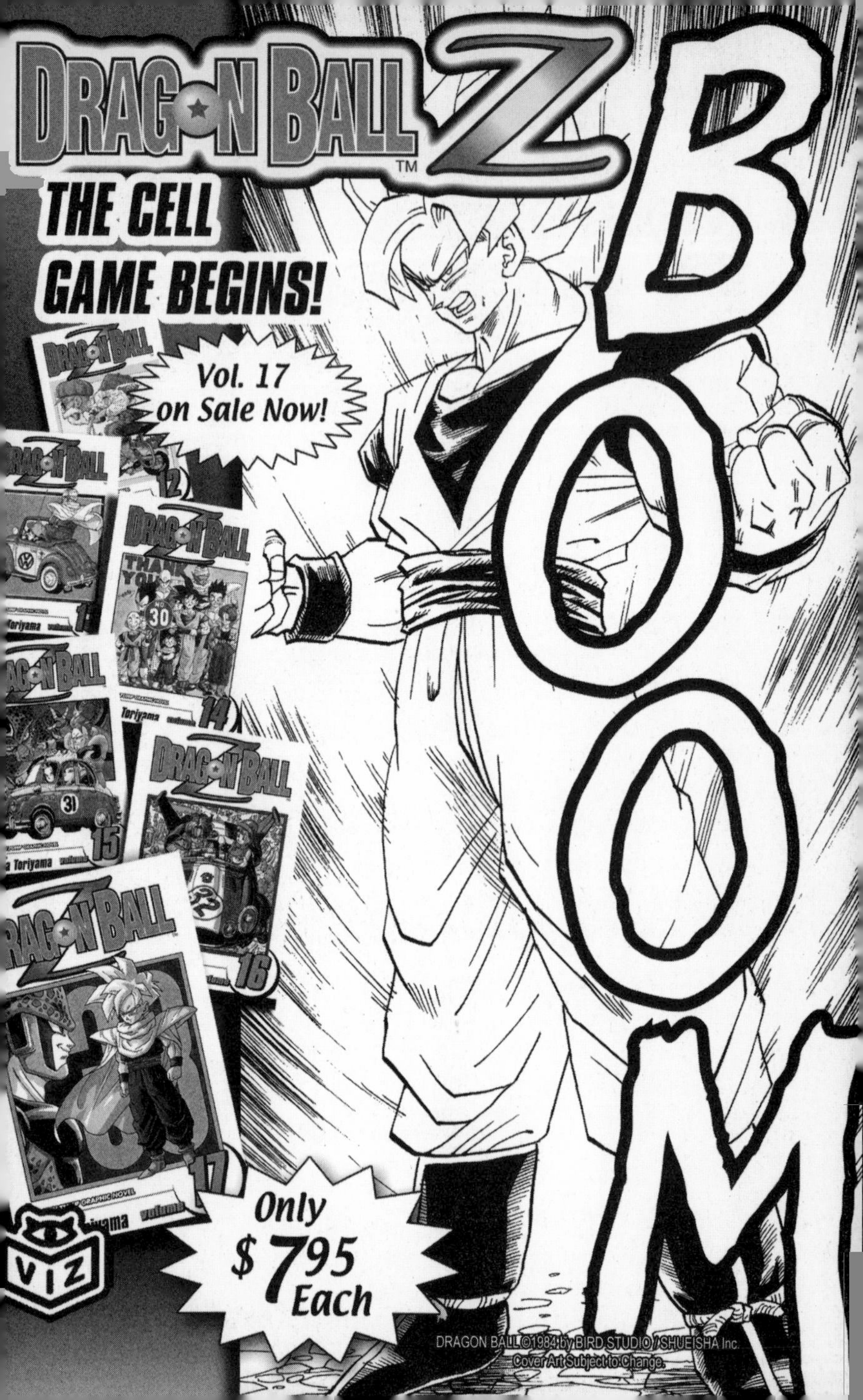

DRAGON BALL Z™
THE CELL GAME BEGINS!
Vol. 17 on Sale Now!
BOOOM
Only $7.95 Each
VIZ
DRAGON BALL ©1984 by BIRD STUDIO / SHUEISHA Inc.
Cover Art Subject to Change.

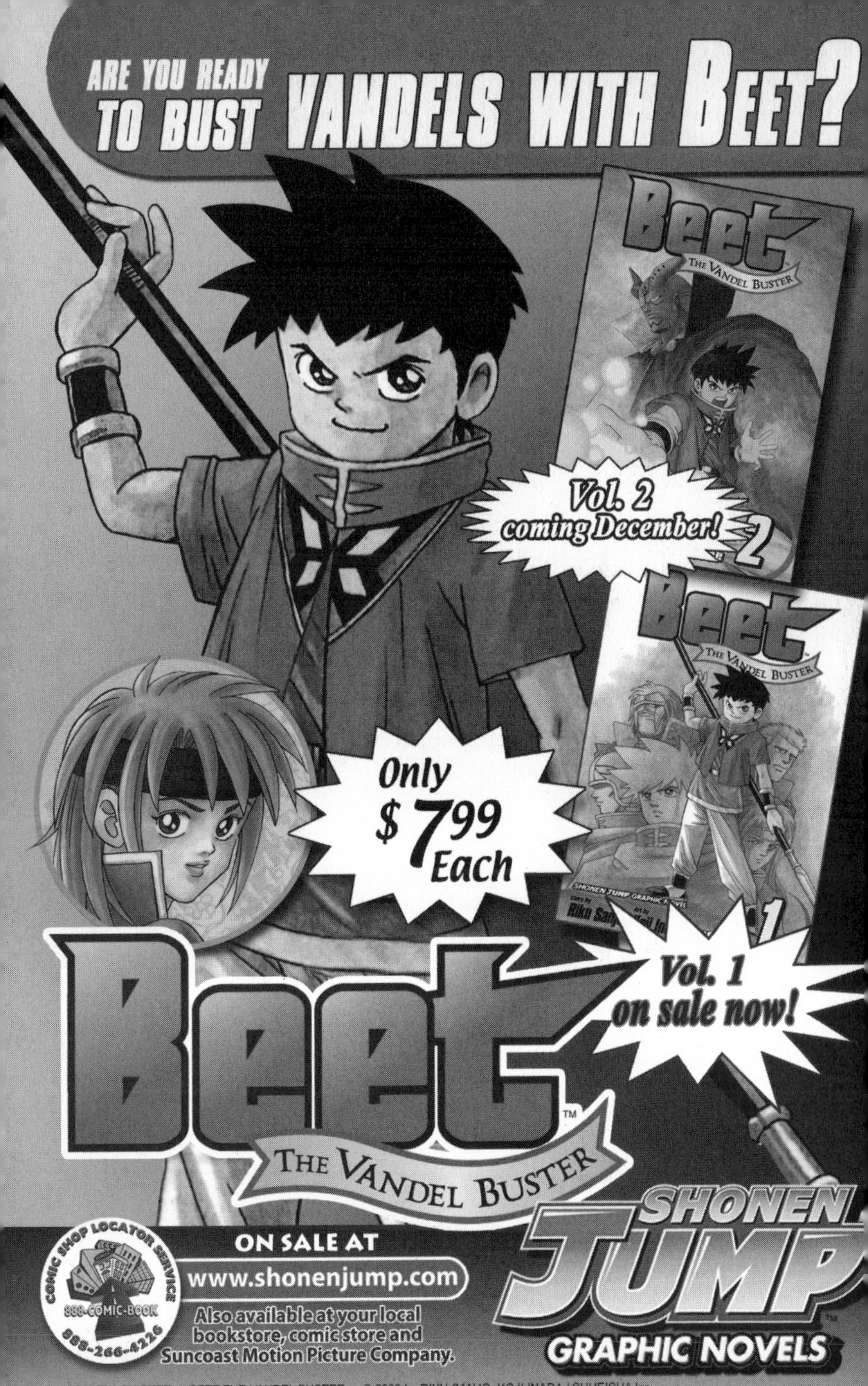
ARE YOU READY TO BUST VANDELS WITH BEET?
Beet THE VANDEL BUSTER
Vol. 2 coming December!
2
Beet THE VANDEL BUSTER
SHONEN JUMP GRAPHIC NOVEL
1
Only $7.99 Each
Vol. 1 on sale now!
Beet™ THE VANDEL BUSTER
COMIC SHOP LOCATOR SERVICE
888-COMIC-BOOK
888-266-4226
ON SALE AT
www.shonenjump.com
Also available at your local bookstore, comic store and Suncoast Motion Picture Company.
SHONEN JUMP™
GRAPHIC NOVELS

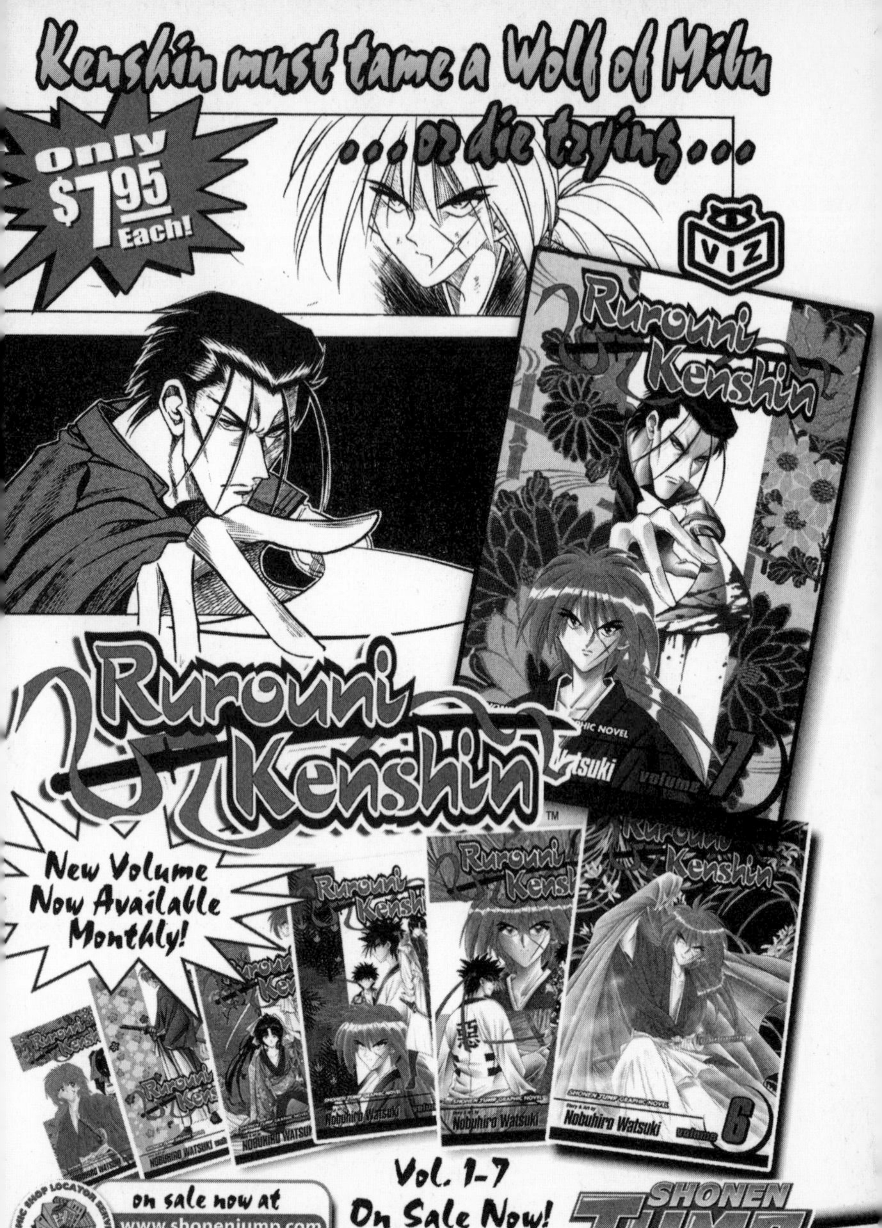
Kenshin must tame a Wolf of Mibu
...or die trying...
Only $7.95 Each!
VIZ
Rurouni Kenshin
New Volume Now Available Monthly!
Vol. 1-7 On Sale Now!
on sale now at
www.shonenjump.com
Also available at your local bookstore, comic store and Suncoast Motion Picture Company.
888-COMIC-BOOK
888-266-4226
SHONEN JUMP GRAPHIC NOVELS

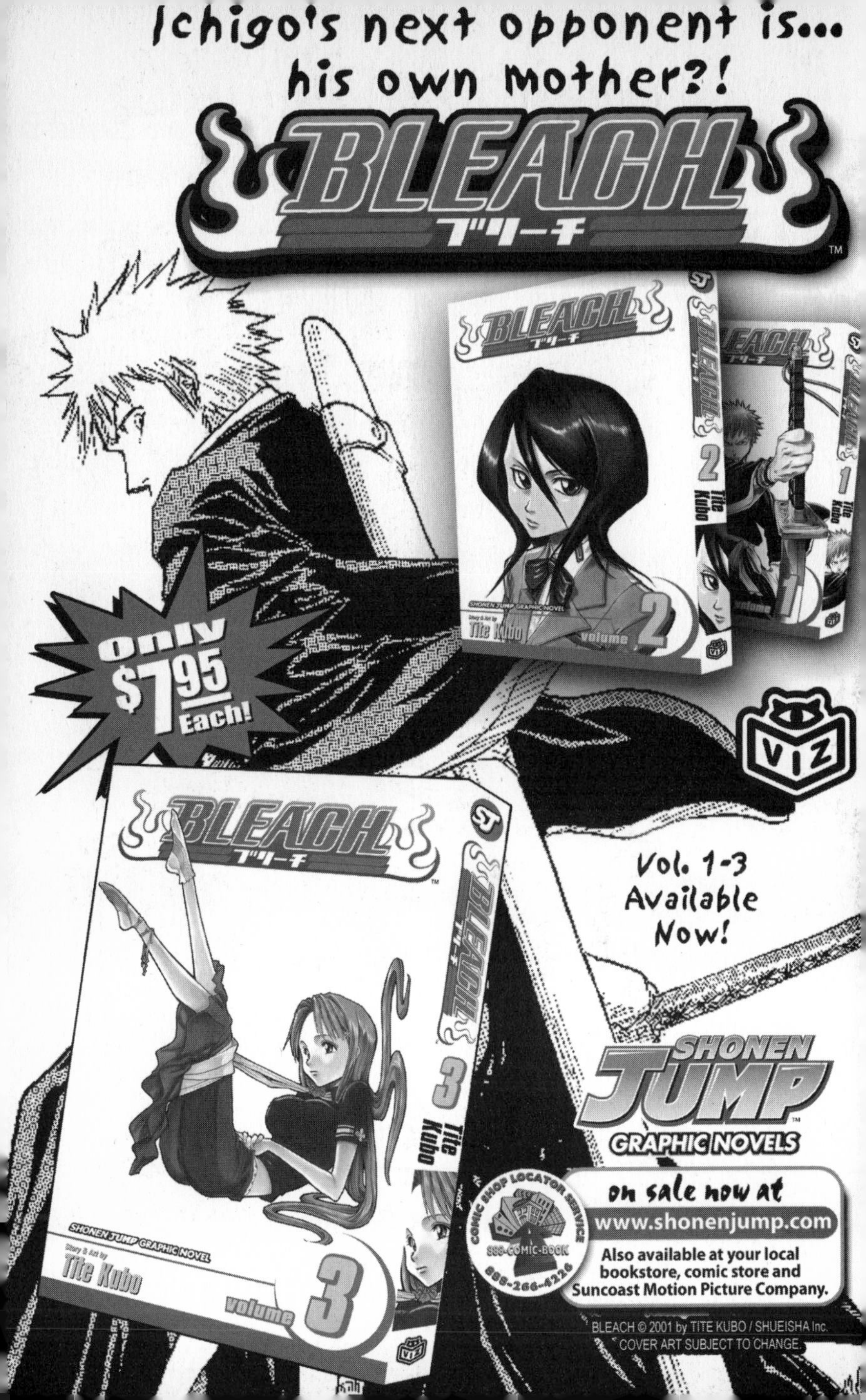

Ichigo's next opponent is...
his own mother?!
BLEACH
ブリーチ
Only $7.95 Each!
Vol. 1-3
Available
Now!
SHONEN JUMP
GRAPHIC NOVELS
on sale now at
www.shonenjump.com
Also available at your local bookstore, comic store and Suncoast Motion Picture Company.
COMIC SHOP LOCATOR SERVICE
888-COMIC-BOOK
888-266-4226
BLEACH © 2001 by TITE KUBO / SHUEISHA Inc.
COVER ART SUBJECT TO CHANGE.

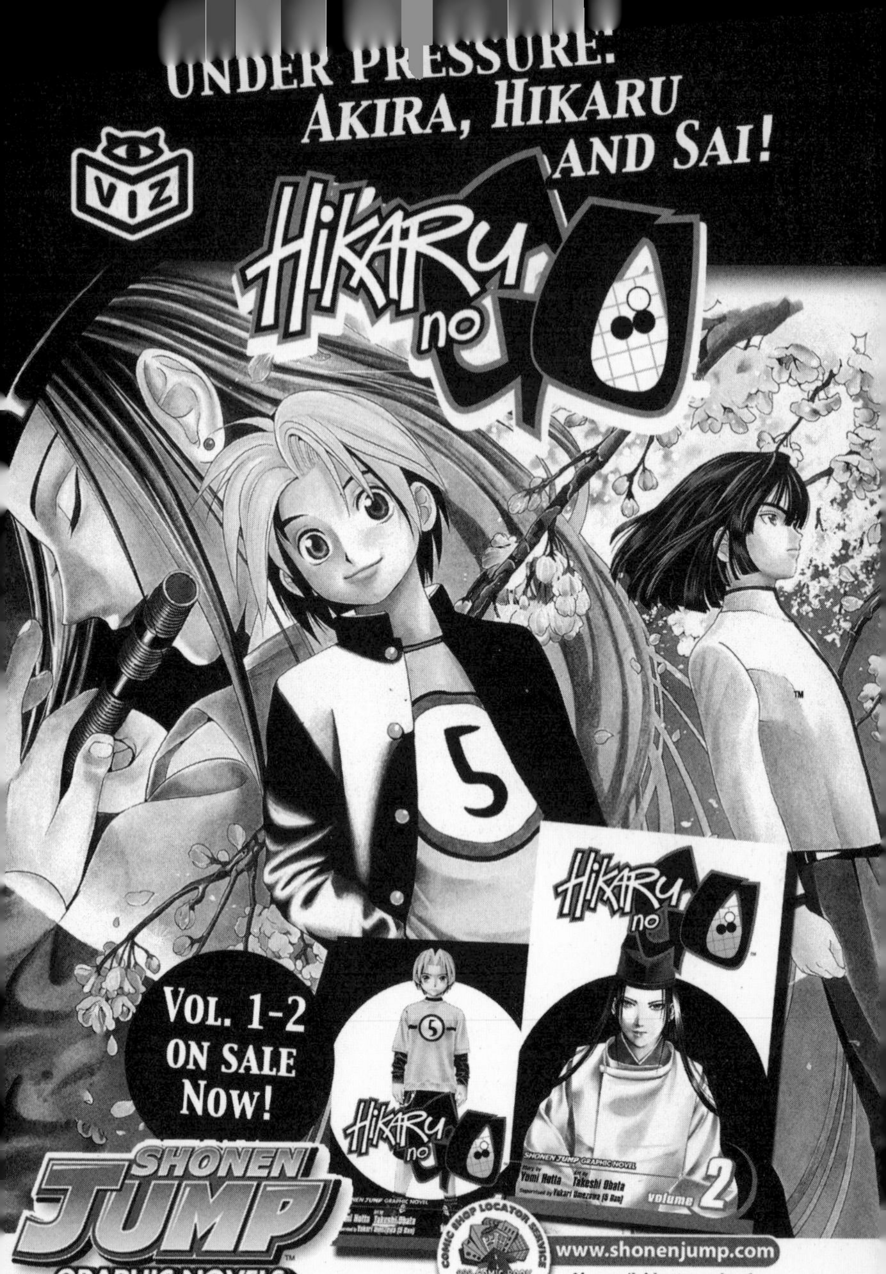
UNDER PRESSURE:
AKIRA, HIKARU
AND SAI!
VIZ
HIKARU no GO
VOL. 1-2
ON SALE
NOW!
SHONEN JUMP GRAPHIC NOVELS
volume 2
COMIC SHOP LOCATOR SERVICE
888-COMIC-BOOK
888-266-4226
www.shonenjump.com
Also available at your local
bookstore, comic store and
Suncoast Motion Picture Company.

COMPLETE OUR SURVEY AND LET US KNOW WHAT YOU THINK!

☐ Please check here if you DO NOT wish to receive information or future offers from VIZ

Name: _____

Address: _____

City: _____ State: _____ Zip: _____

E-mail: _____

☐ Male ☐ Female   Date of Birth (mm/dd/yyyy): ___/___/_____ (Under 13? Parental consent required)

What race/ethnicity do you consider yourself? (please check one)

☐ Asian/Pacific Islander   ☐ Black/African American   ☐ Hispanic/Latino

☐ Native American/Alaskan Native ☐ White/Caucasian   ☐ Other: _____

What SHONEN JUMP Graphic Novel did you purchase? (indicate title purchased)

_____

What other SHONEN JUMP Graphic Novels, if any, do you own? (indicate title(s) owned)

_____

_____

Reason for purchase: (check all that apply)

☐ Special offer   ☐ Favorite title   ☐ Gift

☐ Recommendation   ☐ Read in SHONEN JUMP Magazine

☐ Other _____

Where did you make your purchase? (please check one)

☐ Comic store   ☐ Bookstore   ☐ Mass/Grocery Store

☐ Newsstand   ☐ Video/Video Game Store ☐ Other: _____

☐ Online (site: _____)

Do you read SHONEN JUMP Magazine?

☐ Yes ☐ No **(if no, skip the next two questions)**

Do you subscribe?

☐ Yes ☐ No

If you do not subscribe, how often do you purchase SHONEN JUMP Magazine?

☐ 1-3 issues a year

☐ 4-6 issues a year

☐ more than 7 issues a year

What genre of manga would you like to read as a SHONEN JUMP Graphic Novel?
(please check two)

☐ Adventure ☐ Comic Strip ☐ Science Fiction ☐ Fighting

☐ Horror ☐ Romance ☐ Fantasy ☐ Sports

Which do you prefer? (please check one)

☐ Reading right-to-left

☐ Reading left-to-right

Which do you prefer? (please check one)

☐ Sound effects in English

☐ Sound effects in Japanese with English captions

☐ Sound effects in Japanese only with a glossary at the back

THANK YOU! Please send the completed form to:

VIZ Survey
42 Catharine St.
Poughkeepsie, NY 12601

All information provided will be used for internal purposes only. We promise not to sell or otherwise divulge your information.